SHONEN JUMP MANGA EDITION

DRAGON DRIVE

Vol. 7
DECISIVE BATTLE

STORY & ART BY
KEN-ICHI SAKURA
IN COLLABORATION WITH BANDAI • CHAN'S • ORG

CHARACTERS

Reiji Ozora

A JUNIOR HIGH SCHOOL STUDENT WHO NEVER APPLIED HIMSELF, BUT HE'S TOTALLY GETTING INTO DRAGON DRIVE.

Maiko Yukino

SHE'S KNOWN REIJI SINCE CHILDHOOD. HER DRAGON PARTNER IS GORAO.

Chibi

REIJI'S DRAGON PARTNER. IN RIKYU, HE'S KNOWN AS SENKOKURA.

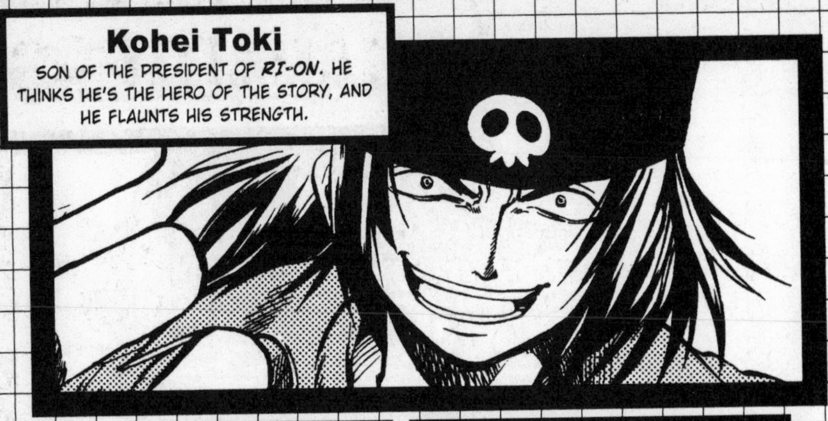
Kohei Toki
SON OF THE PRESIDENT OF *RI-ON*. HE THINKS HE'S THE HERO OF THE STORY, AND HE FLAUNTS HIS STRENGTH.

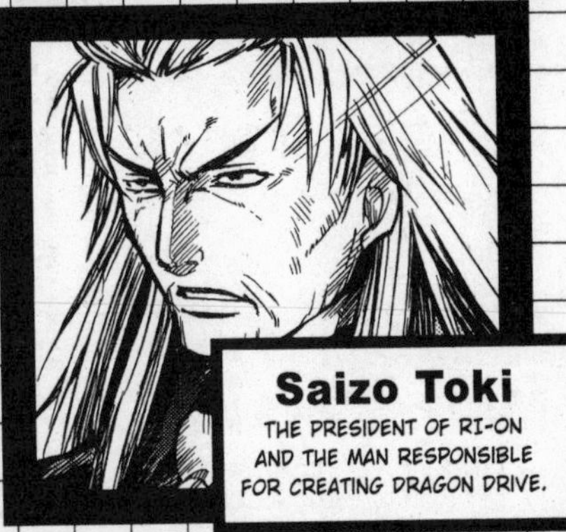
Saizo Toki
THE PRESIDENT OF RI-ON AND THE MAN RESPONSIBLE FOR CREATING DRAGON DRIVE.

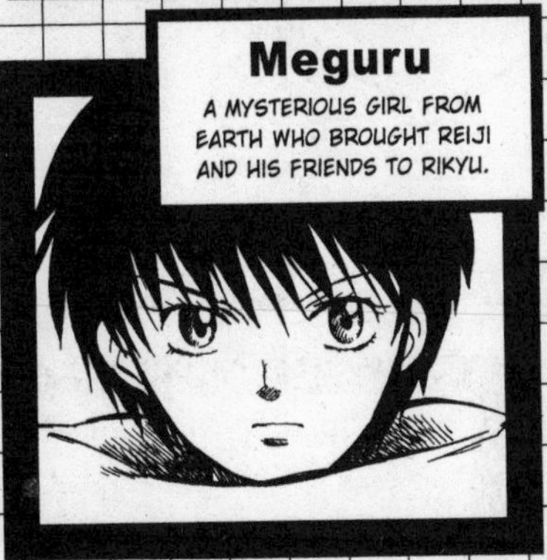
Meguru
A MYSTERIOUS GIRL FROM EARTH WHO BROUGHT REIJI AND HIS FRIENDS TO RIKYU.

STORY

DRAGON DRIVE IS A VIRTUAL REALITY GAME THAT ONLY KIDS CAN PLAY. THE THRILL OF THE GAME GRIPS REIJI, A BOY WHO WAS NEVER REALLY GOOD AT ANYTHING. A GIRL NAMED MEGURU LEADS REIJI AND HIS FRIENDS TO RIKYU, AN ALTERNATE EARTH. THERE, THEY LEARN THAT RI-ON, THE ORGANIZATION RUNNING DRAGON DRIVE, IS PLOTTING TO ACQUIRE THE JINRYU STONE. WITH IT, RION CAN CONTROL ALL THE DRAGONS OF RIKYU AND CONQUER BOTH WORLDS. TO WIN THE STONE HIMSELF, REIJI ENTERS THE DRAGONIC HEAVEN COMPETITION IN RIKYU, BUT KOHEI CHEATS AND SEIZES THE STONE. HOWEVER, THE STONE THAT KOHEI TAKES IS JUST THE KEY TO ACCESS THE SHRINE WHERE THE REAL JINRYU STONE LIES.

TO STOP RI-ON'S PLAN AND SAVE RIKYU, REIJI WINS THE ALLEGIANCE OF THE LEGENDARY DRAGON SHINSABER. HE HEADS INTO BATTLE TO STOP THE TOKI FAMILY'S REIGN OF TERROR!

Vol. 7 DECISIVE BATTLE
CONTENTS

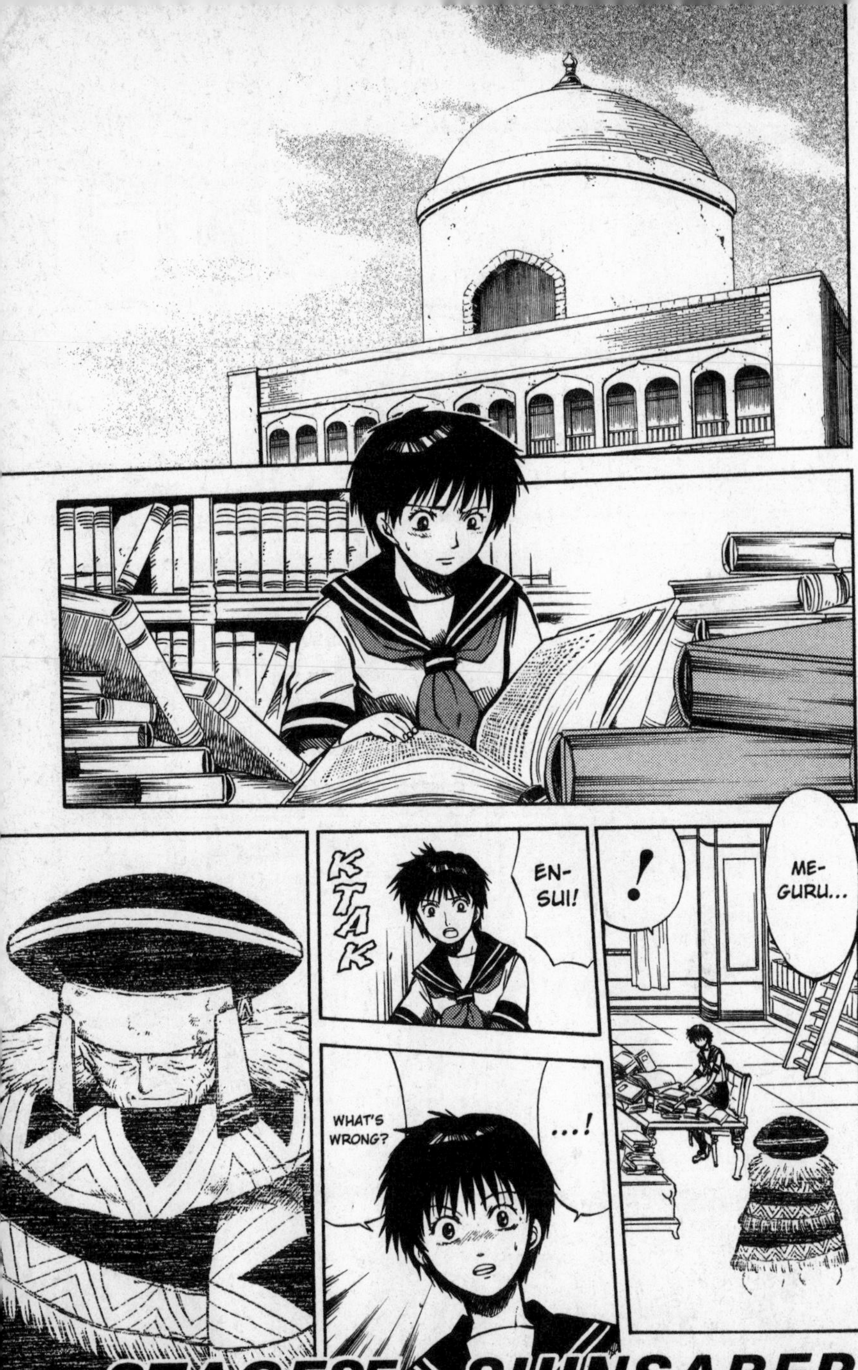
ME-GURU...
!
EN-SUI!
KTAK
...!
WHAT'S WRONG?

STAGE25 SHINSABER

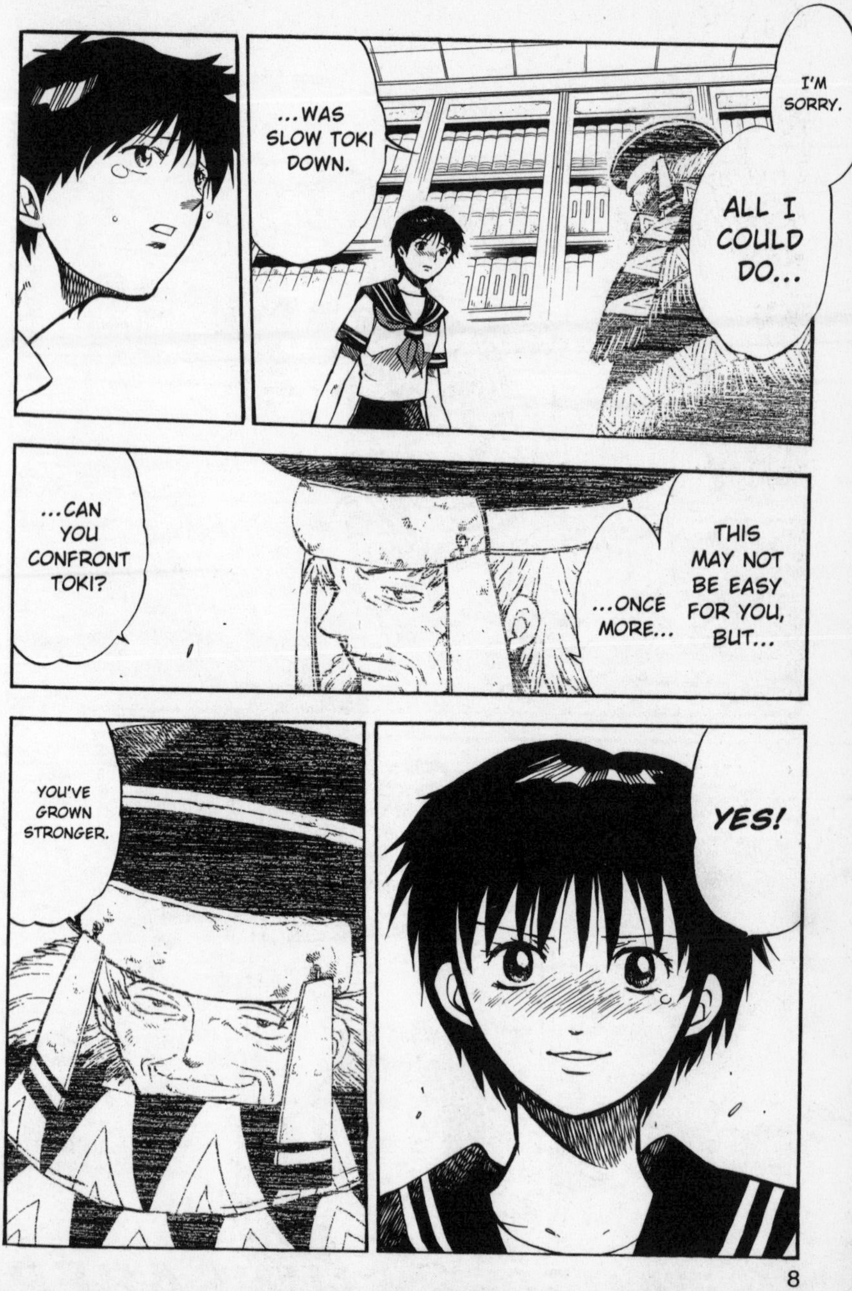
I'M SORRY.
ALL I COULD DO...
...WAS SLOW TOKI DOWN.
THIS MAY NOT BE EASY FOR YOU, BUT...
...ONCE MORE...
...CAN YOU CONFRONT TOKI?
YES!
YOU'VE GROWN STRONGER.

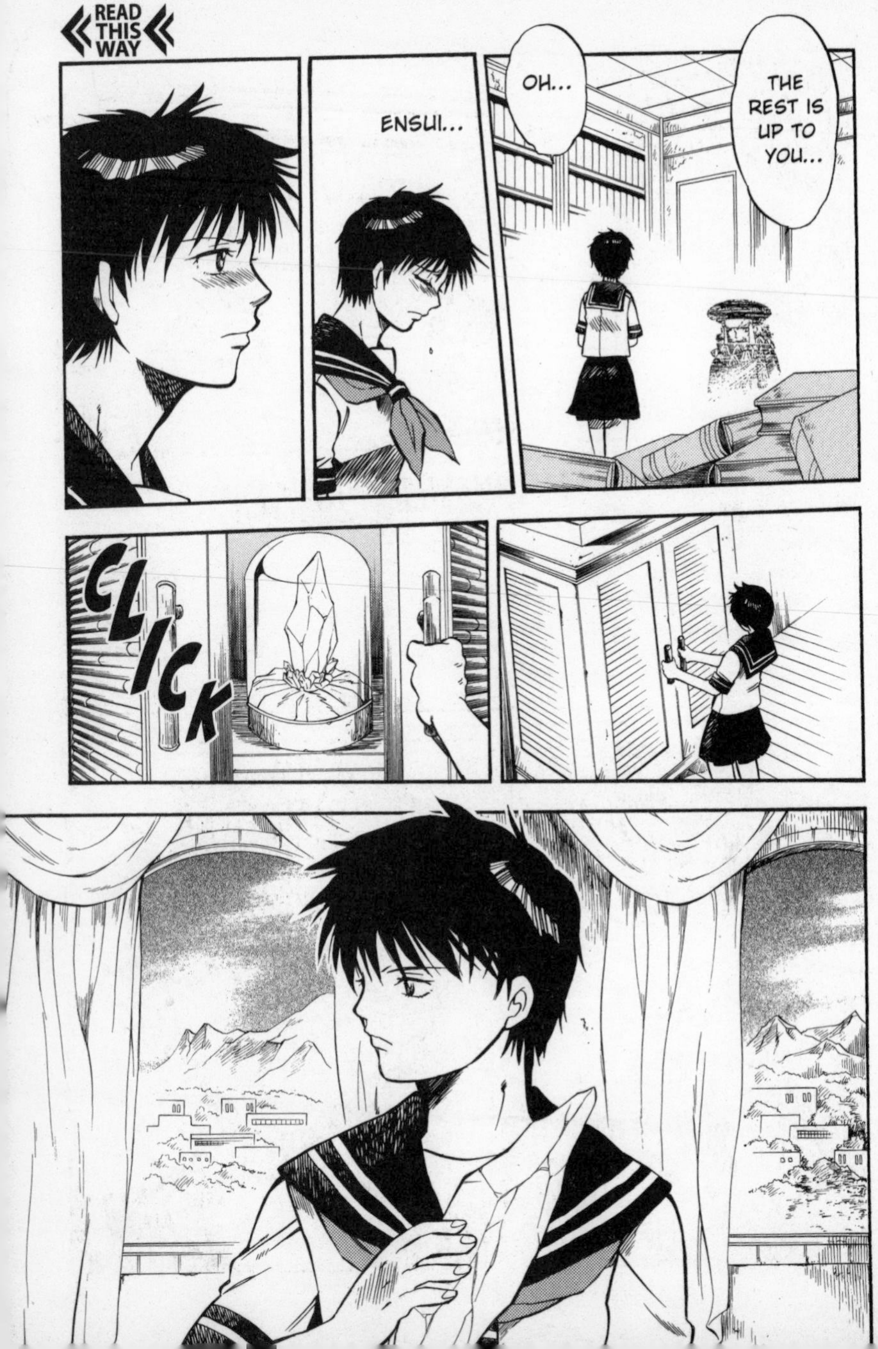
READ THIS WAY
THE REST IS UP TO YOU...
OH...
ENSUI...
CLICK

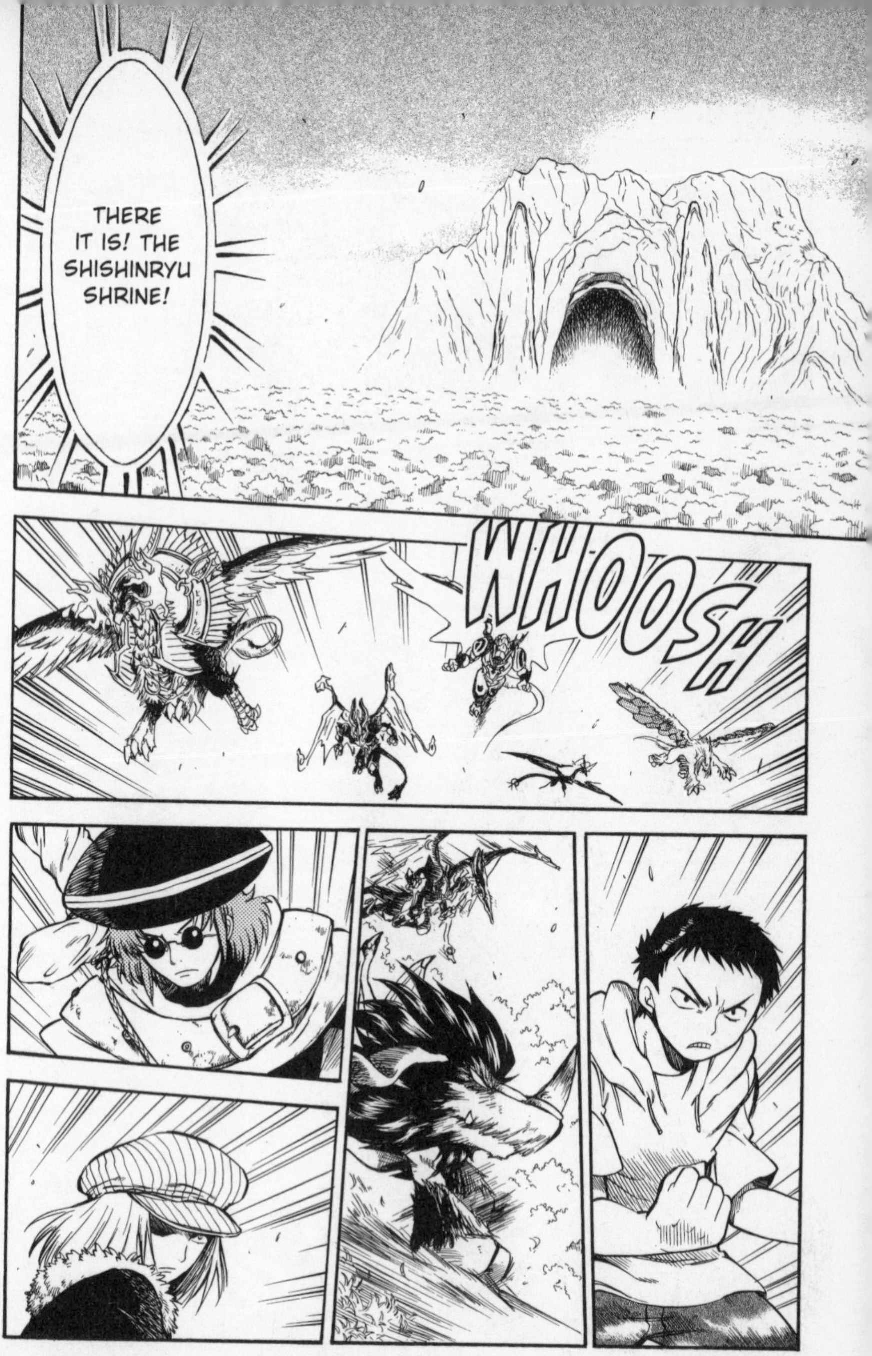
THERE IT IS! THE SHISHINRYU SHRINE!
WHOOSH

READ THIS WAY

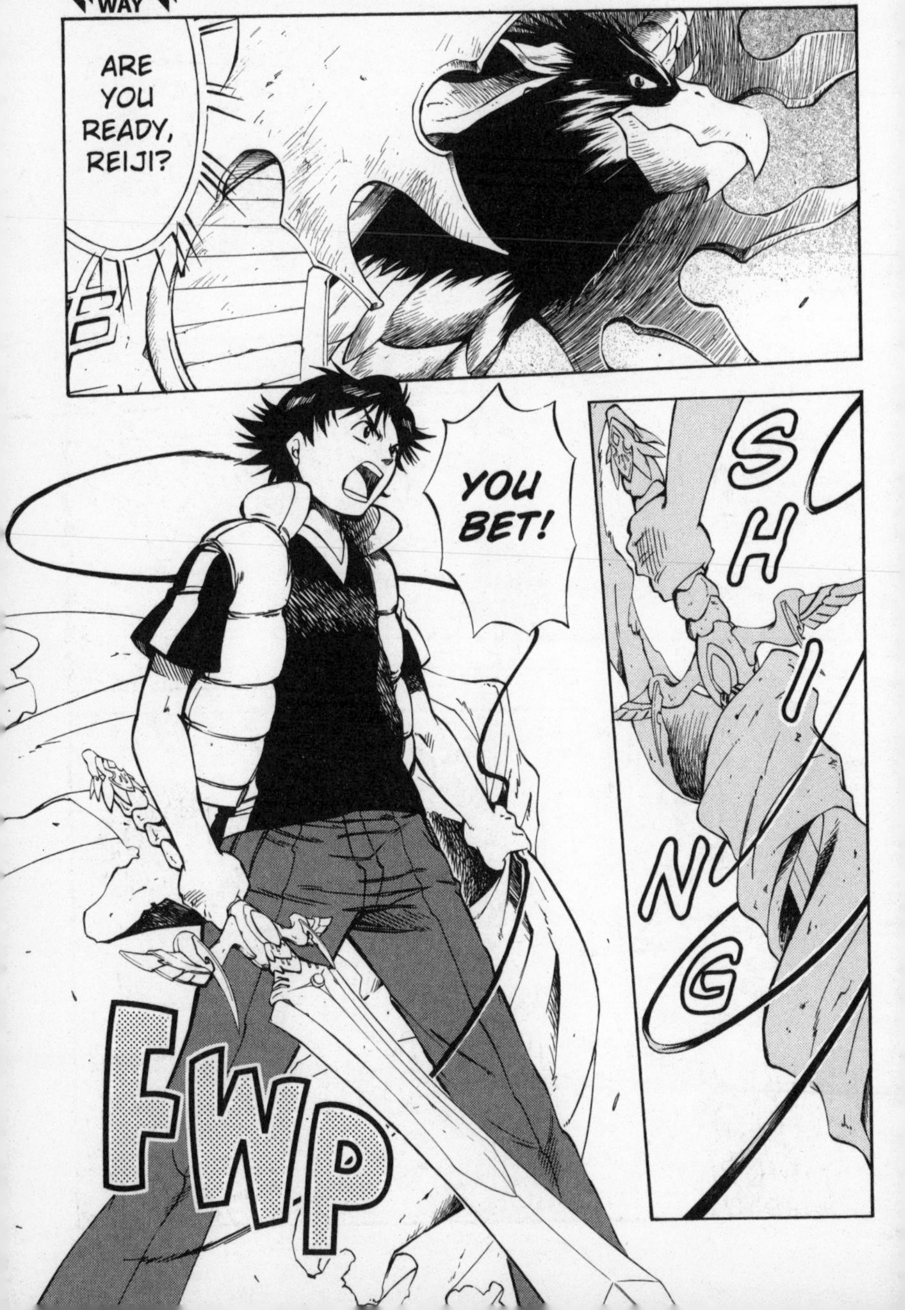
ARE YOU READY, REIJI?
SHIING
YOU BET!
FWP

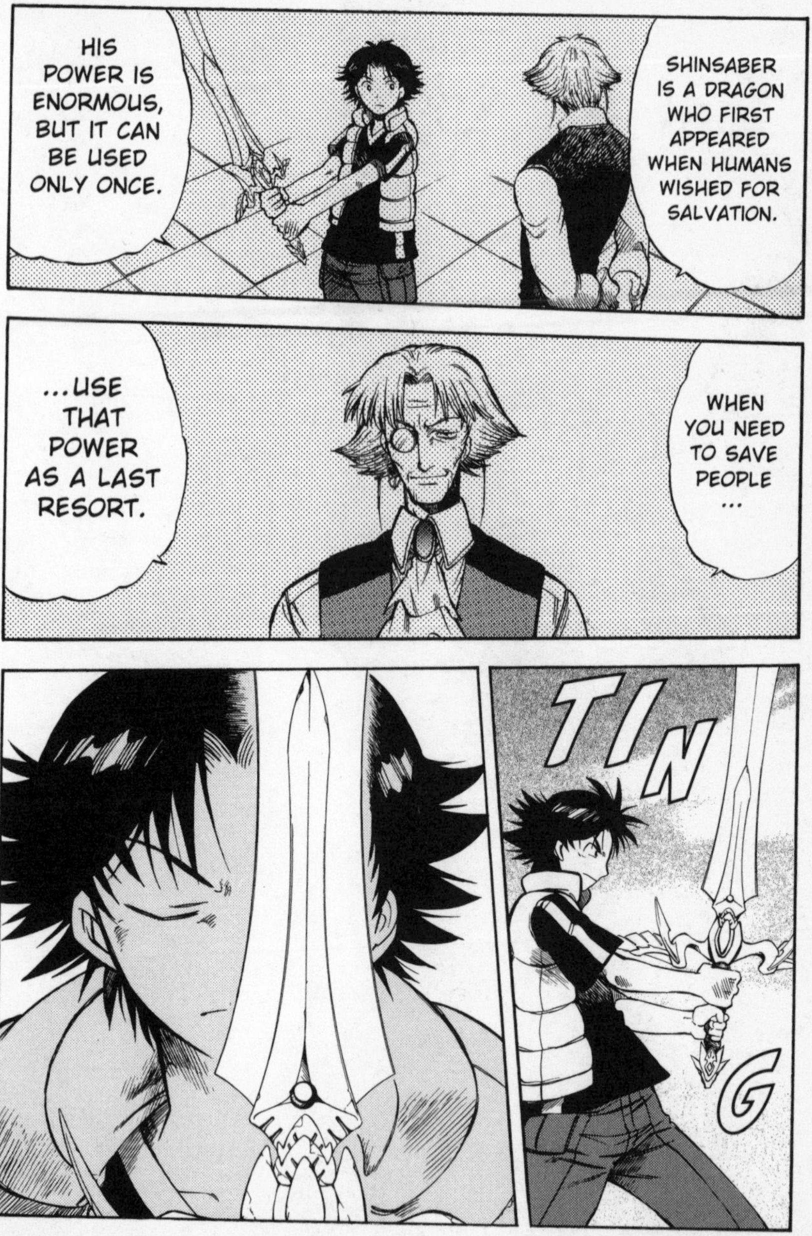
SHINSABER IS A DRAGON WHO FIRST APPEARED WHEN HUMANS WISHED FOR SALVATION.
HIS POWER IS ENORMOUS, BUT IT CAN BE USED ONLY ONCE.
WHEN YOU NEED TO SAVE PEOPLE ...
...USE THAT POWER AS A LAST RESORT.
TING

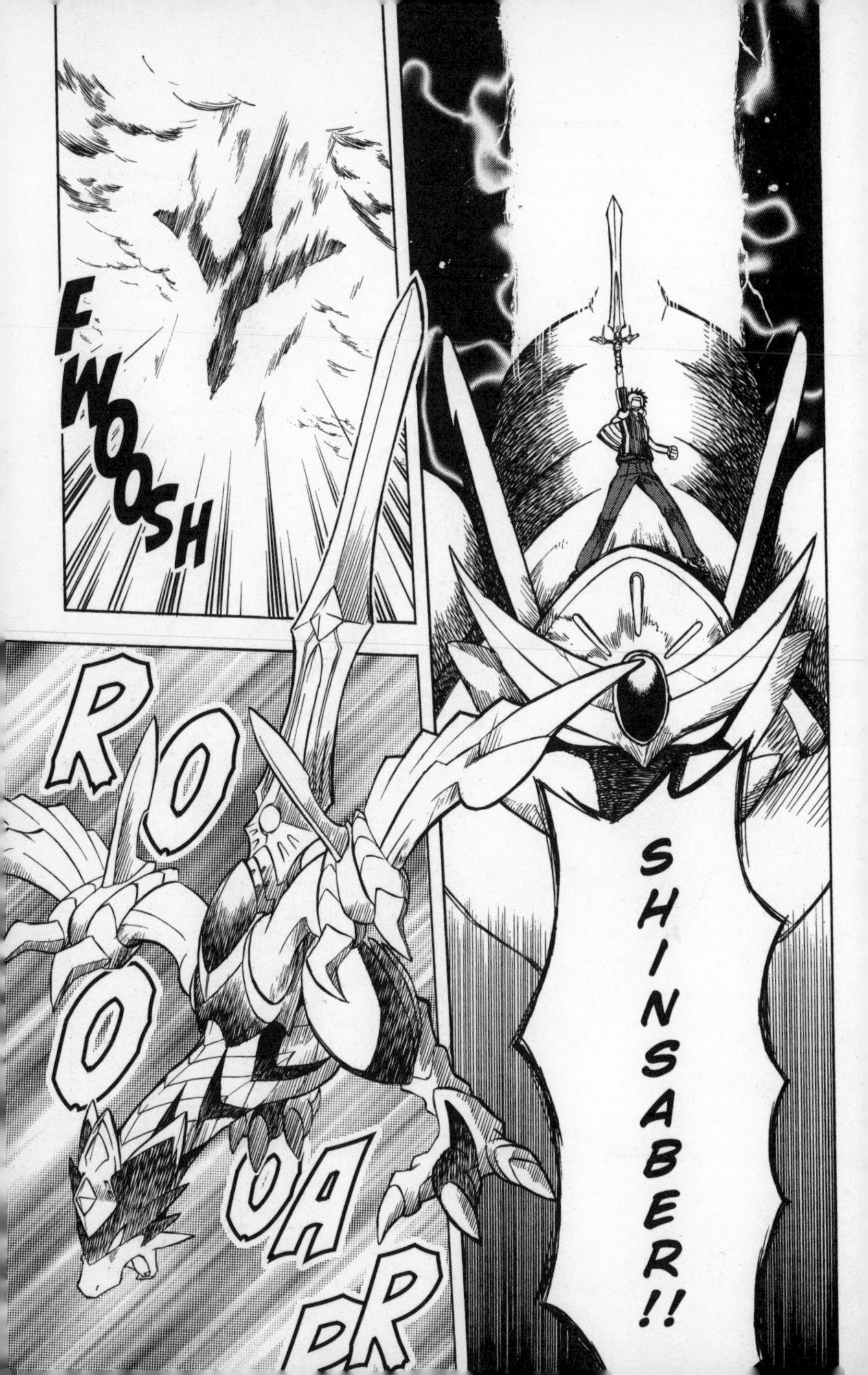
SHINSABER!!
FWOOSH
ROOOAR

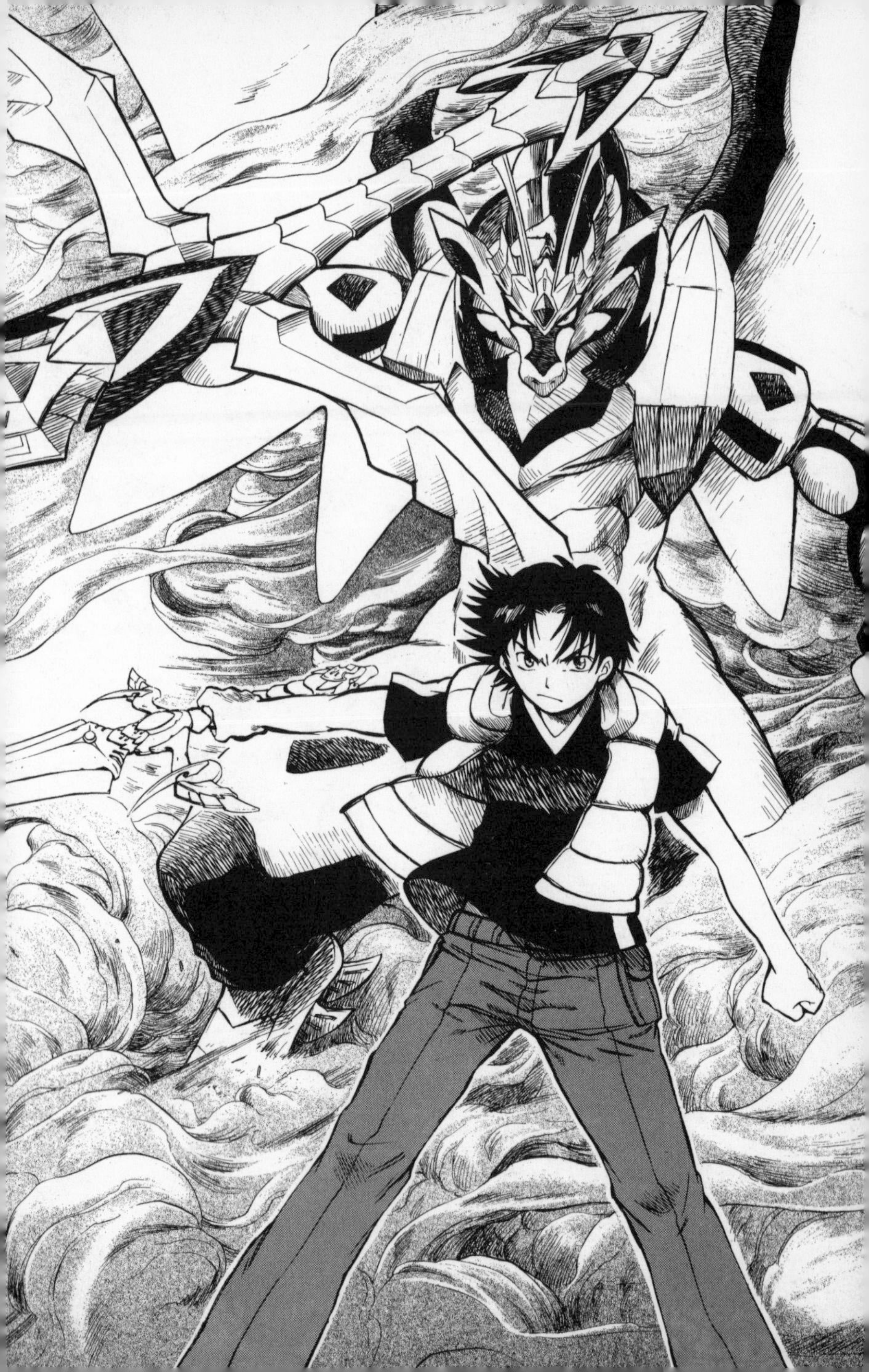

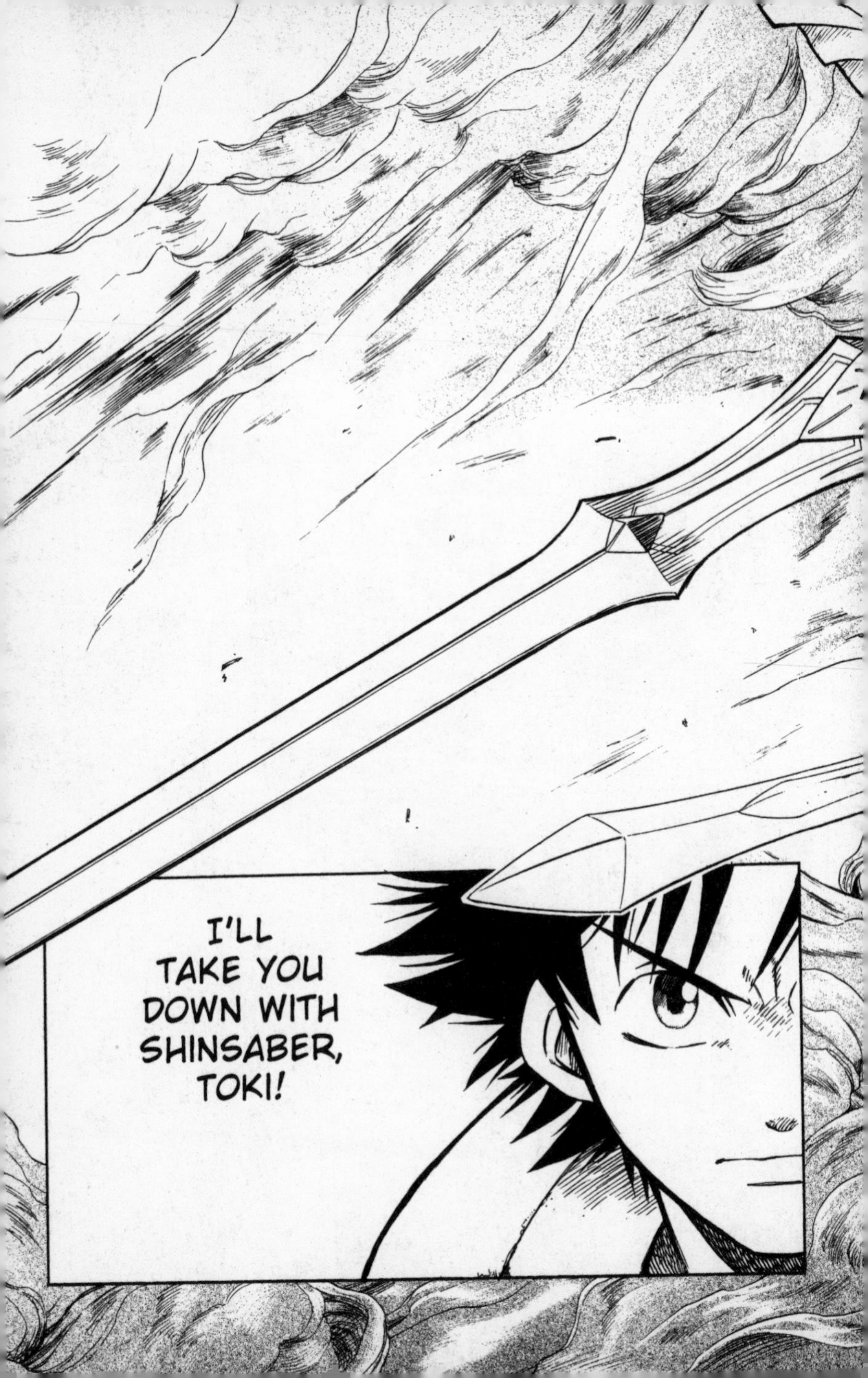
I'LL TAKE YOU DOWN WITH SHINSABER, TOKI!

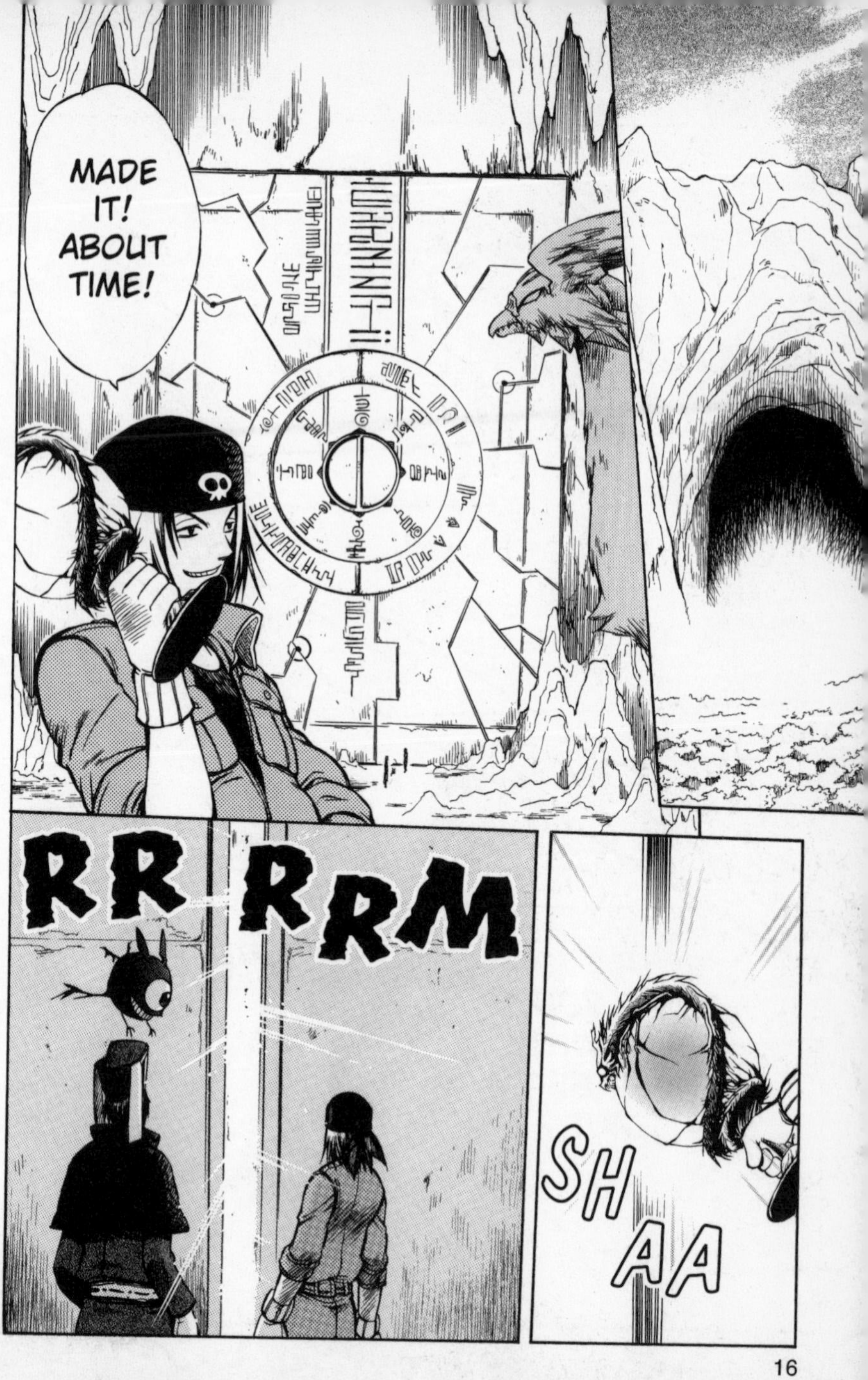

MADE IT! ABOUT TIME!
SHAA
RRRRM

READ THIS WAY

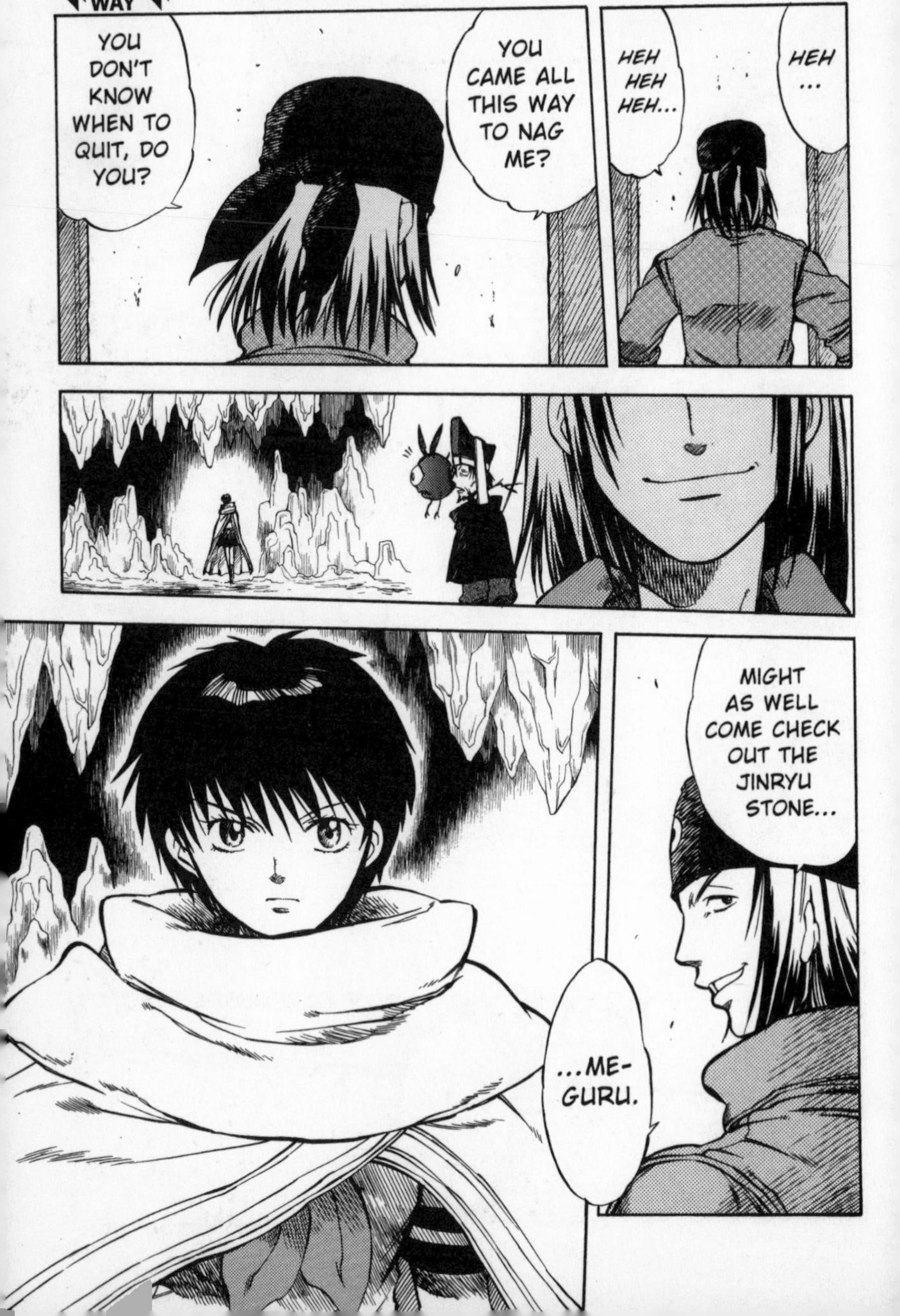
HEH ...
HEH HEH HEH...
YOU CAME ALL THIS WAY TO NAG ME?
YOU DON'T KNOW WHEN TO QUIT, DO YOU?
MIGHT AS WELL COME CHECK OUT THE JINRYU STONE...
...ME-GURU.

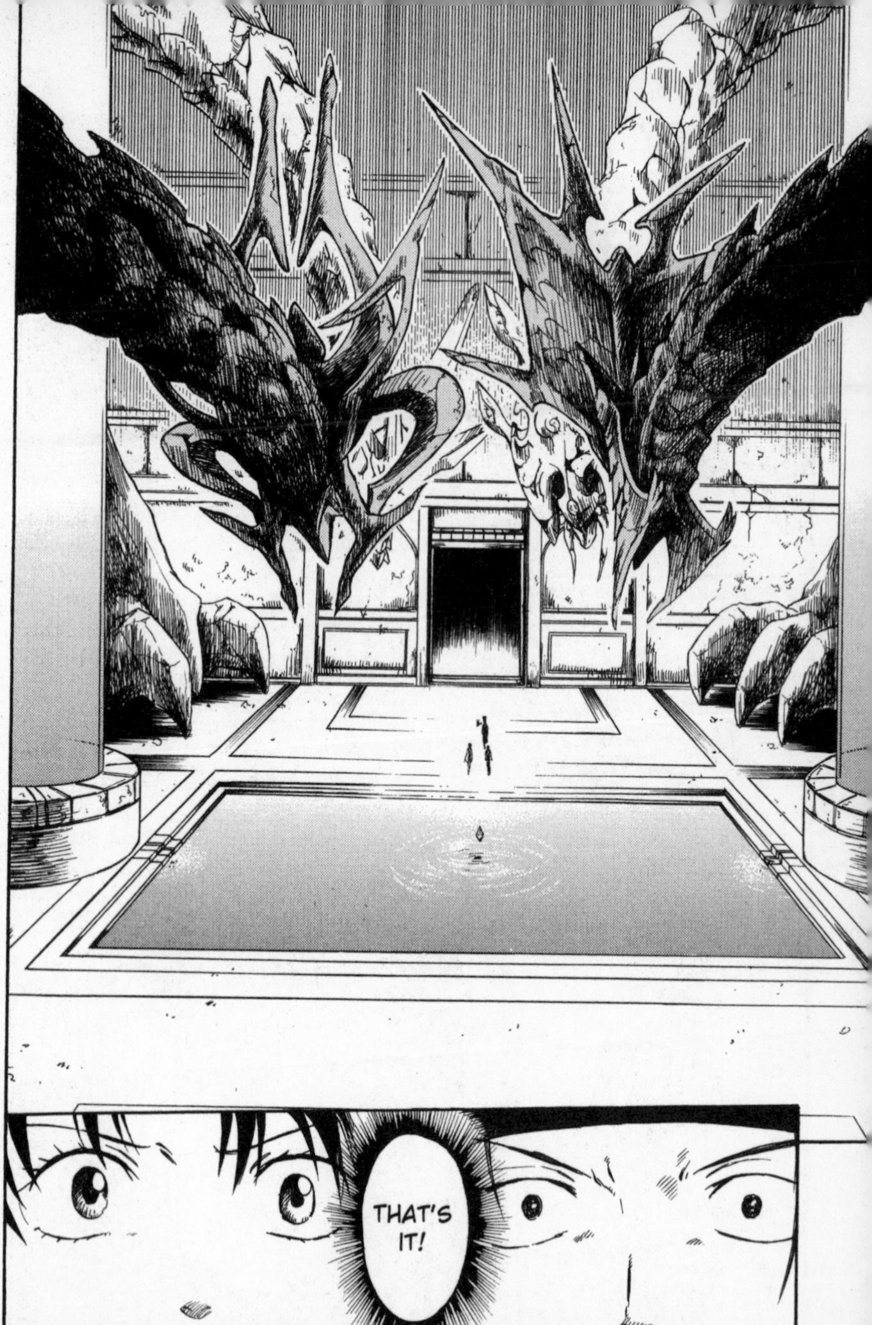
THAT'S IT!

READ THIS WAY

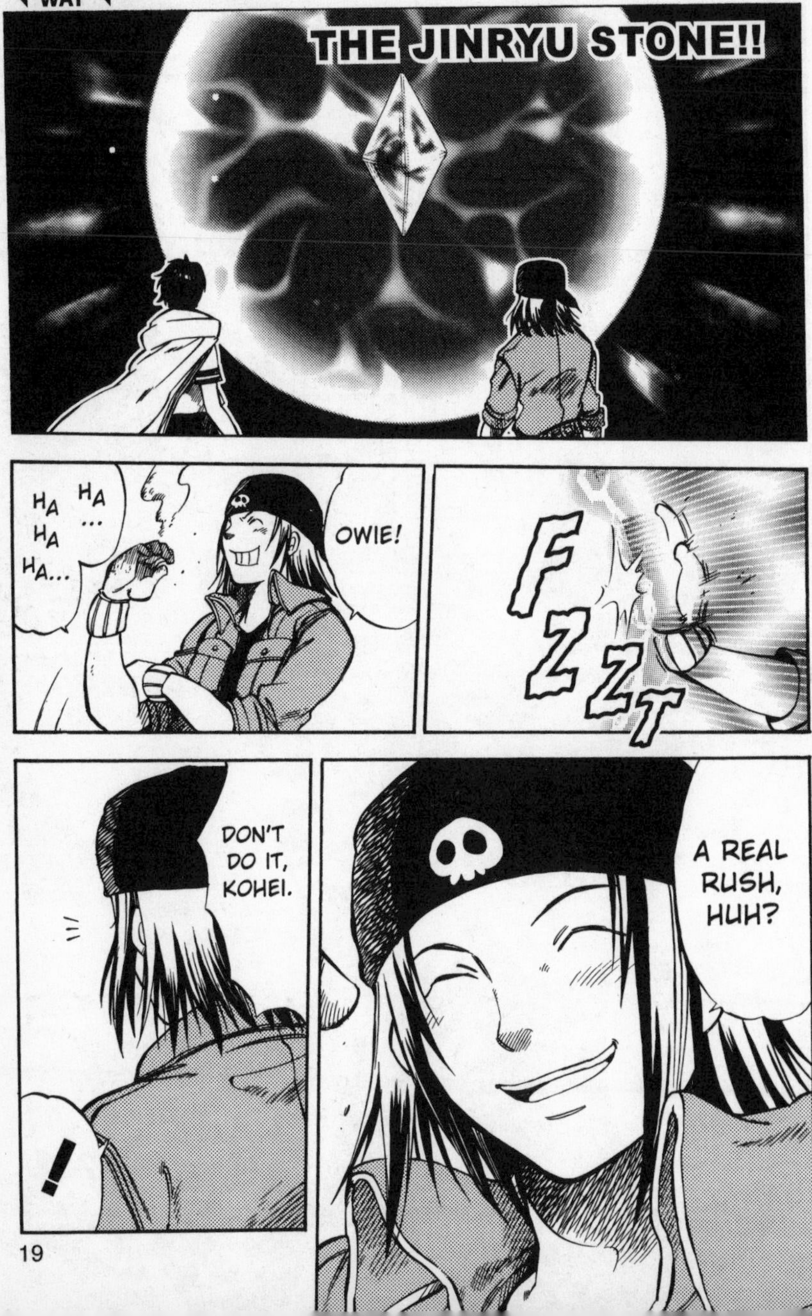
THE JINRYU STONE!!
FZZT
OWIE!
HA HA... HA HA HA...
A REAL RUSH, HUH?
DON'T DO IT, KOHEI.
!

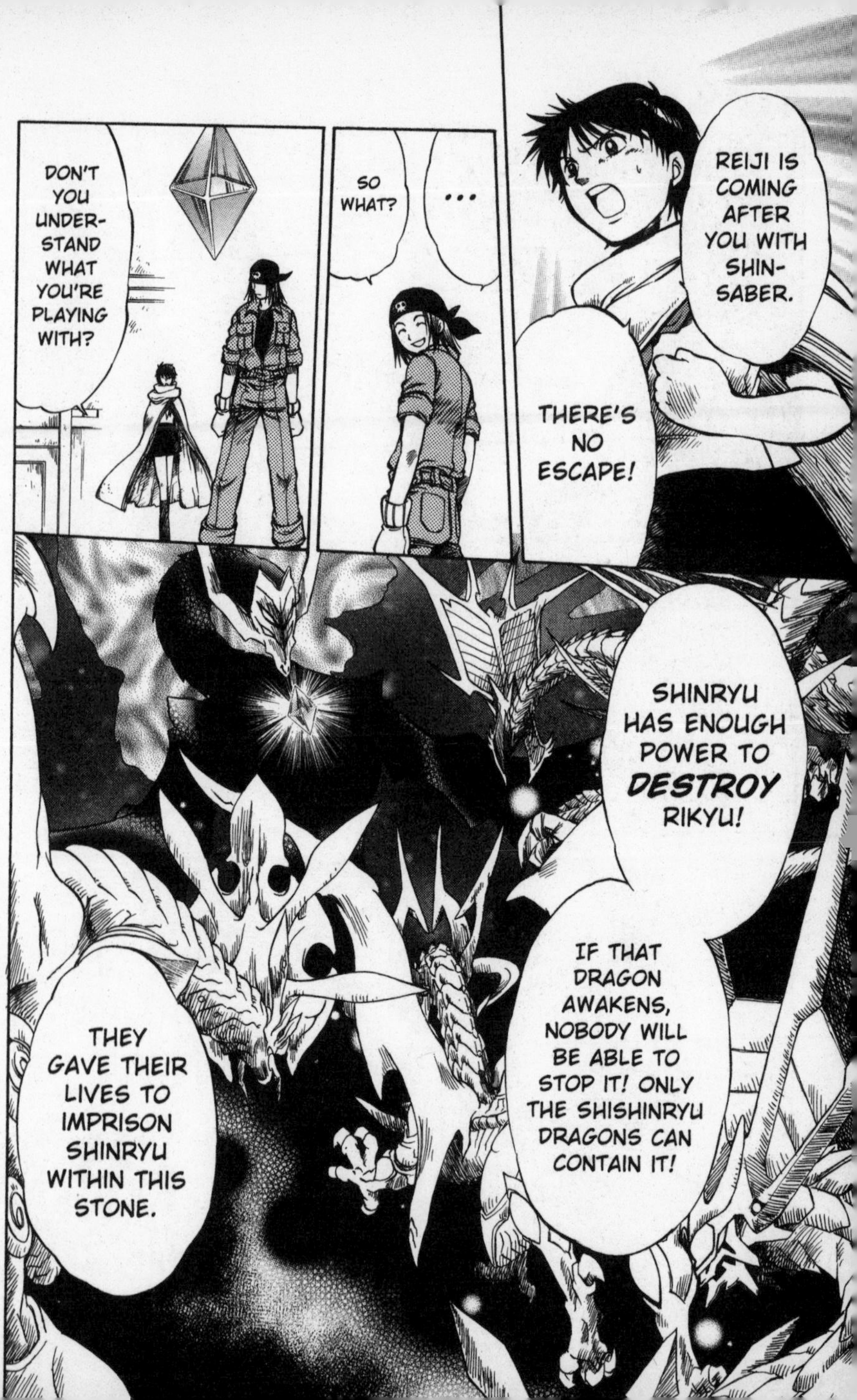
REIJI IS COMING AFTER YOU WITH SHIN-SABER.
THERE'S NO ESCAPE!
...
SO WHAT?
DON'T YOU UNDER-STAND WHAT YOU'RE PLAYING WITH?
SHINRYU HAS ENOUGH POWER TO ***DESTROY*** RIKYU!
IF THAT DRAGON AWAKENS, NOBODY WILL BE ABLE TO STOP IT! ONLY THE SHISHINRYU DRAGONS CAN CONTAIN IT!
THEY GAVE THEIR LIVES TO IMPRISON SHINRYU WITHIN THIS STONE.

READ THIS WAY

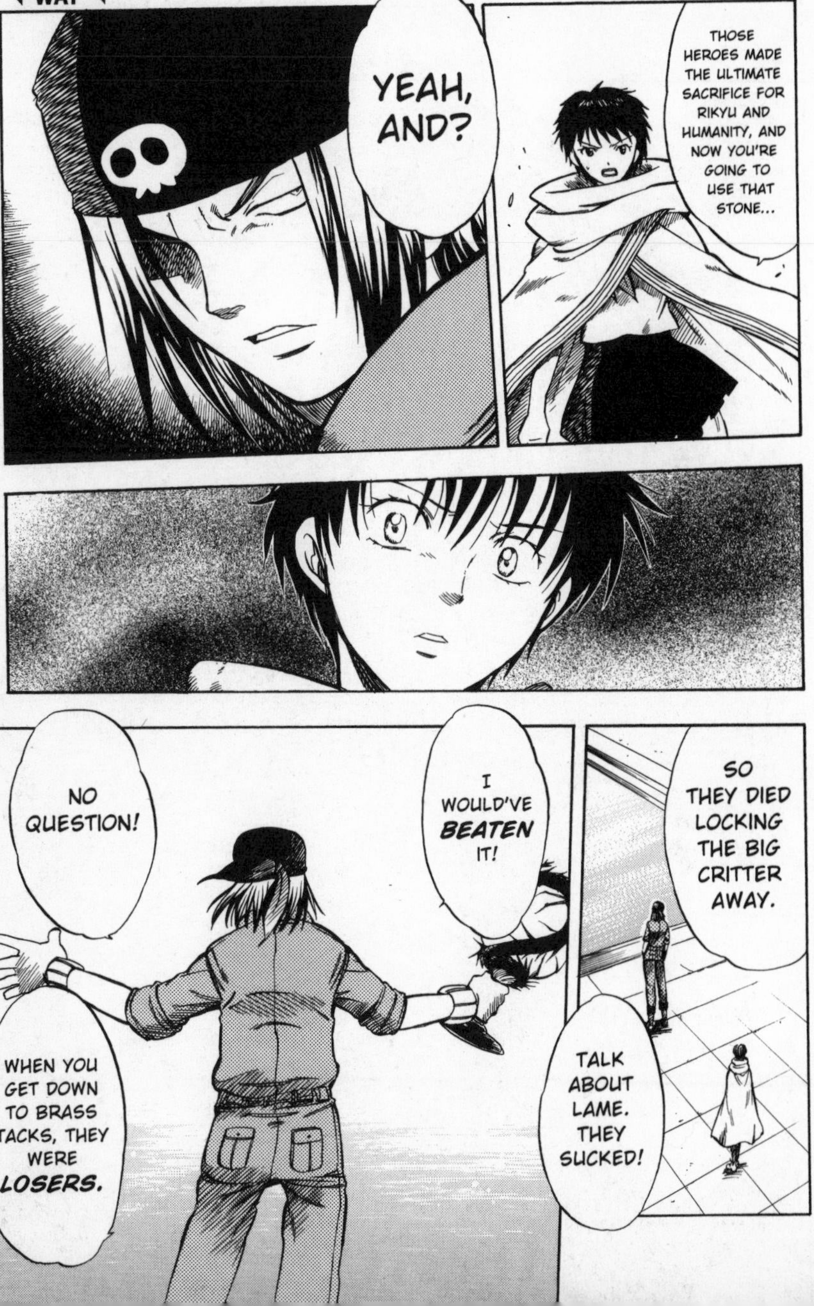
THOSE HEROES MADE THE ULTIMATE SACRIFICE FOR RIKYU AND HUMANITY, AND NOW YOU'RE GOING TO USE THAT STONE...
YEAH, AND?
SO THEY DIED LOCKING THE BIG CRITTER AWAY.
TALK ABOUT LAME. THEY SUCKED!
I WOULD'VE *BEATEN* IT!
NO QUESTION!
WHEN YOU GET DOWN TO BRASS TACKS, THEY WERE *LOSERS.*

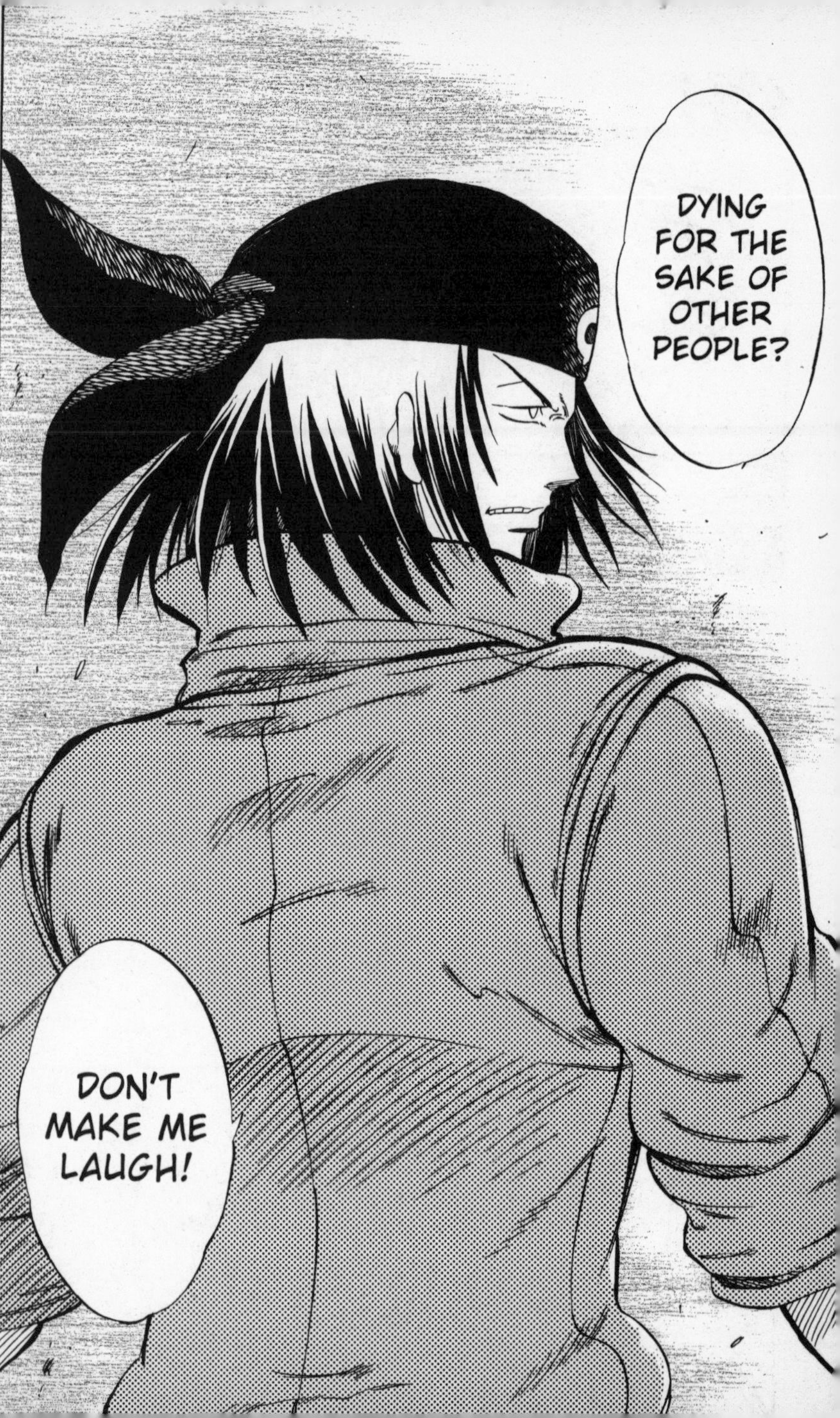
DYING FOR THE SAKE OF OTHER PEOPLE?
DON'T MAKE ME LAUGH!

READ THIS WAY

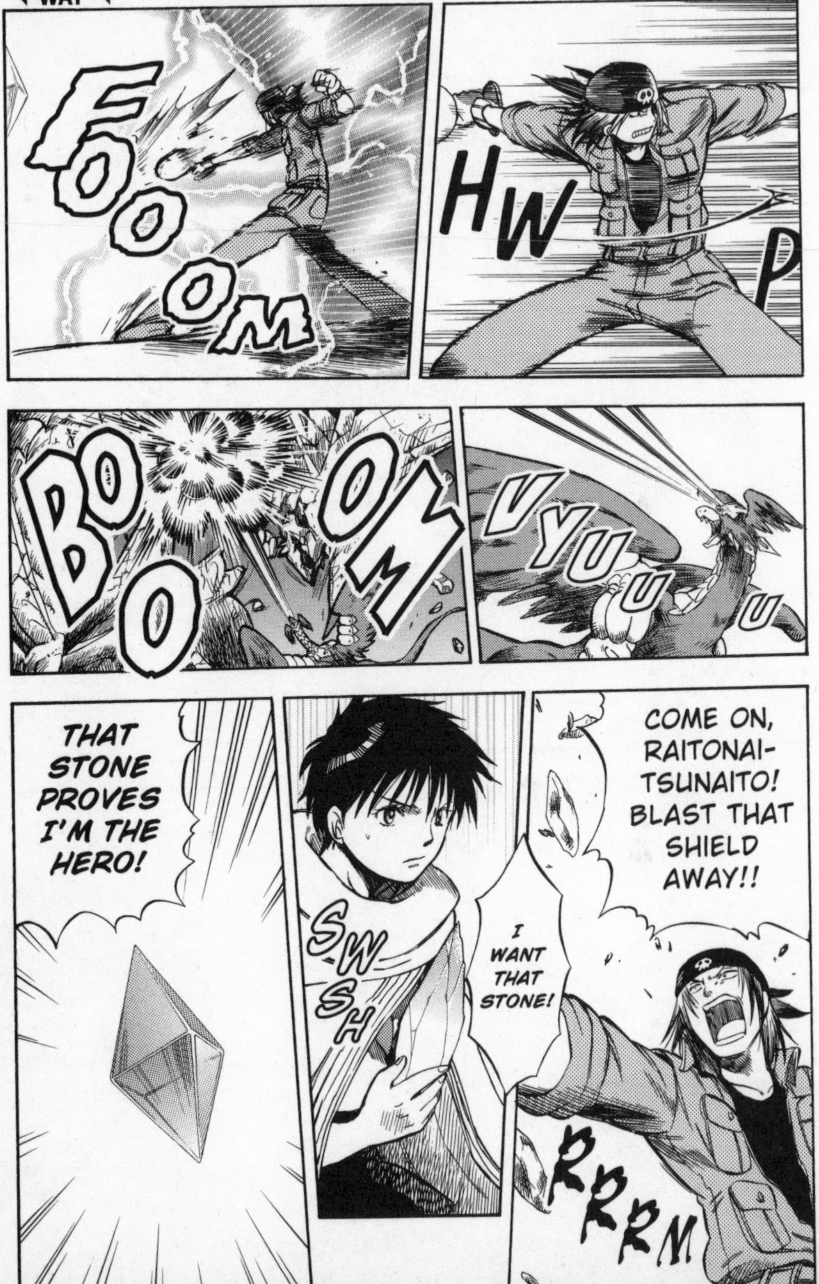
HWP
FOOOM
VYUUUU
BOOOM
COME ON, RAITONAI-TSUNAITO! BLAST THAT SHIELD AWAY!!
I WANT THAT STONE!
RRRRM
SWSH
THAT STONE PROVES I'M THE HERO!

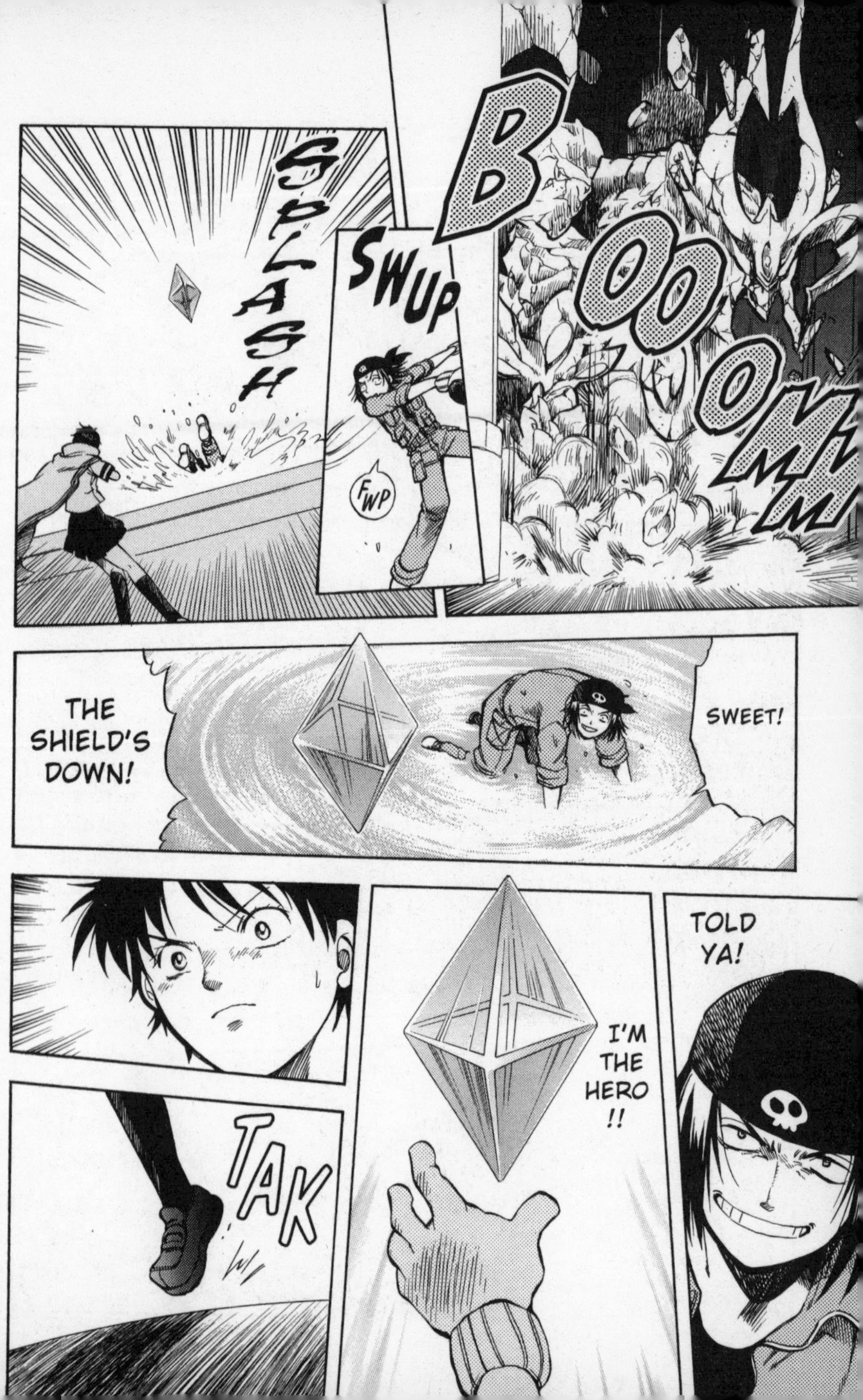
BOOOOMMM
SWUP
FWP
SPLASH
SWEET!
THE SHIELD'S DOWN!
TOLD YA!
I'M THE HERO!!
TAK

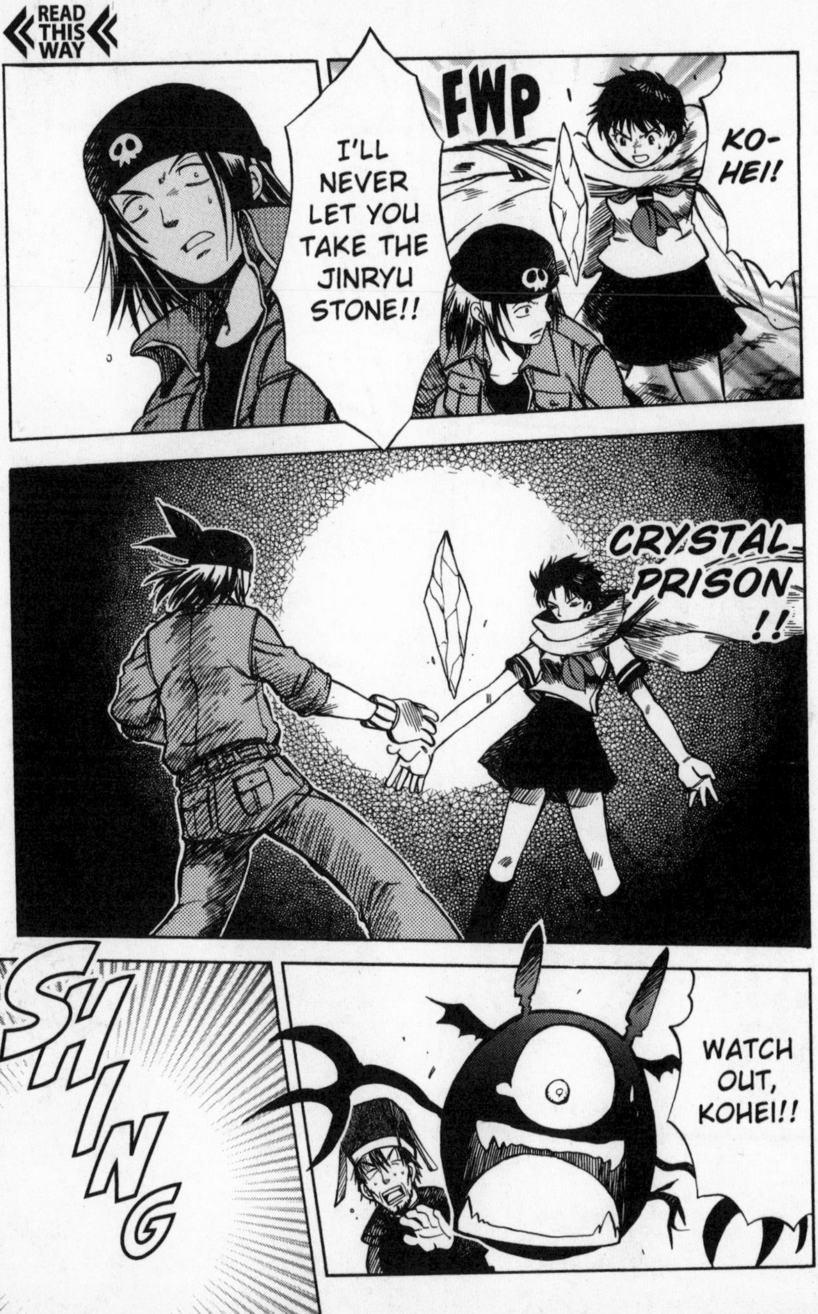
READ THIS WAY
FWP
KO-HEI!
I'LL NEVER LET YOU TAKE THE JINRYU STONE!!
CRYSTAL PRISON!!
WATCH OUT, KOHEI!!
SHING

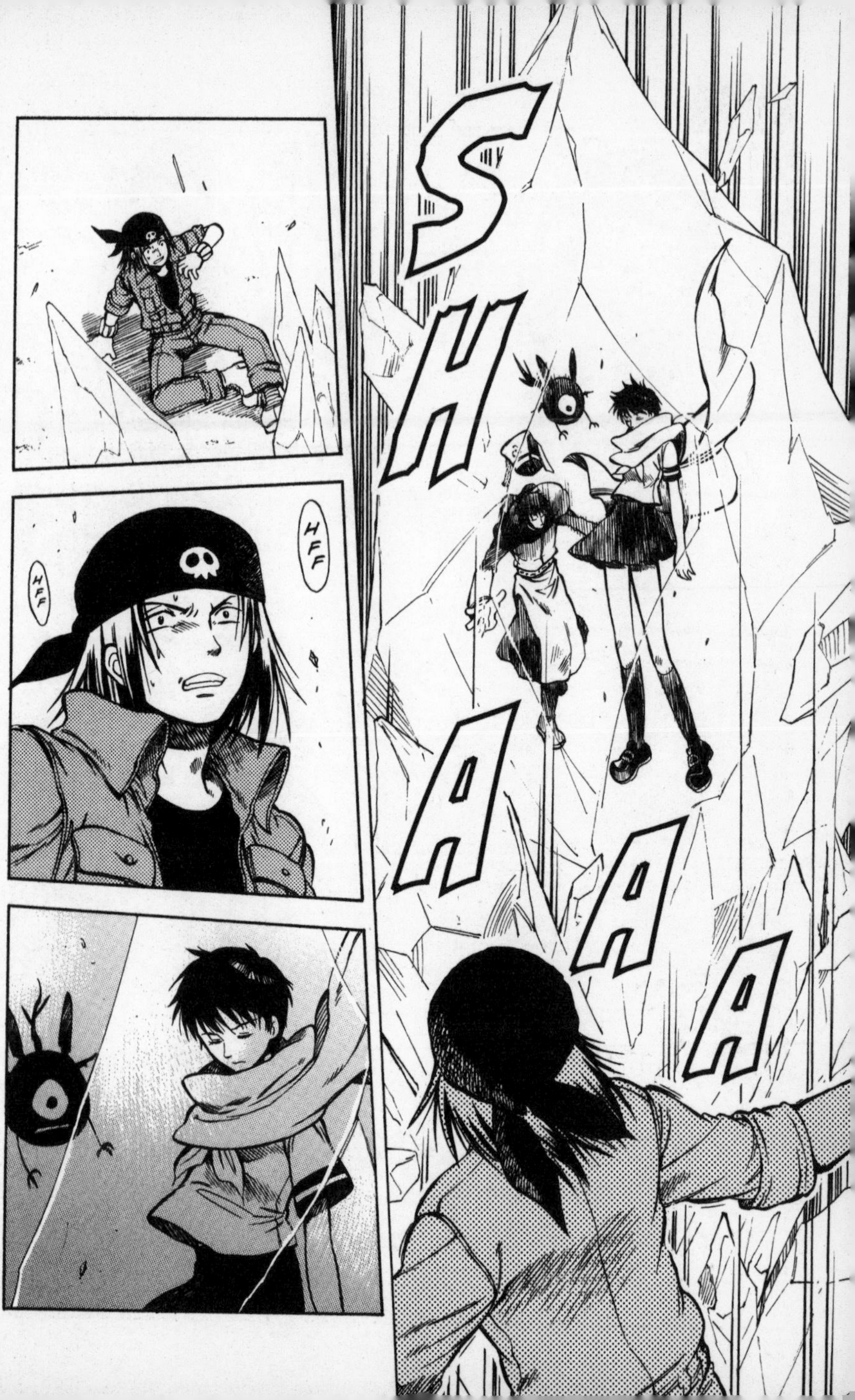
SHAAAA
HFF
HFF

READ THIS WAY

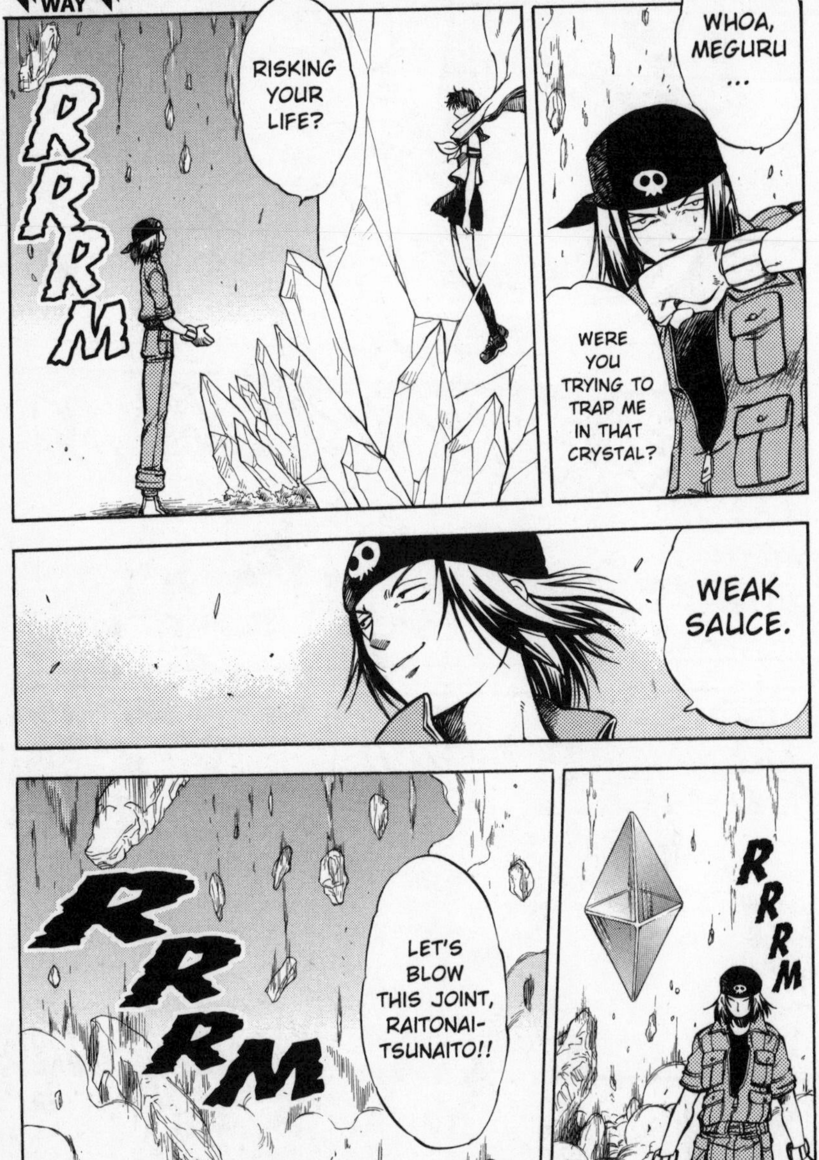
WHOA, MEGURU ...
WERE YOU TRYING TO TRAP ME IN THAT CRYSTAL?
RISKING YOUR LIFE?
RRRM
WEAK SAUCE.
RRRM
LET'S BLOW THIS JOINT, RAITONAI-TSUNAITO!!
RRRM

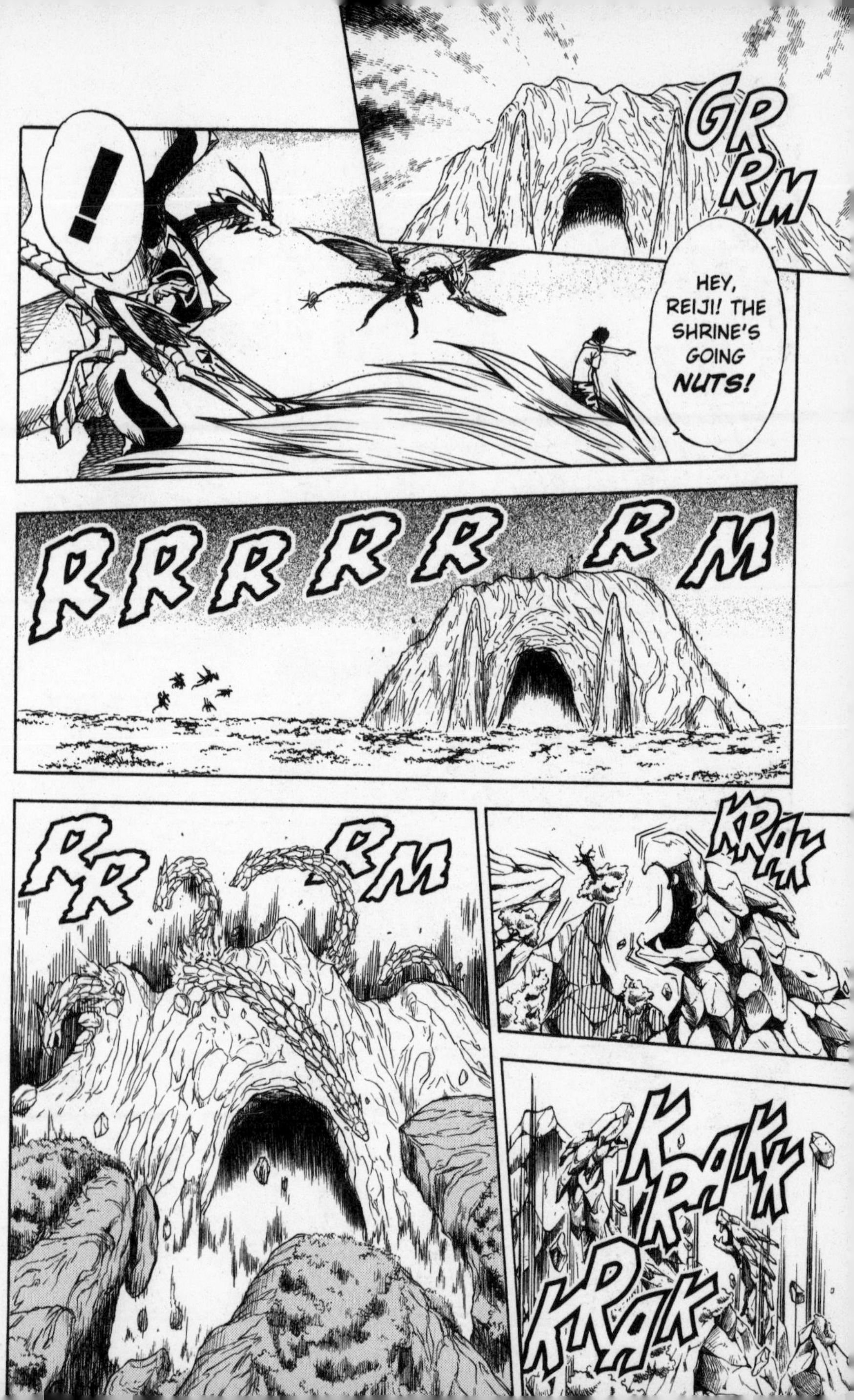
GRRM
HEY, REIJI! THE SHRINE'S GOING NUTS!
!
RRRRR RM
KRAK
KRAK
KRAK
RR RM

READ THIS WAY

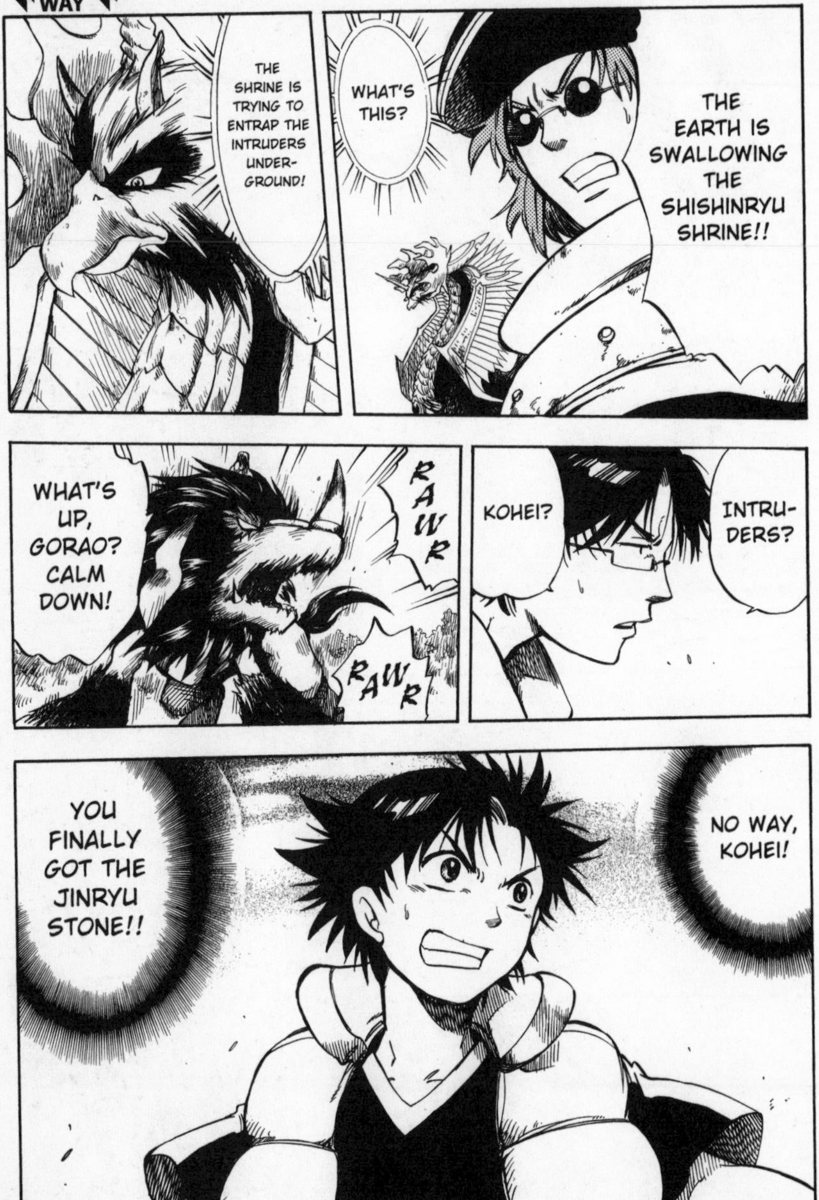
THE EARTH IS SWALLOWING THE SHISHINRYU SHRINE!!
WHAT'S THIS?
THE SHRINE IS TRYING TO ENTRAP THE INTRUDERS UNDER-GROUND!
INTRU-DERS?
KOHEI?
RAWR
WHAT'S UP, GORAO? CALM DOWN!
RAWR
NO WAY, KOHEI!
YOU FINALLY GOT THE JINRYU STONE!!

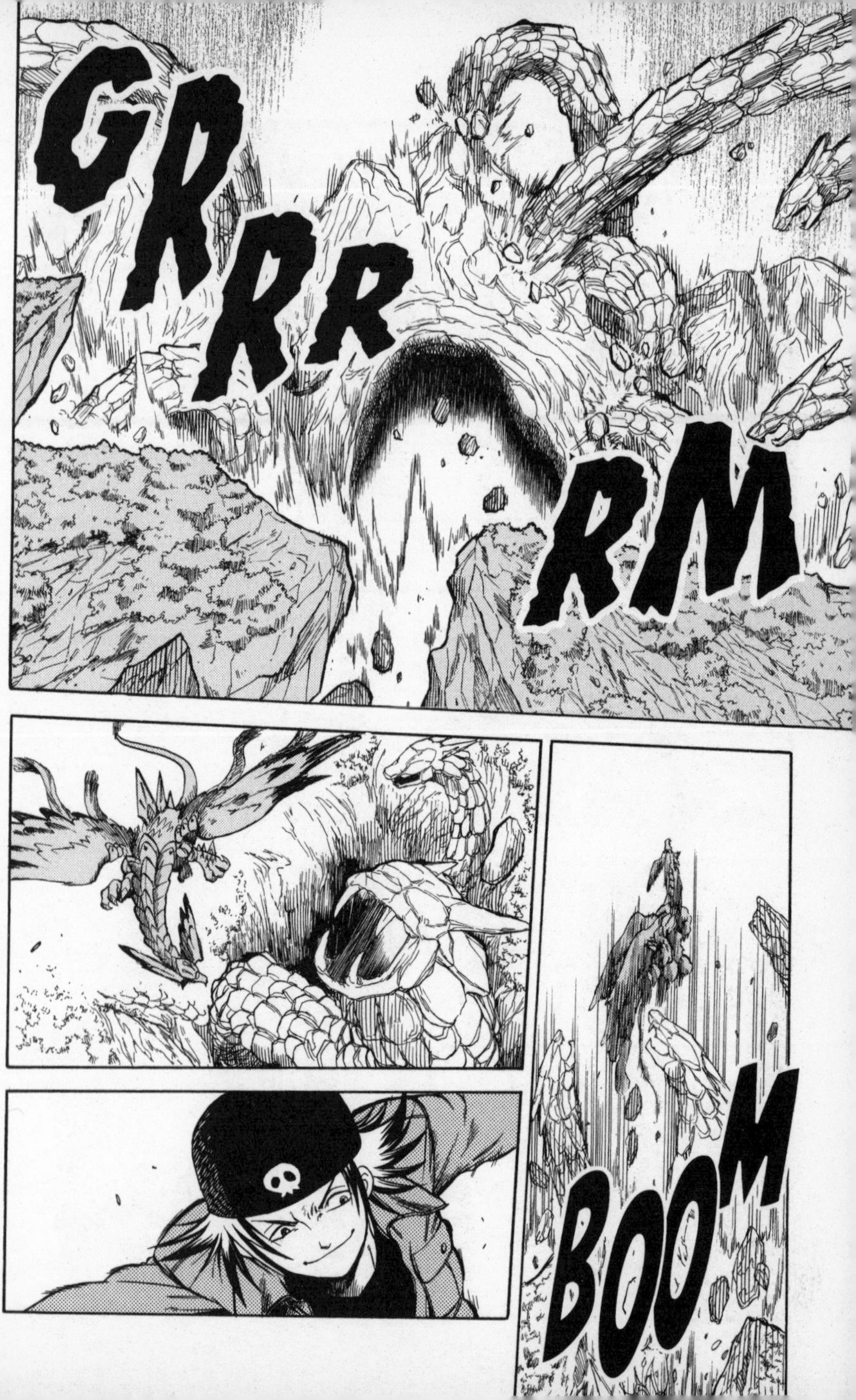
GRRRRM
BOOM

READ THIS WAY

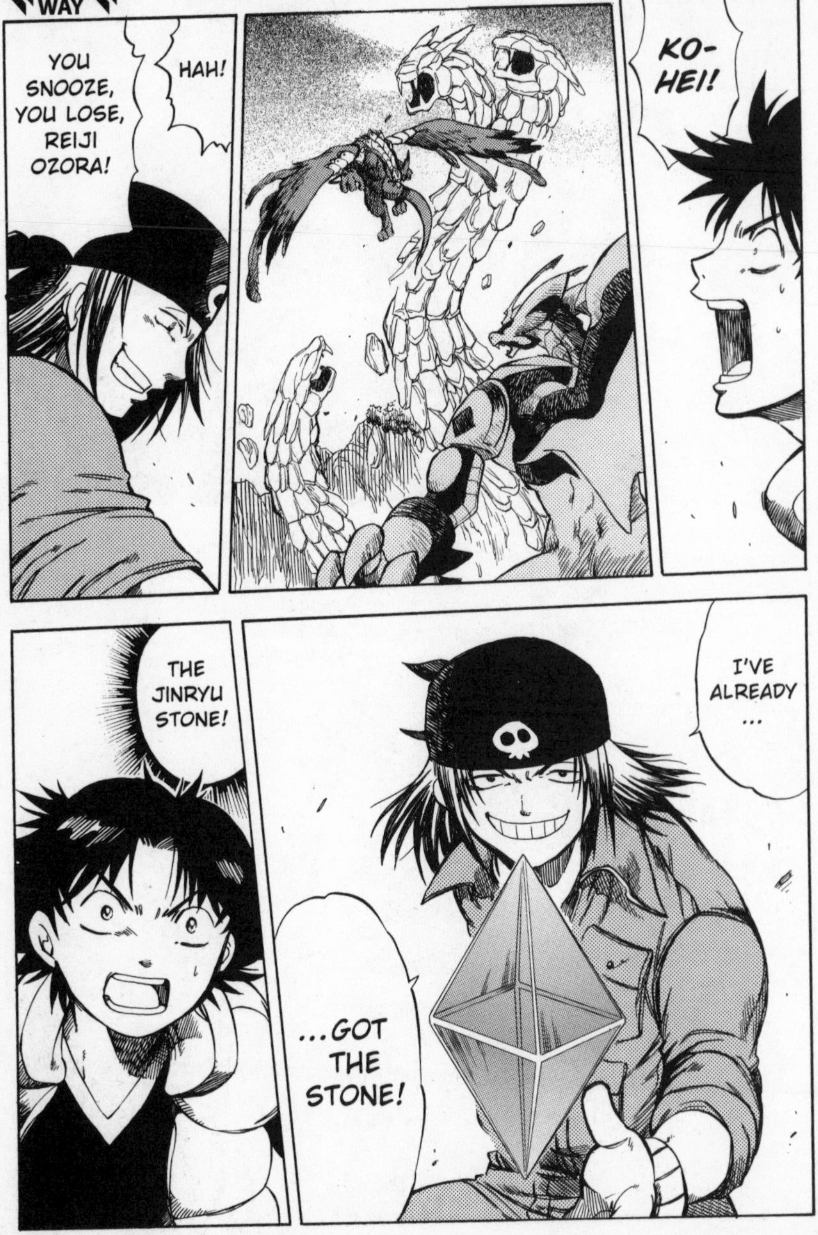
KO-HEI!
HAH!
YOU SNOOZE, YOU LOSE, REIJI OZORA!
I'VE ALREADY ...
...GOT THE STONE!
THE JINRYU STONE!

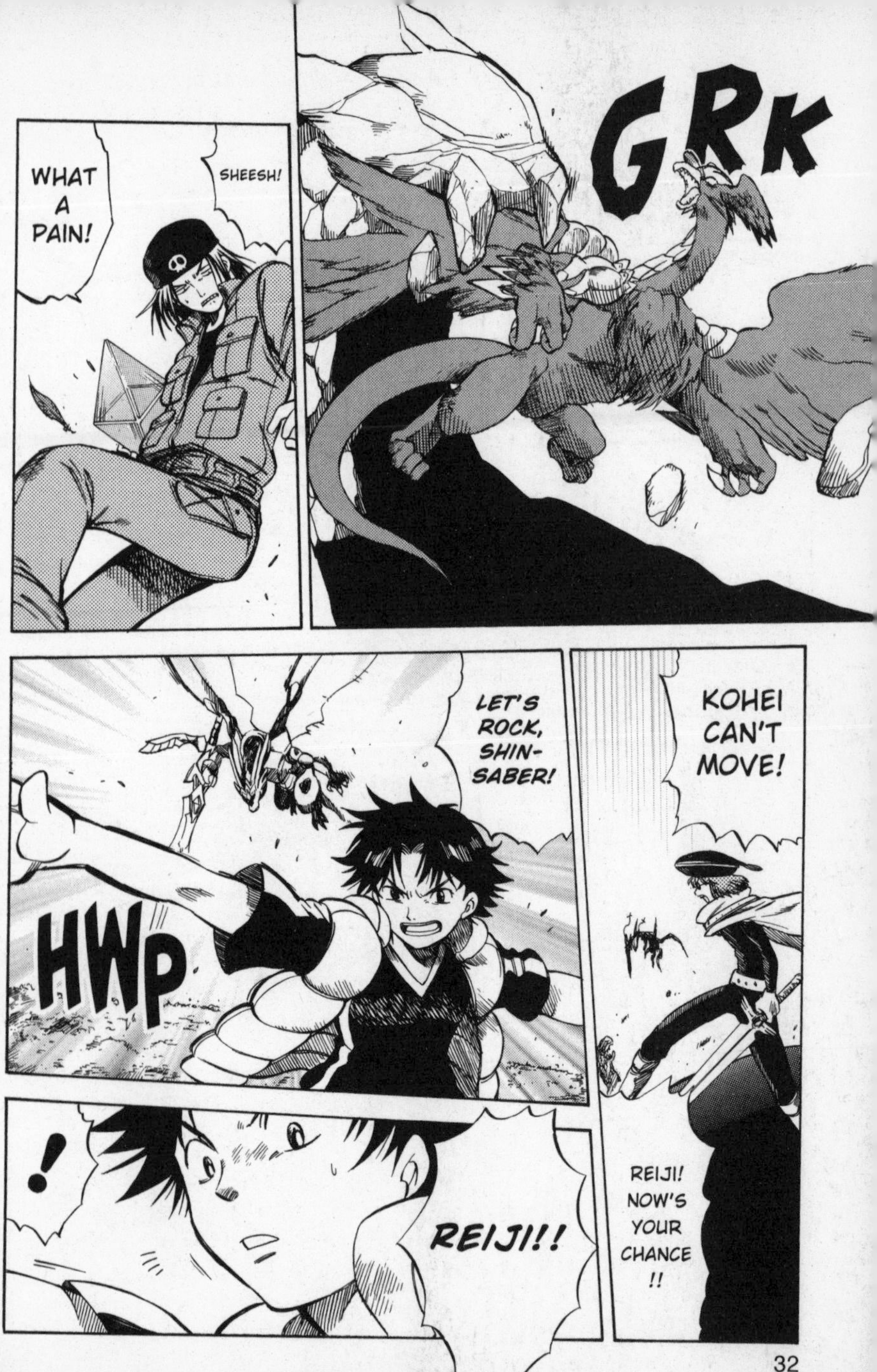
GRK
SHEESH!
WHAT A PAIN!
KOHEI CAN'T MOVE!
REIJI! NOW'S YOUR CHANCE !!
LET'S ROCK, SHIN-SABER!
HWP
!
REIJI!!

READ THIS WAY

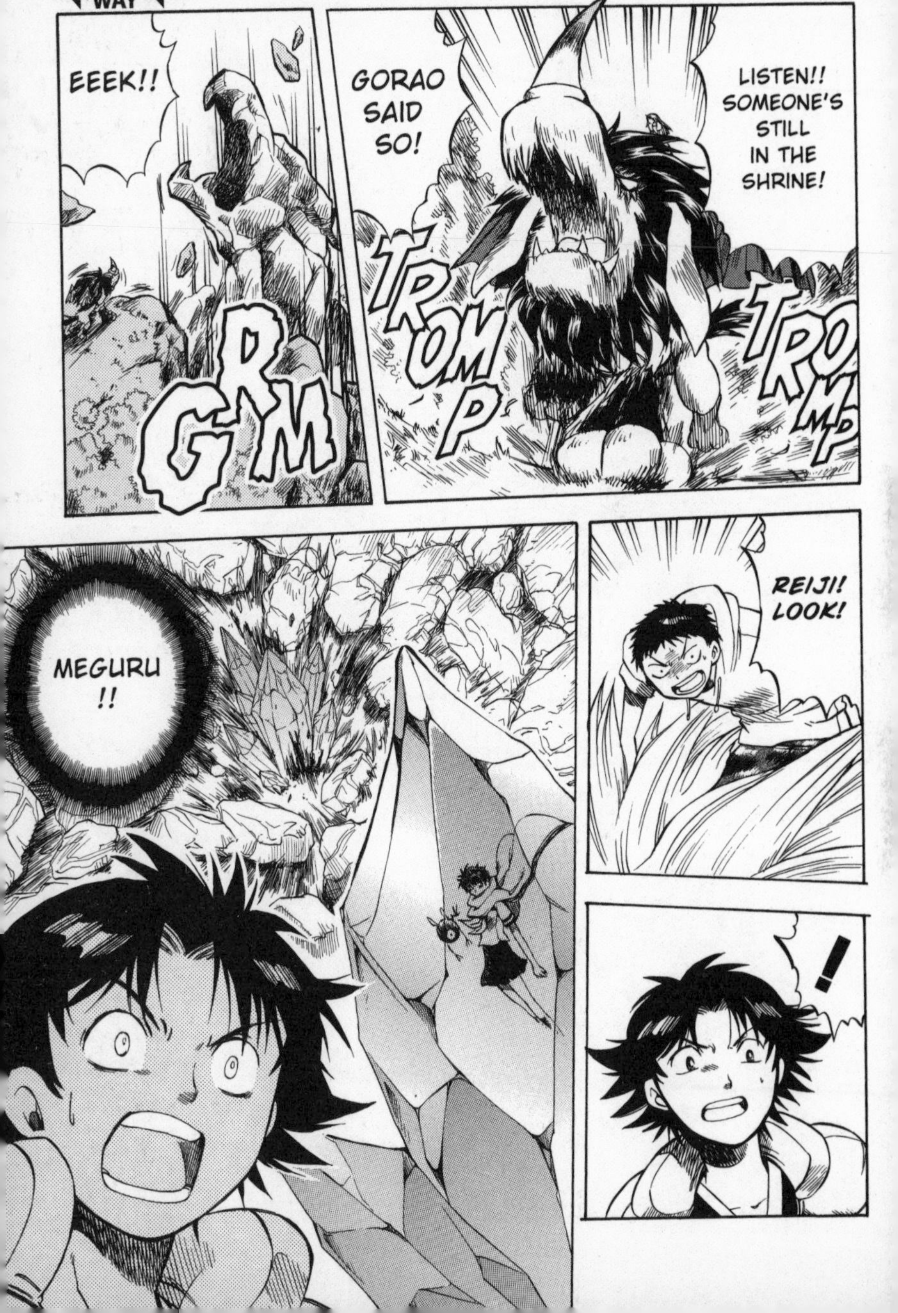

LISTEN!! SOMEONE'S STILL IN THE SHRINE!
GORAO SAID SO!
TROMP
TROMP
EEEK!!
GRGM
REIJI! LOOK!
!
MEGURU !!

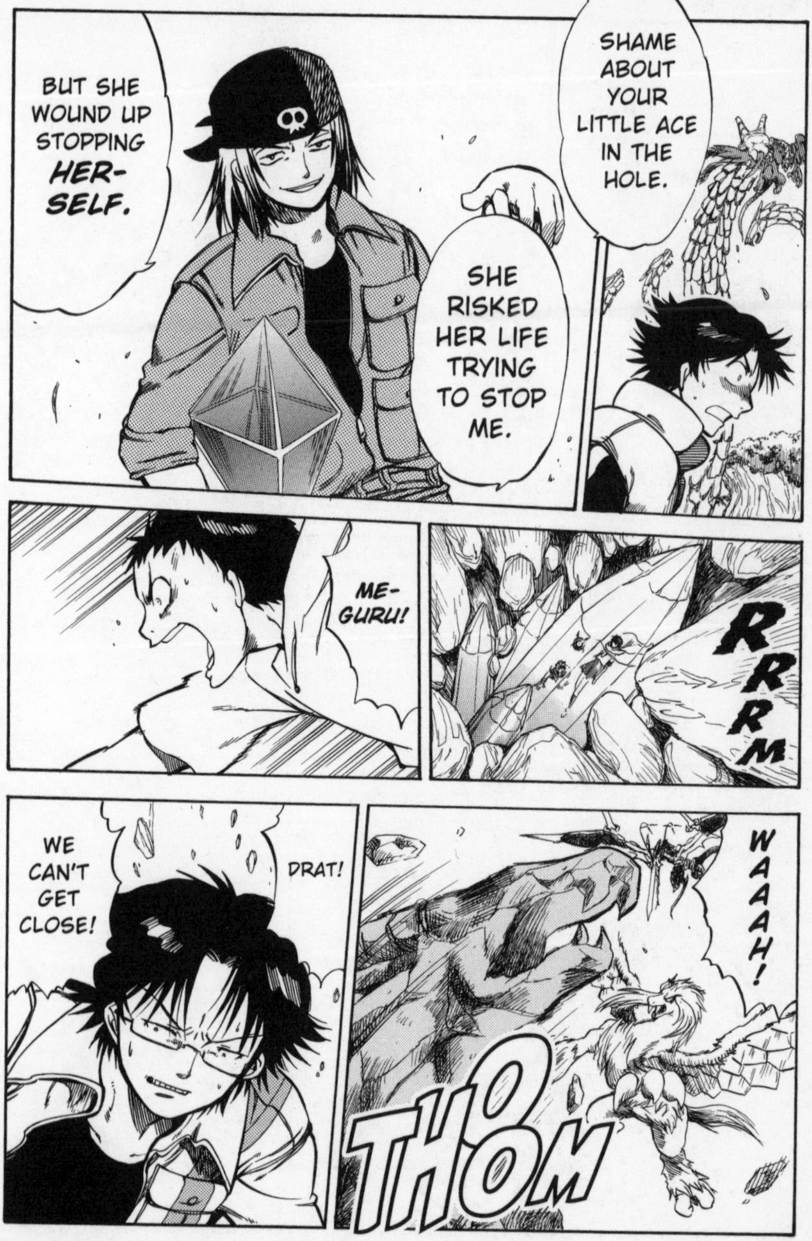
SHAME ABOUT YOUR LITTLE ACE IN THE HOLE.
SHE RISKED HER LIFE TRYING TO STOP ME.
BUT SHE WOUND UP STOPPING *HER-SELF*.
RRRRM
ME-GURU!
WAAAAH!
THOOM
DRAT!
WE CAN'T GET CLOSE!

READ THIS WAY

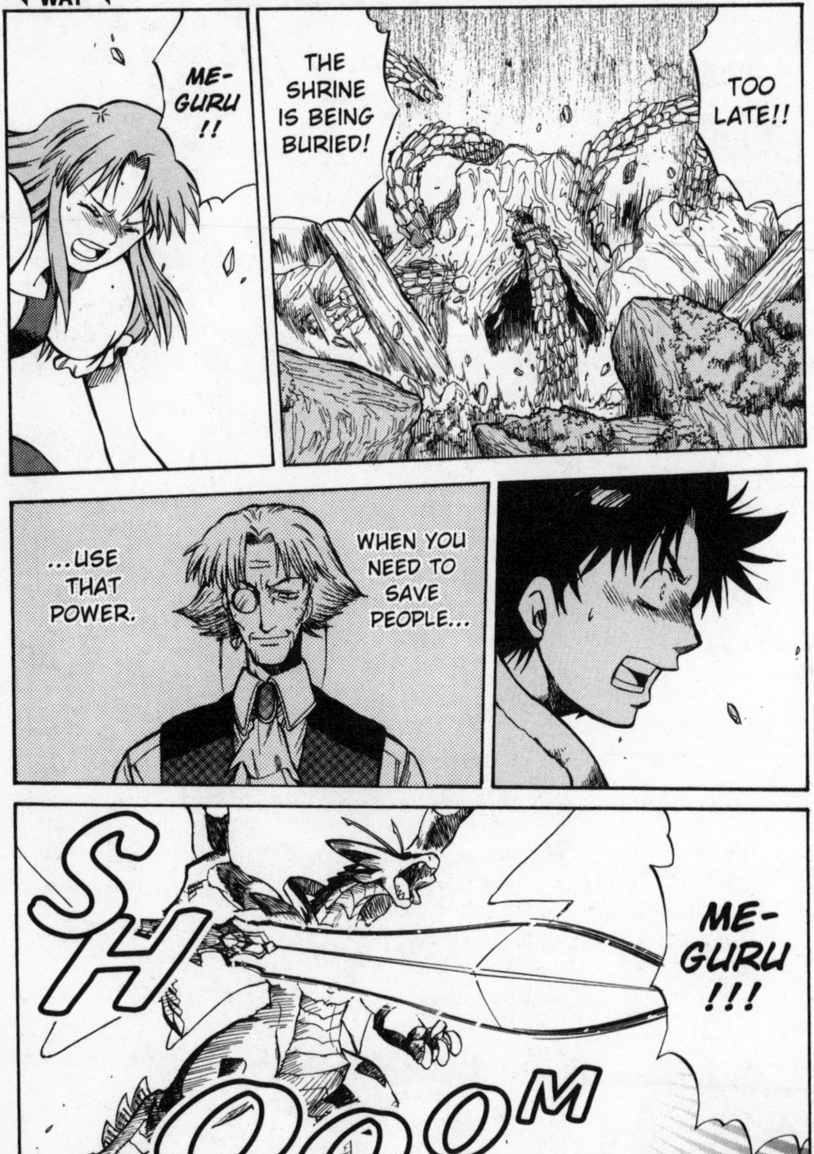
TOO LATE!!
THE SHRINE IS BEING BURIED!
ME-GURU!!
WHEN YOU NEED TO SAVE PEOPLE...
...USE THAT POWER.
ME-GURU!!!
SHOOOOM

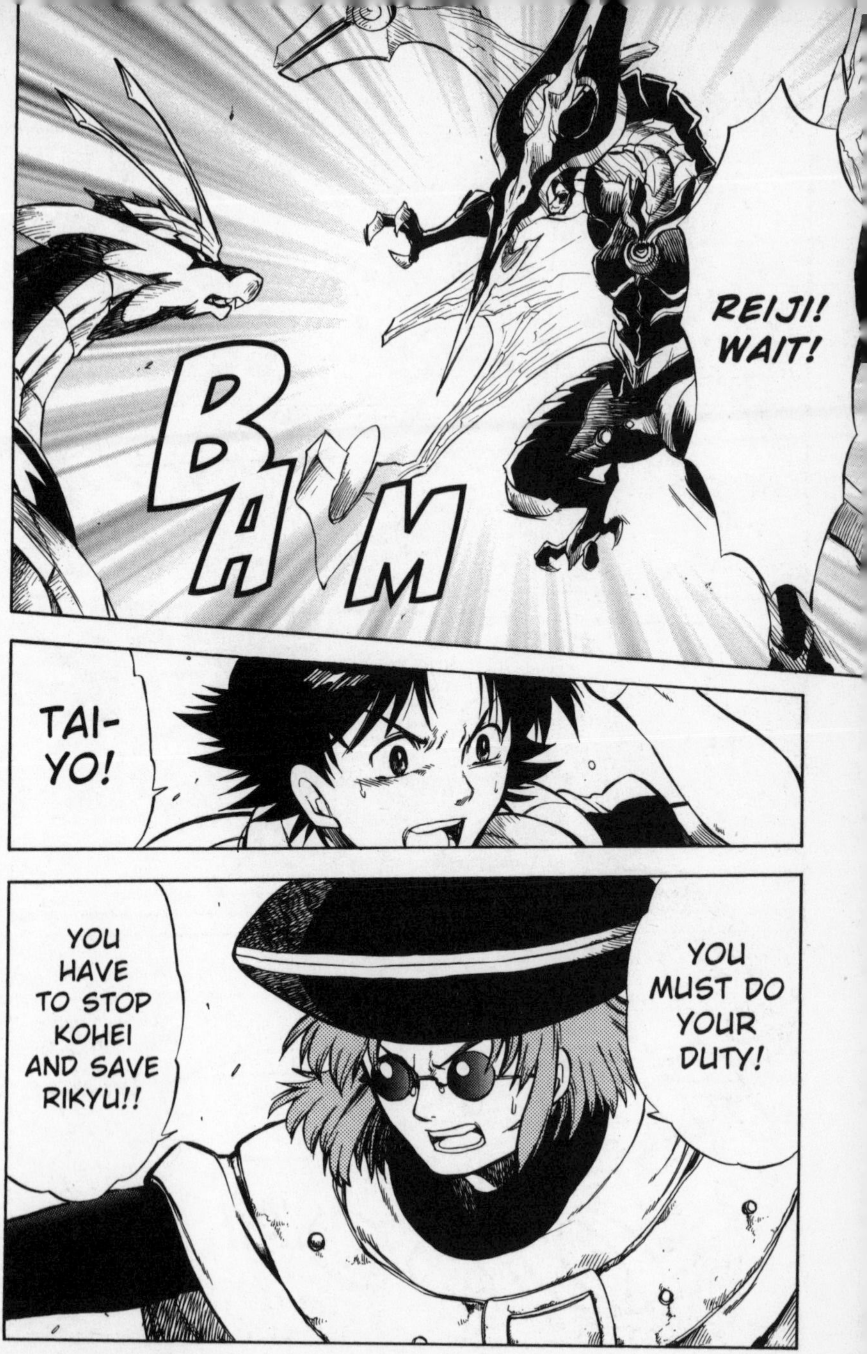
REIJI! WAIT!
BAM
TAI-YO!
YOU MUST DO YOUR DUTY!
YOU HAVE TO STOP KOHEI AND SAVE RIKYU!!

READ THIS WAY

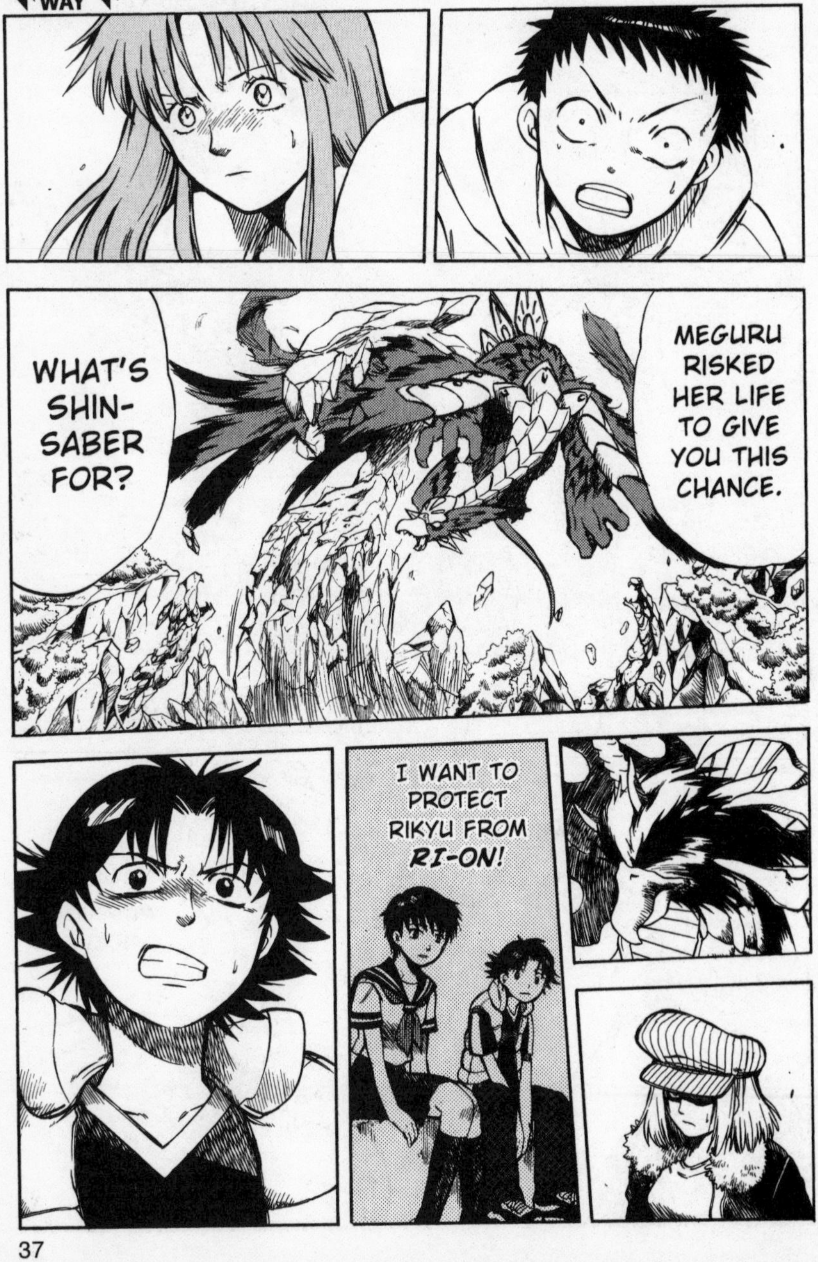
MEGURU RISKED HER LIFE TO GIVE YOU THIS CHANCE.
WHAT'S SHIN-SABER FOR?
I WANT TO PROTECT RIKYU FROM *RI-ON*!

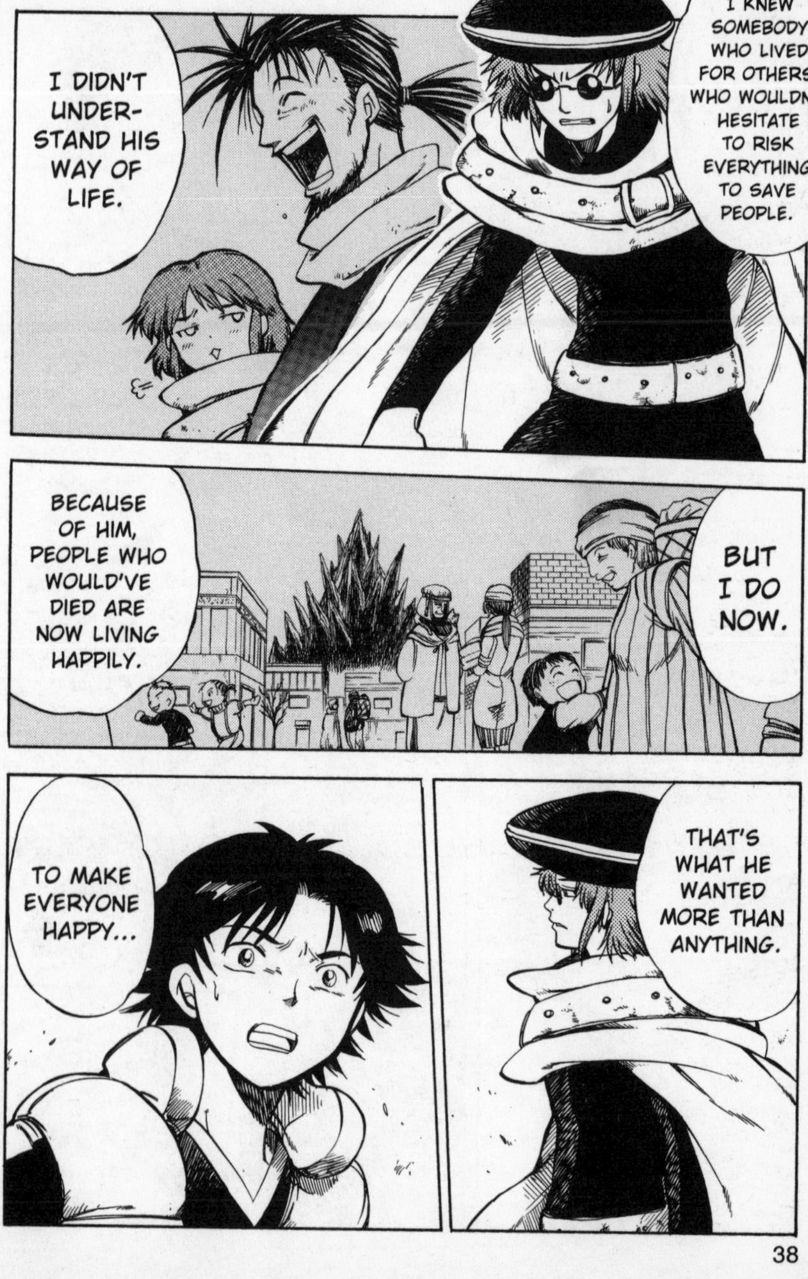
I KNEW SOMEBODY WHO LIVED FOR OTHERS, WHO WOULDN'T HESITATE TO RISK EVERYTHING TO SAVE PEOPLE.
I DIDN'T UNDER-STAND HIS WAY OF LIFE.
BUT I DO NOW.
BECAUSE OF HIM, PEOPLE WHO WOULD'VE DIED ARE NOW LIVING HAPPILY.
THAT'S WHAT HE WANTED MORE THAN ANYTHING.
TO MAKE EVERYONE HAPPY...

READ THIS WAY

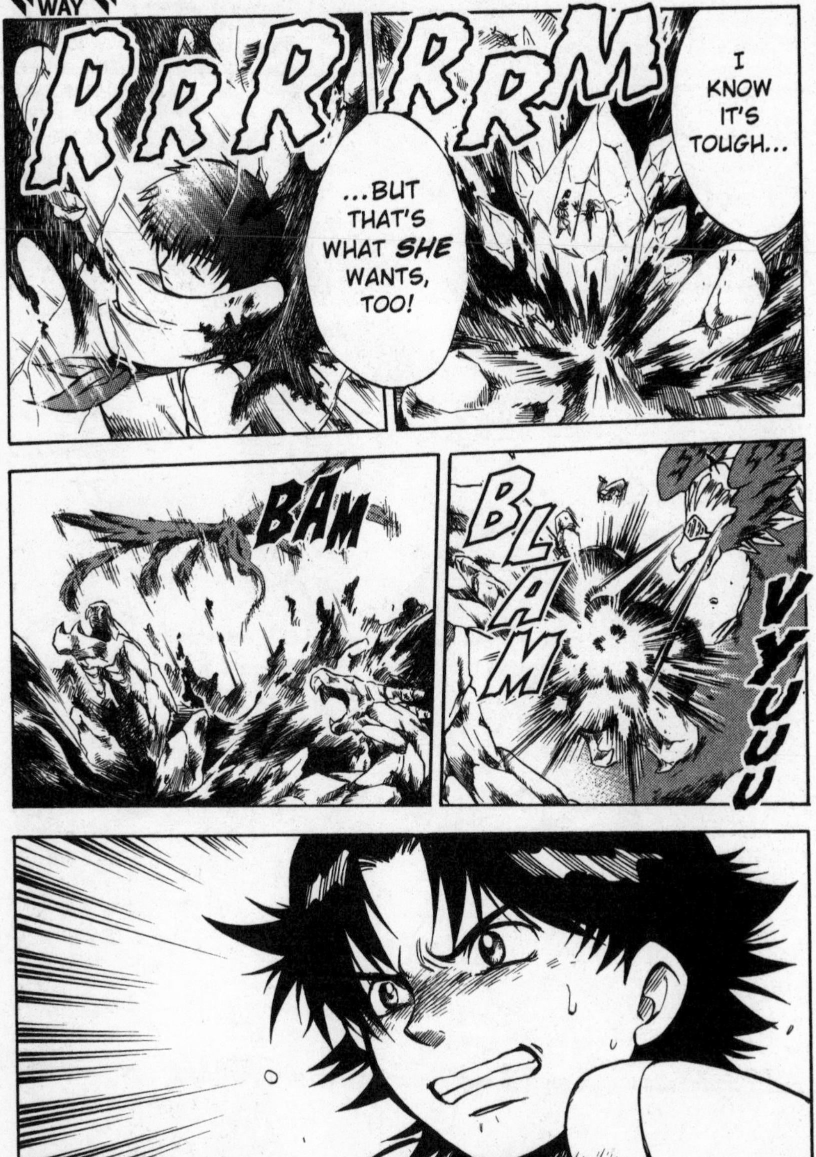
RRRRRM
I KNOW IT'S TOUGH...
...BUT THAT'S WHAT *SHE* WANTS, TOO!
VYUUU
BLAM
BAM

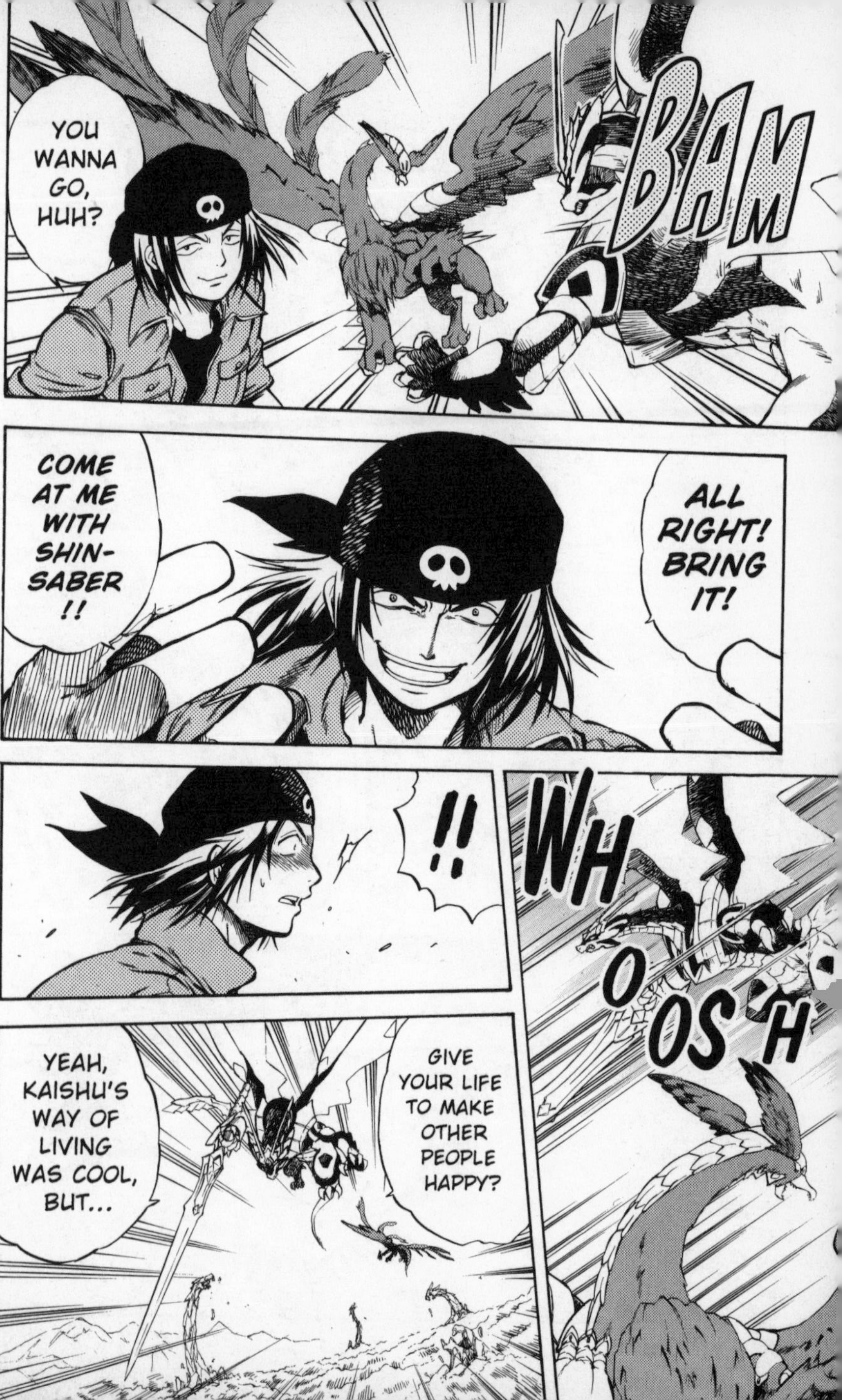
BAM
YOU WANNA GO, HUH?
ALL RIGHT! BRING IT!
COME AT ME WITH SHIN-SABER!!
WHOOSH
!!
GIVE YOUR LIFE TO MAKE OTHER PEOPLE HAPPY?
YEAH, KAISHU'S WAY OF LIVING WAS COOL, BUT...

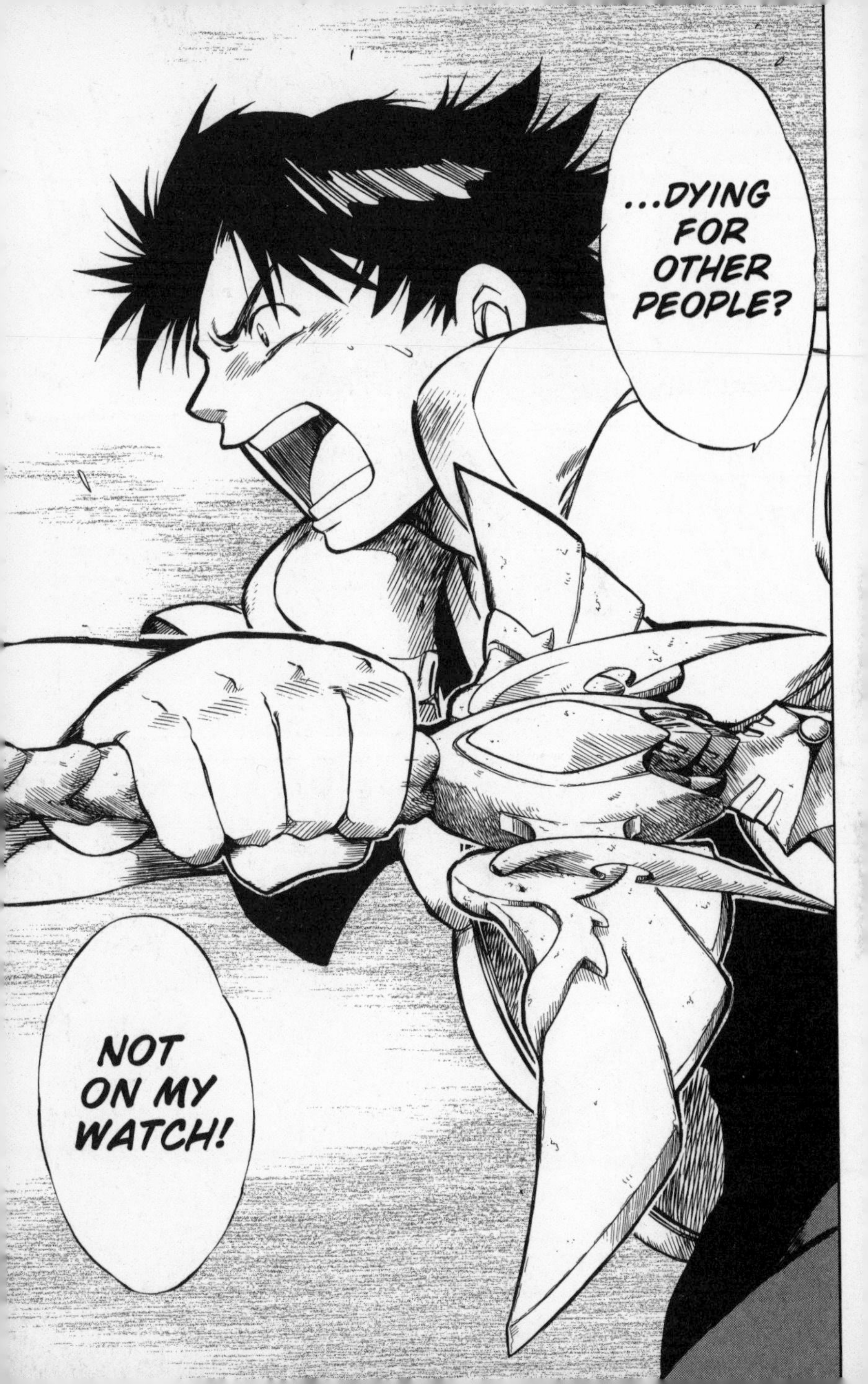
...DYING FOR OTHER PEOPLE?
NOT ON MY WATCH!

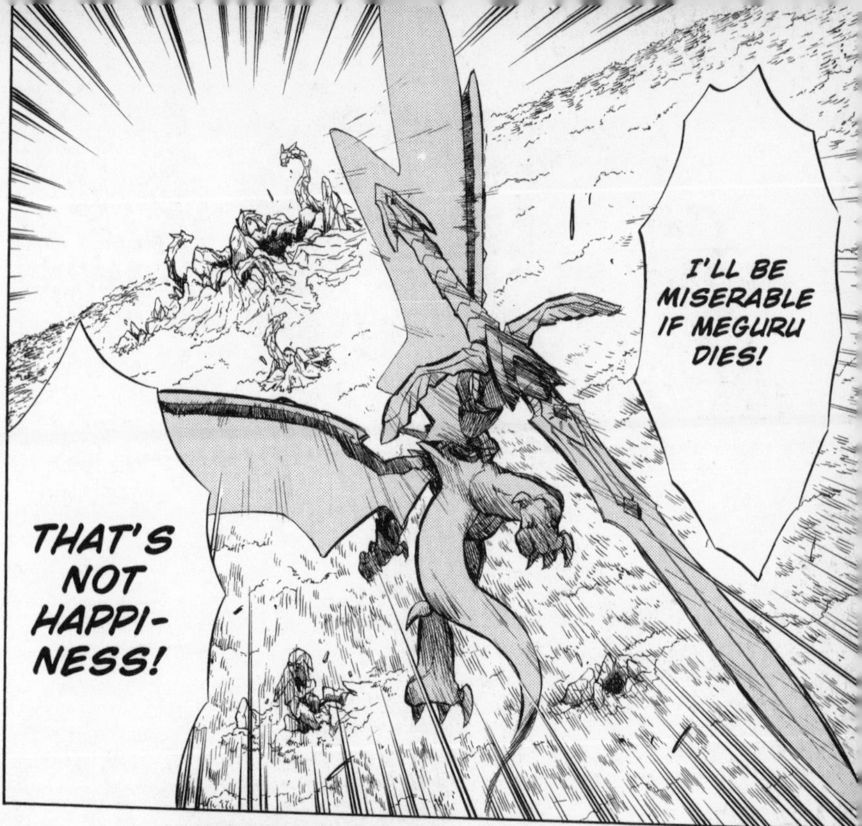
I'LL BE MISERABLE IF MEGURU DIES!
THAT'S NOT HAPPI-NESS!
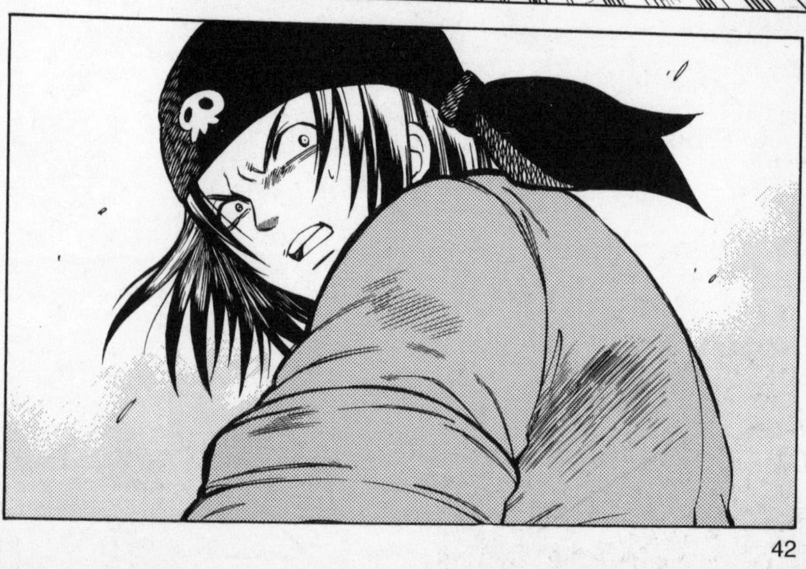

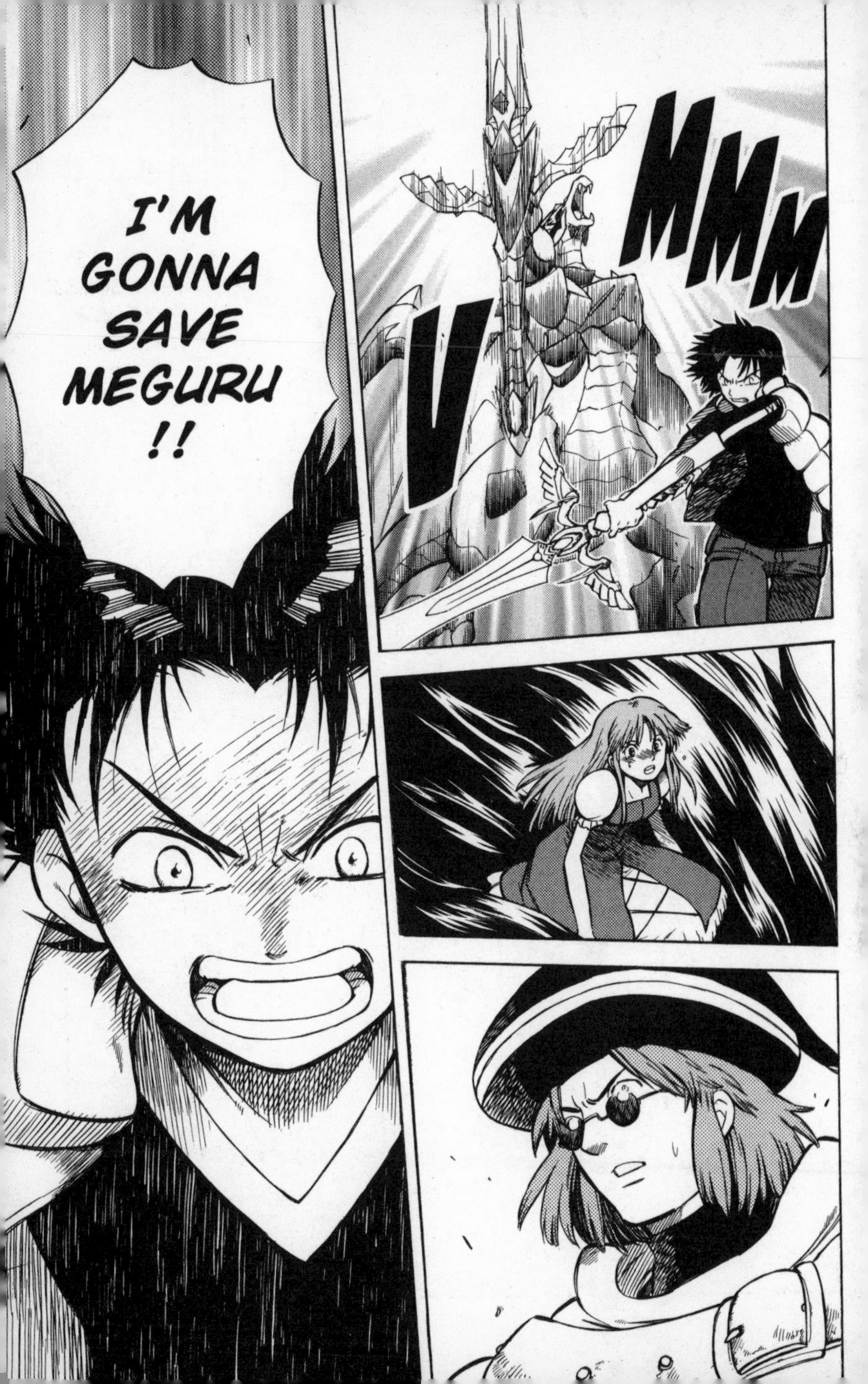

VMMMM
I'M GONNA SAVE MEGURU!!

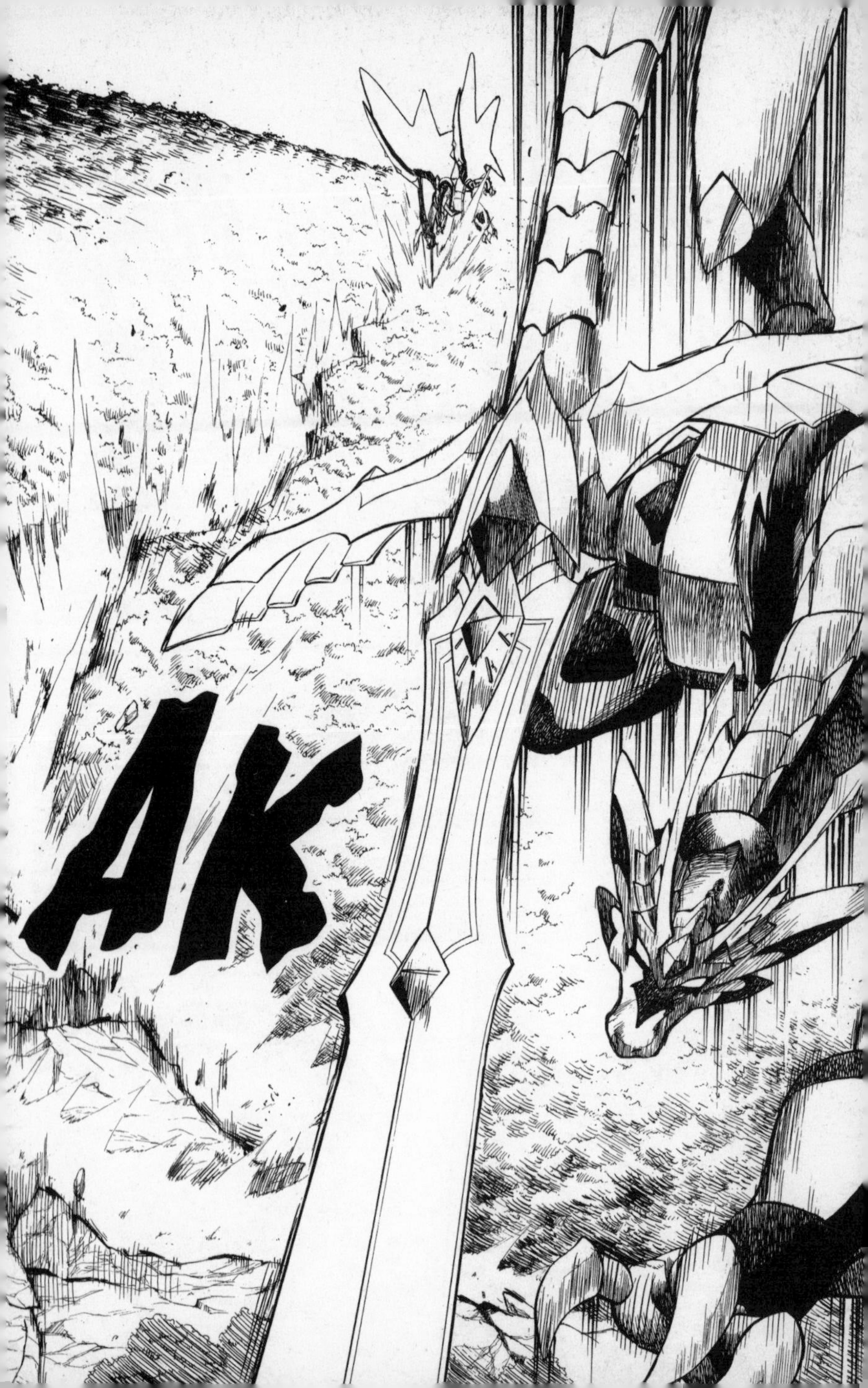
AK

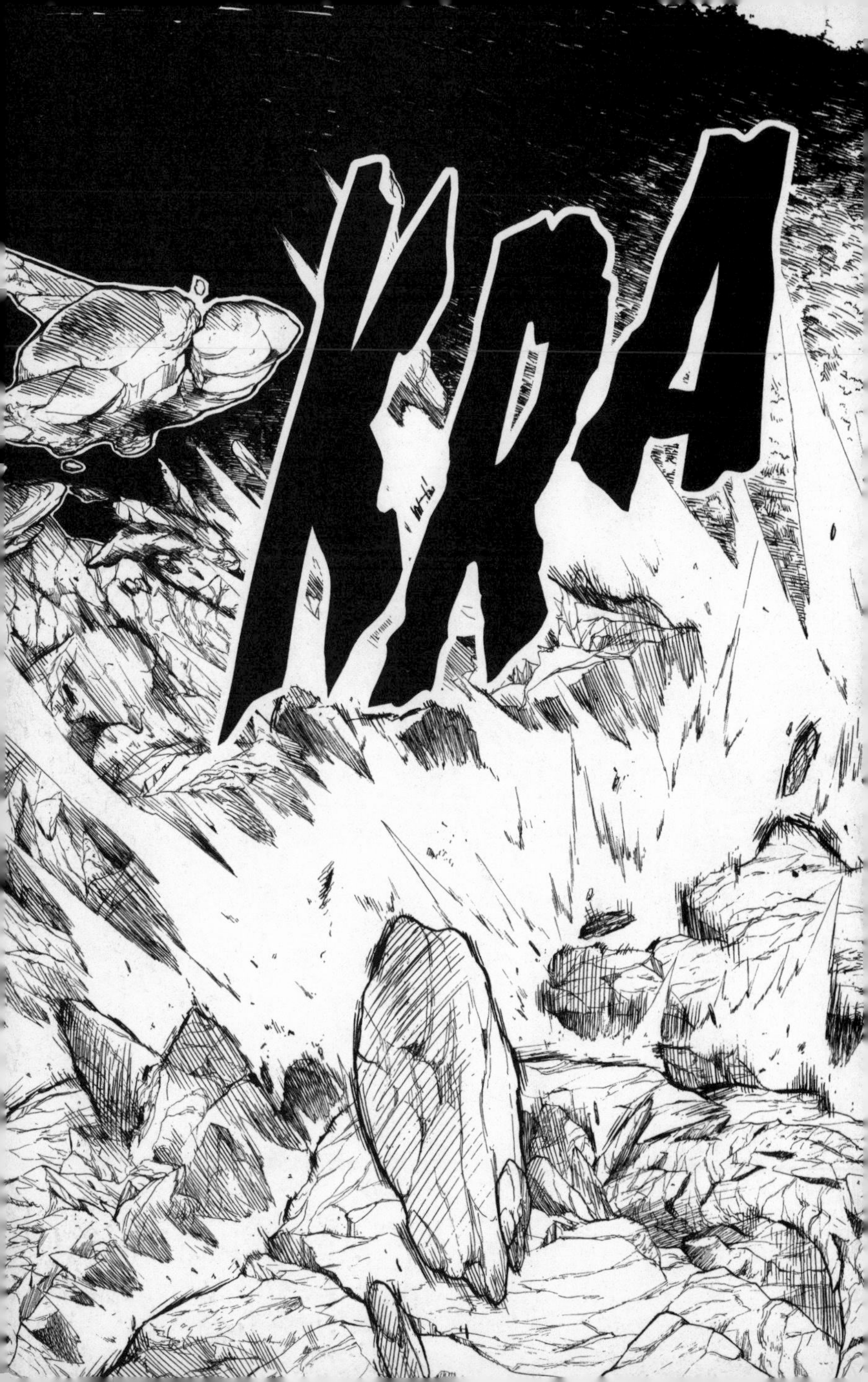
KRA

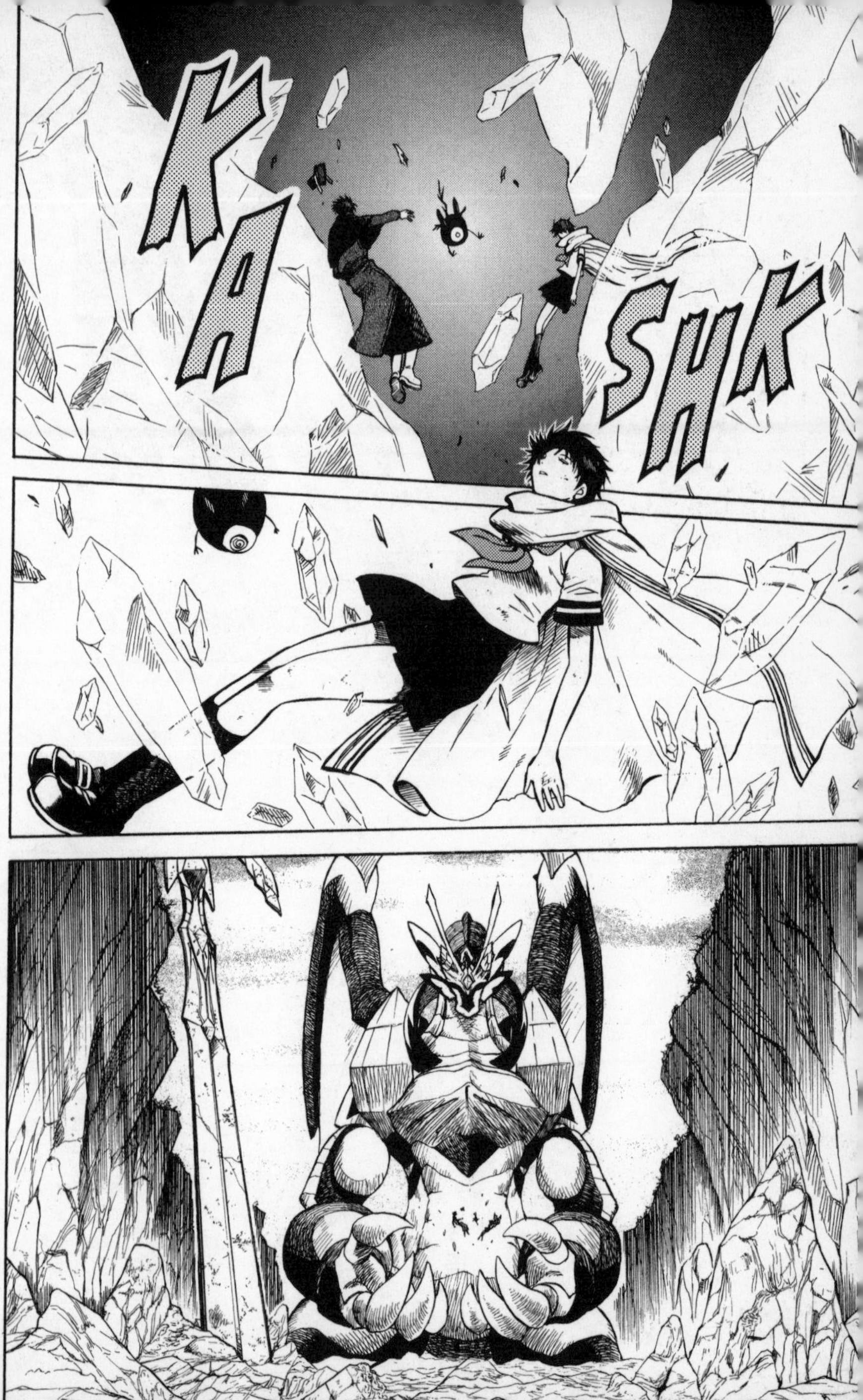
KA
SHK

READ THIS WAY

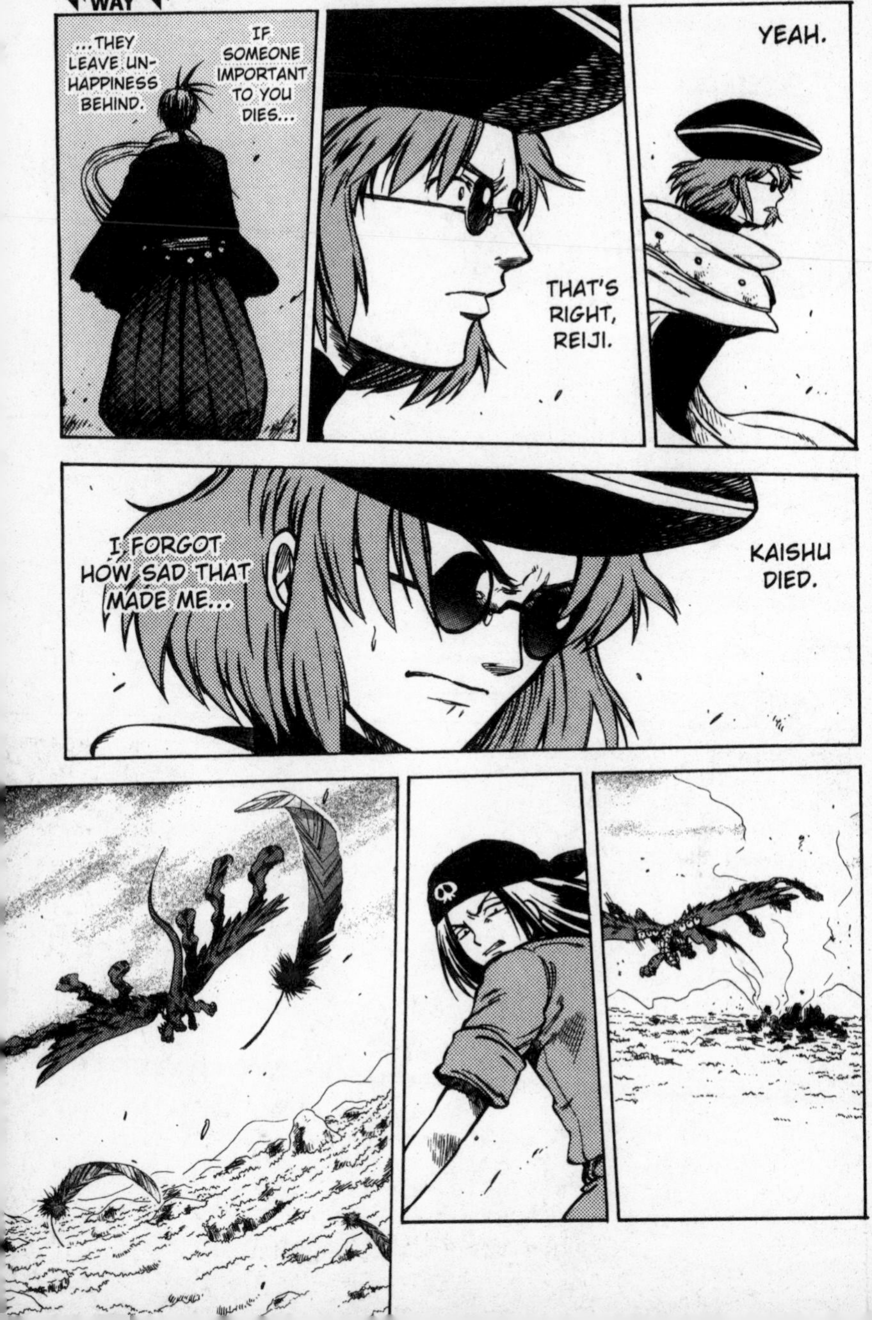
YEAH.
THAT'S RIGHT, REIJI.
IF SOMEONE IMPORTANT TO YOU DIES...
...THEY LEAVE UN-HAPPINESS BEHIND.
KAISHU DIED.
I FORGOT HOW SAD THAT MADE ME...

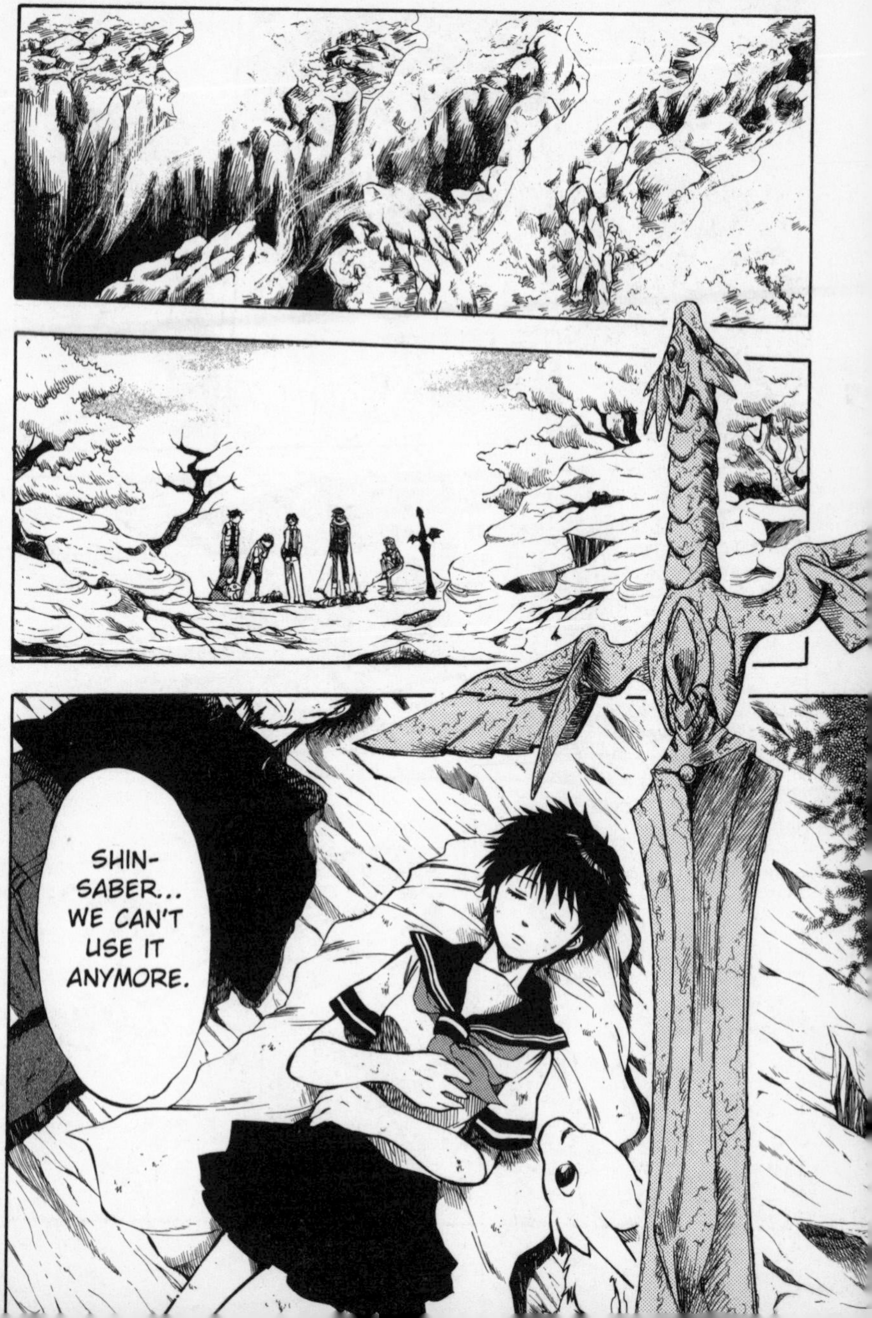
SHIN-SABER... WE CAN'T USE IT ANYMORE.

READ THIS WAY

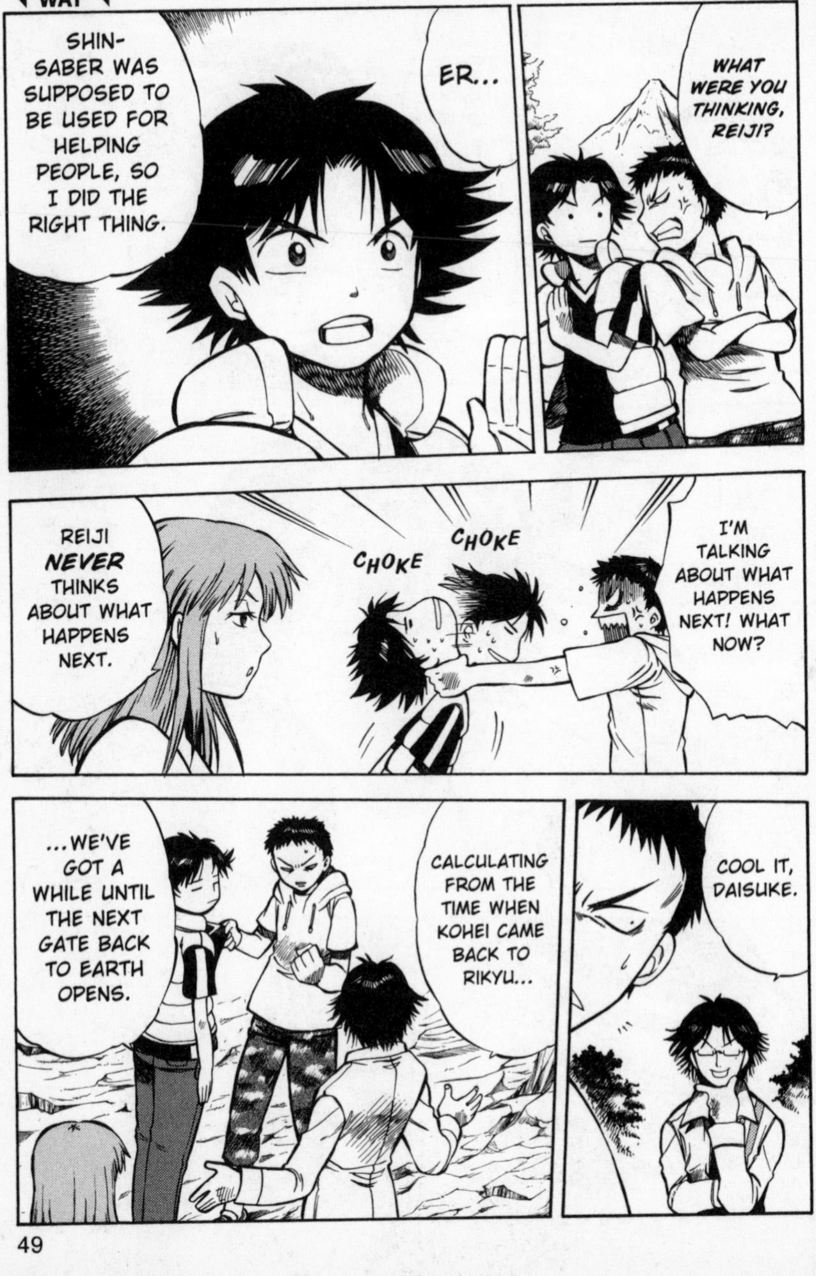
WHAT WERE YOU THINKING, REIJI?
ER...
SHIN-SABER WAS SUPPOSED TO BE USED FOR HELPING PEOPLE, SO I DID THE RIGHT THING.
I'M TALKING ABOUT WHAT HAPPENS NEXT! WHAT NOW?
CHOKE
CHOKE
REIJI **NEVER** THINKS ABOUT WHAT HAPPENS NEXT.
COOL IT, DAISUKE.
CALCULATING FROM THE TIME WHEN KOHEI CAME BACK TO RIKYU...
...WE'VE GOT A WHILE UNTIL THE NEXT GATE BACK TO EARTH OPENS.

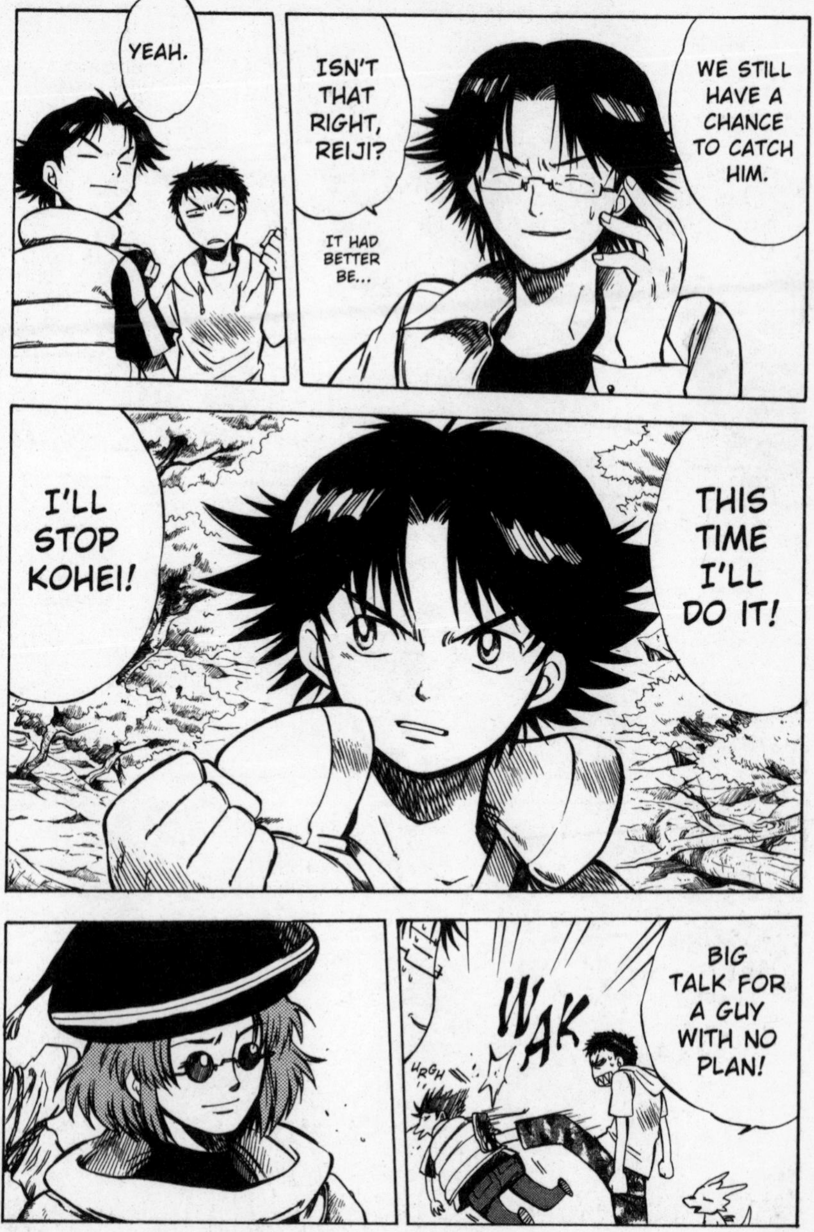
WE STILL HAVE A CHANCE TO CATCH HIM.
ISN'T THAT RIGHT, REIJI?
IT HAD BETTER BE...
YEAH.
THIS TIME I'LL DO IT!
I'LL STOP KOHEI!
BIG TALK FOR A GUY WITH NO PLAN!
WAK
URGH

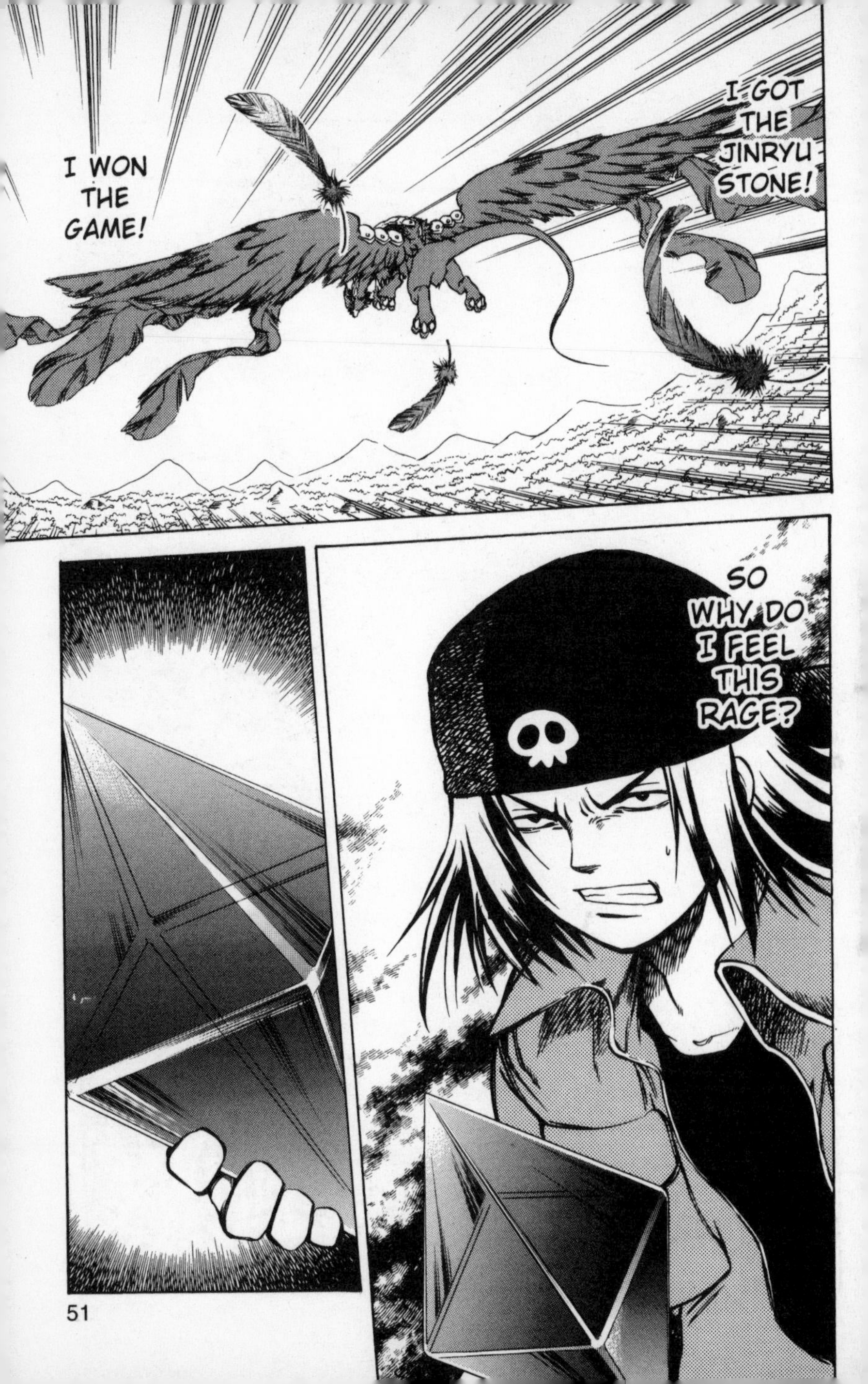
I GOT THE JINRYU STONE!
I WON THE GAME!
SO WHY DO I FEEL THIS RAGE?

Disappearing Knife

BY NAGI

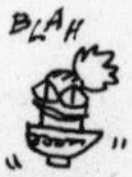
BLAH

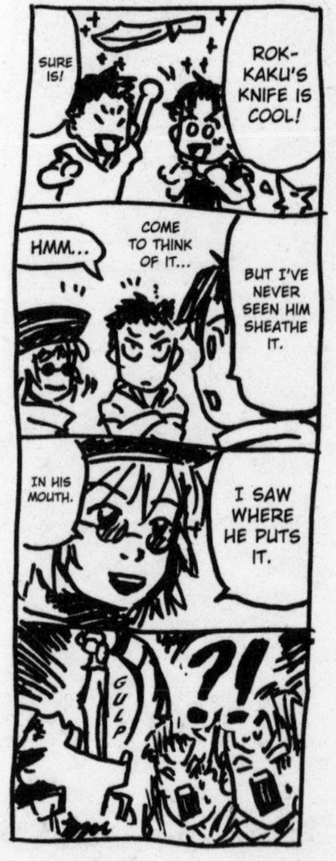
ROK-KAKU'S KNIFE IS COOL!
SURE IS!
BUT I'VE NEVER SEEN HIM SHEATHE IT.
COME TO THINK OF IT...
HMM...
I SAW WHERE HE PUTS IT.
IN HIS MOUTH.
?!
GULP

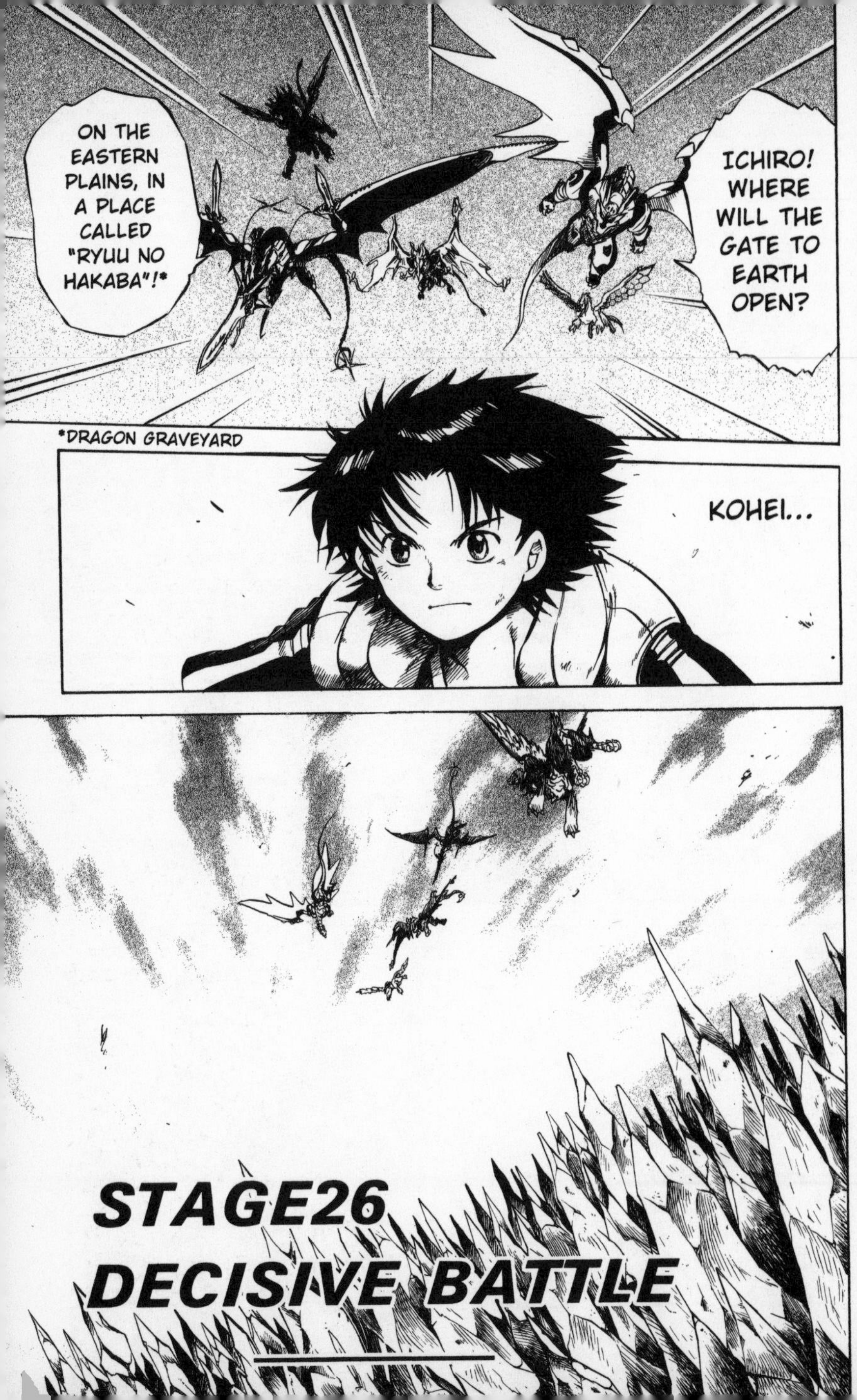
ICHIRO! WHERE WILL THE GATE TO EARTH OPEN?
ON THE EASTERN PLAINS, IN A PLACE CALLED "RYUU NO HAKABA"!*
*DRAGON GRAVEYARD
KOHEI...
STAGE26
DECISIVE BATTLE

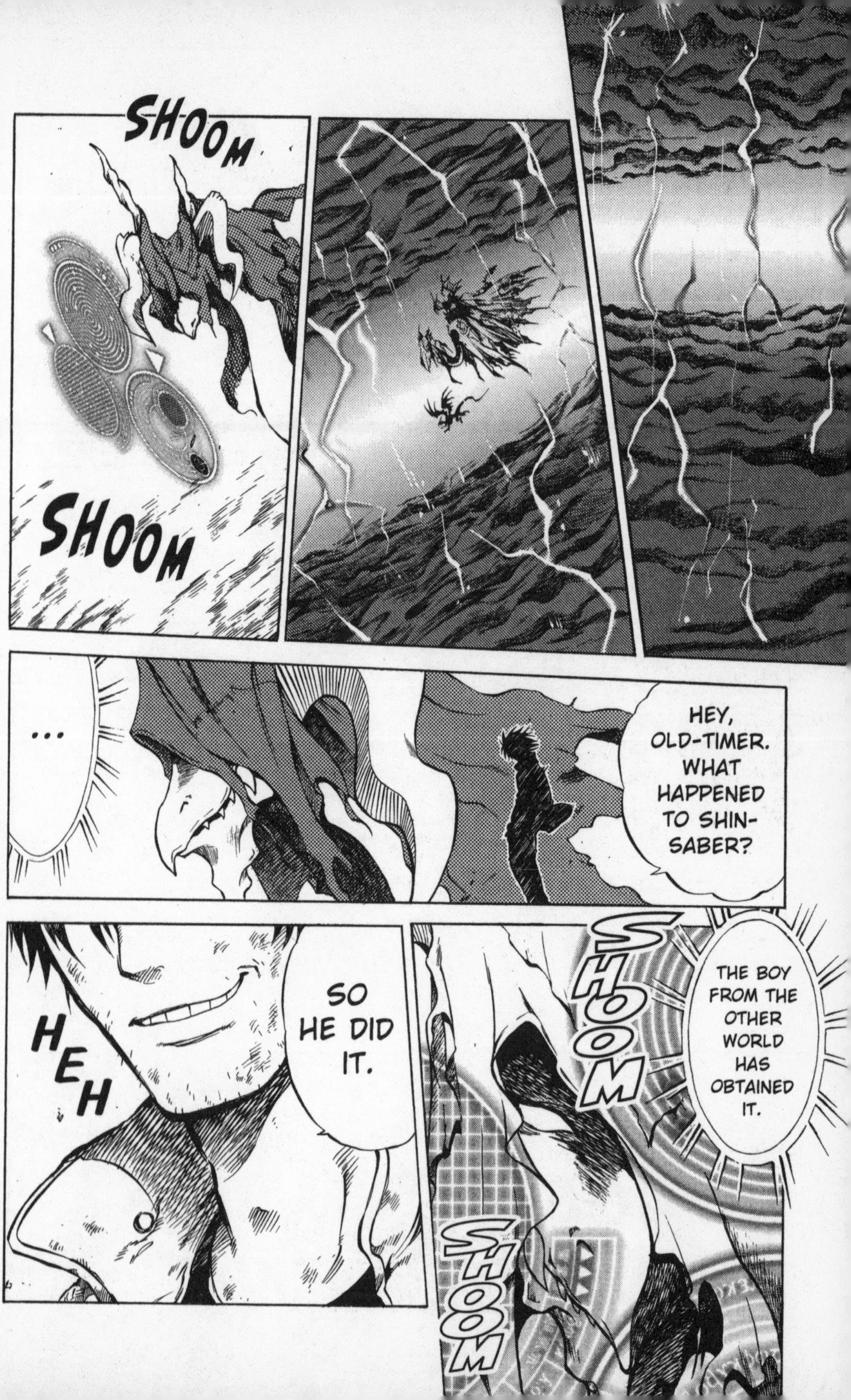
SHOOM
SHOOM
HEY, OLD-TIMER. WHAT HAPPENED TO SHIN-SABER?
...
SHOOM
THE BOY FROM THE OTHER WORLD HAS OBTAINED IT.
SHOOM
SO HE DID IT.
HEH

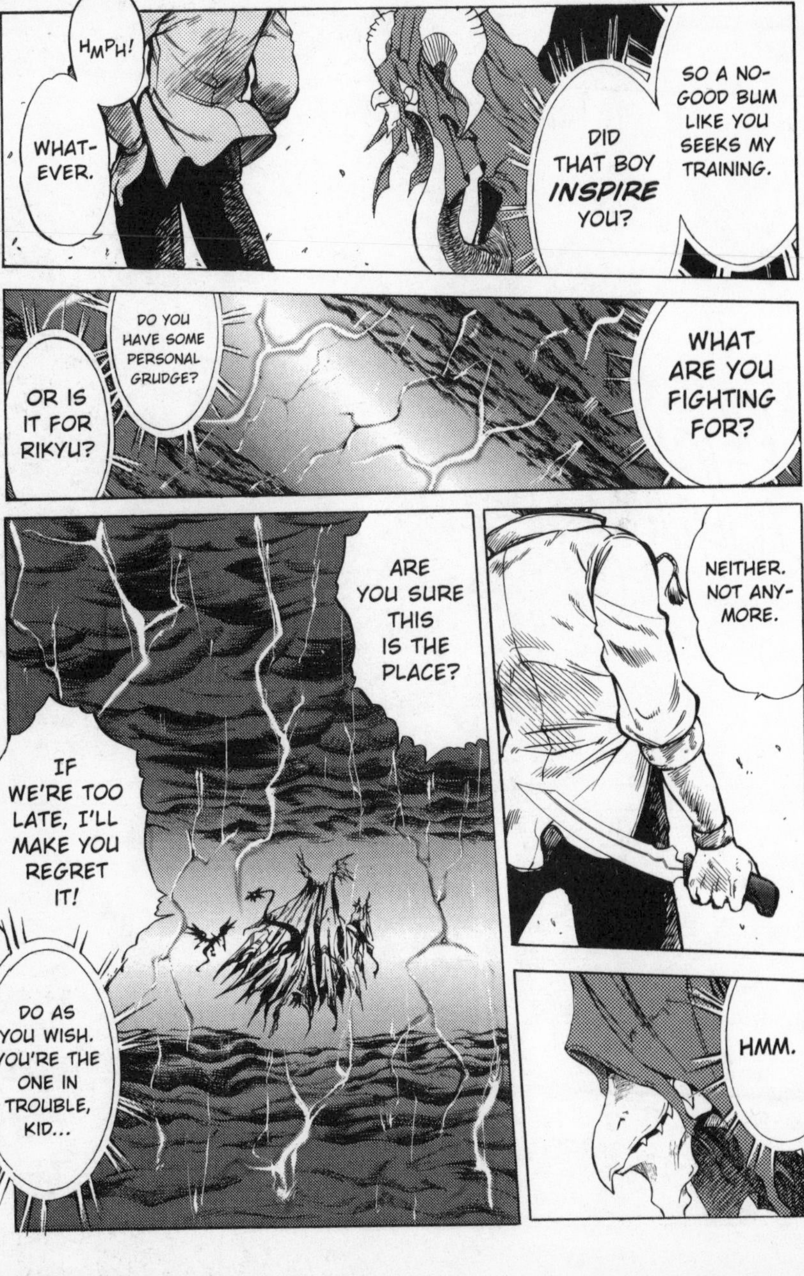
SO A NO-GOOD BUM LIKE YOU SEEKS MY TRAINING.
DID THAT BOY INSPIRE YOU?
HMPH!
WHAT-EVER.
WHAT ARE YOU FIGHTING FOR?
DO YOU HAVE SOME PERSONAL GRUDGE?
OR IS IT FOR RIKYU?
NEITHER. NOT ANY-MORE.
HMM.
ARE YOU SURE THIS IS THE PLACE?
IF WE'RE TOO LATE, I'LL MAKE YOU REGRET IT!
DO AS YOU WISH. YOU'RE THE ONE IN TROUBLE, KID...

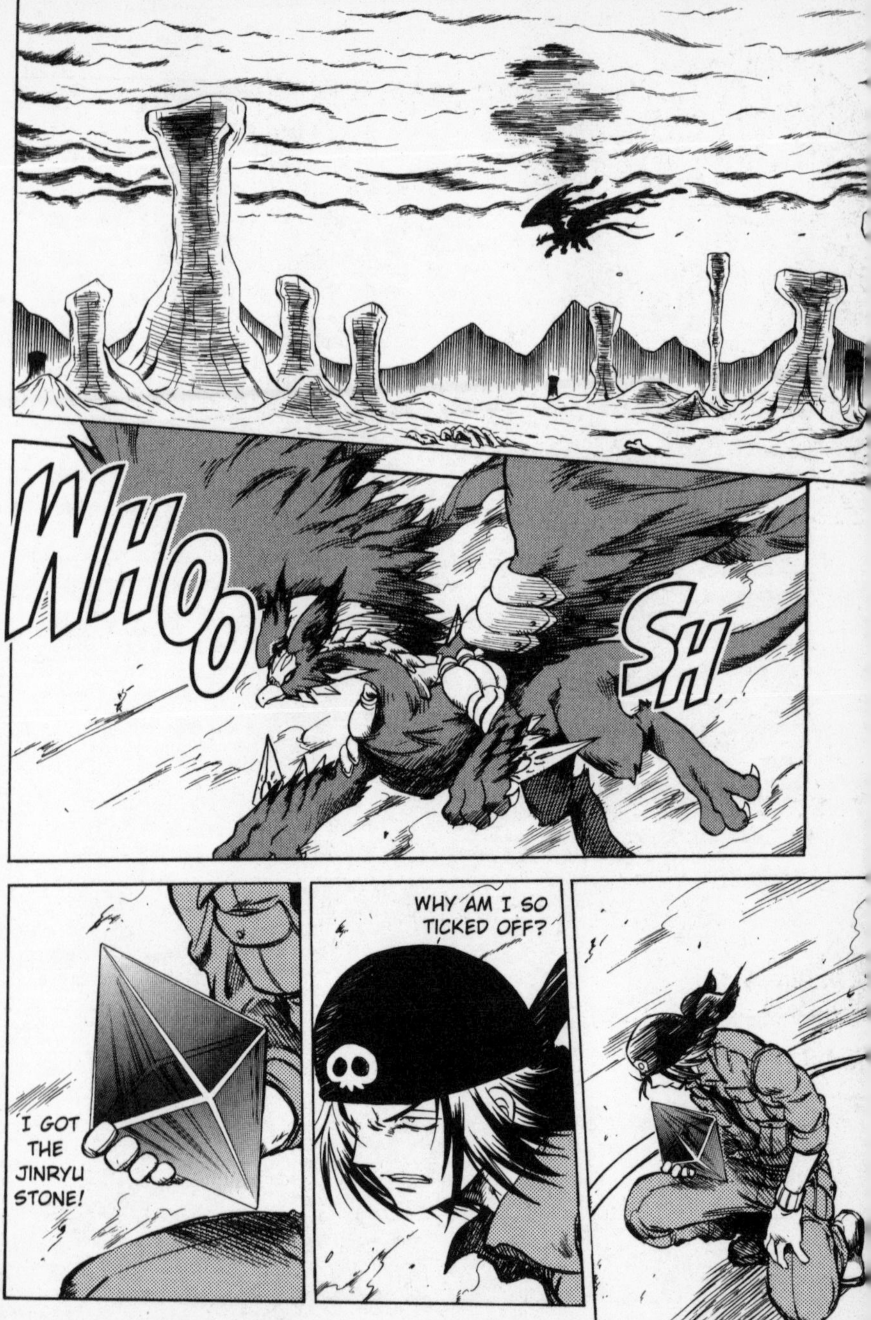
WHOOSH
WHY AM I SO TICKED OFF?
I GOT THE JINRYU STONE!

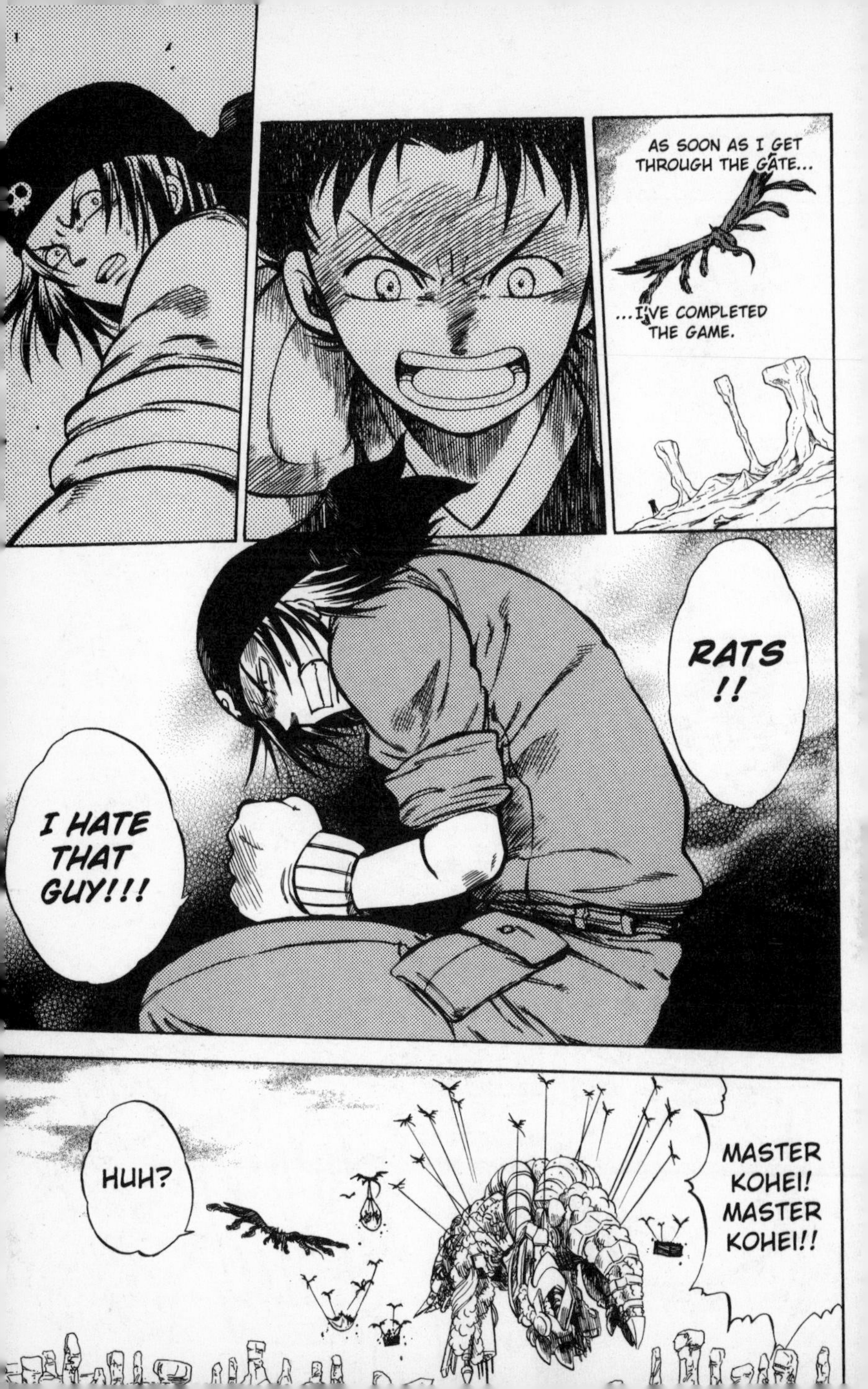
AS SOON AS I GET THROUGH THE GATE...
...I'VE COMPLETED THE GAME.
RATS!!
I HATE THAT GUY!!!
MASTER KOHEI! MASTER KOHEI!!
HUH?

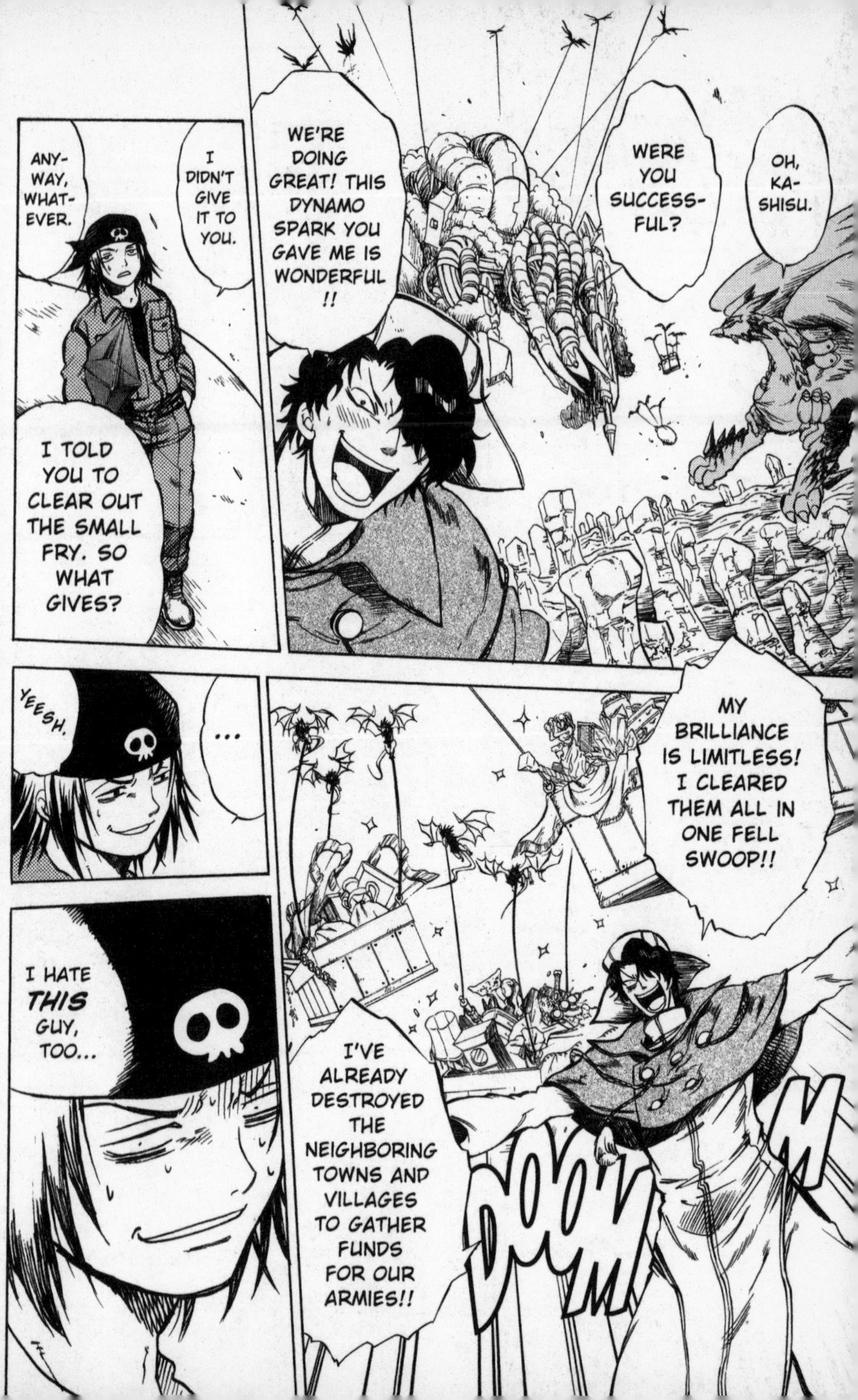
OH, KA-SHISU.
WERE YOU SUCCESS-FUL?
WE'RE DOING GREAT! THIS DYNAMO SPARK YOU GAVE ME IS WONDERFUL!!
I DIDN'T GIVE IT TO YOU.
ANY-WAY, WHAT-EVER.
I TOLD YOU TO CLEAR OUT THE SMALL FRY. SO WHAT GIVES?
MY BRILLIANCE IS LIMITLESS! I CLEARED THEM ALL IN ONE FELL SWOOP!!
I'VE ALREADY DESTROYED THE NEIGHBORING TOWNS AND VILLAGES TO GATHER FUNDS FOR OUR ARMIES!!
DOOOM
...
YEESH.
I HATE *THIS* GUY, TOO...

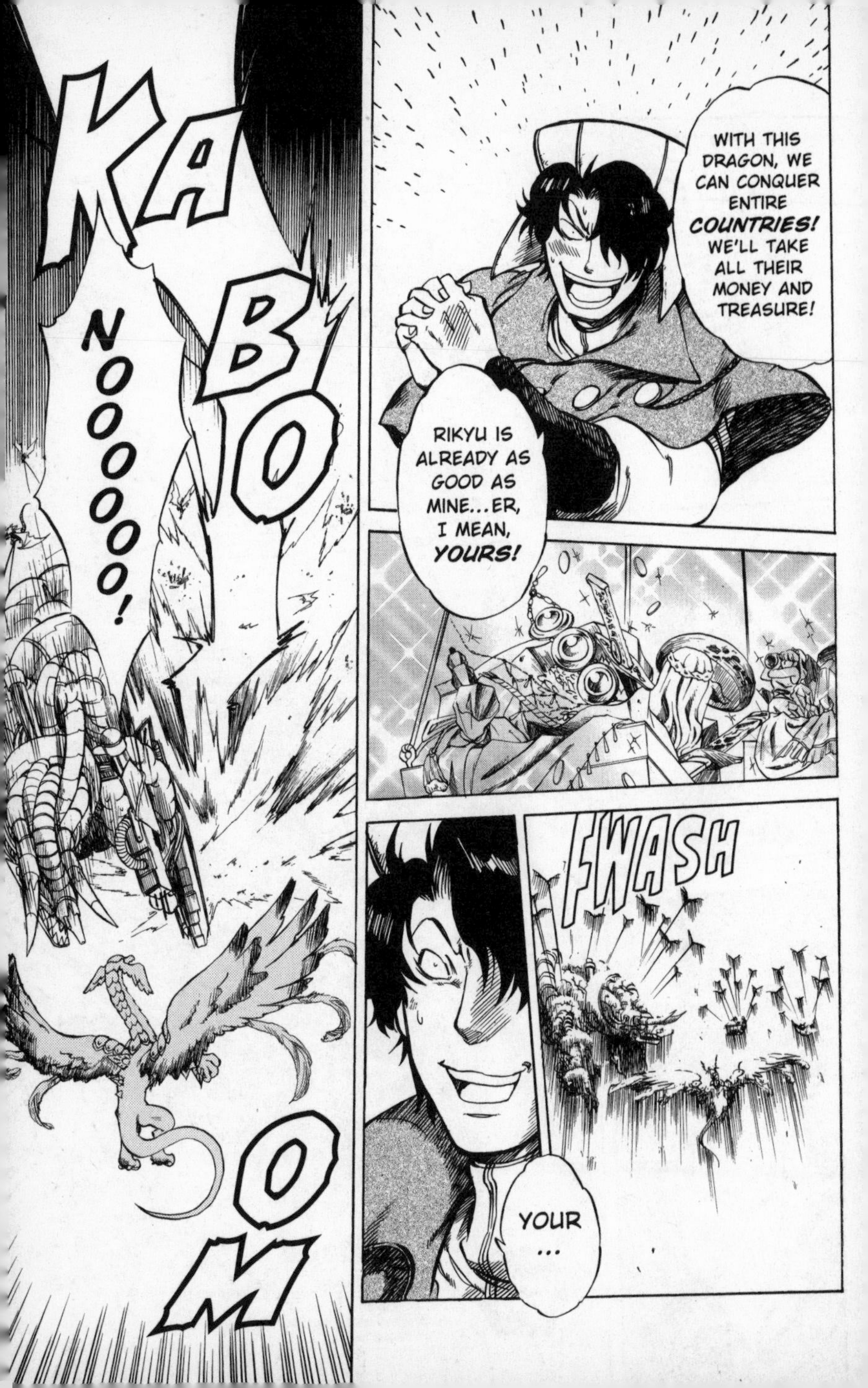
WITH THIS DRAGON, WE CAN CONQUER ENTIRE COUNTRIES! WE'LL TAKE ALL THEIR MONEY AND TREASURE!
RIKYU IS ALREADY AS GOOD AS MINE...ER, I MEAN, YOURS!
FWASH
YOUR ...
KABOOOM
NOOOOOOO!

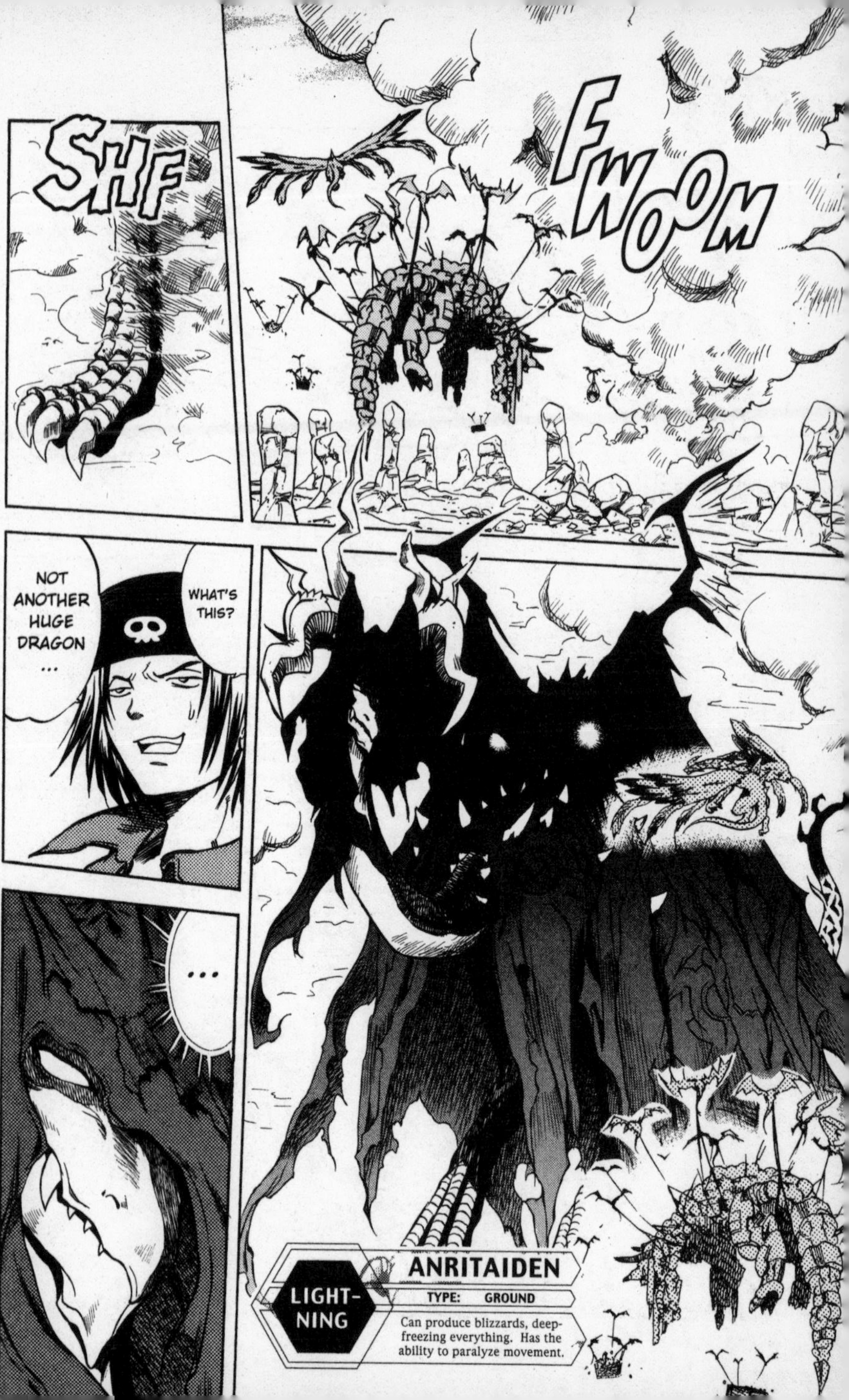
FWOOM
SHF
WHAT'S THIS?
NOT ANOTHER HUGE DRAGON ...
...
ANRITAIDEN
LIGHT-NING
TYPE: GROUND
Can produce blizzards, deep-freezing everything. Has the ability to paralyze movement.

READ THIS WAY

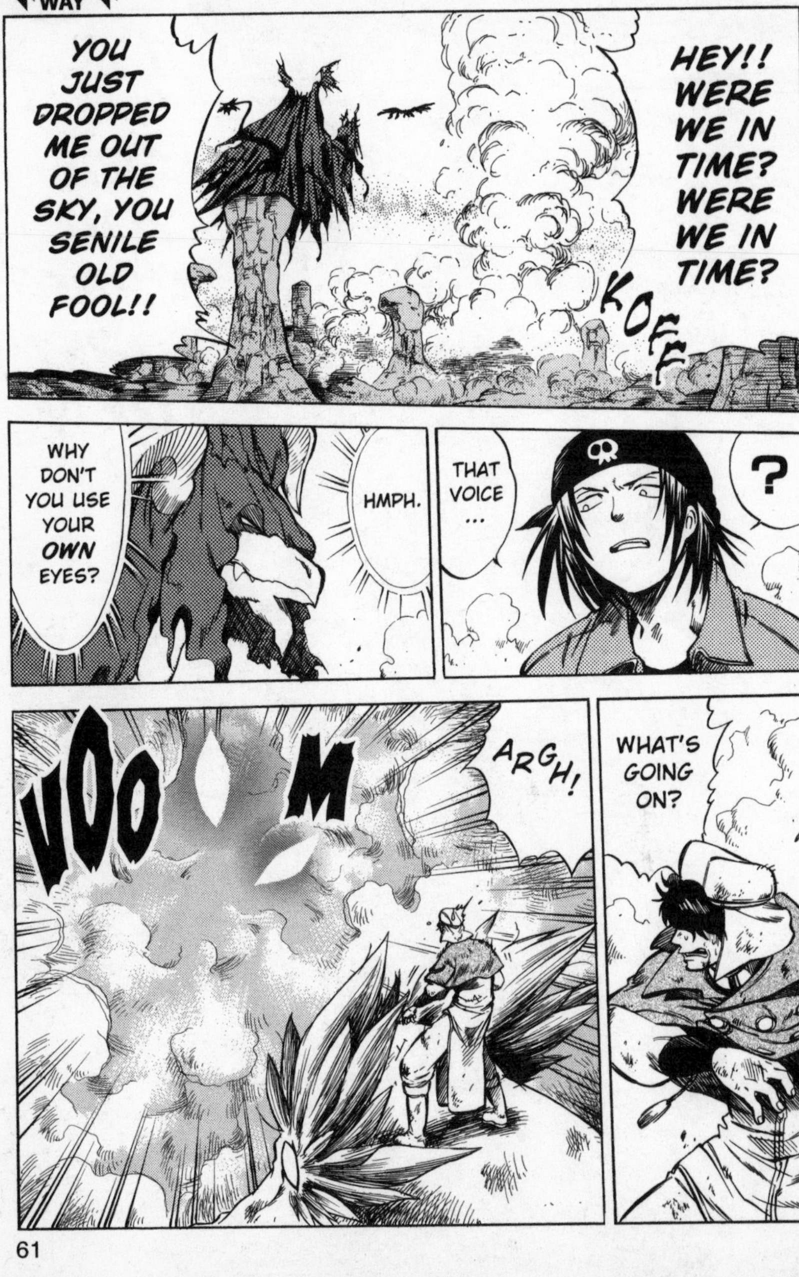
HEY!! WERE WE IN TIME? WERE WE IN TIME?
KOFF
YOU JUST DROPPED ME OUT OF THE SKY, YOU SENILE OLD FOOL!!
?
THAT VOICE ...
HMPH.
WHY DON'T YOU USE YOUR OWN EYES?
WHAT'S GOING ON?
ARGH!
VOOOM

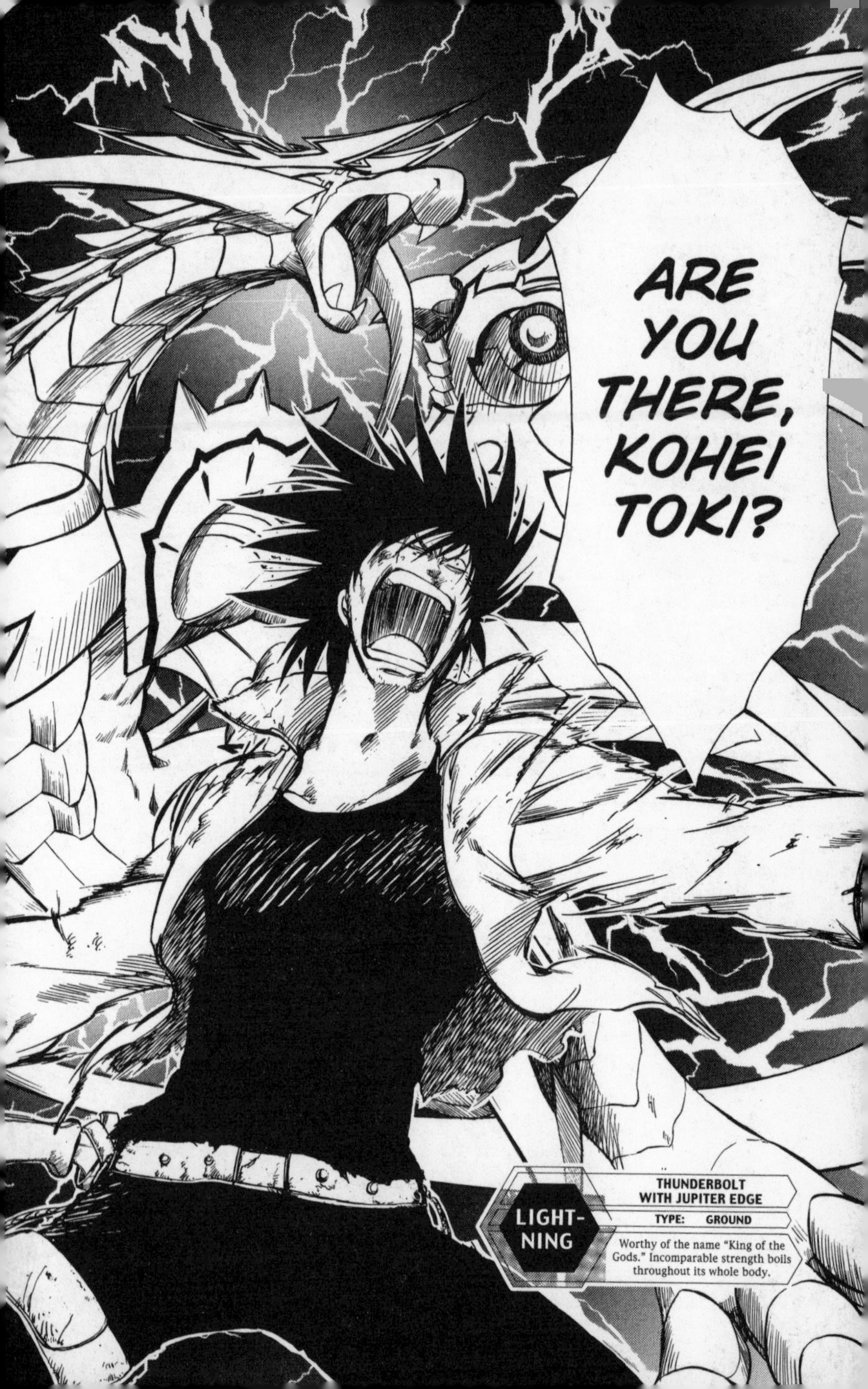
ARE YOU THERE, KOHEI TOKI?
LIGHT-NING
THUNDERBOLT WITH JUPITER EDGE
TYPE: GROUND
Worthy of the name "King of the Gods." Incomparable strength boils throughout its whole body.

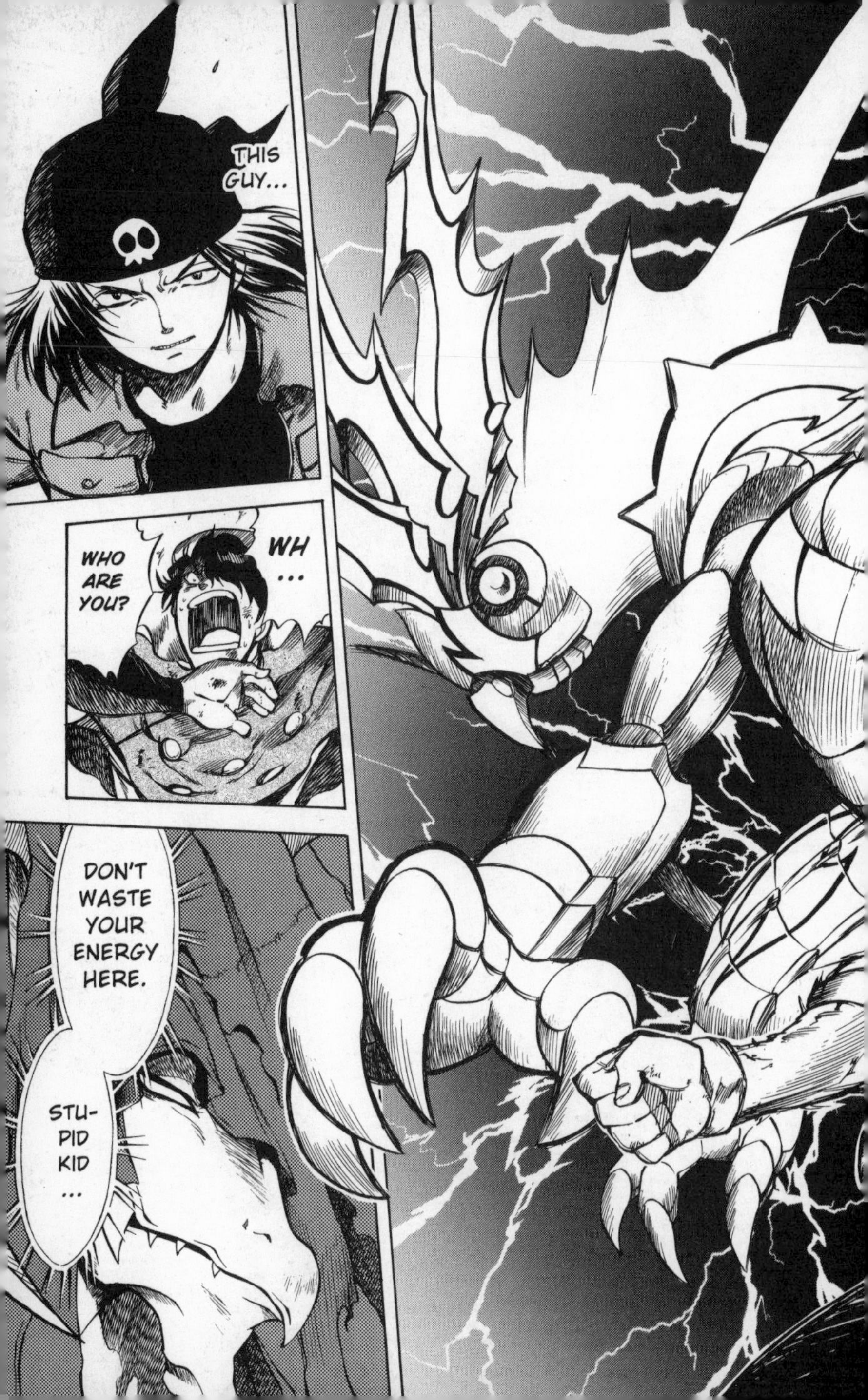
THIS GUY...
WH ...
WHO ARE YOU?
DON'T WASTE YOUR ENERGY HERE.
STU-PID KID ...

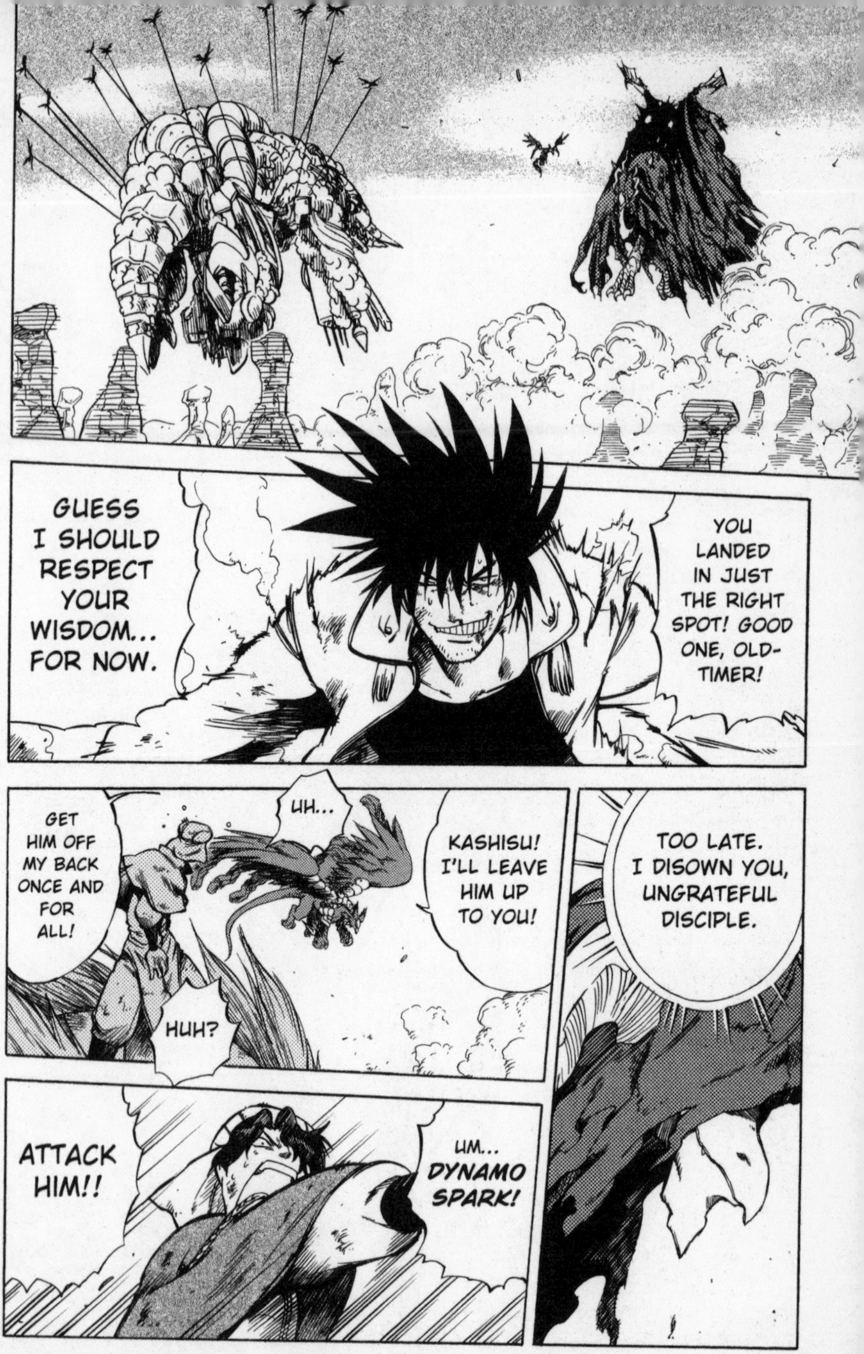
YOU LANDED IN JUST THE RIGHT SPOT! GOOD ONE, OLD-TIMER!
GUESS I SHOULD RESPECT YOUR WISDOM... FOR NOW.
TOO LATE. I DISOWN YOU, UNGRATEFUL DISCIPLE.
KASHISU! I'LL LEAVE HIM UP TO YOU!
UH...
GET HIM OFF MY BACK ONCE AND FOR ALL!
HUH?
UM... DYNAMO SPARK!
ATTACK HIM!!

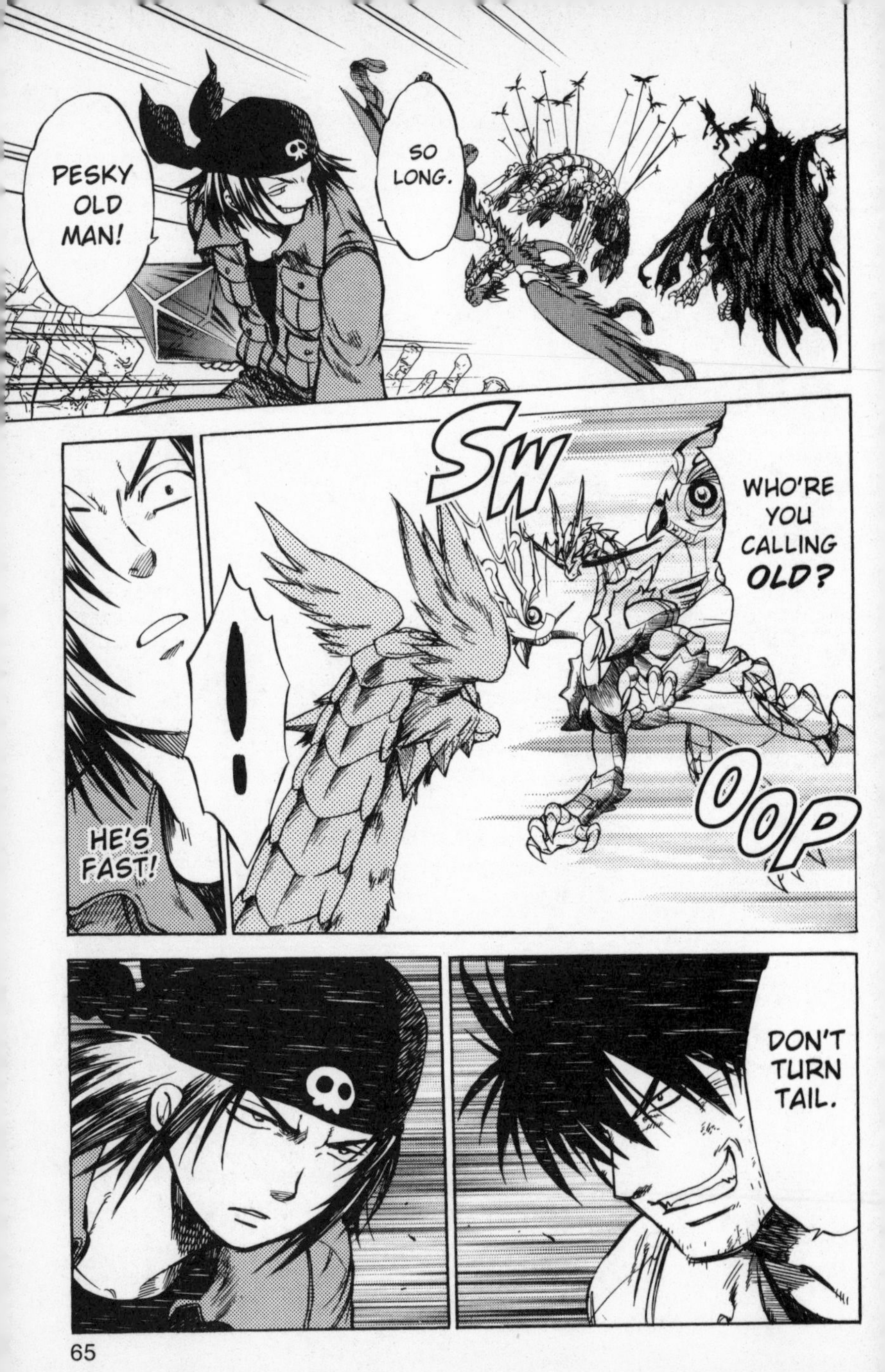
SO LONG.
PESKY OLD MAN!
WHO'RE YOU CALLING OLD?
SW
OOP
!
HE'S FAST!
DON'T TURN TAIL.

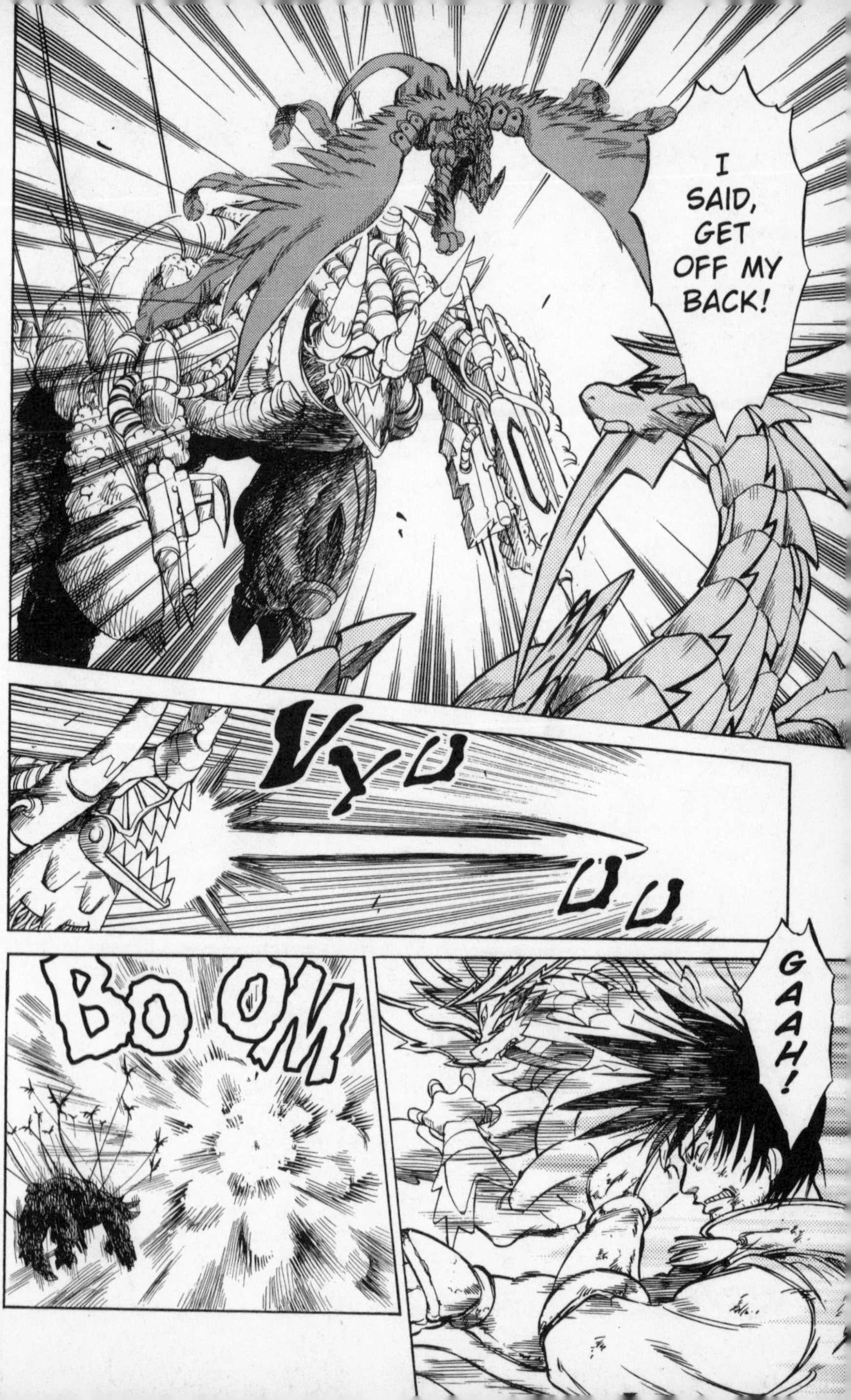
I SAID, GET OFF MY BACK!
VYUUU
GAAH!
BOOM

READ THIS WAY

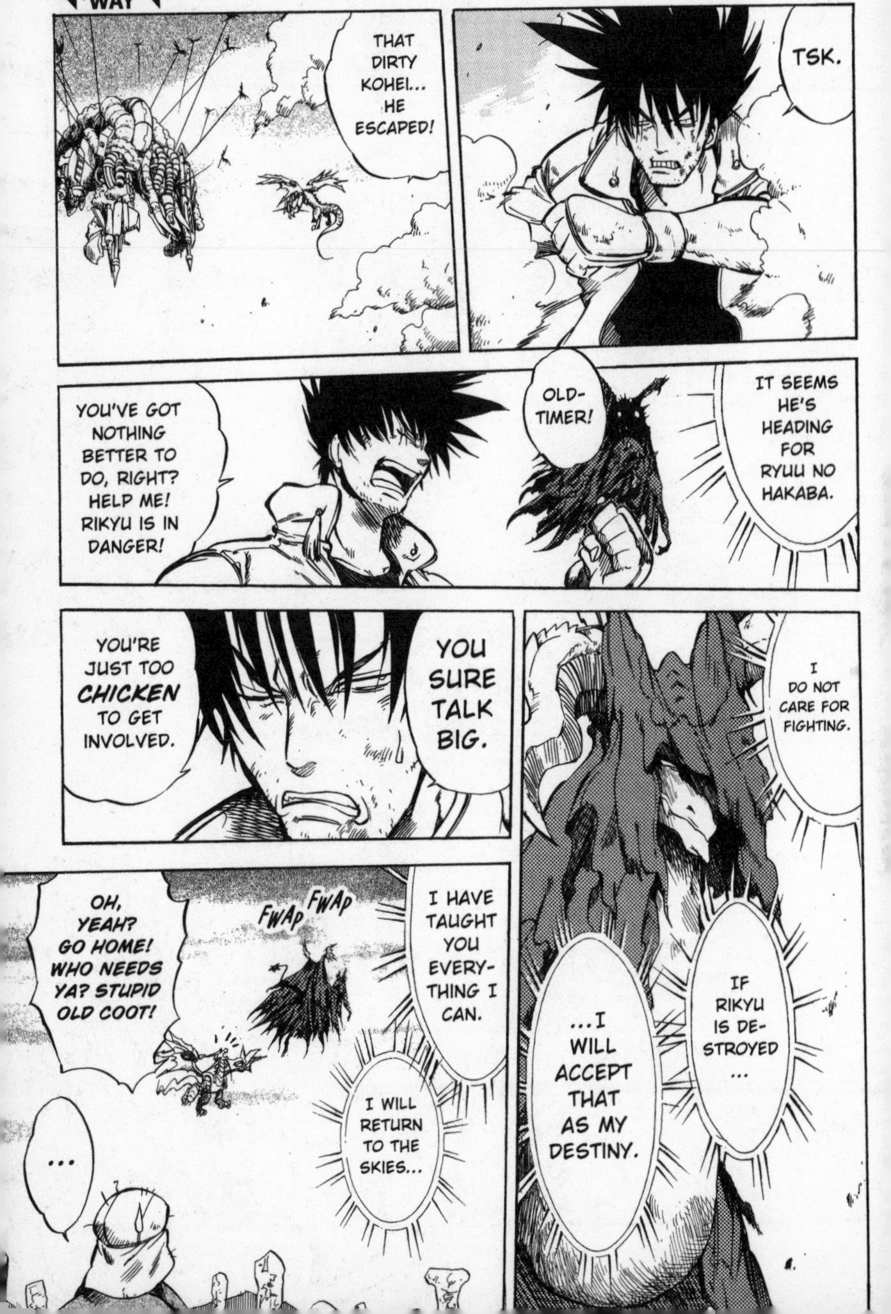

TSK.
THAT DIRTY KOHEI... HE ESCAPED!
IT SEEMS HE'S HEADING FOR RYUU NO HAKABA.
OLD-TIMER!
YOU'VE GOT NOTHING BETTER TO DO, RIGHT? HELP ME! RIKYU IS IN DANGER!
I DO NOT CARE FOR FIGHTING.
IF RIKYU IS DE-STROYED ...
...I WILL ACCEPT THAT AS MY DESTINY.
YOU SURE TALK BIG.
YOU'RE JUST TOO CHICKEN TO GET INVOLVED.
I HAVE TAUGHT YOU EVERY-THING I CAN.
I WILL RETURN TO THE SKIES...
FWAP FWAP
OH, YEAH? GO HOME! WHO NEEDS YA? STUPID OLD COOT!
...

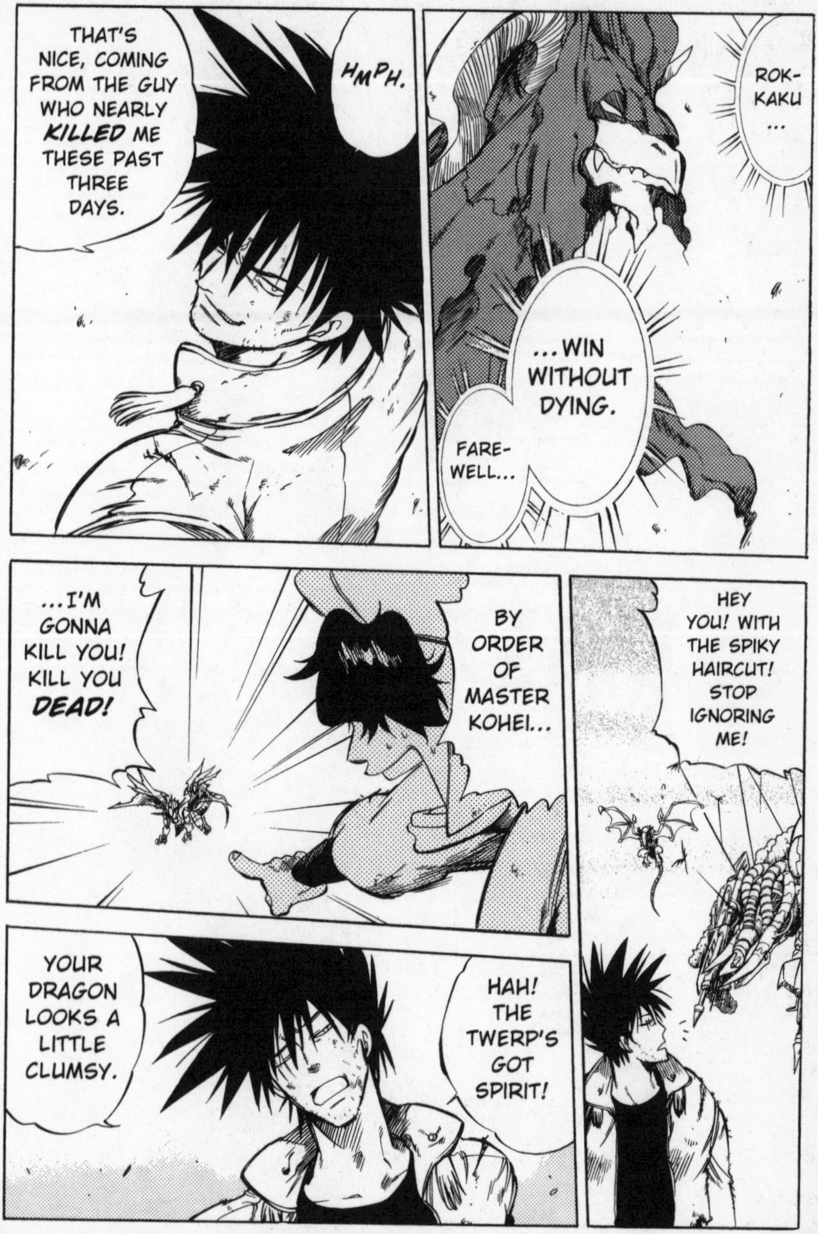
ROK-KAKU...
...WIN WITHOUT DYING.
FARE-WELL...
HMPH.
THAT'S NICE, COMING FROM THE GUY WHO NEARLY KILLED ME THESE PAST THREE DAYS.
HEY YOU! WITH THE SPIKY HAIRCUT! STOP IGNORING ME!
BY ORDER OF MASTER KOHEI...
...I'M GONNA KILL YOU! KILL YOU DEAD!
HAH! THE TWERP'S GOT SPIRIT!
YOUR DRAGON LOOKS A LITTLE CLUMSY.

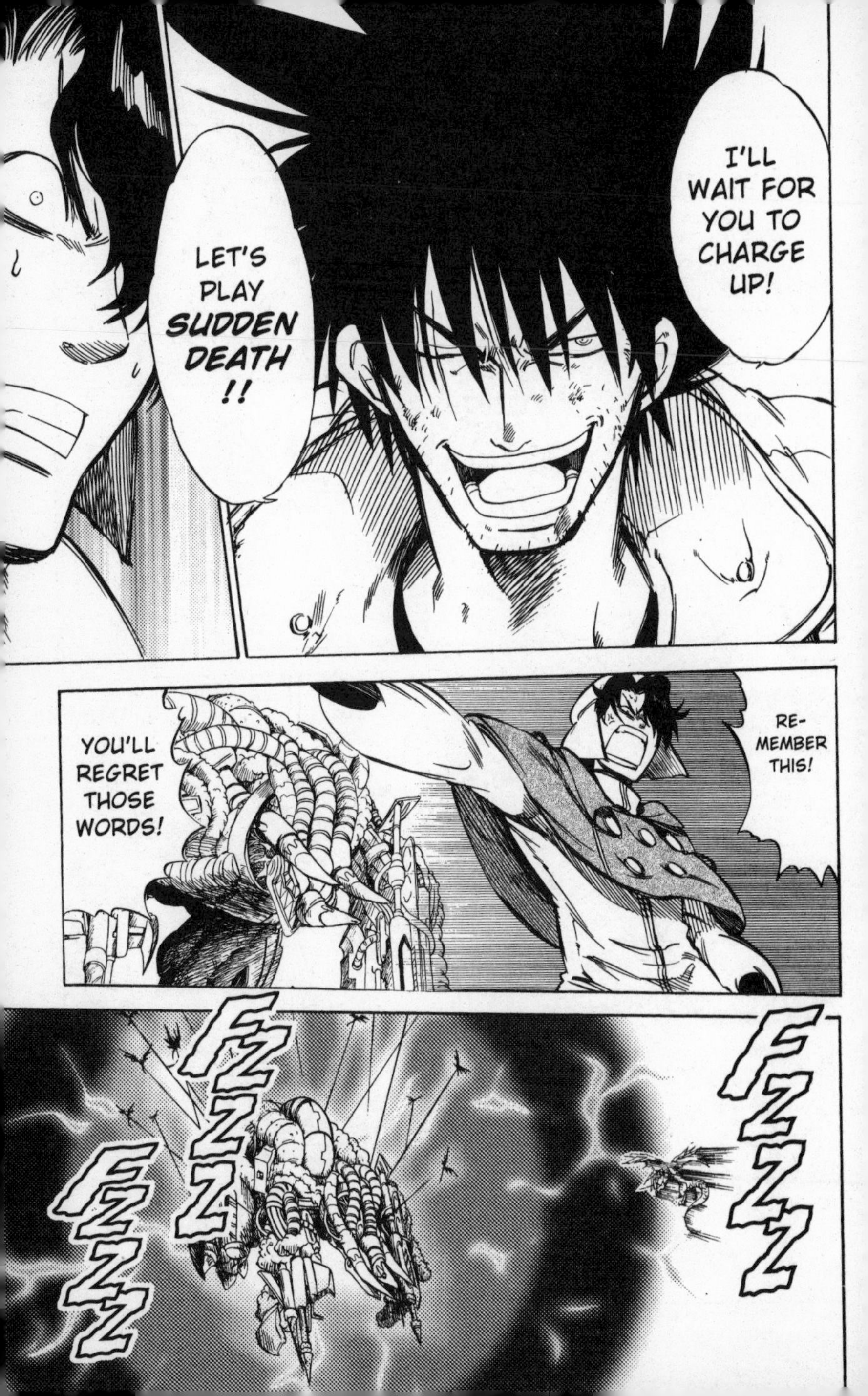
I'LL WAIT FOR YOU TO CHARGE UP!
LET'S PLAY SUDDEN DEATH!!
RE-MEMBER THIS!
YOU'LL REGRET THOSE WORDS!
FZZZ
FZZZ
FZZZ

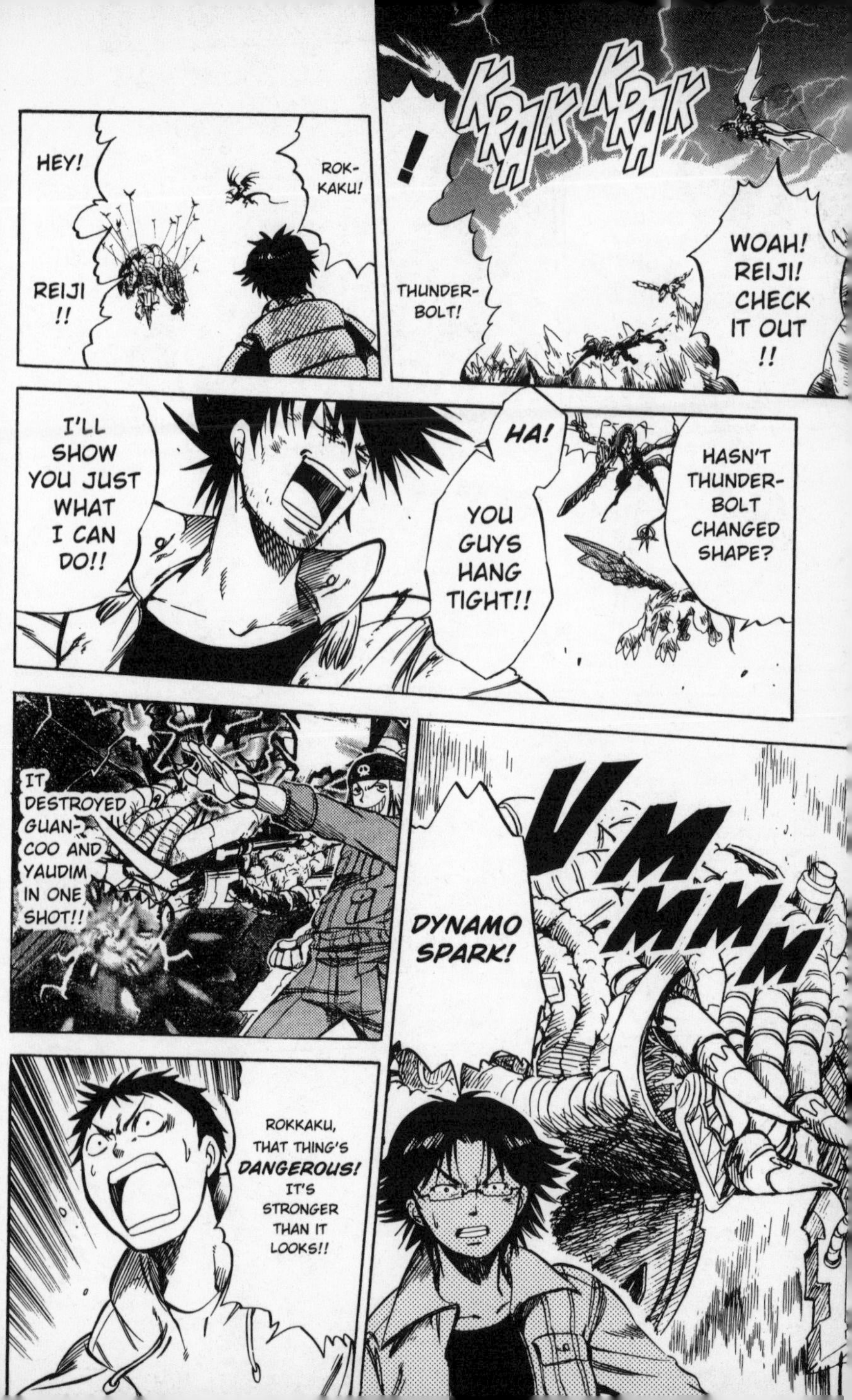
WOAH! REIJI! CHECK IT OUT!!
KRAK KRAK
!
THUNDER-BOLT!
ROK-KAKU!
HEY!
REIJI!!
HASN'T THUNDER-BOLT CHANGED SHAPE?
HA!
YOU GUYS HANG TIGHT!!
I'LL SHOW YOU JUST WHAT I CAN DO!!
VMMMM
DYNAMO SPARK!
IT DESTROYED GUAN-COO AND YAUDIM IN ONE SHOT!!
ROKKAKU, THAT THING'S DANGEROUS! IT'S STRONGER THAN IT LOOKS!!

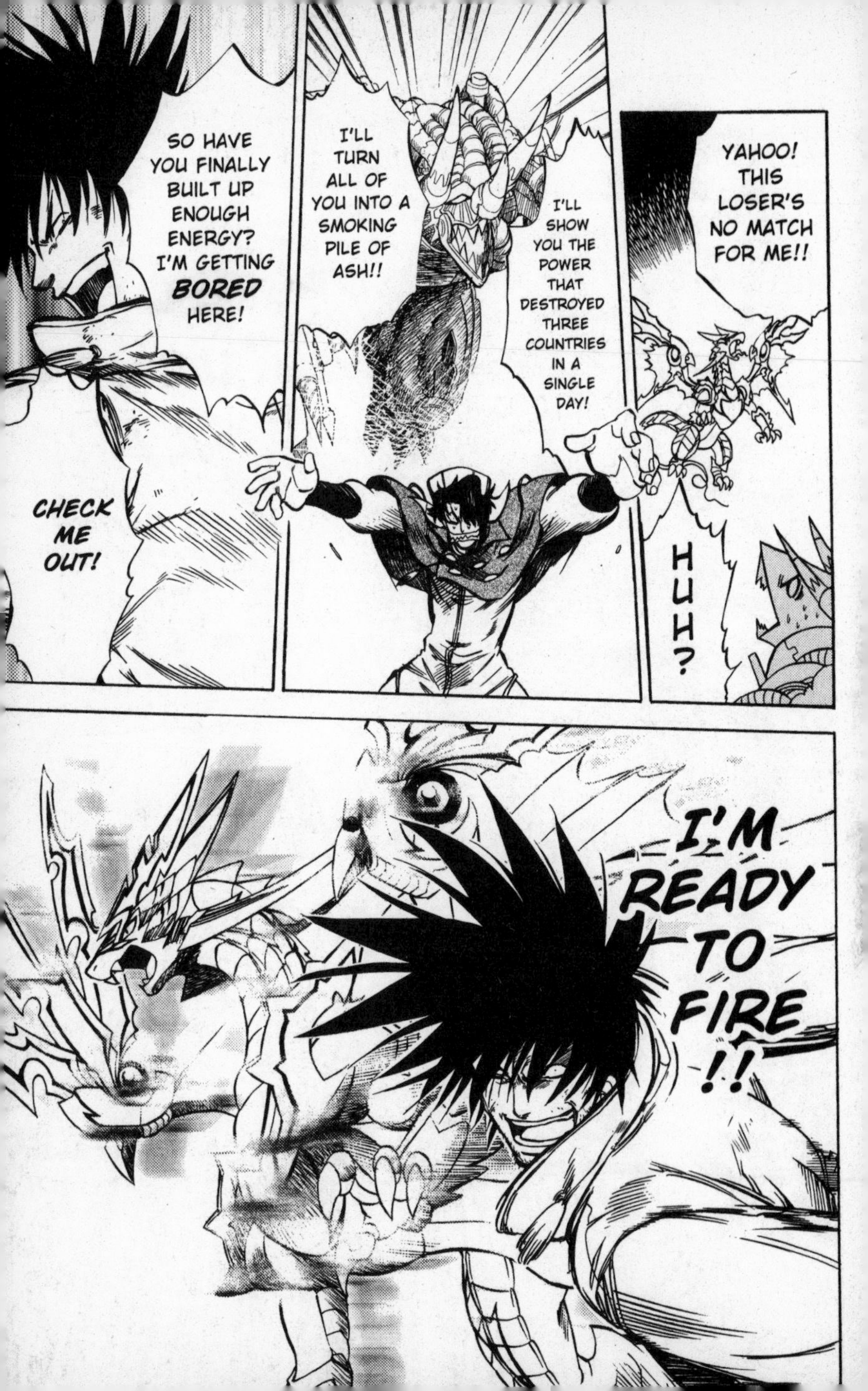
YAHOO! THIS LOSER'S NO MATCH FOR ME!!
HUH?
I'LL SHOW YOU THE POWER THAT DESTROYED THREE COUNTRIES IN A SINGLE DAY!
I'LL TURN ALL OF YOU INTO A SMOKING PILE OF ASH!!
SO HAVE YOU FINALLY BUILT UP ENOUGH ENERGY? I'M GETTING BORED HERE!
CHECK ME OUT!
I'M READY TO FIRE!!

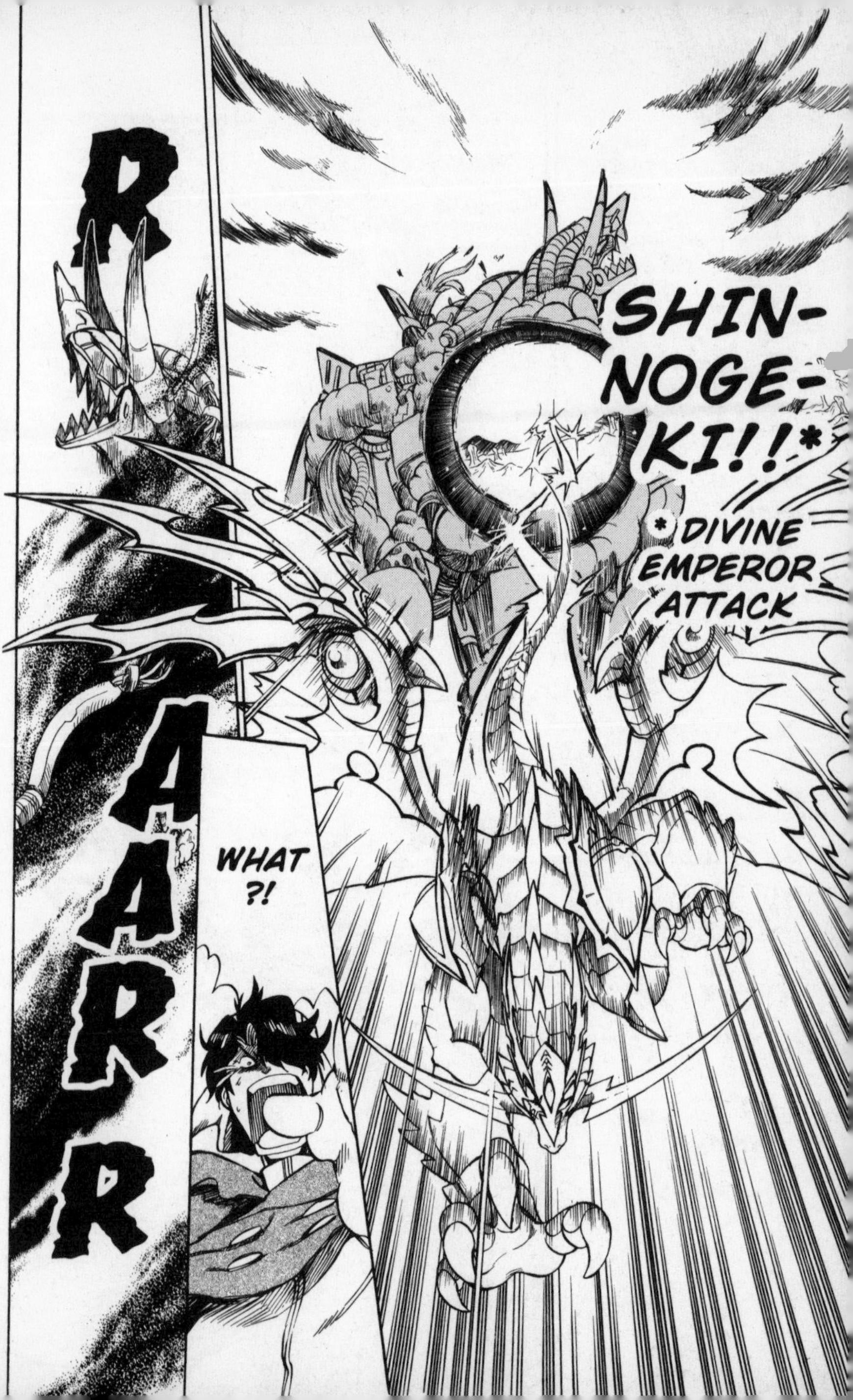
SHIN-NOGE-KI!!*
*DIVINE EMPEROR ATTACK
WHAT ?!
RAARR

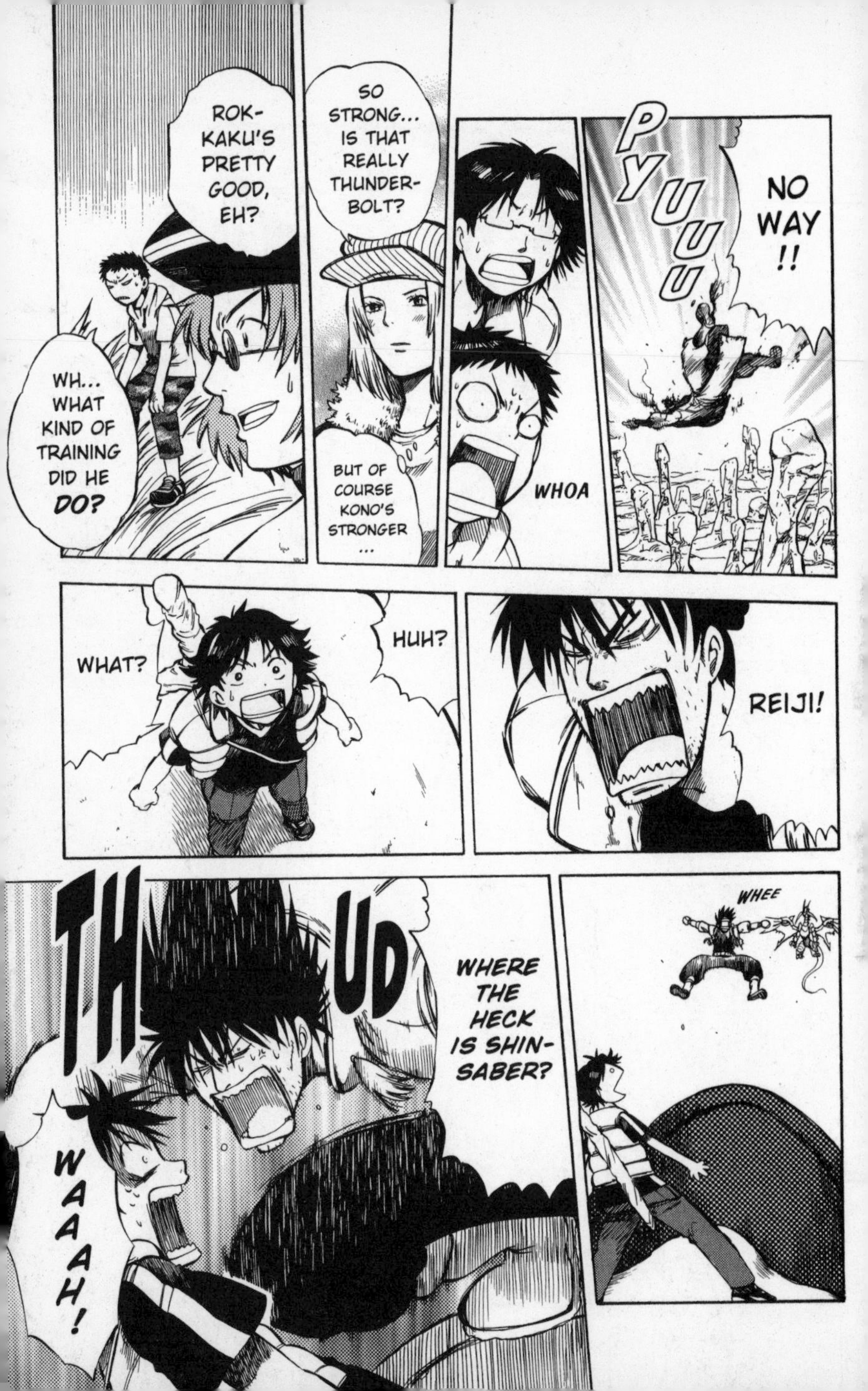
PYUUU
NO WAY!!
WHOA
SO STRONG... IS THAT REALLY THUNDER-BOLT?
BUT OF COURSE KONO'S STRONGER ...
ROK-KAKU'S PRETTY GOOD, EH?
WH... WHAT KIND OF TRAINING DID HE *DO?*
REIJI!
HUH?
WHAT?
WHEE
WHERE THE HECK IS SHIN-SABER?
THUD
WAAAH!

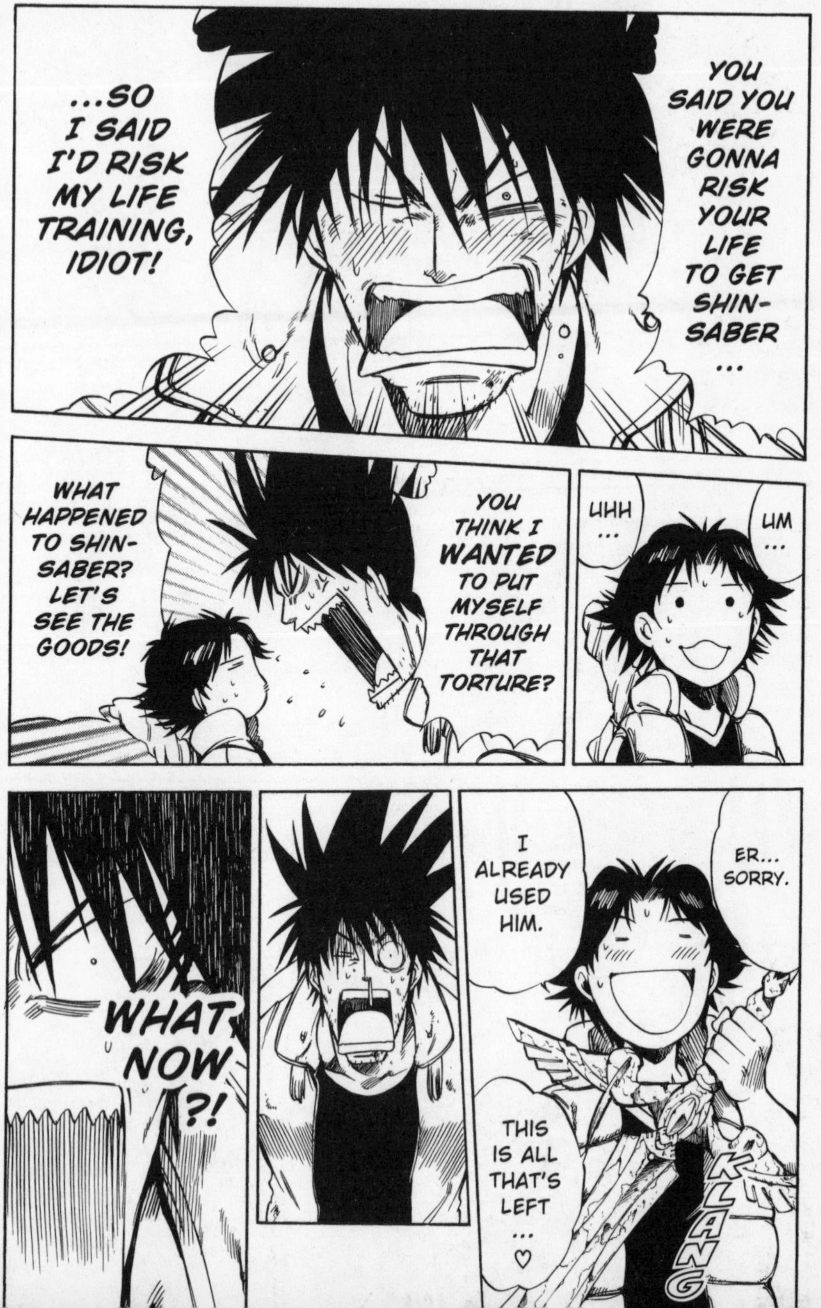
YOU SAID YOU WERE GONNA RISK YOUR LIFE TO GET SHIN-SABER...
...SO I SAID I'D RISK MY LIFE TRAINING, IDIOT!
UM...
UHH...
YOU THINK I WANTED TO PUT MYSELF THROUGH THAT TORTURE?
WHAT HAPPENED TO SHIN-SABER? LET'S SEE THE GOODS!
ER... SORRY.
I ALREADY USED HIM.
KLANG
THIS IS ALL THAT'S LEFT... ♡
WHAT NOW?!

READ THIS WAY

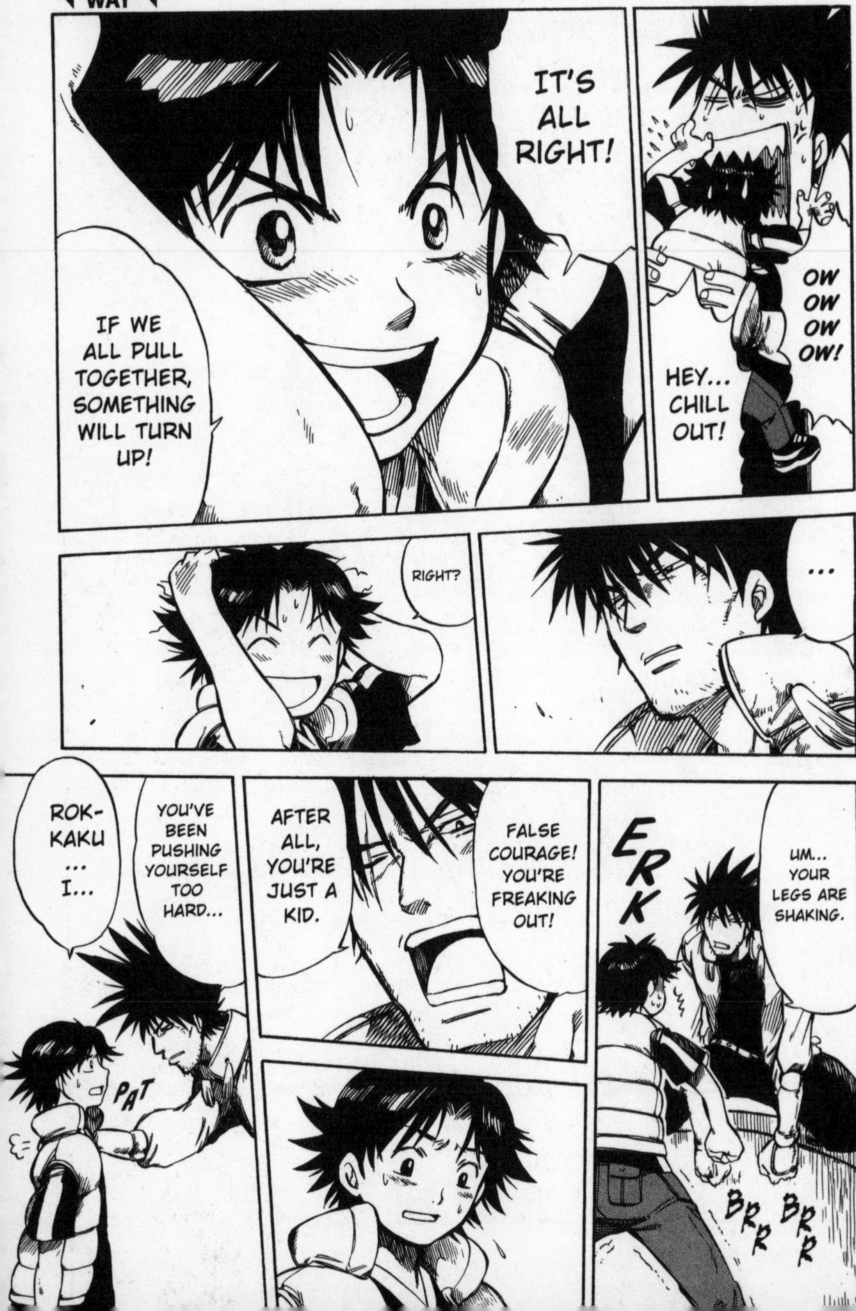
OW OW OW OW!
HEY... CHILL OUT!
IT'S ALL RIGHT!
IF WE ALL PULL TOGETHER, SOMETHING WILL TURN UP!
...
RIGHT?
UM... YOUR LEGS ARE SHAKING.
ERK
BRRR BRRR
FALSE COURAGE! YOU'RE FREAKING OUT!
AFTER ALL, YOU'RE JUST A KID.
YOU'VE BEEN PUSHING YOURSELF TOO HARD...
ROK-KAKU ... I...
PAT

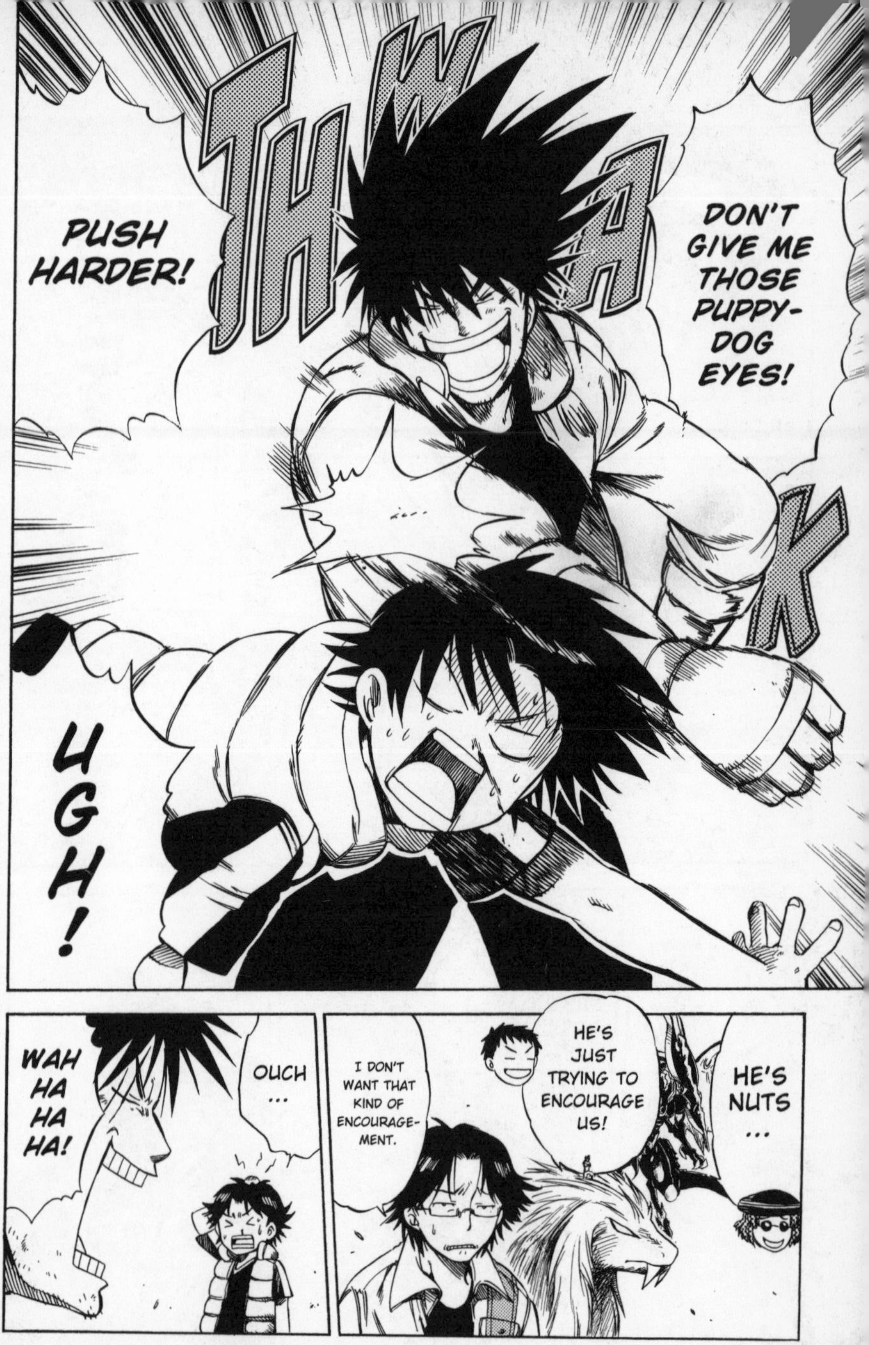

THWACK
DON'T GIVE ME THOSE PUPPY-DOG EYES!
PUSH HARDER!
UGH!
HE'S NUTS...
HE'S JUST TRYING TO ENCOURAGE US!
I DON'T WANT THAT KIND OF ENCOURAGE-MENT.
OUCH...
WAH HA HA HA!

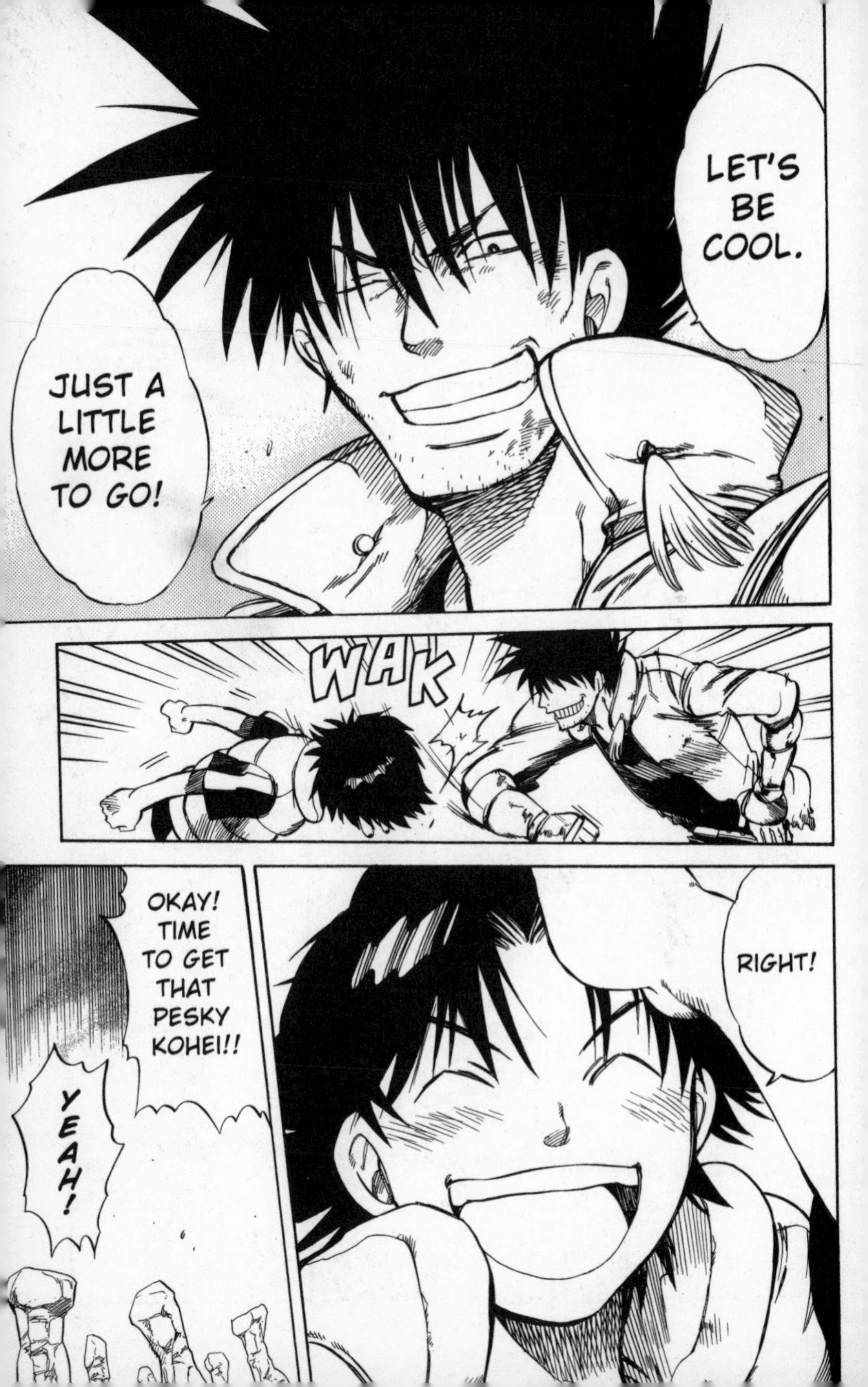
LET'S BE COOL.
JUST A LITTLE MORE TO GO!
WAK
RIGHT!
OKAY! TIME TO GET THAT PESKY KOHEI!!
YEAH!

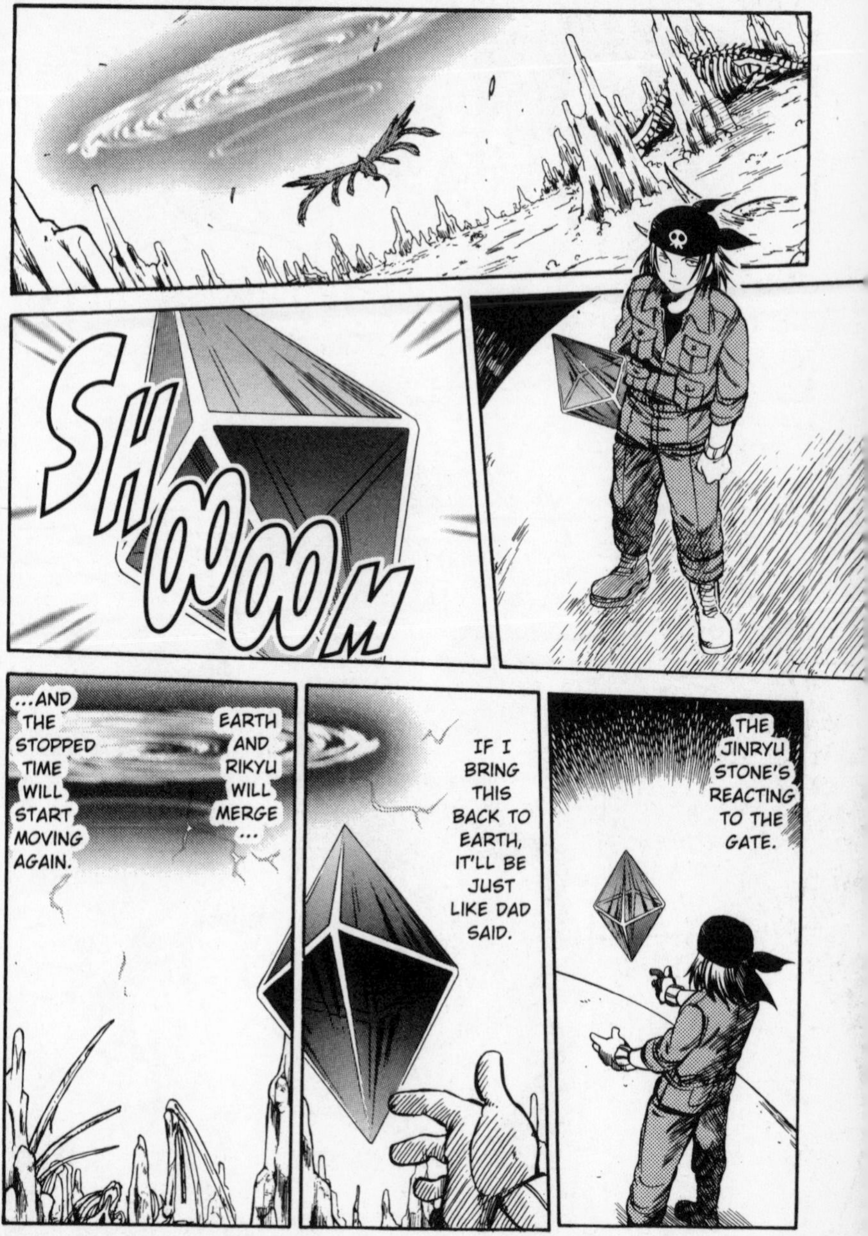
SHOOOOM
THE JINRYU STONE'S REACTING TO THE GATE.
IF I BRING THIS BACK TO EARTH, IT'LL BE JUST LIKE DAD SAID.
EARTH AND RIKYU WILL MERGE...
...AND THE STOPPED TIME WILL START MOVING AGAIN.

READ THIS WAY

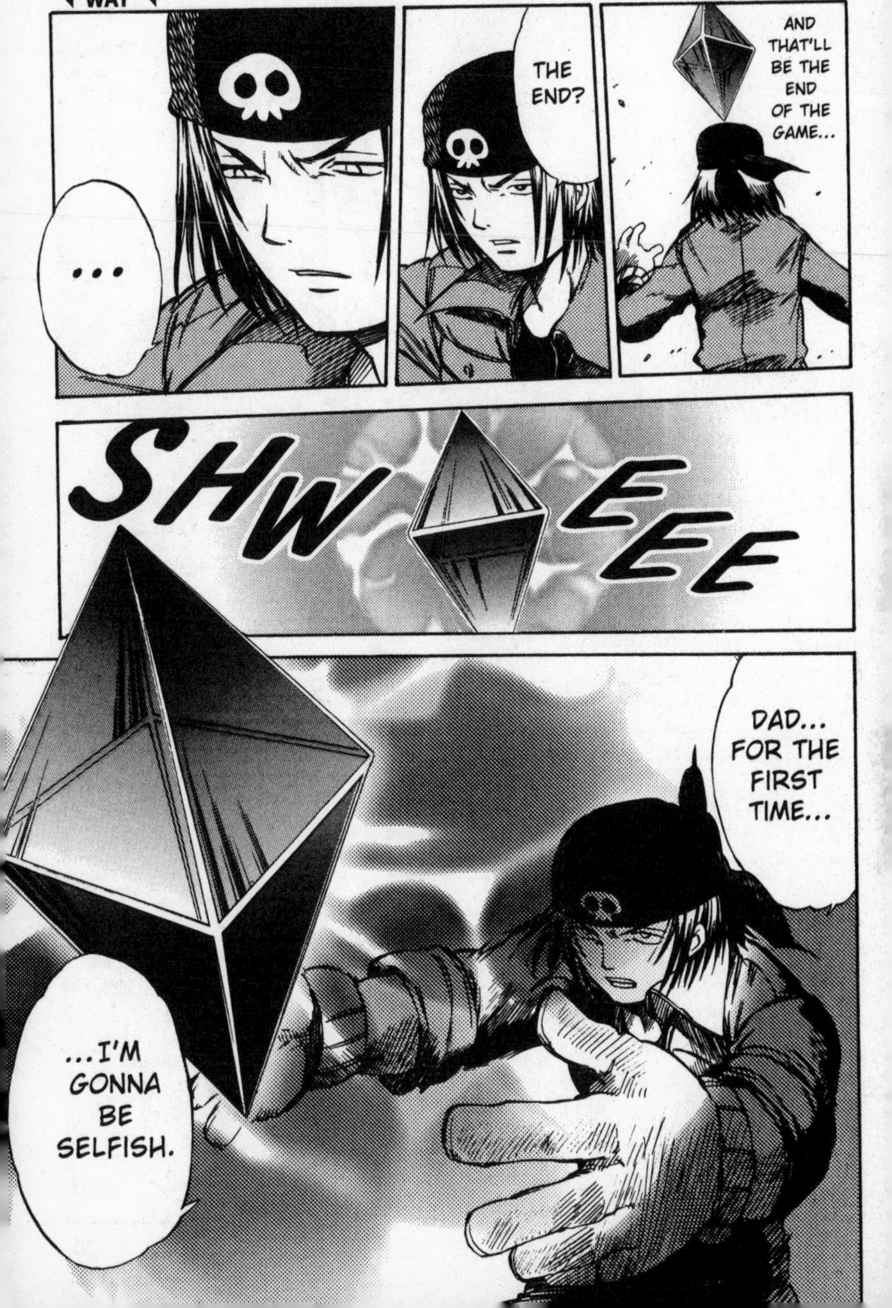
AND THAT'LL BE THE END OF THE GAME...
THE END?
...
SHWEEE
DAD... FOR THE FIRST TIME...
...I'M GONNA BE SELFISH.

I CAN'T FINISH YET.
THERE'S SOMEONE I WANT TO BEAT DOWN...
RRRRRM
SHING

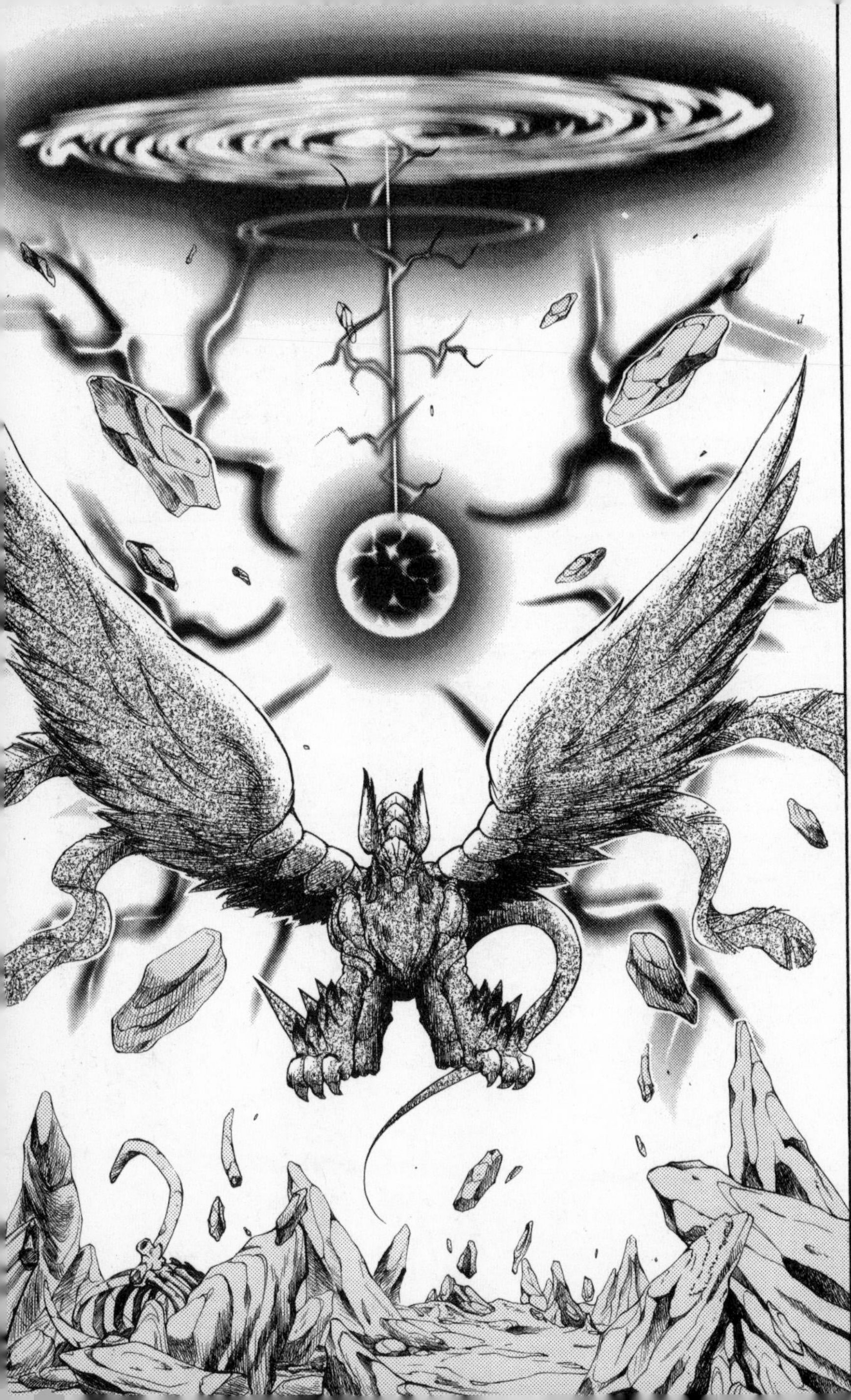

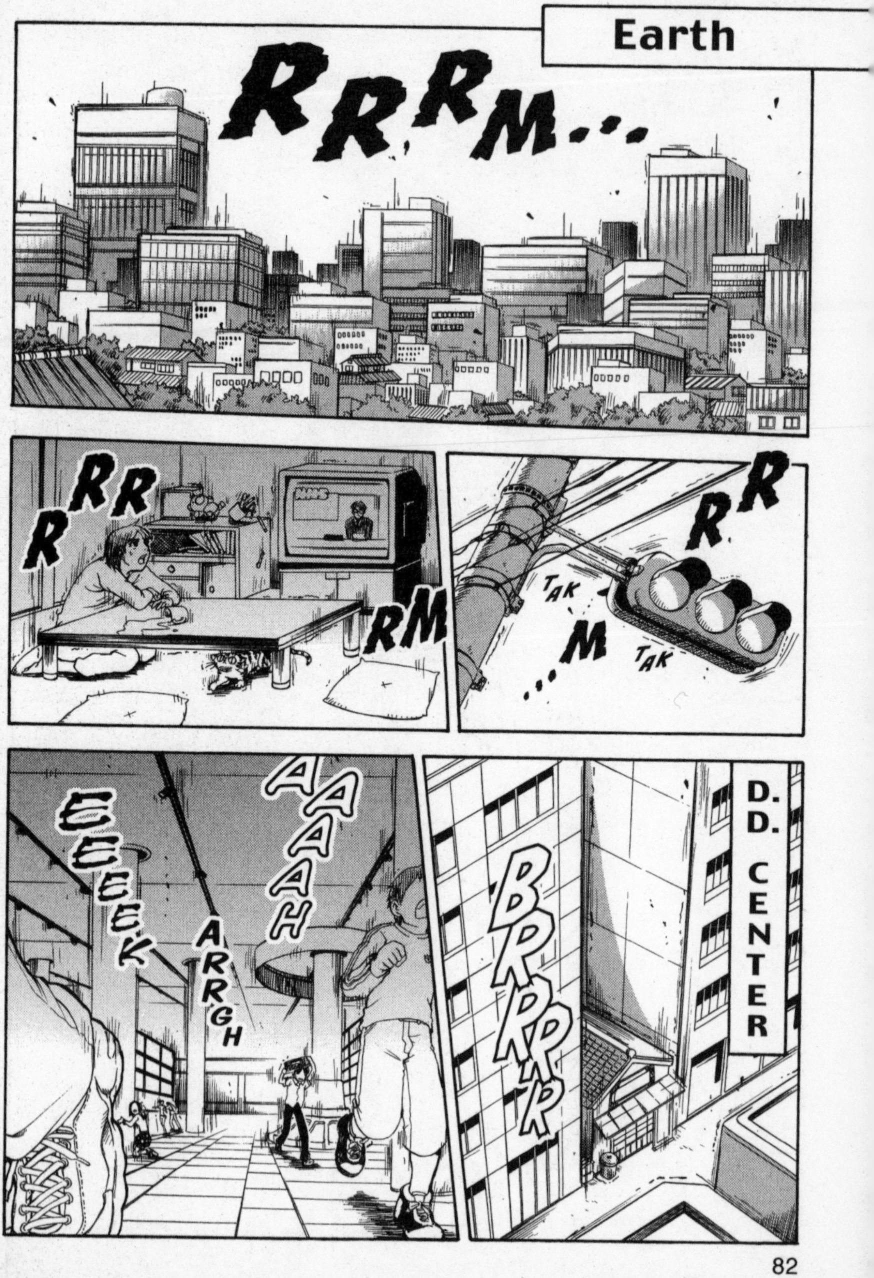
Earth
RRRM...
RRR
TAK
...M
TAK
RRR
RM
D.D. CENTER
BRRRR
AAAAAH
EEEEEK
ARRGH

READ THIS WAY

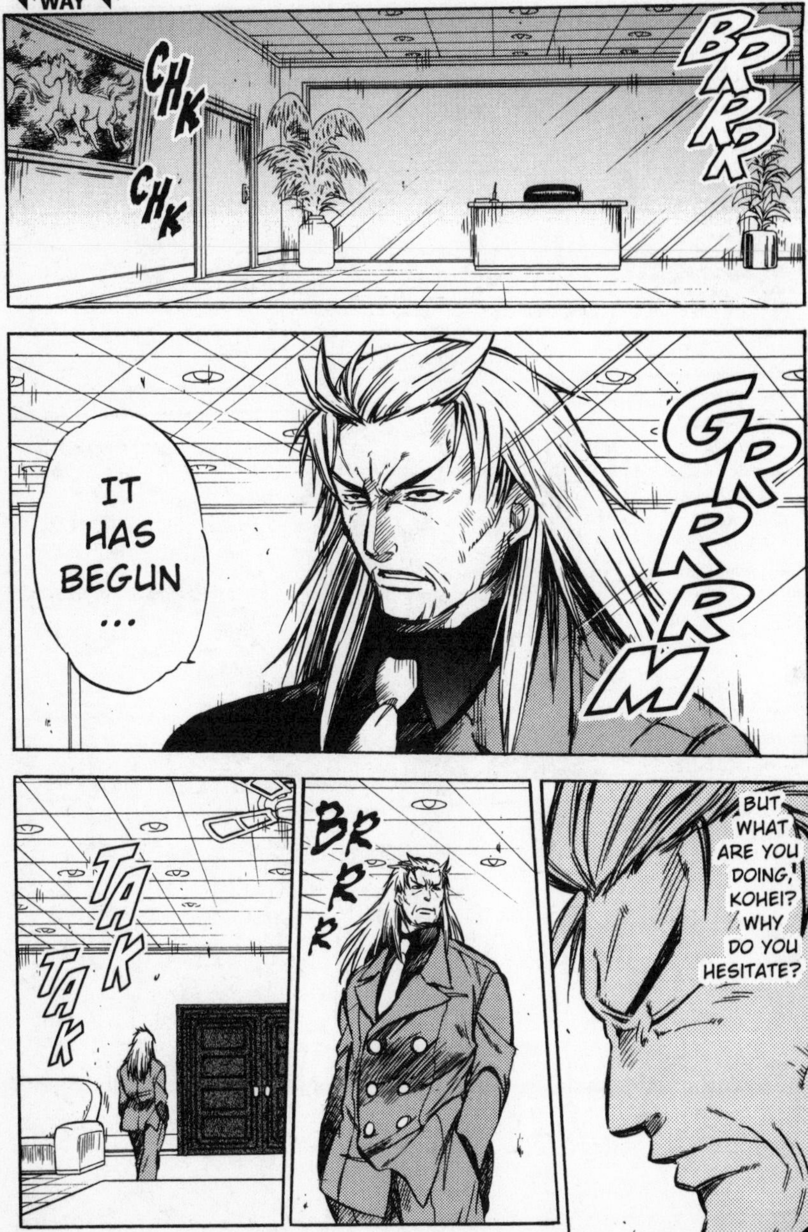
BRRRR
CHK
CHK
GRRRM
IT HAS BEGUN ...
BUT WHAT ARE YOU DOING, KOHEI? WHY DO YOU HESITATE?
BRRR
TAK
TAK

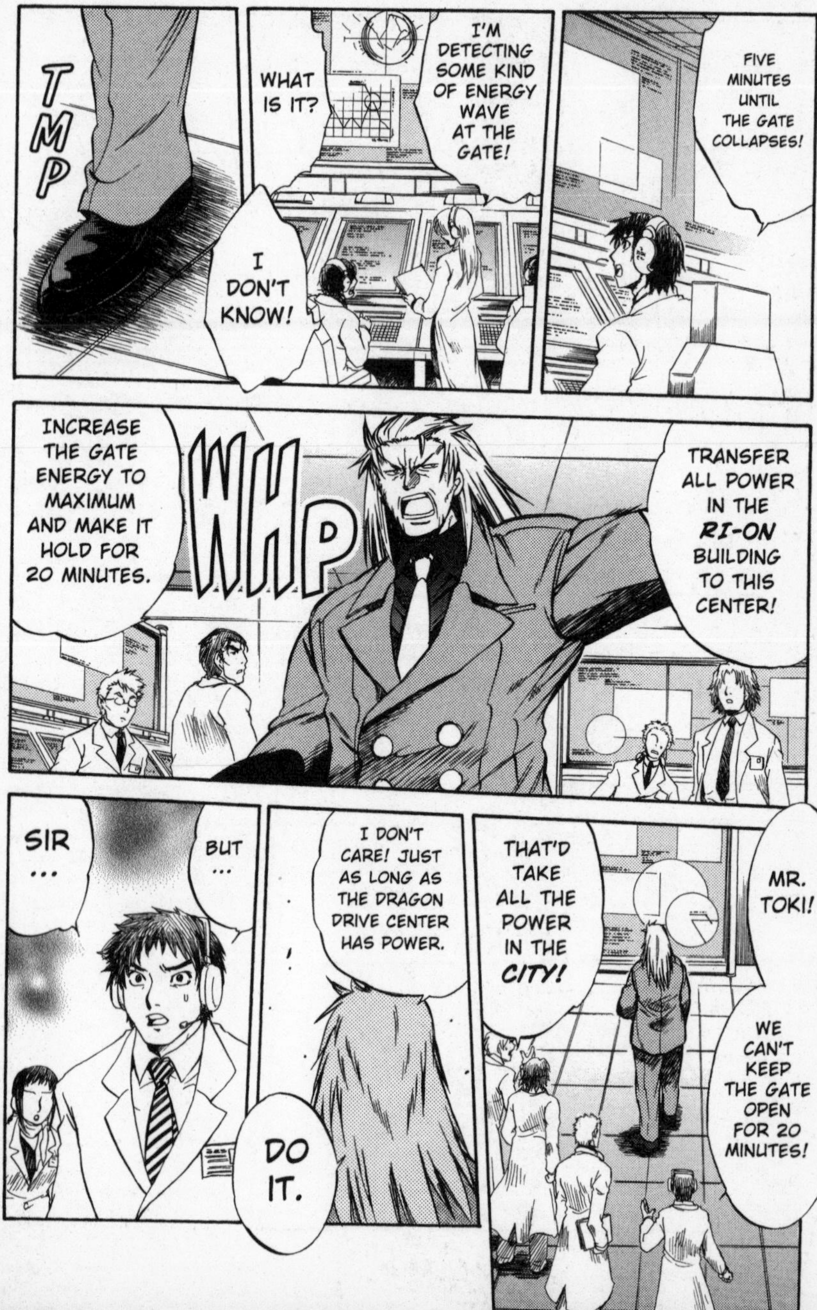
FIVE MINUTES UNTIL THE GATE COLLAPSES!
I'M DETECTING SOME KIND OF ENERGY WAVE AT THE GATE!
WHAT IS IT?
I DON'T KNOW!
TMP
TRANSFER ALL POWER IN THE RI-ON BUILDING TO THIS CENTER!
WHP
INCREASE THE GATE ENERGY TO MAXIMUM AND MAKE IT HOLD FOR 20 MINUTES.
MR. TOKI!
THAT'D TAKE ALL THE POWER IN THE CITY!
WE CAN'T KEEP THE GATE OPEN FOR 20 MINUTES!
I DON'T CARE! JUST AS LONG AS THE DRAGON DRIVE CENTER HAS POWER.
DO IT.
BUT ...
SIR ...

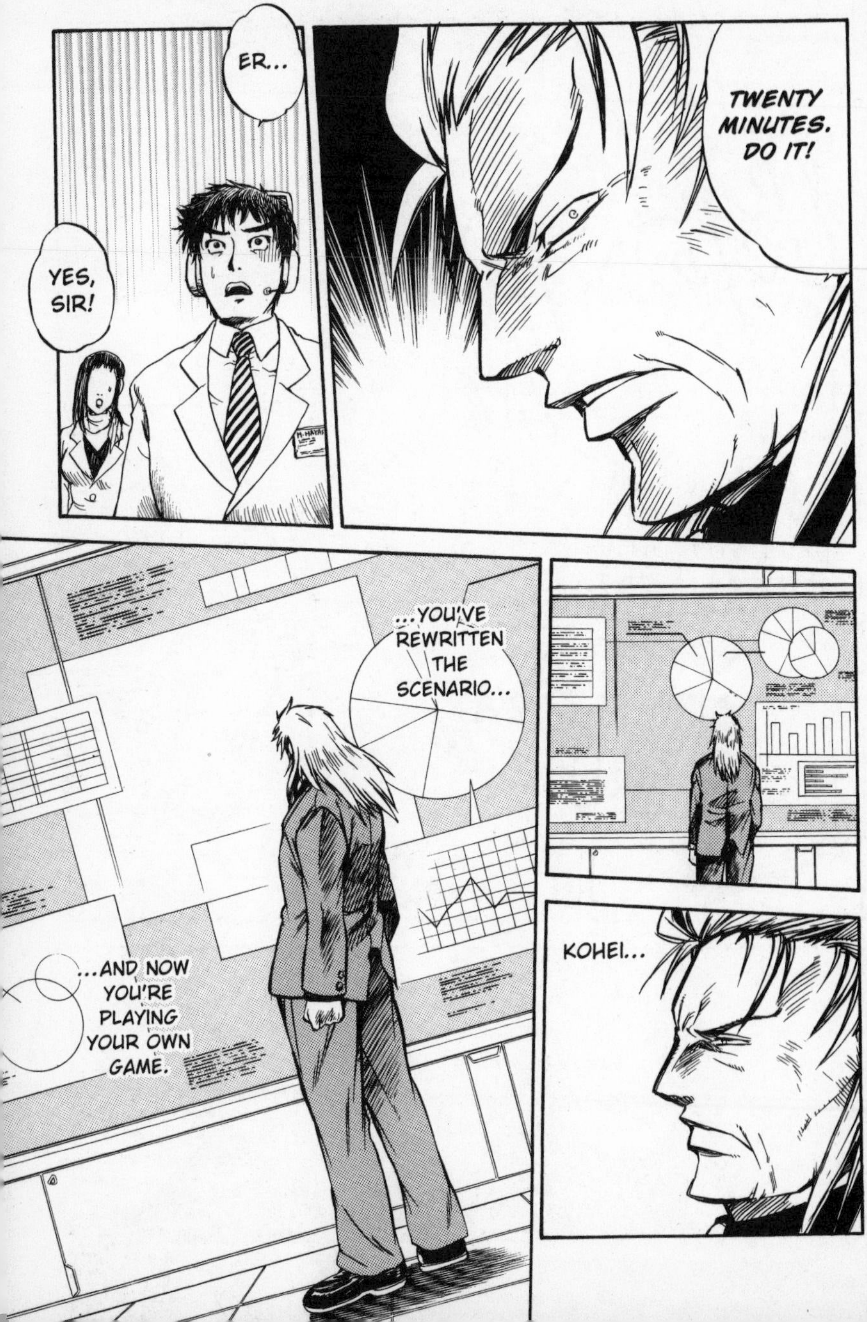
TWENTY MINUTES. DO IT!
ER...
YES, SIR!
KOHEI...
...YOU'VE REWRITTEN THE SCENARIO...
...AND NOW YOU'RE PLAYING YOUR OWN GAME.

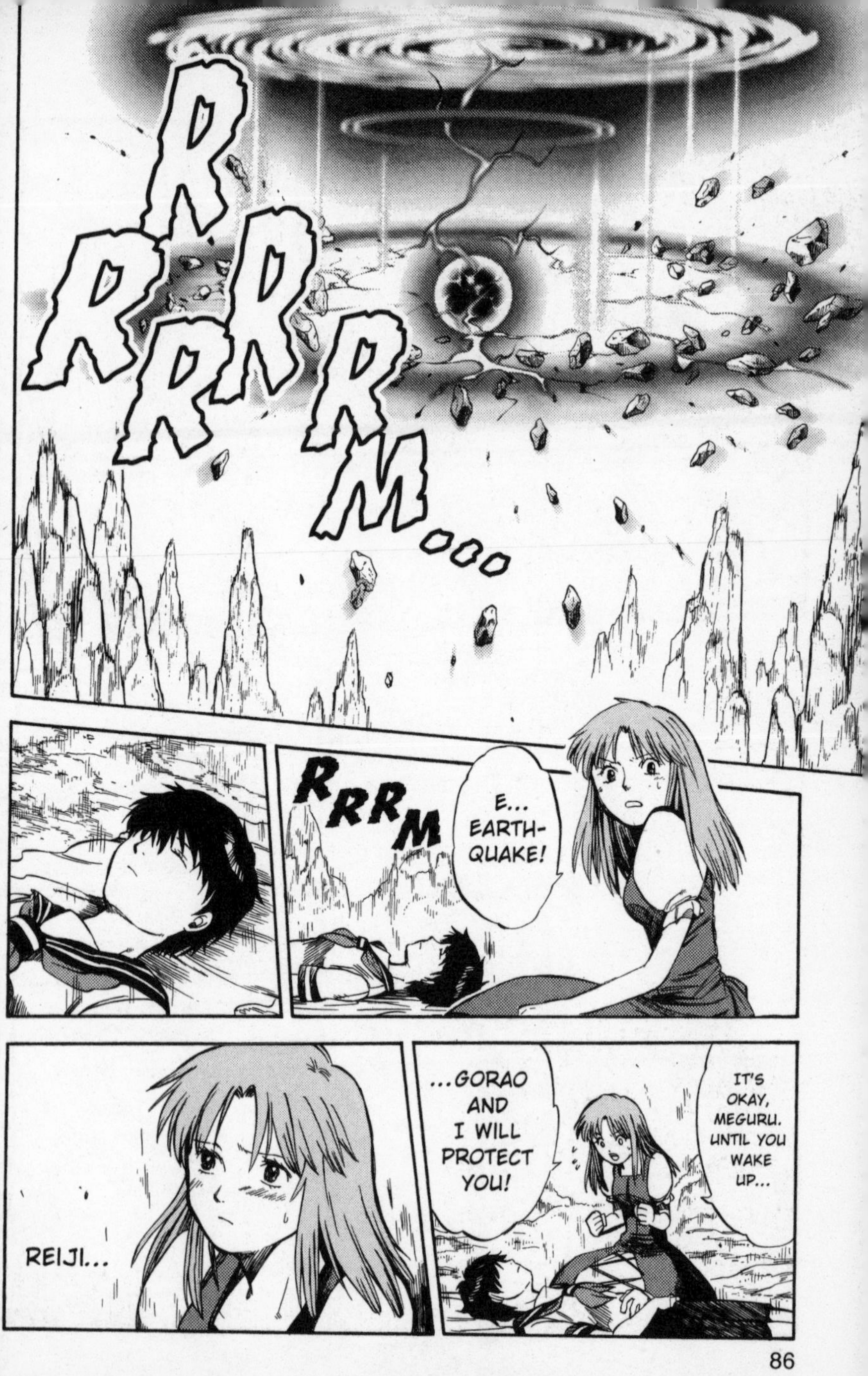
RRRRRMooo
RRRM
E... EARTH-QUAKE!
IT'S OKAY, MEGURU. UNTIL YOU WAKE UP...
...GORAO AND I WILL PROTECT YOU!
REIJI...

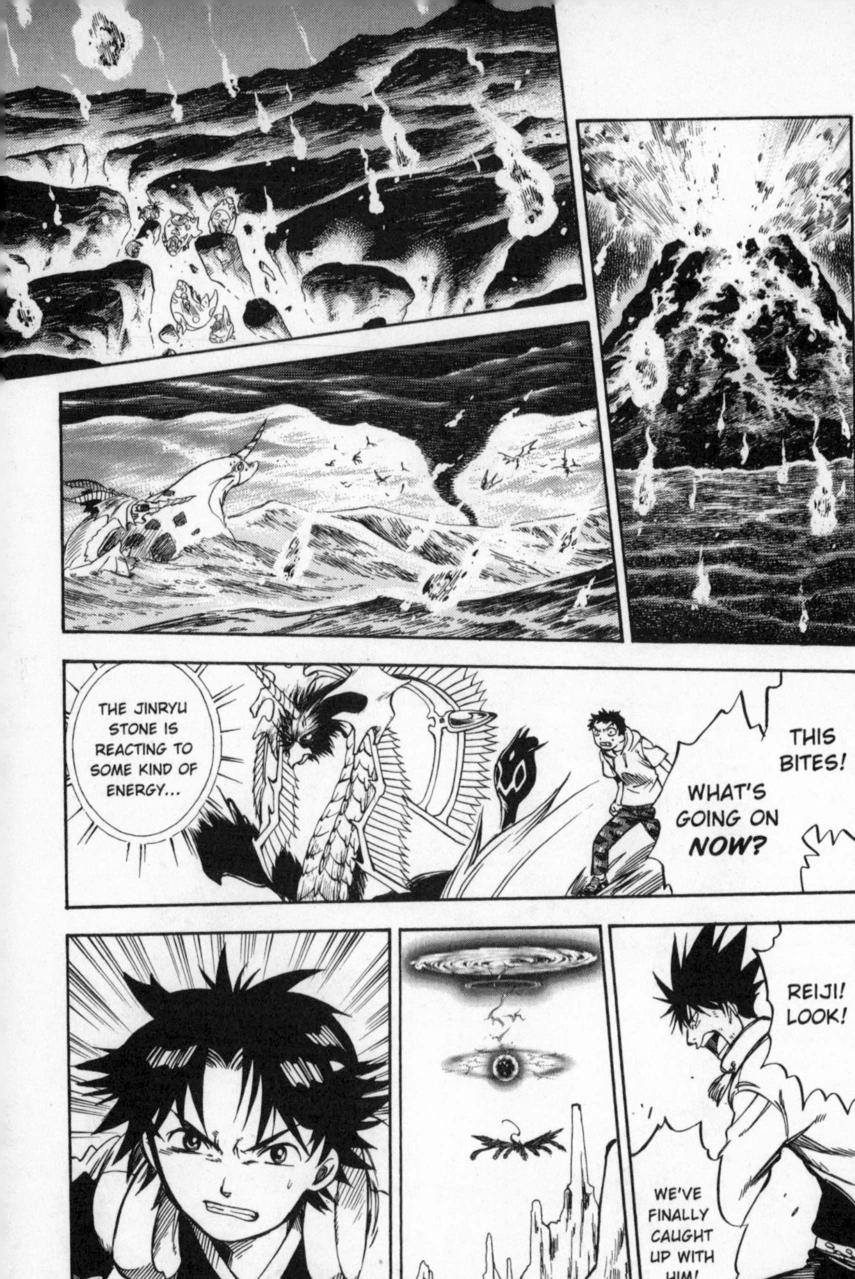
THIS BITES!
WHAT'S GOING ON NOW?
THE JINRYU STONE IS REACTING TO SOME KIND OF ENERGY...
REIJI! LOOK!
WE'VE FINALLY CAUGHT UP WITH HIM!

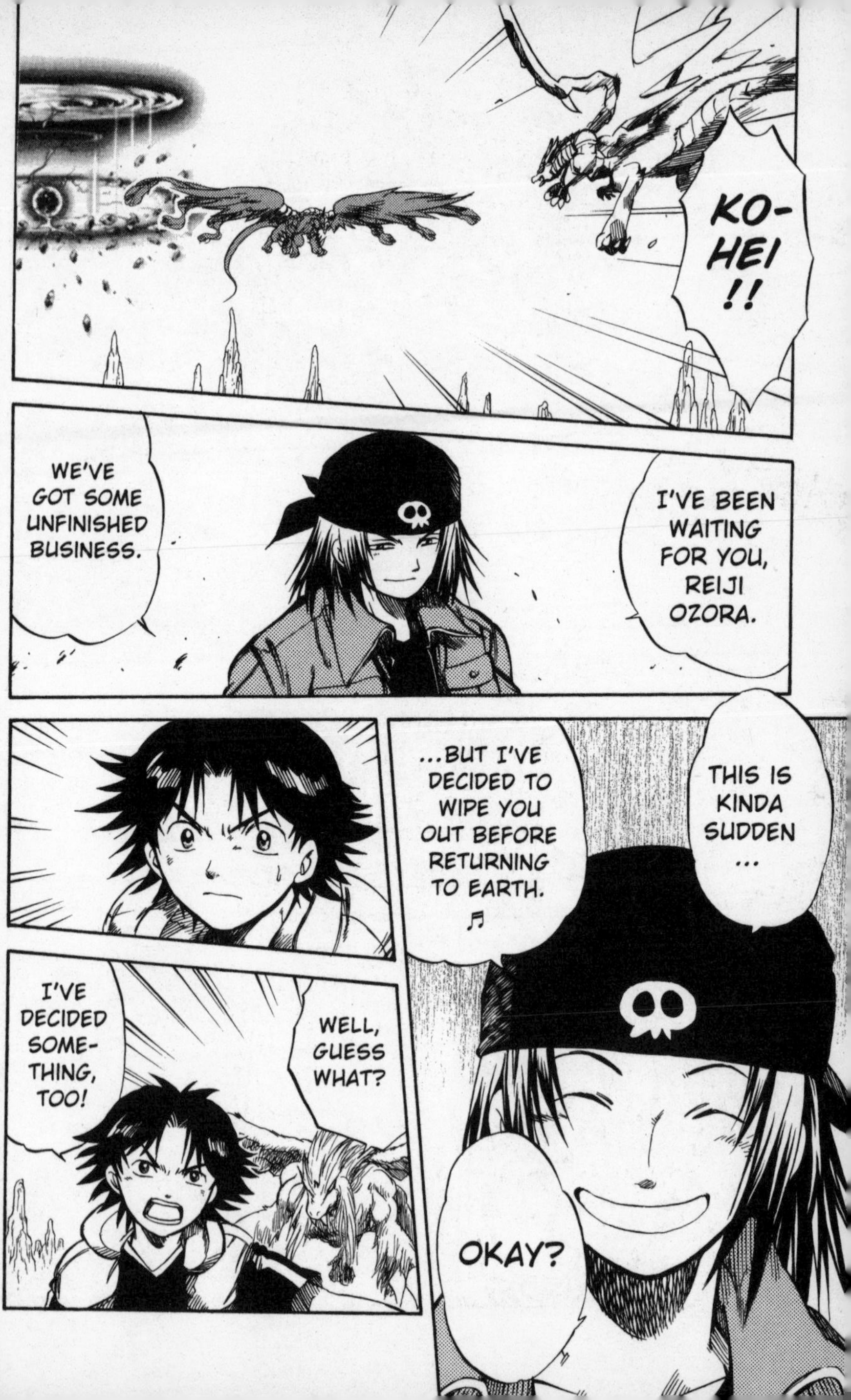
KO-HEI!!
I'VE BEEN WAITING FOR YOU, REIJI OZORA.
WE'VE GOT SOME UNFINISHED BUSINESS.
THIS IS KINDA SUDDEN...
...BUT I'VE DECIDED TO WIPE YOU OUT BEFORE RETURNING TO EARTH. ♬
OKAY?
WELL, GUESS WHAT?
I'VE DECIDED SOMETHING, TOO!

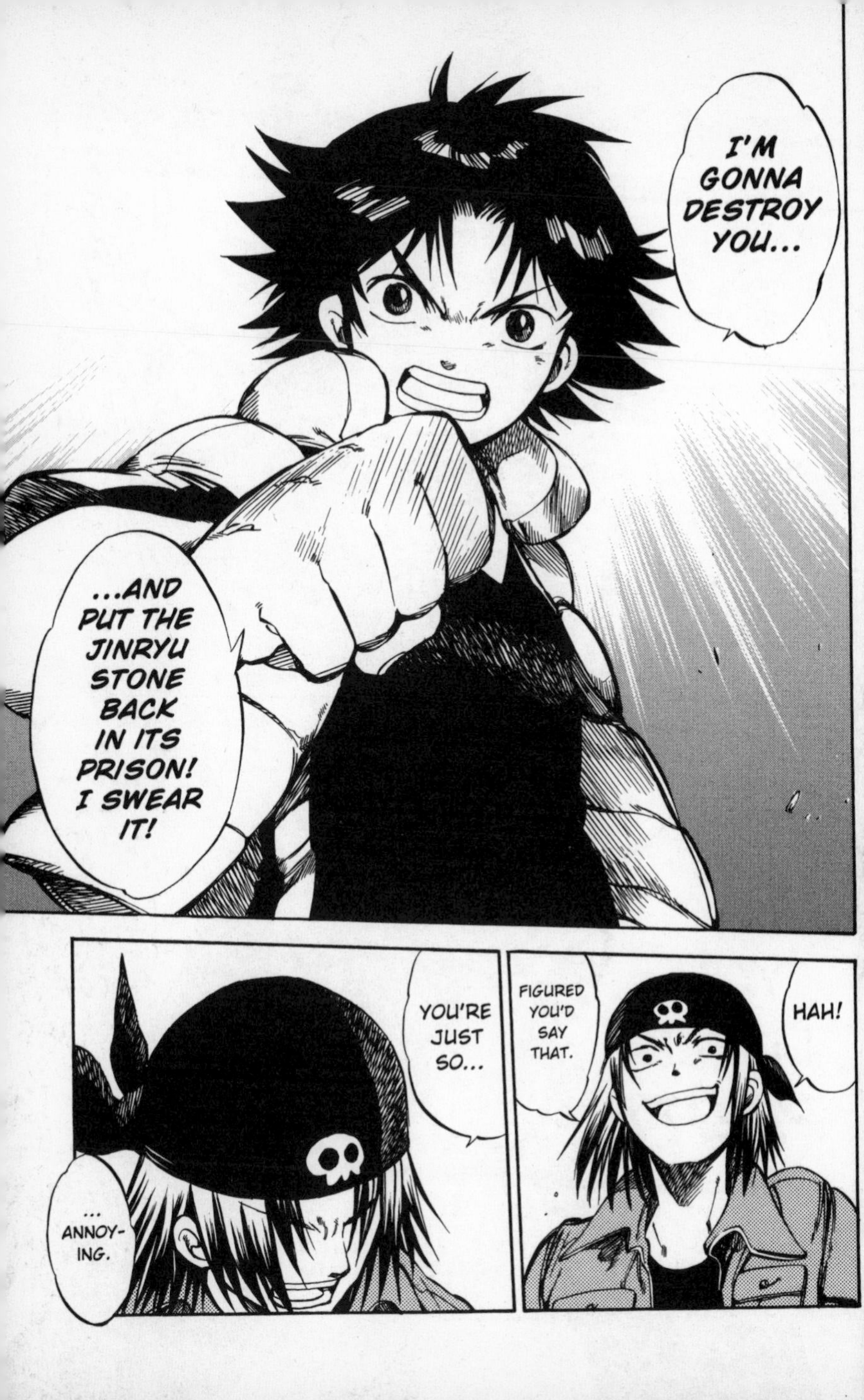
I'M GONNA DESTROY YOU...
...AND PUT THE JINRYU STONE BACK IN ITS PRISON! I SWEAR IT!
HAH!
FIGURED YOU'D SAY THAT.
YOU'RE JUST SO...
... ANNOY-ING.

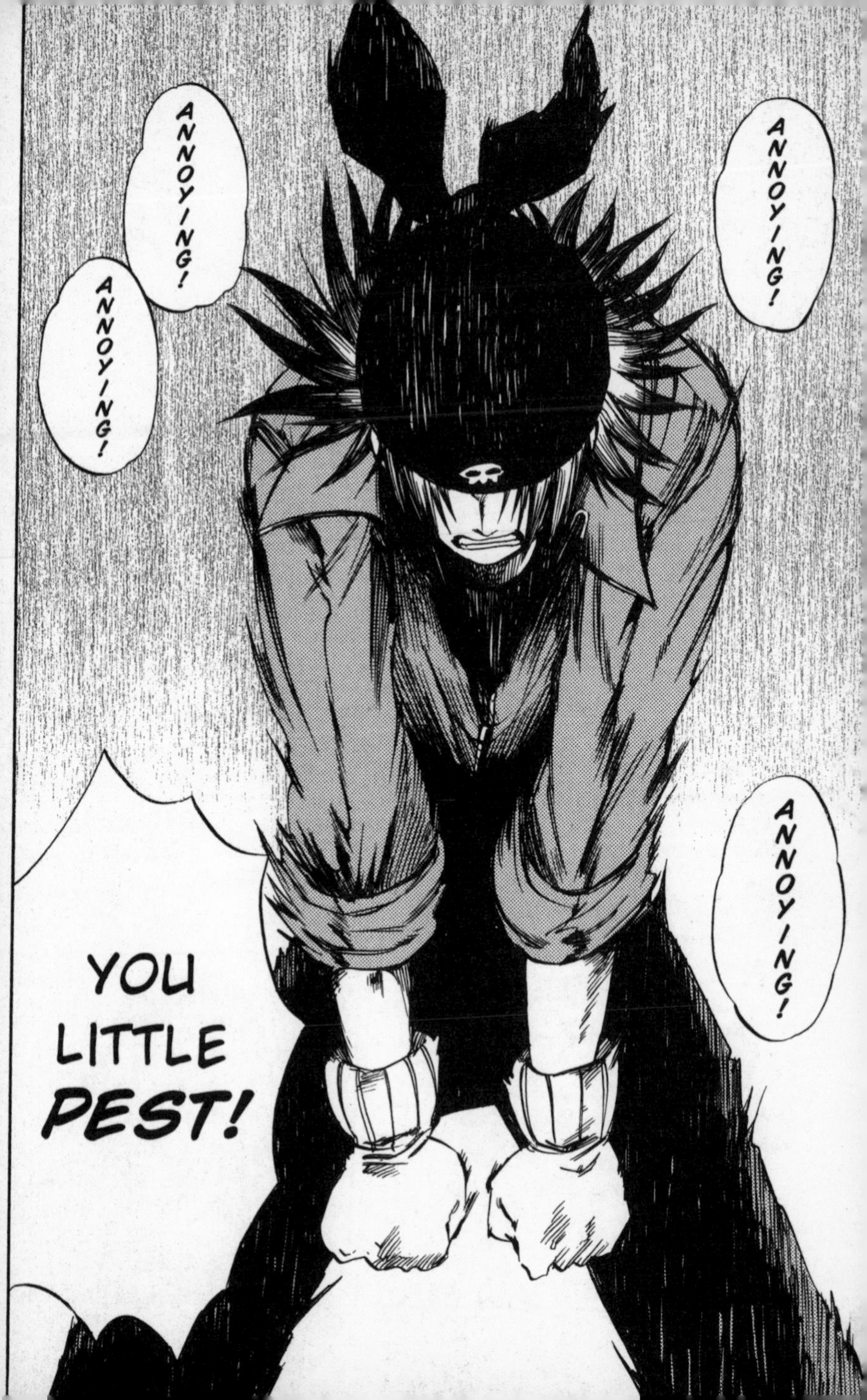
ANNOYING!
ANNOYING!
ANNOYING!
ANNOYING!
YOU LITTLE PEST!

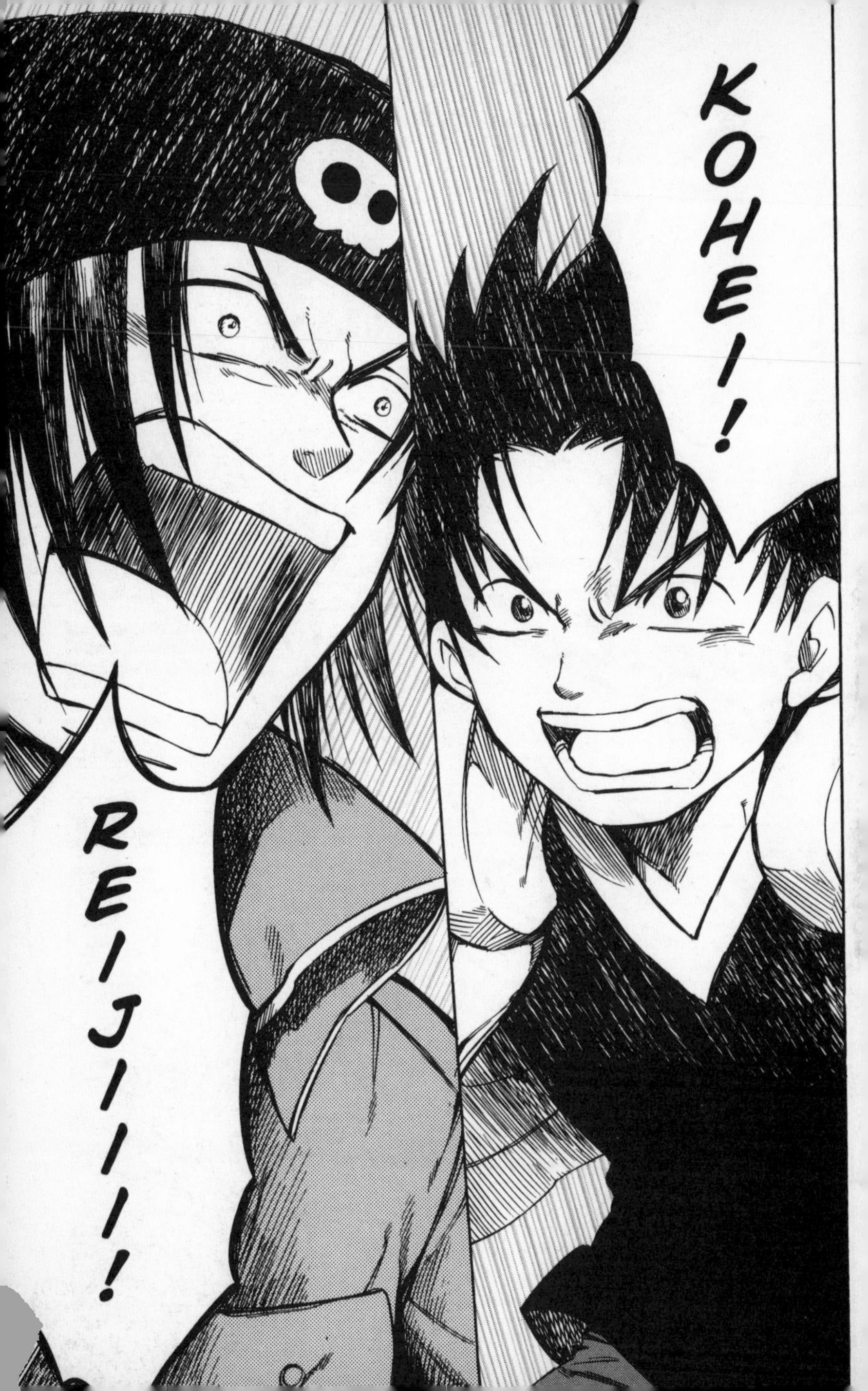
KOHEI!!
REIJIIII!

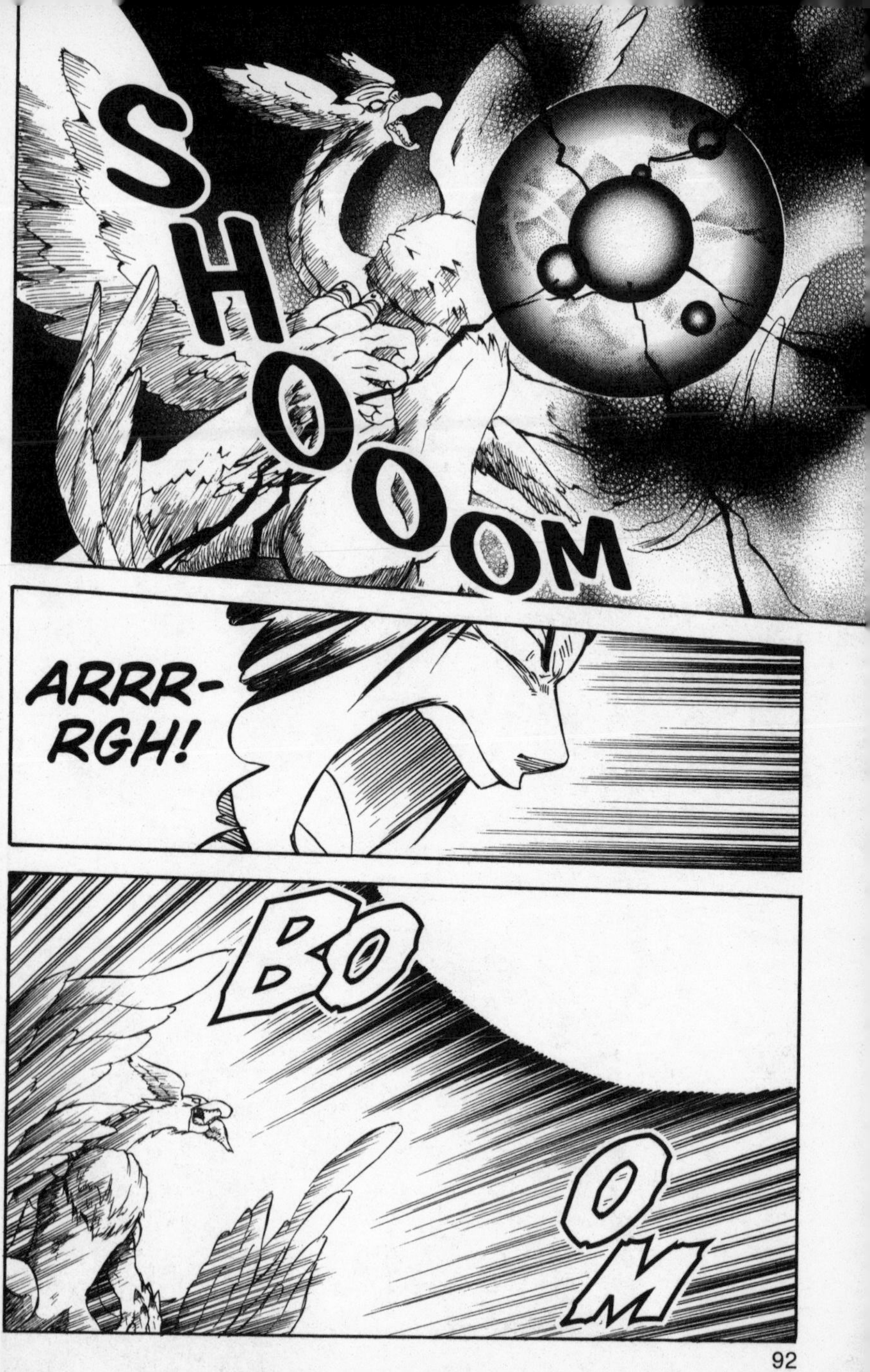
SHOOOOM
ARRR-
RGH!
BOOM

READ THIS WAY

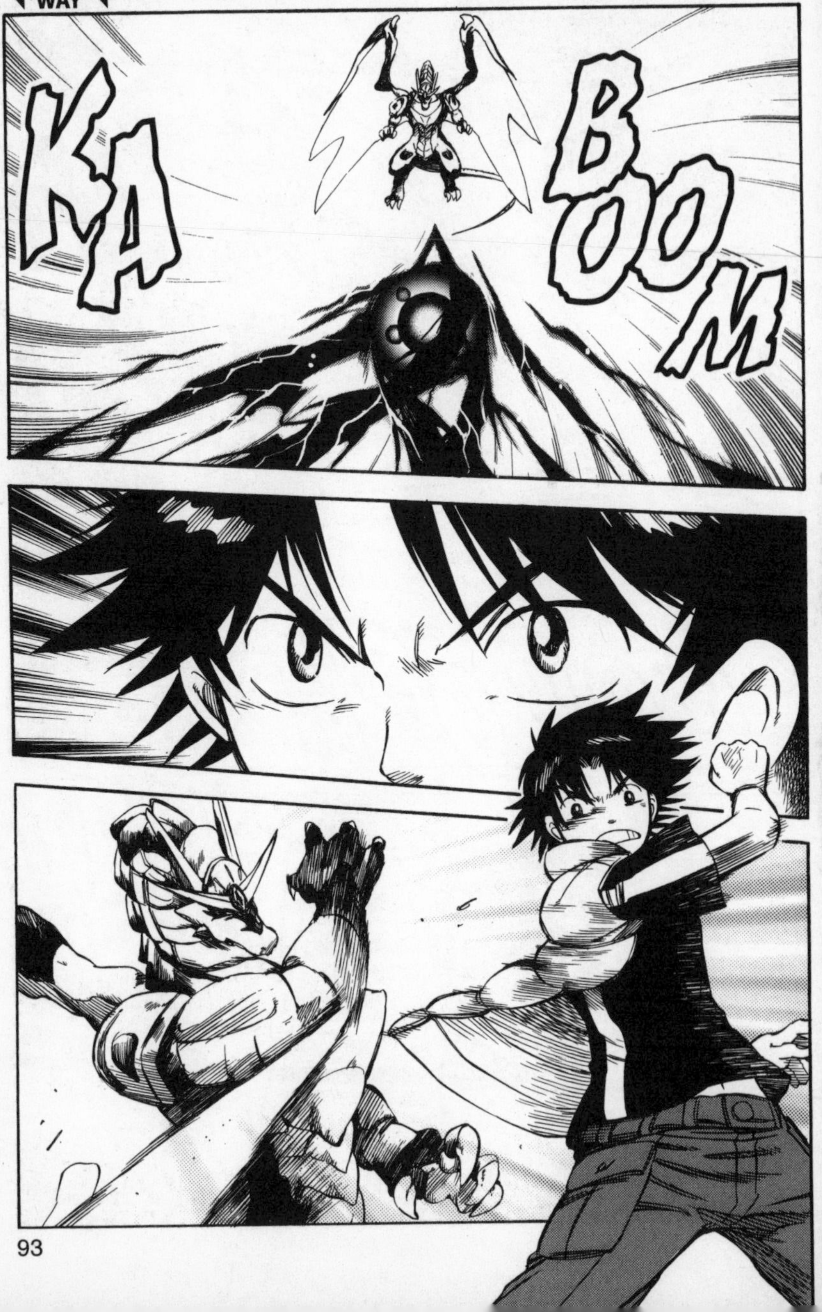
KA
BOOM

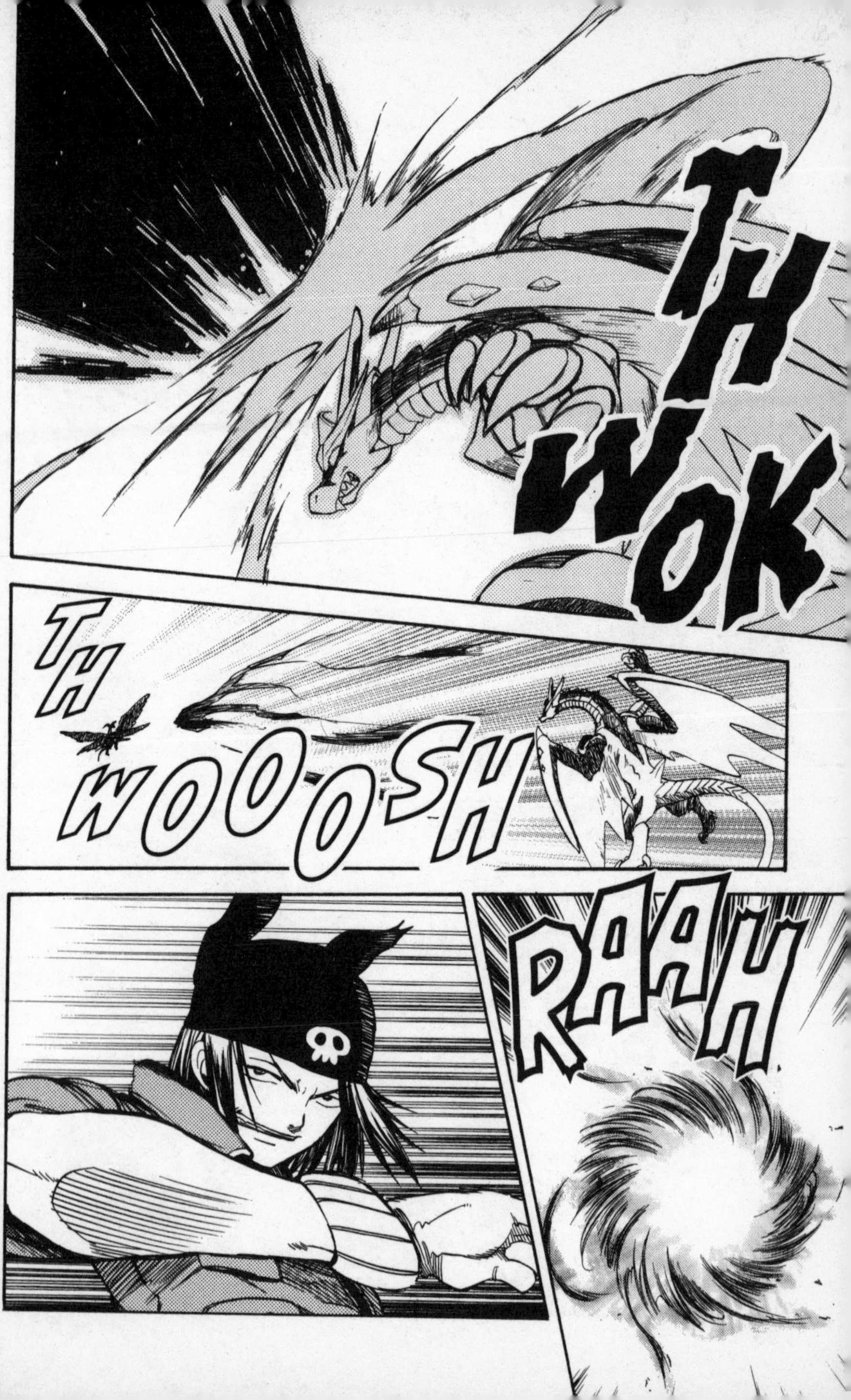
THWOK
THWOOOSH
RAAH

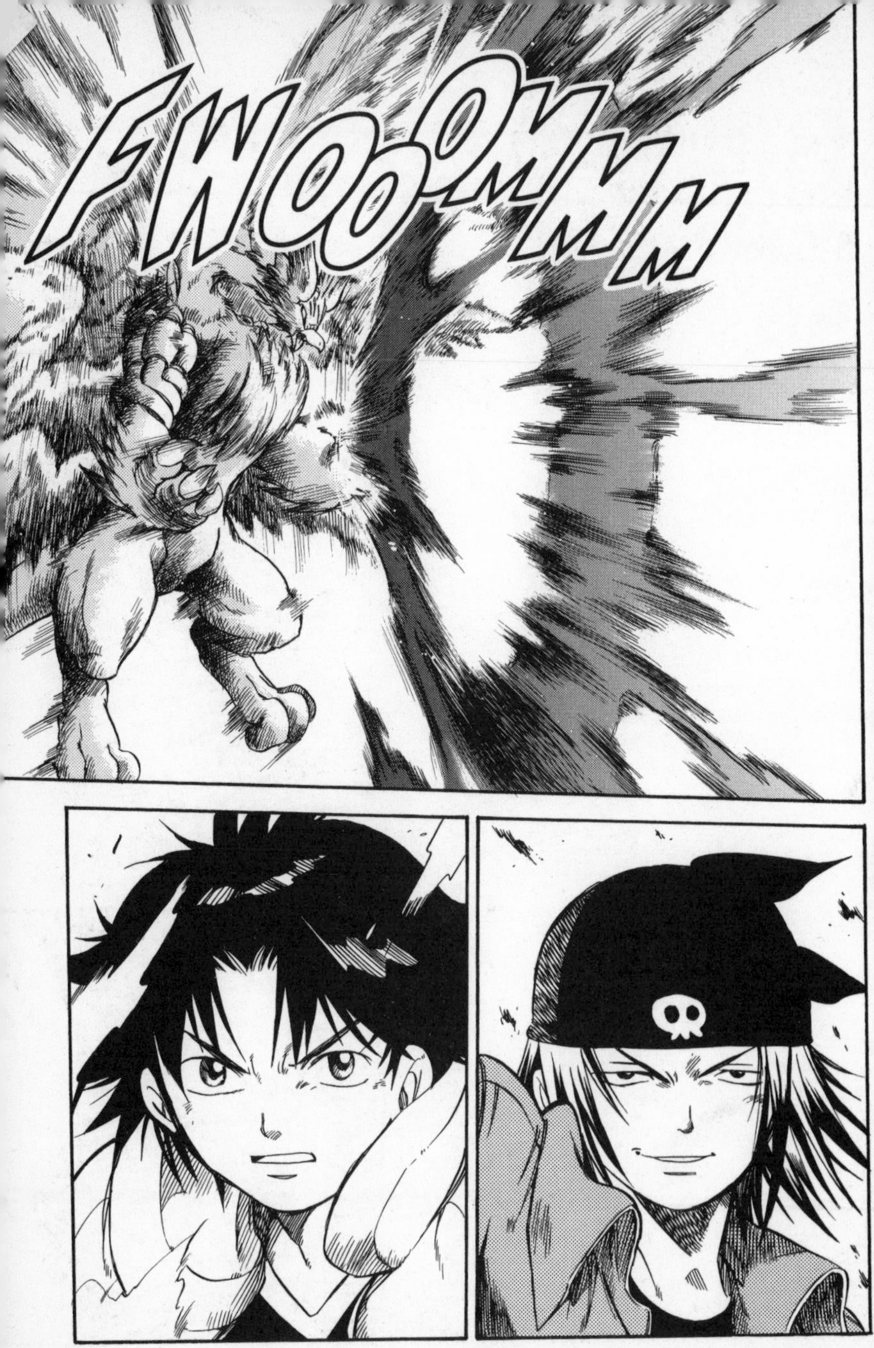
FWOOOMMM

Go Agent S!

BY NAGI

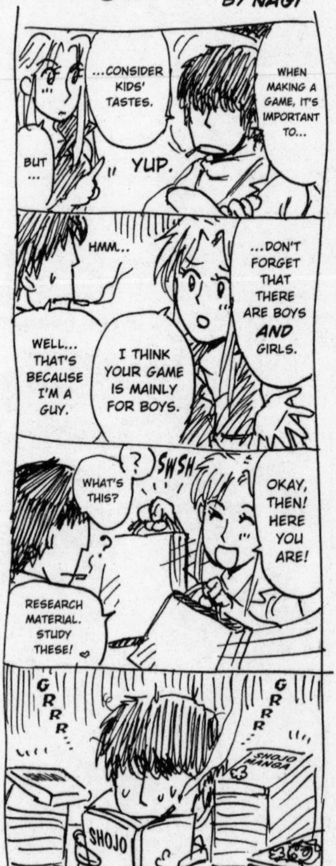

WHEN MAKING A GAME, IT'S IMPORTANT TO...
...CONSIDER KIDS' TASTES.
YUP.
BUT...
...DON'T FORGET THAT THERE ARE BOYS **AND** GIRLS.
HMM...
I THINK YOUR GAME IS MAINLY FOR BOYS.
WELL... THAT'S BECAUSE I'M A GUY.
OKAY, THEN! HERE YOU ARE!
SWSH
WHAT'S THIS?
RESEARCH MATERIAL. STUDY THESE!
GRRR...
GRRR...
SHOJO MANGA
SHOJO

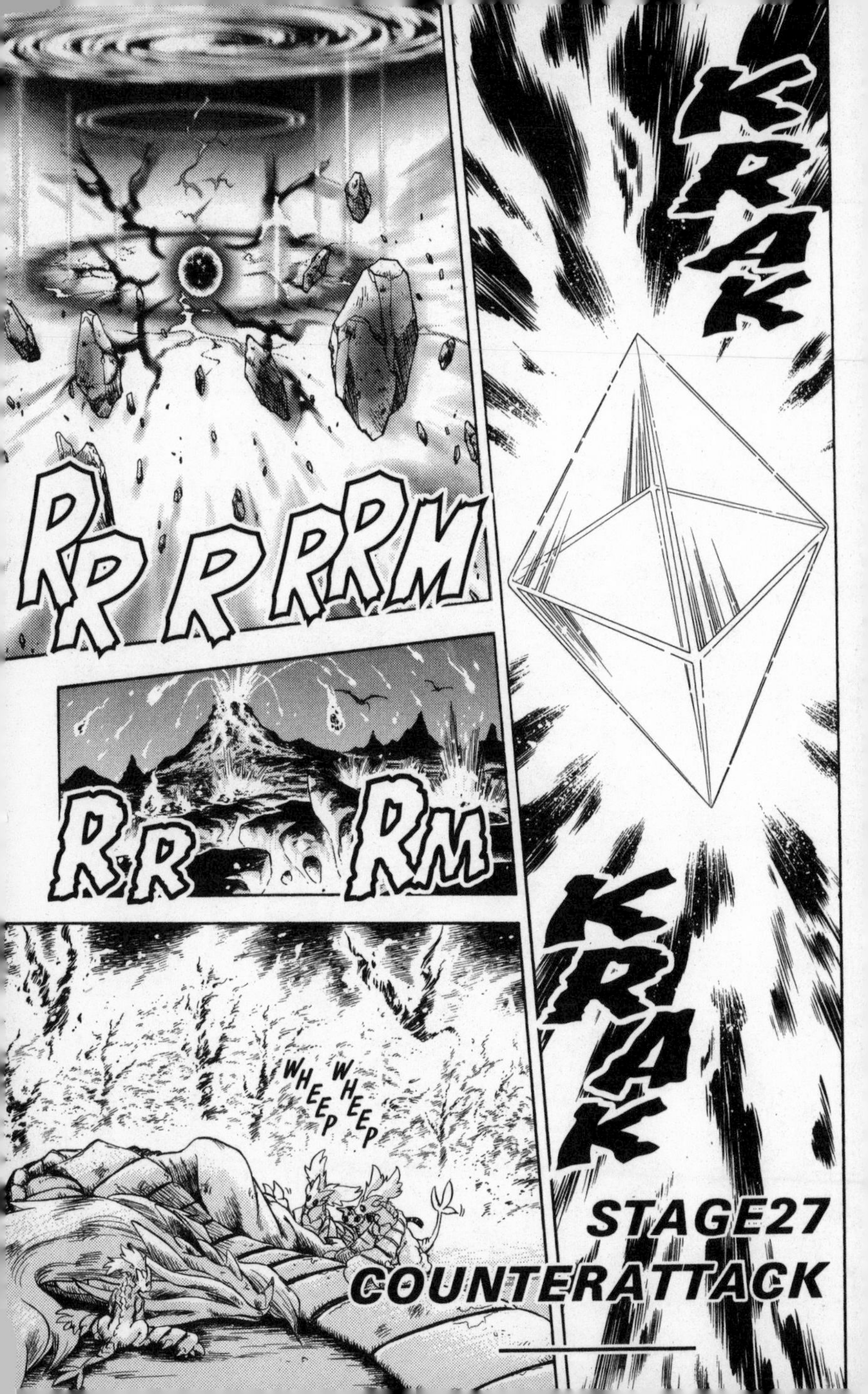
KRAK
KRAK
STAGE27
COUNTERATTACK
RRRRRM
R-R RM
WHEEP WHEEP

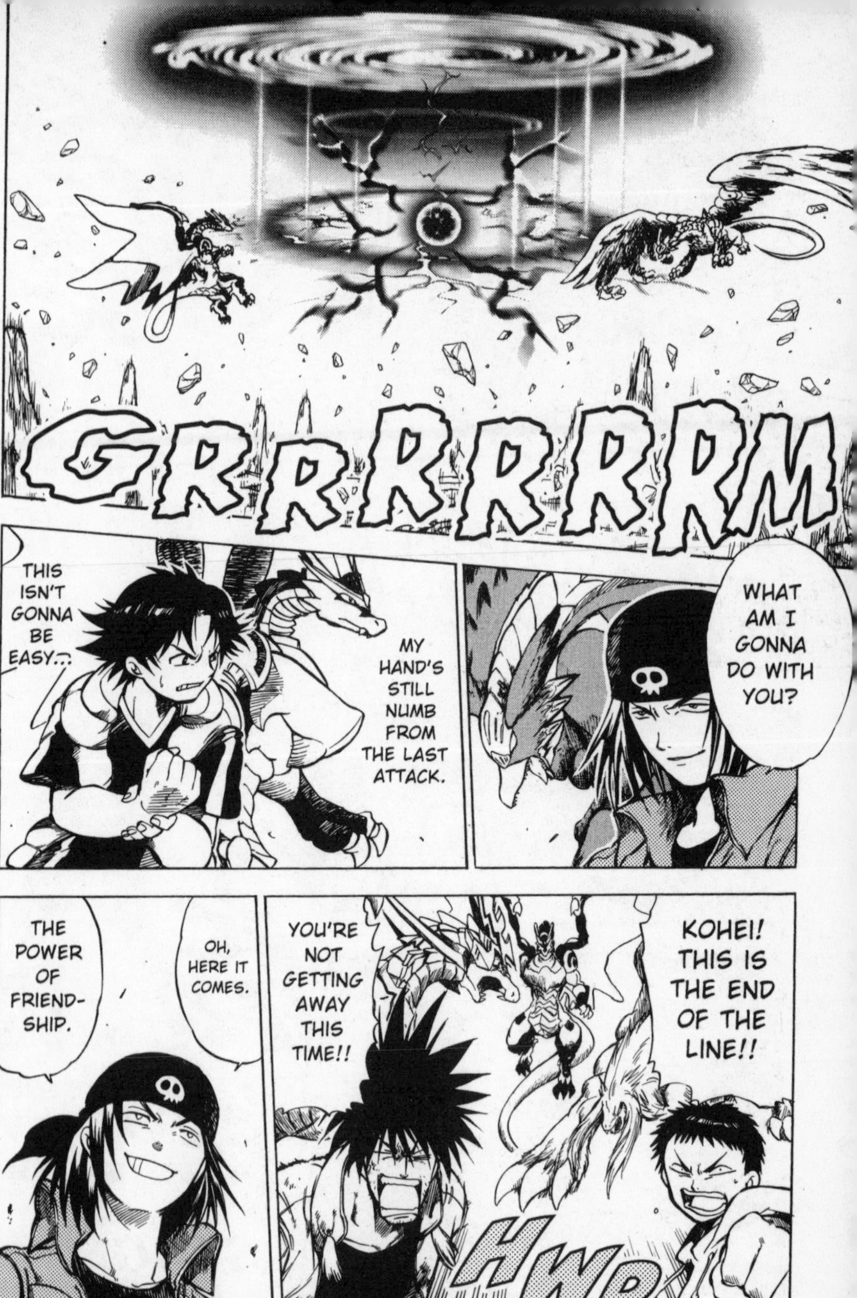
GRRRRRM
WHAT AM I GONNA DO WITH YOU?
THIS ISN'T GONNA BE EASY...
MY HAND'S STILL NUMB FROM THE LAST ATTACK.
KOHEI! THIS IS THE END OF THE LINE!!
YOU'RE NOT GETTING AWAY THIS TIME!!
HWP
OH, HERE IT COMES.
THE POWER OF FRIEND-SHIP.

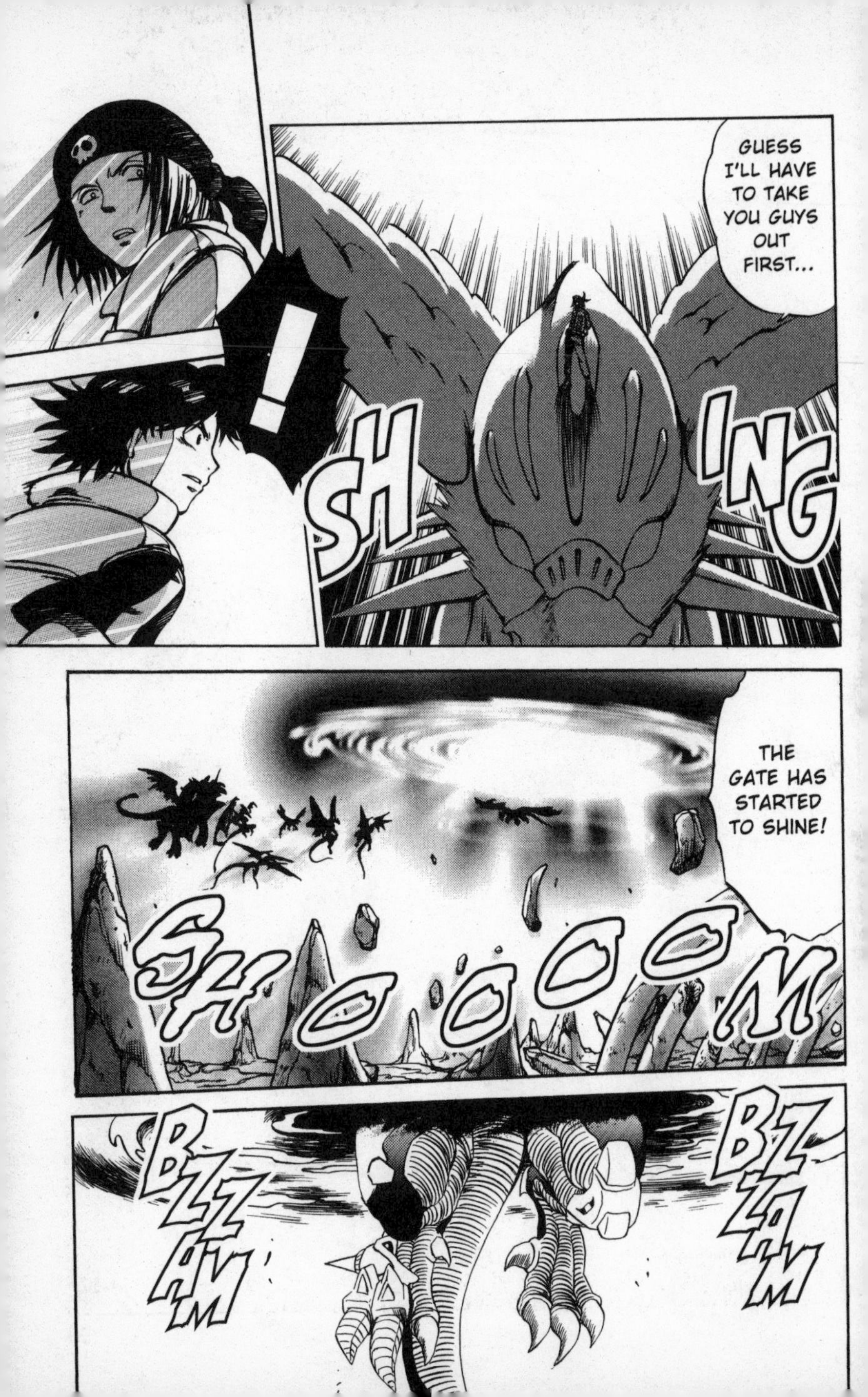
GUESS I'LL HAVE TO TAKE YOU GUYS OUT FIRST...
SHING
!
THE GATE HAS STARTED TO SHINE!
SHOOOOOM
BZZAM
BZZAM

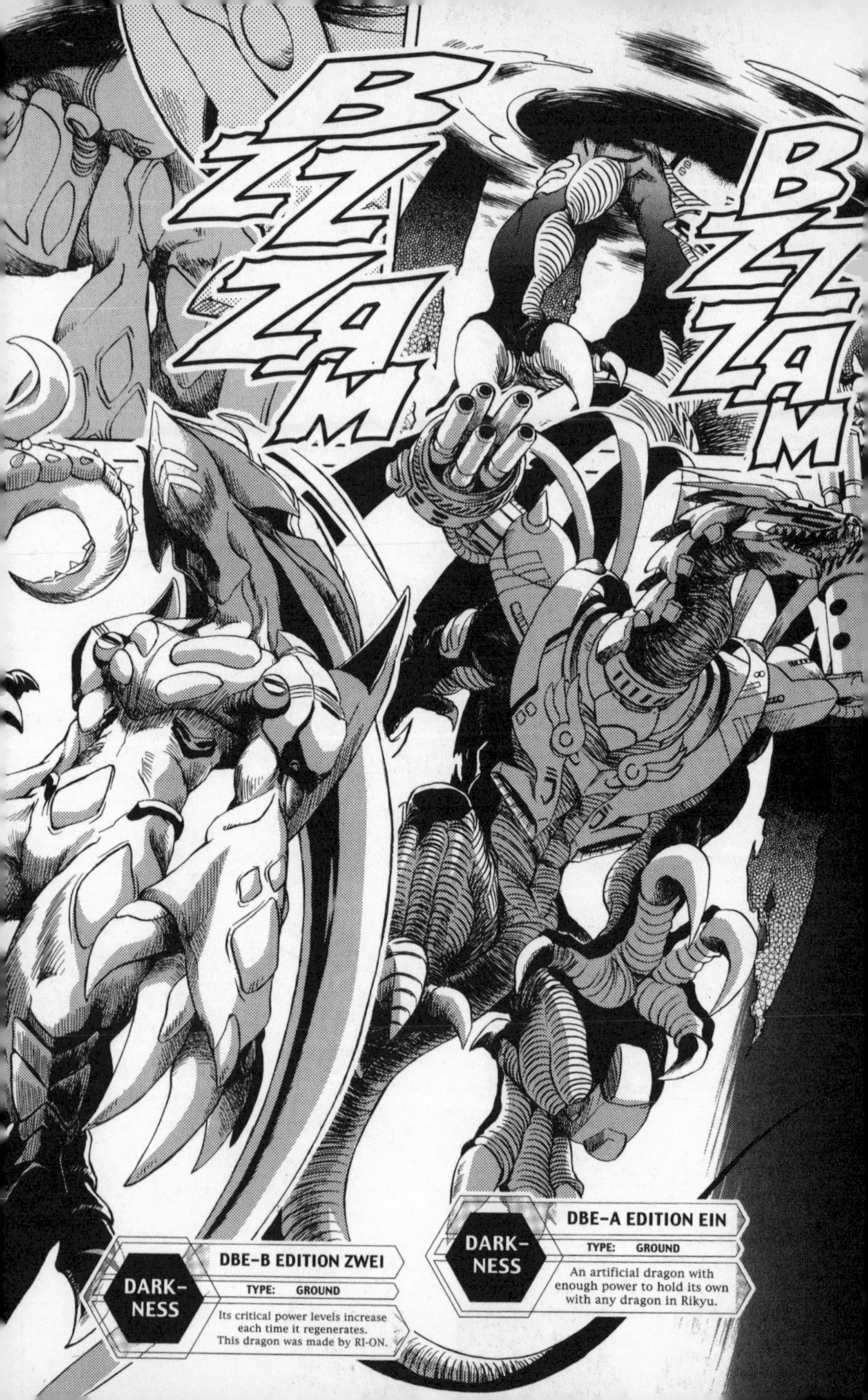
BZZZAM
BZZZAM
DARK-NESS
DBE-A EDITION EIN
TYPE: GROUND
An artificial dragon with enough power to hold its own with any dragon in Rikyu.
DARK-NESS
DBE-B EDITION ZWEI
TYPE: GROUND
Its critical power levels increase each time it regenerates. This dragon was made by RI-ON.

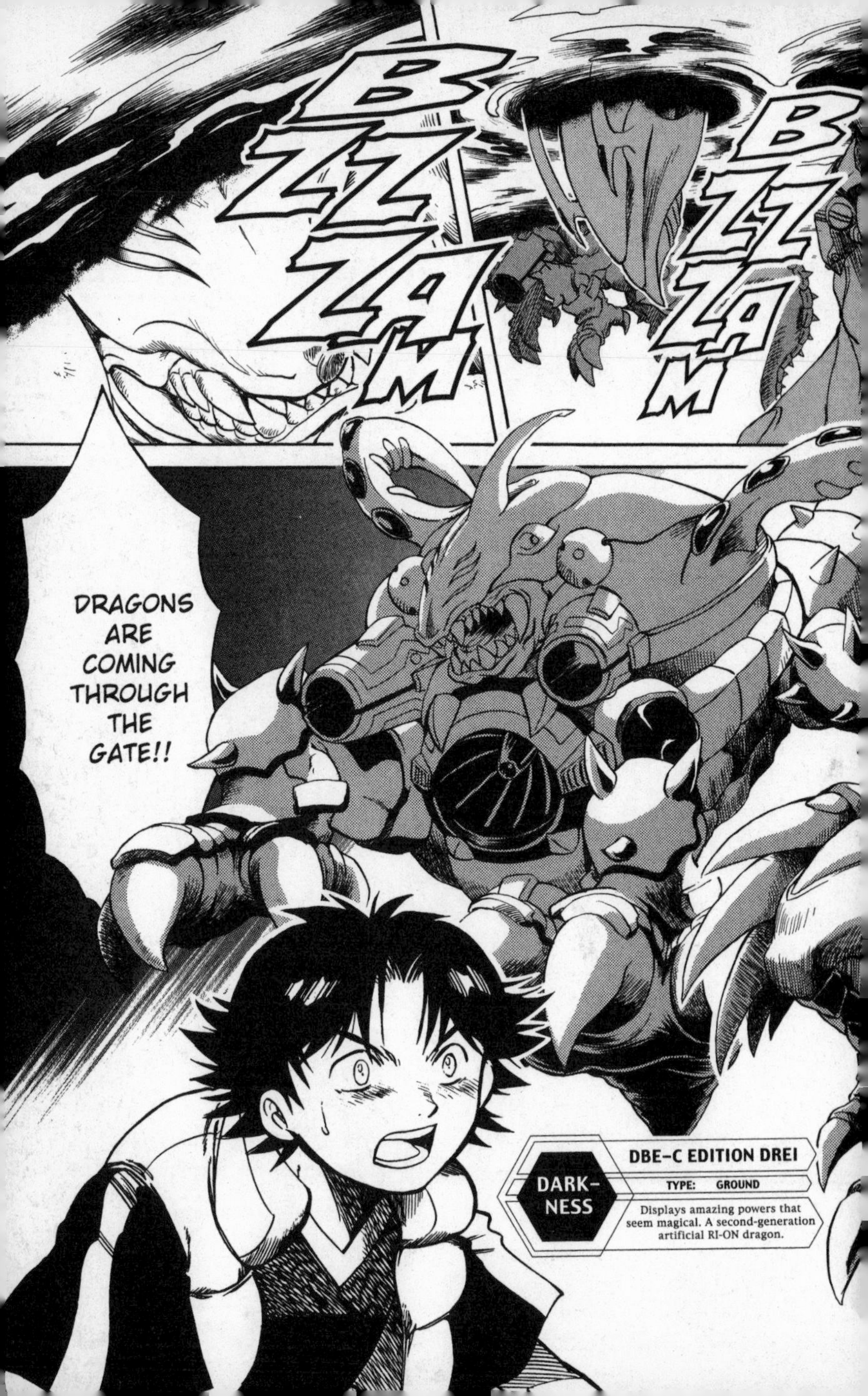
BZZZAM
BZZZAM
DRAGONS ARE COMING THROUGH THE GATE!!
DBE-C EDITION DREI
DARK-NESS
TYPE: GROUND
Displays amazing powers that seem magical. A second-generation artificial RI-ON dragon.

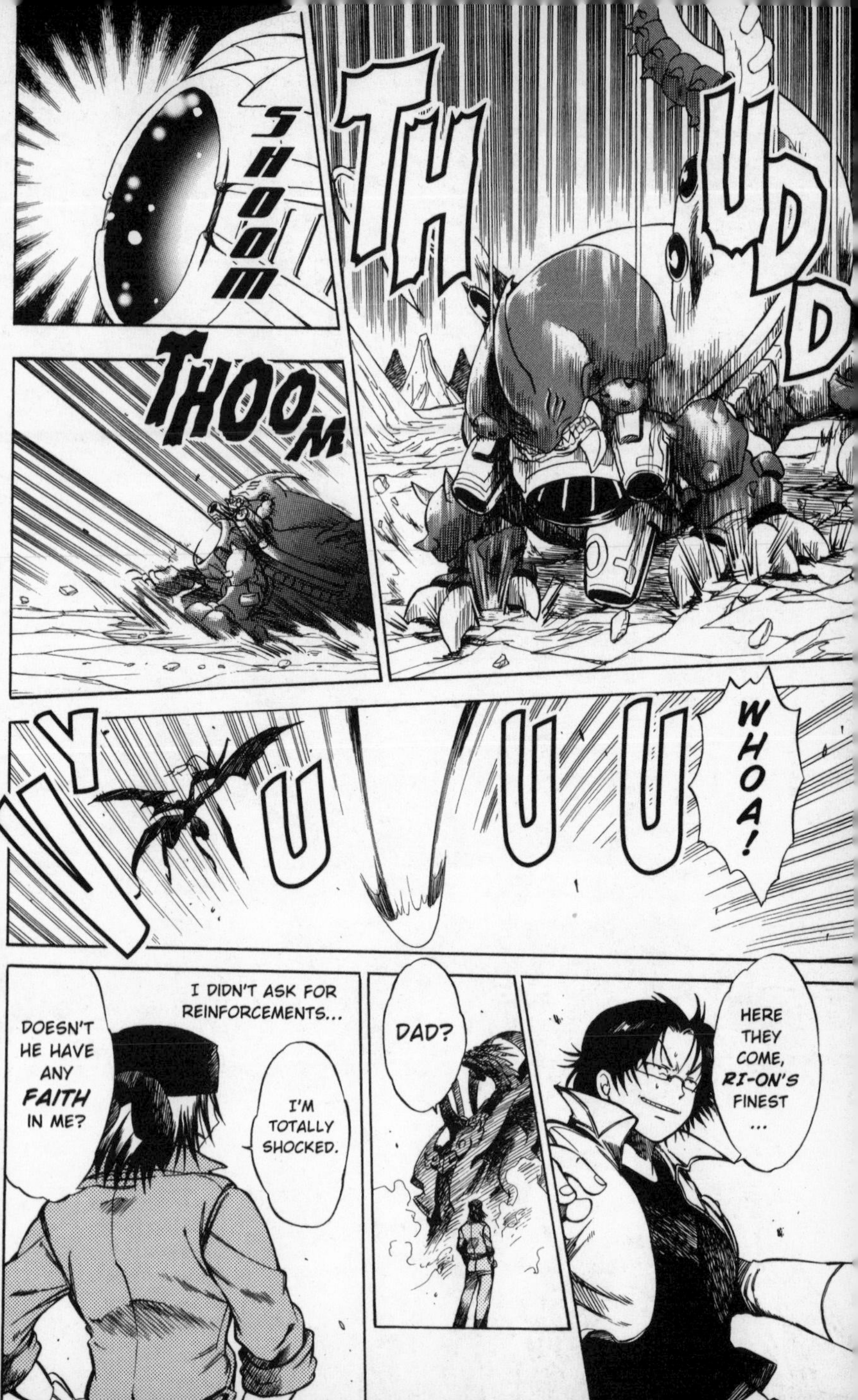

THUDD
SHOOOM
THOOM
WHOA!
VYUUUU
HERE THEY COME, RI-ON'S FINEST ...
DAD?
I DIDN'T ASK FOR REINFORCEMENTS...
DOESN'T HE HAVE ANY FAITH IN ME?
I'M TOTALLY SHOCKED.

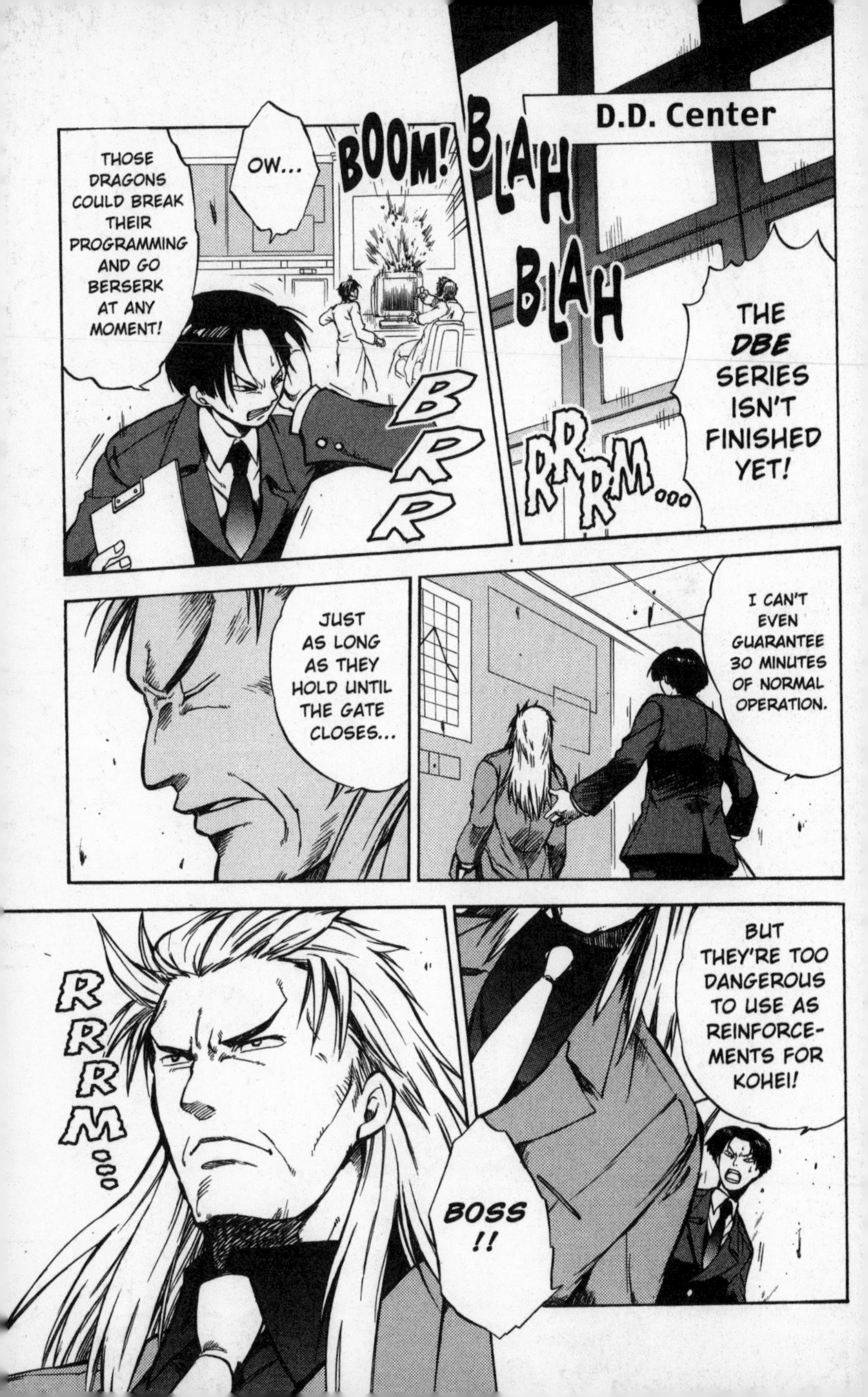
D.D. Center
BLAH BLAH
THE DBE SERIES ISN'T FINISHED YET!
RRRM...
BOOM!
OW...
THOSE DRAGONS COULD BREAK THEIR PROGRAMMING AND GO BERSERK AT ANY MOMENT!
BRRR
I CAN'T EVEN GUARANTEE 30 MINUTES OF NORMAL OPERATION.
JUST AS LONG AS THEY HOLD UNTIL THE GATE CLOSES...
BUT THEY'RE TOO DANGEROUS TO USE AS REINFORCEMENTS FOR KOHEI!
BOSS!!
RRRM...

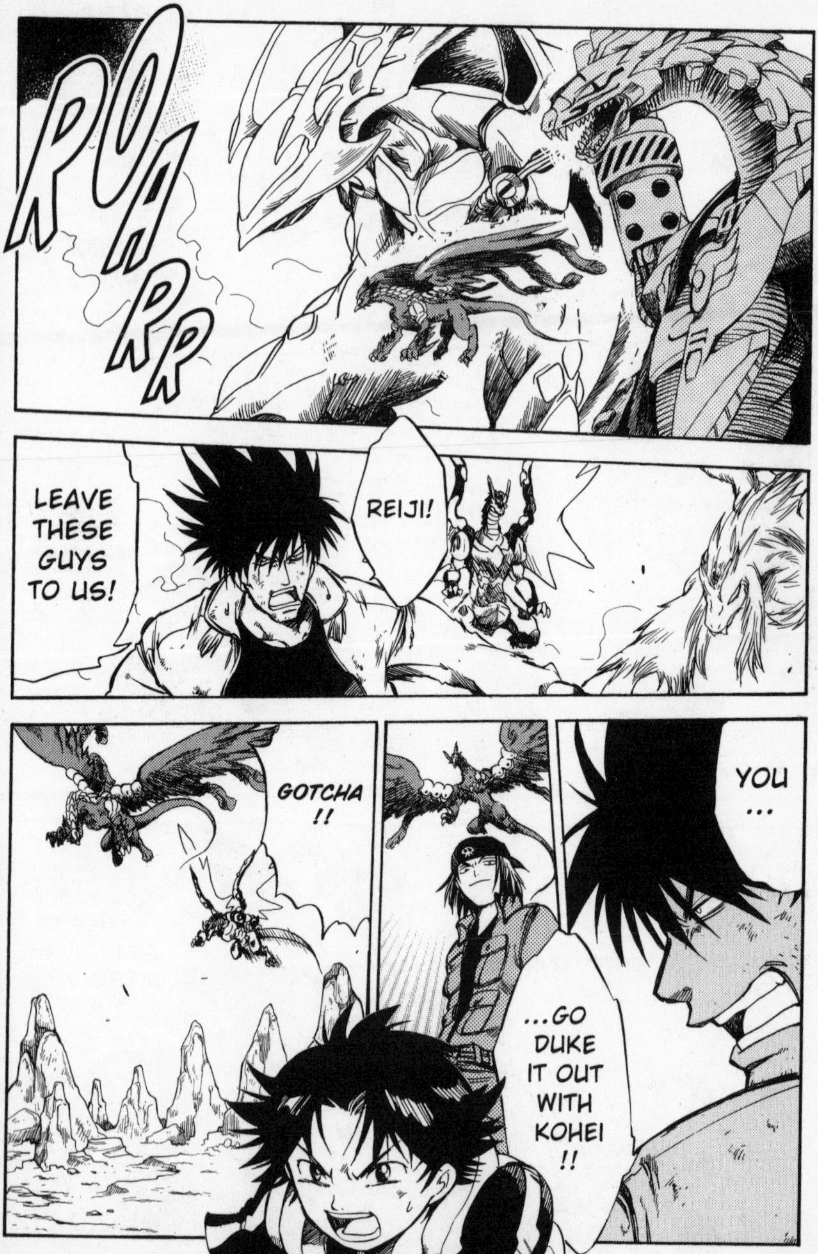
ROARR
REIJI!
LEAVE THESE GUYS TO US!
YOU...
...GO DUKE IT OUT WITH KOHEI!!
GOTCHA!!

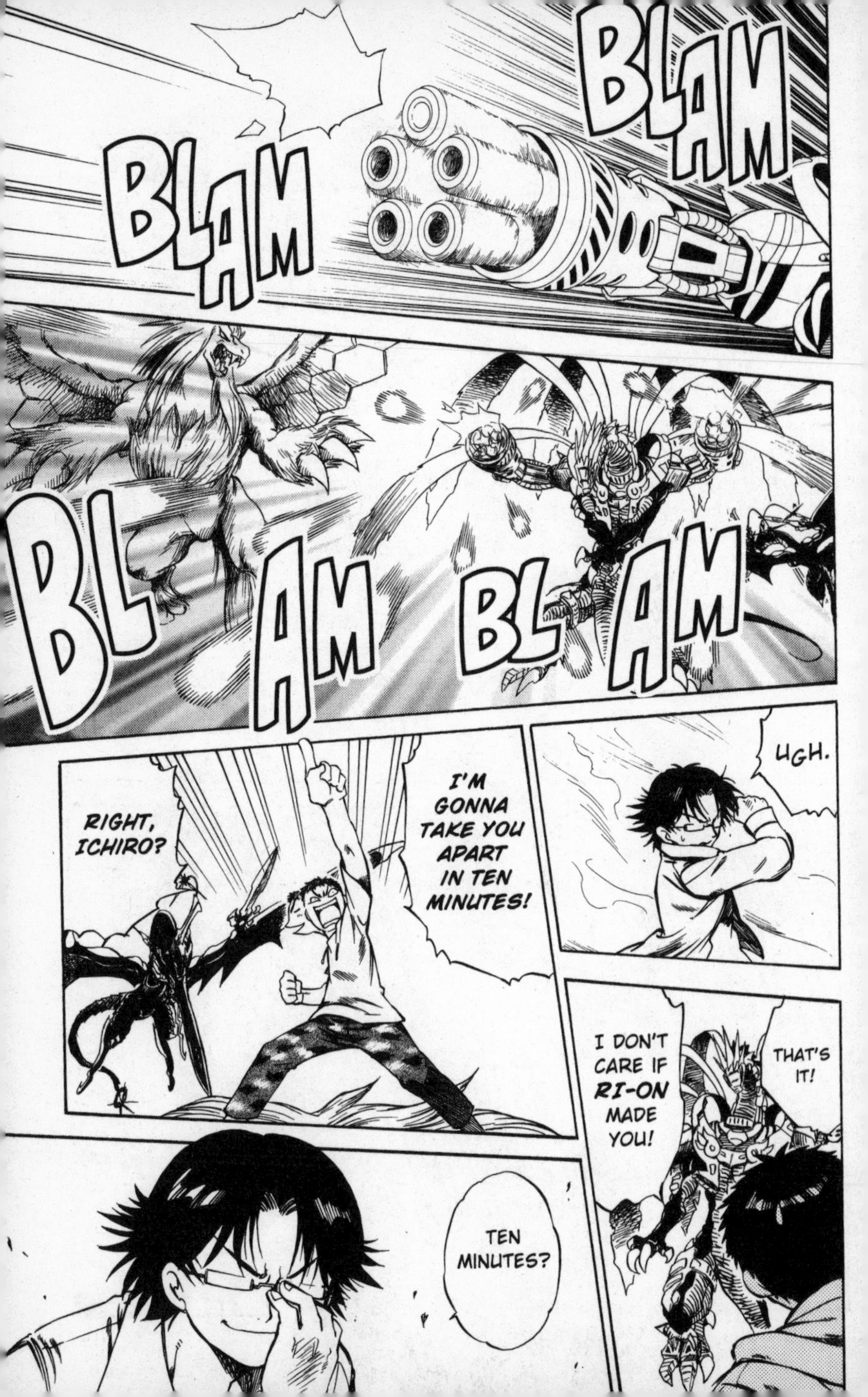
BLAM
BLAM
BLAM
BLAM
UGH.
I'M GONNA TAKE YOU APART IN TEN MINUTES!
RIGHT, ICHIRO?
THAT'S IT!
I DON'T CARE IF RI-ON MADE YOU!
TEN MINUTES?

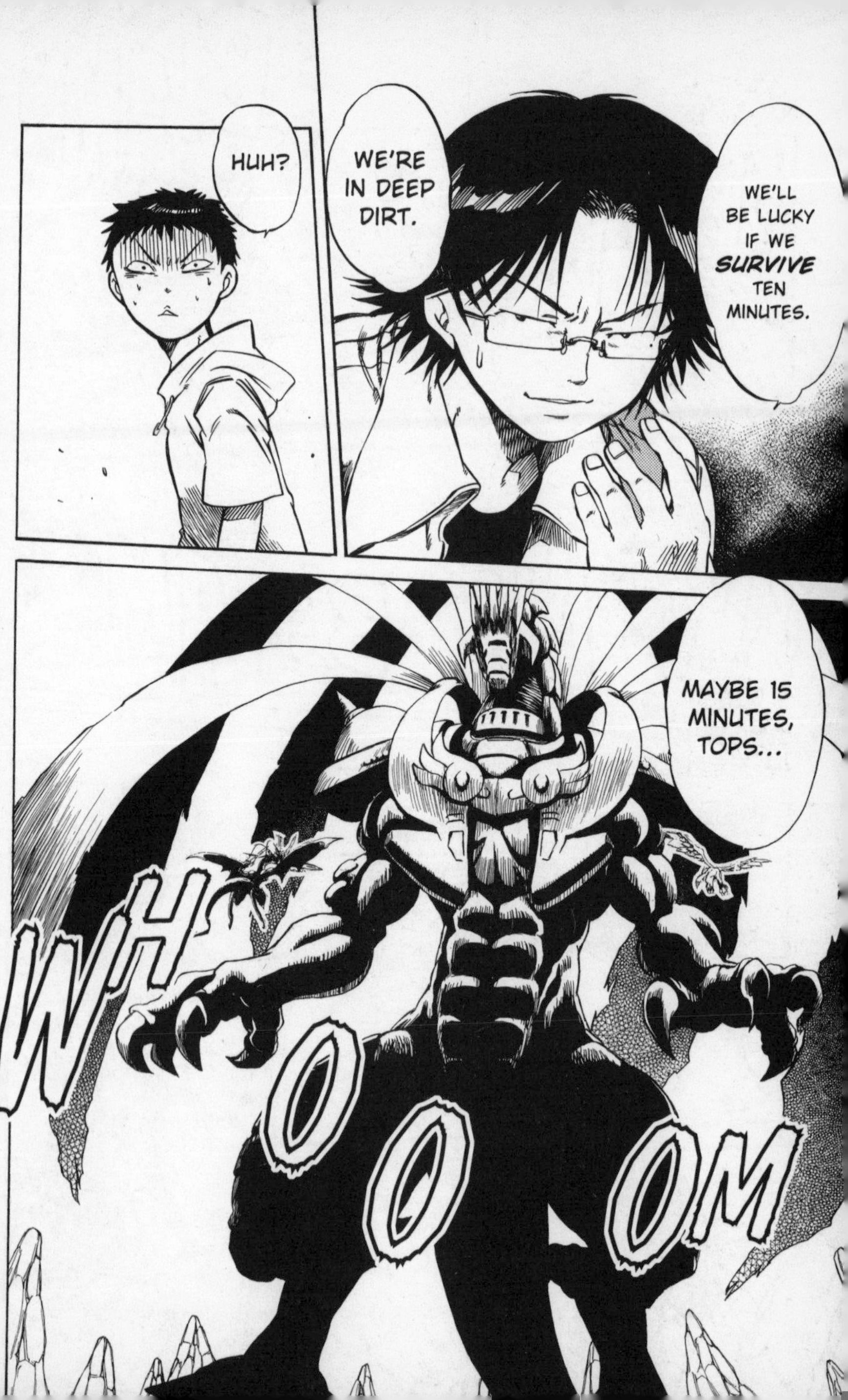
WE'RE IN DEEP DIRT.
WE'LL BE LUCKY IF WE SURVIVE TEN MINUTES.
HUH?
MAYBE 15 MINUTES, TOPS...
WHOOOOM

READ THIS WAY

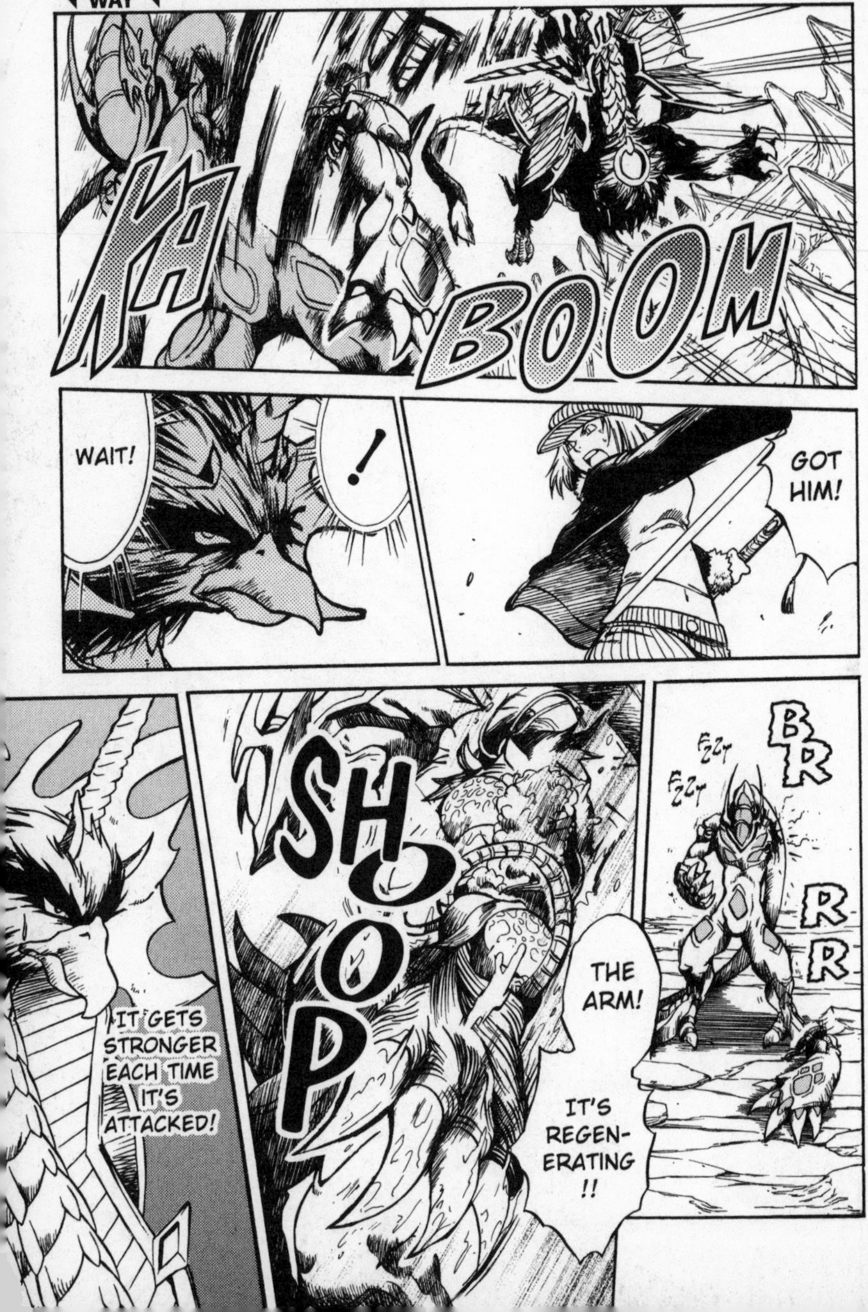

KA
BOOM
GOT HIM!
!
WAIT!
BRRR
FZZT
FZZT
THE ARM!
IT'S REGENERATING!!
SHOOP
IT GETS STRONGER EACH TIME IT'S ATTACKED!

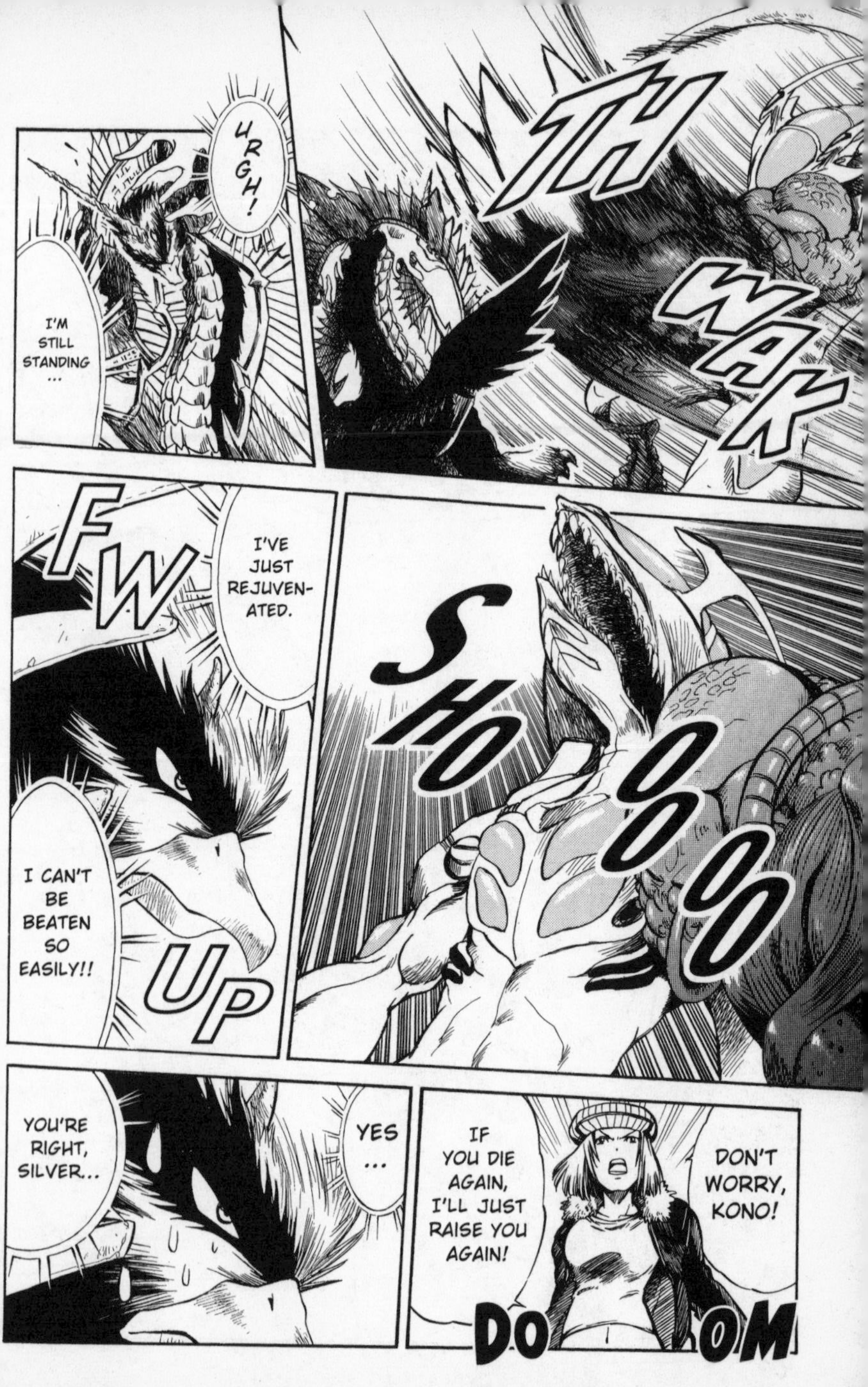
THWAK
URGH!
I'M STILL STANDING...
SHOOOOO
I'VE JUST REJUVENATED.
FW
UP
I CAN'T BE BEATEN SO EASILY!!
DON'T WORRY, KONO!
IF YOU DIE AGAIN, I'LL JUST RAISE YOU AGAIN!
DO
OM
YES...
YOU'RE RIGHT, SILVER...

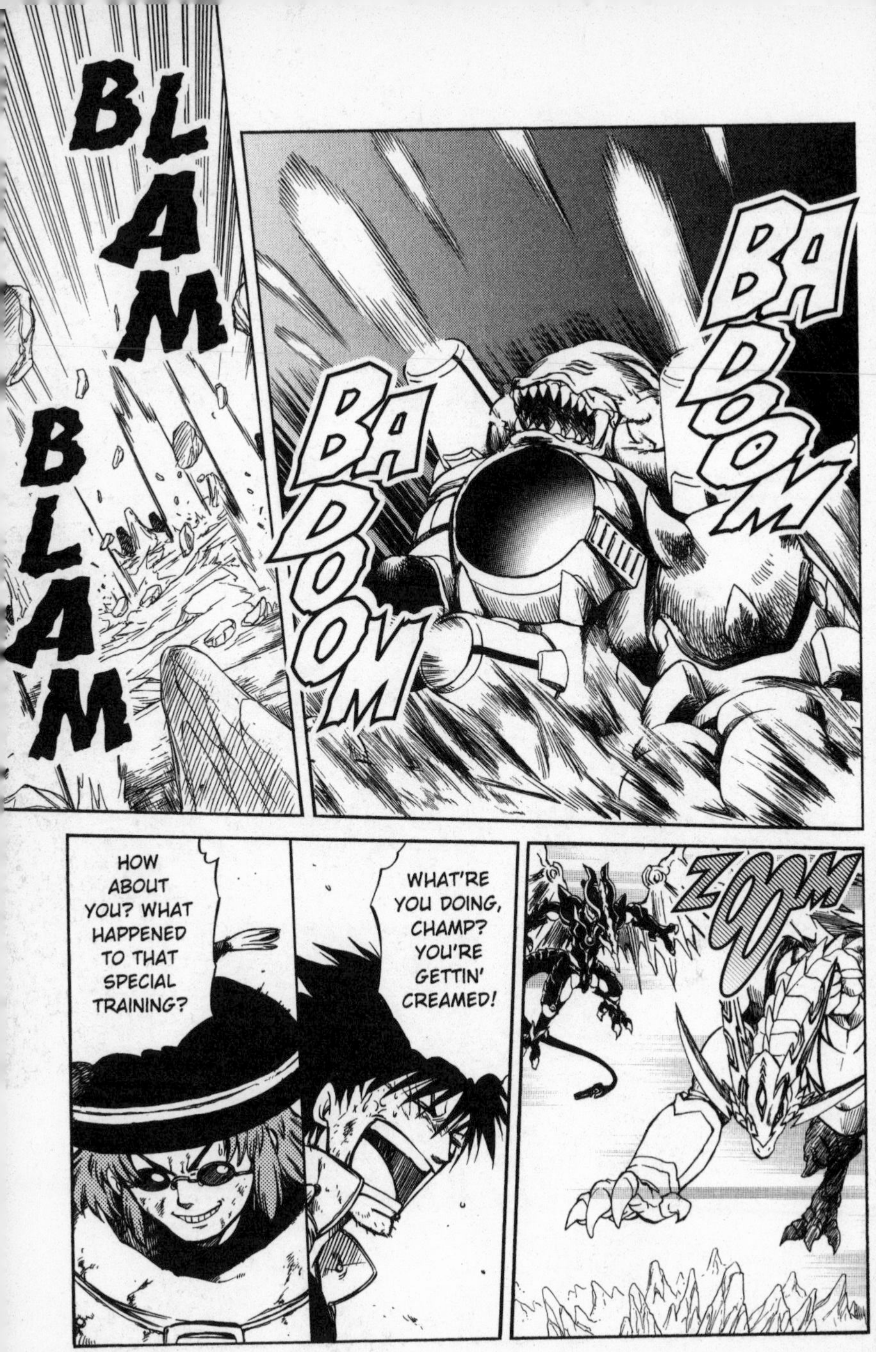
BADOOM
BADOOM
BLAM
BLAM
ZOOM
WHAT'RE YOU DOING, CHAMP? YOU'RE GETTIN' CREAMED!
HOW ABOUT YOU? WHAT HAPPENED TO THAT SPECIAL TRAINING?

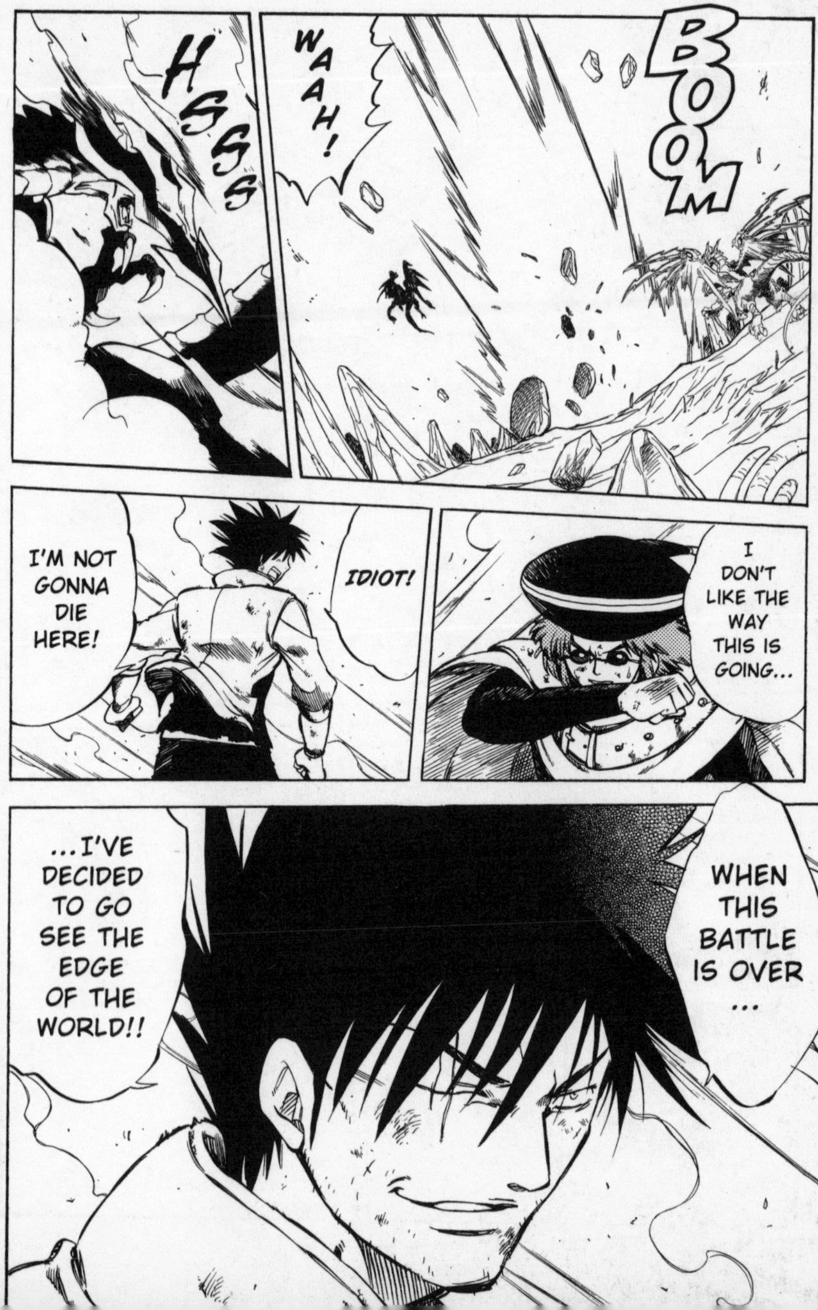
BOOM
WAAH!
HSSS
I DON'T LIKE THE WAY THIS IS GOING...
IDIOT!
I'M NOT GONNA DIE HERE!
WHEN THIS BATTLE IS OVER...
...I'VE DECIDED TO GO SEE THE EDGE OF THE WORLD!!

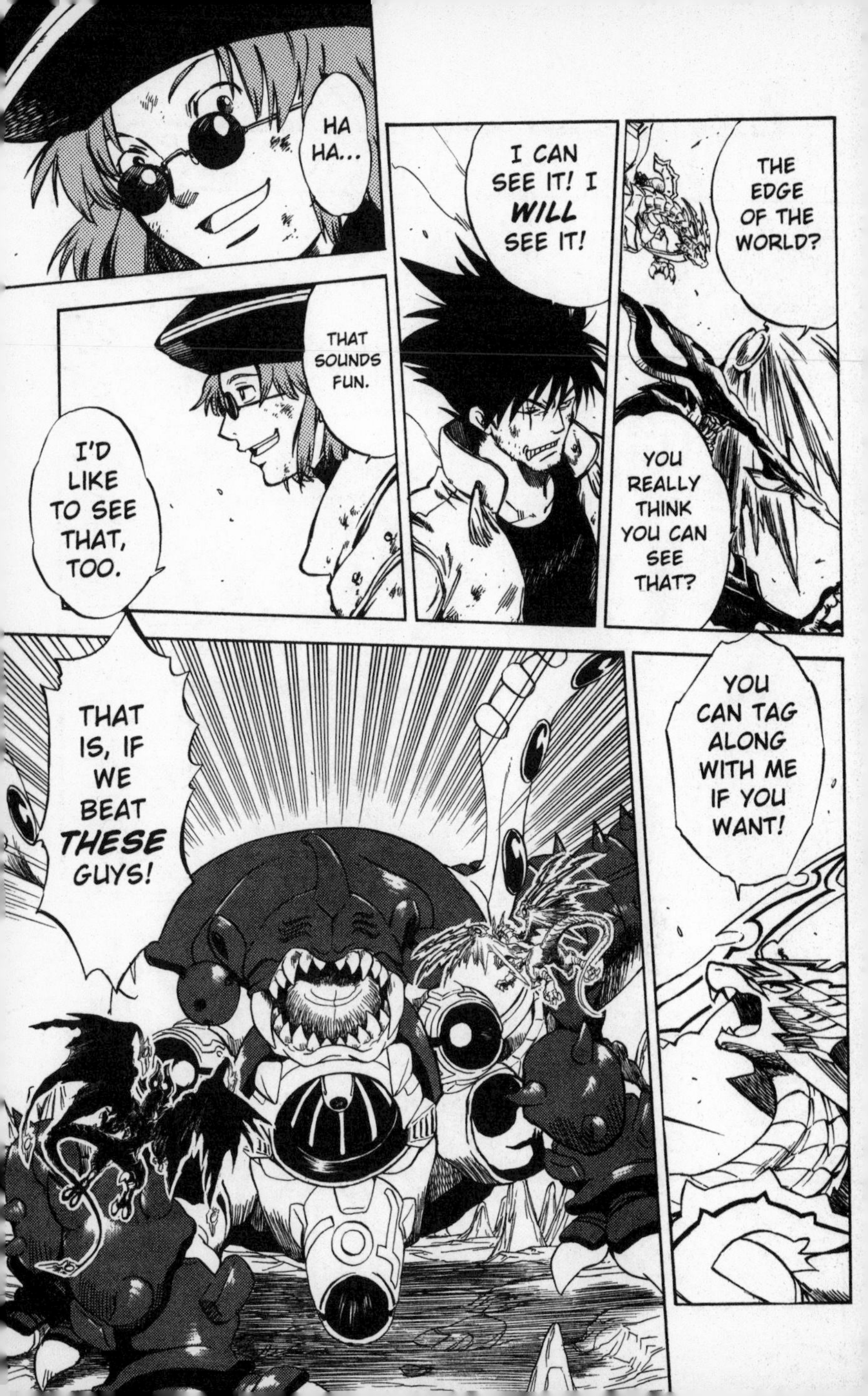
THE EDGE OF THE WORLD?
YOU REALLY THINK YOU CAN SEE THAT?
I CAN SEE IT! I *WILL* SEE IT!
HA HA...
THAT SOUNDS FUN.
I'D LIKE TO SEE THAT, TOO.
YOU CAN TAG ALONG WITH ME IF YOU WANT!
THAT IS, IF WE BEAT *THESE* GUYS!

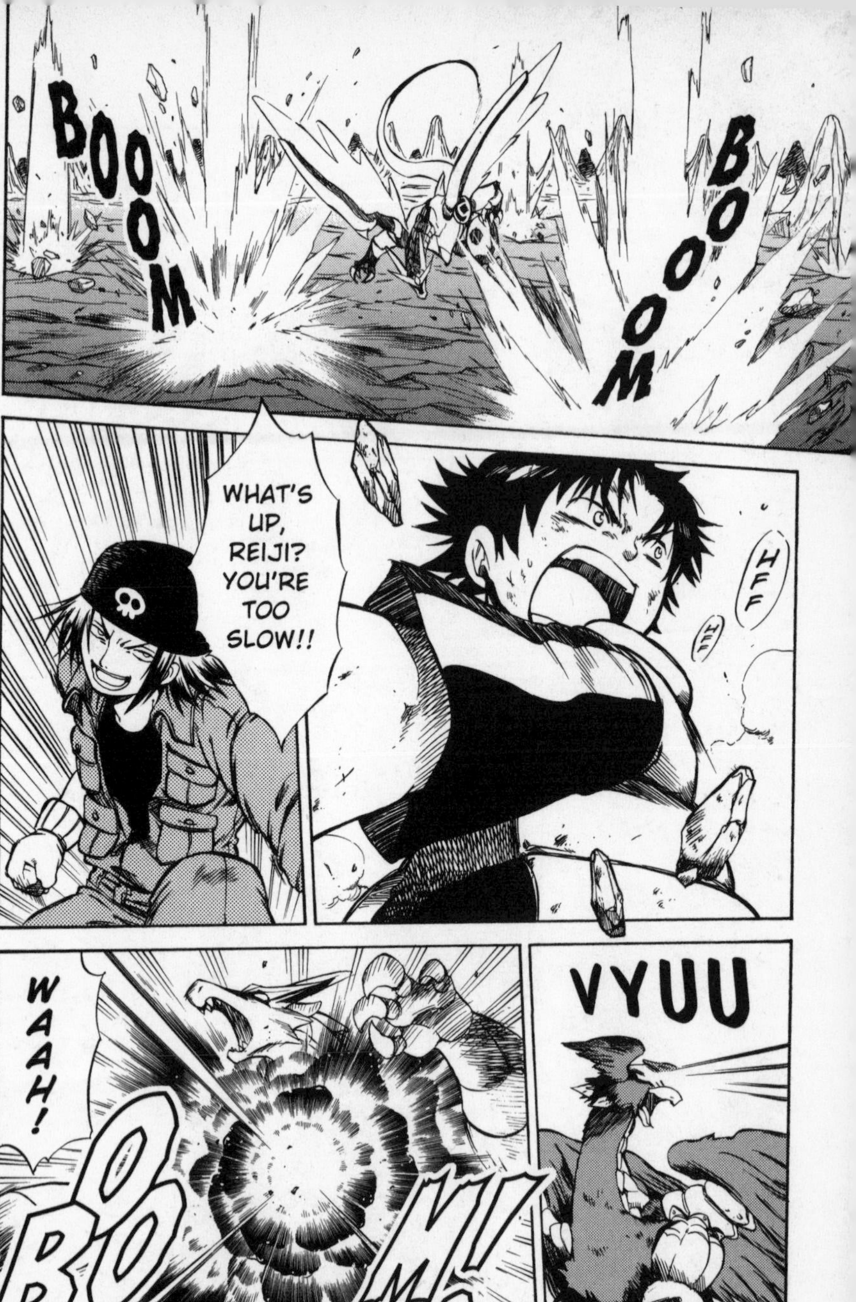
BOOOM
BOOOM
HFF
HFF
WHAT'S UP, REIJI? YOU'RE TOO SLOW!!
VYUU
WAAH!
BOOM!

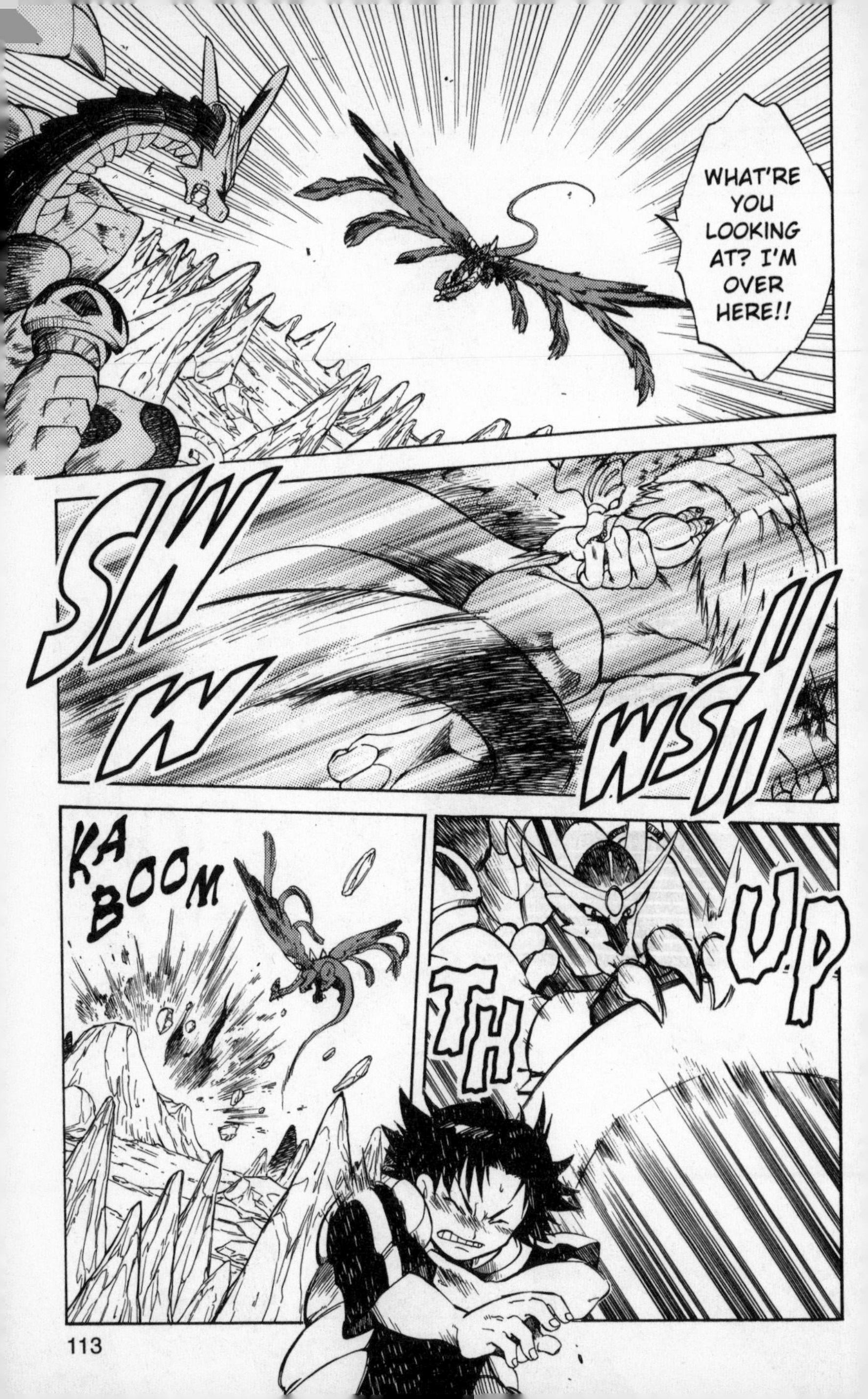
WHAT'RE YOU LOOKING AT? I'M OVER HERE!!
SHWNSH
SHWN
THUP
KA BOOM

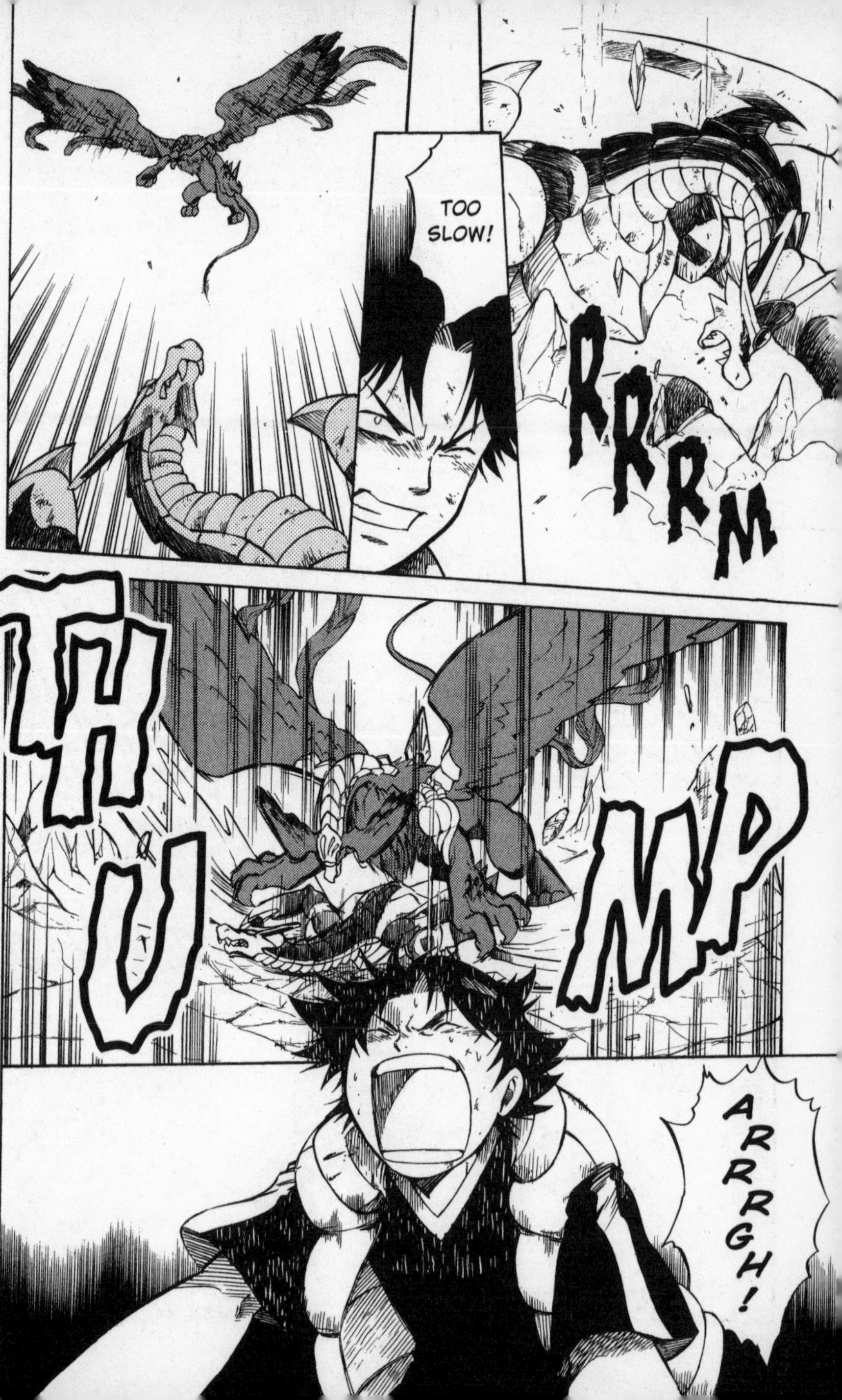
RRRM
TOO SLOW!
THUMP
ARRRGH!

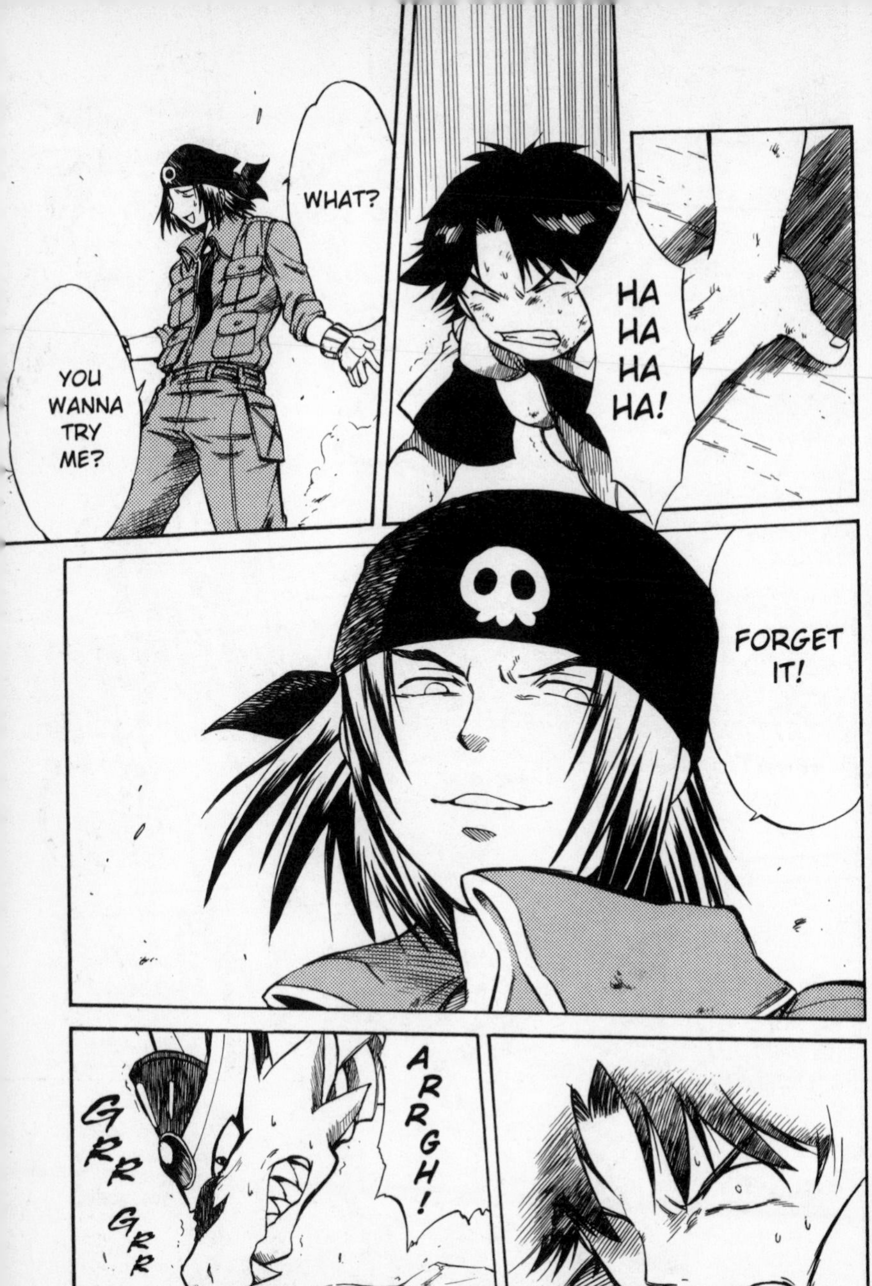
HA HA HA HA!
WHAT?
YOU WANNA TRY ME?
FORGET IT!
ARRGH!
GRR GRR

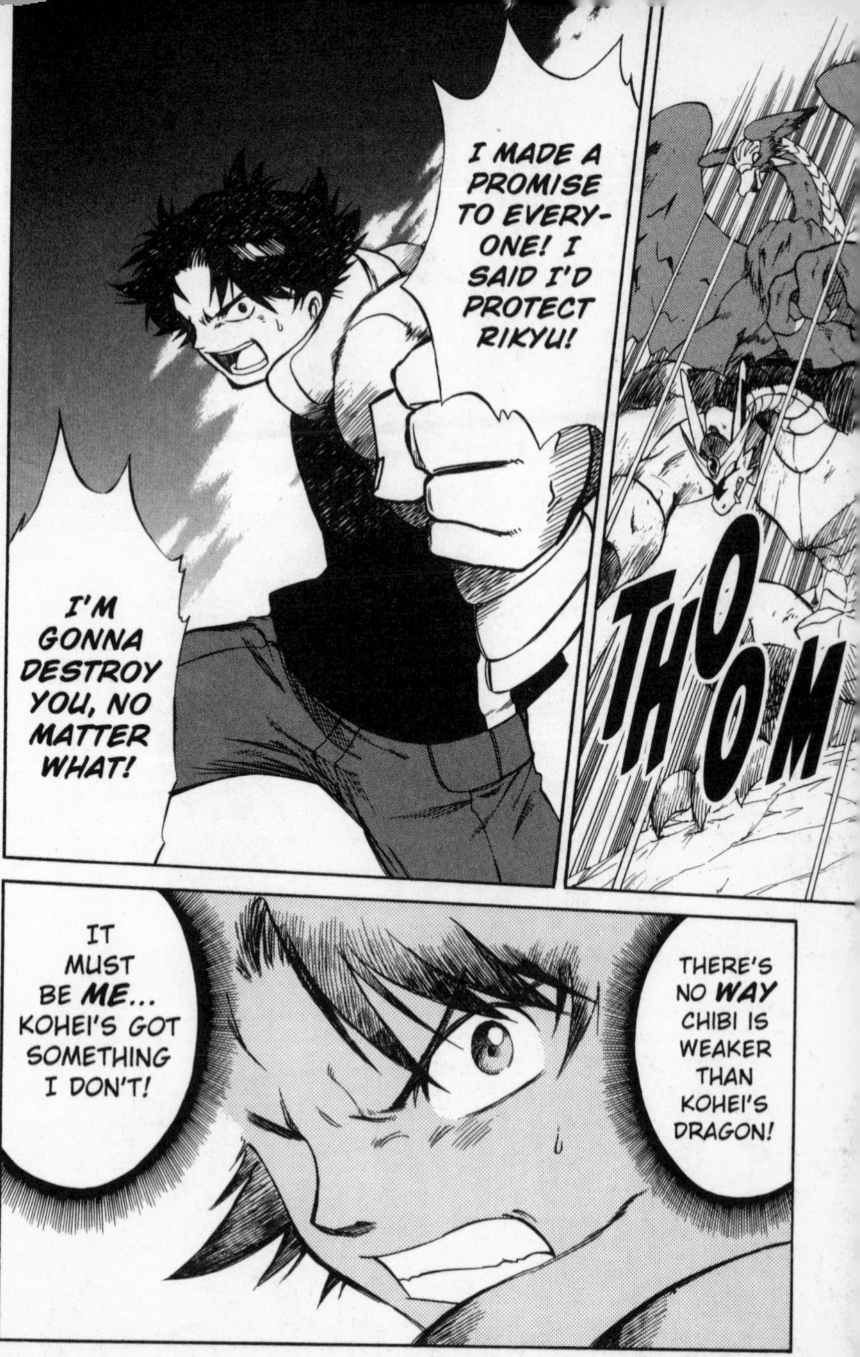
THOOM
I MADE A PROMISE TO EVERY-ONE! I SAID I'D PROTECT RIKYU!
I'M GONNA DESTROY YOU, NO MATTER WHAT!
THERE'S NO **WAY** CHIBI IS WEAKER THAN KOHEI'S DRAGON!
IT MUST BE **ME**... KOHEI'S GOT SOMETHING I DON'T!

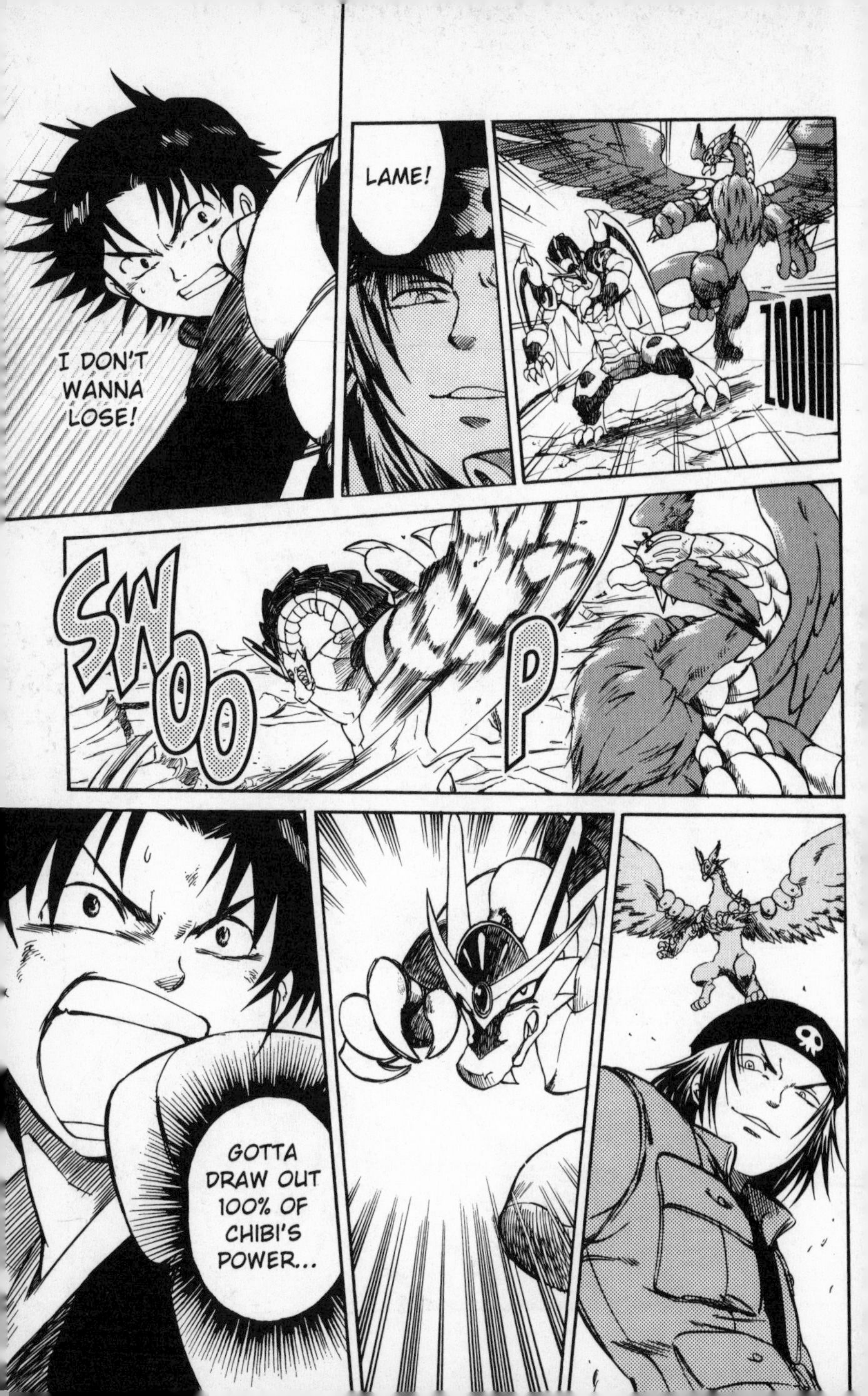
ZOOM
LAME!
I DON'T WANNA LOSE!
SWOOOP
GOTTA DRAW OUT 100% OF CHIBI'S POWER...

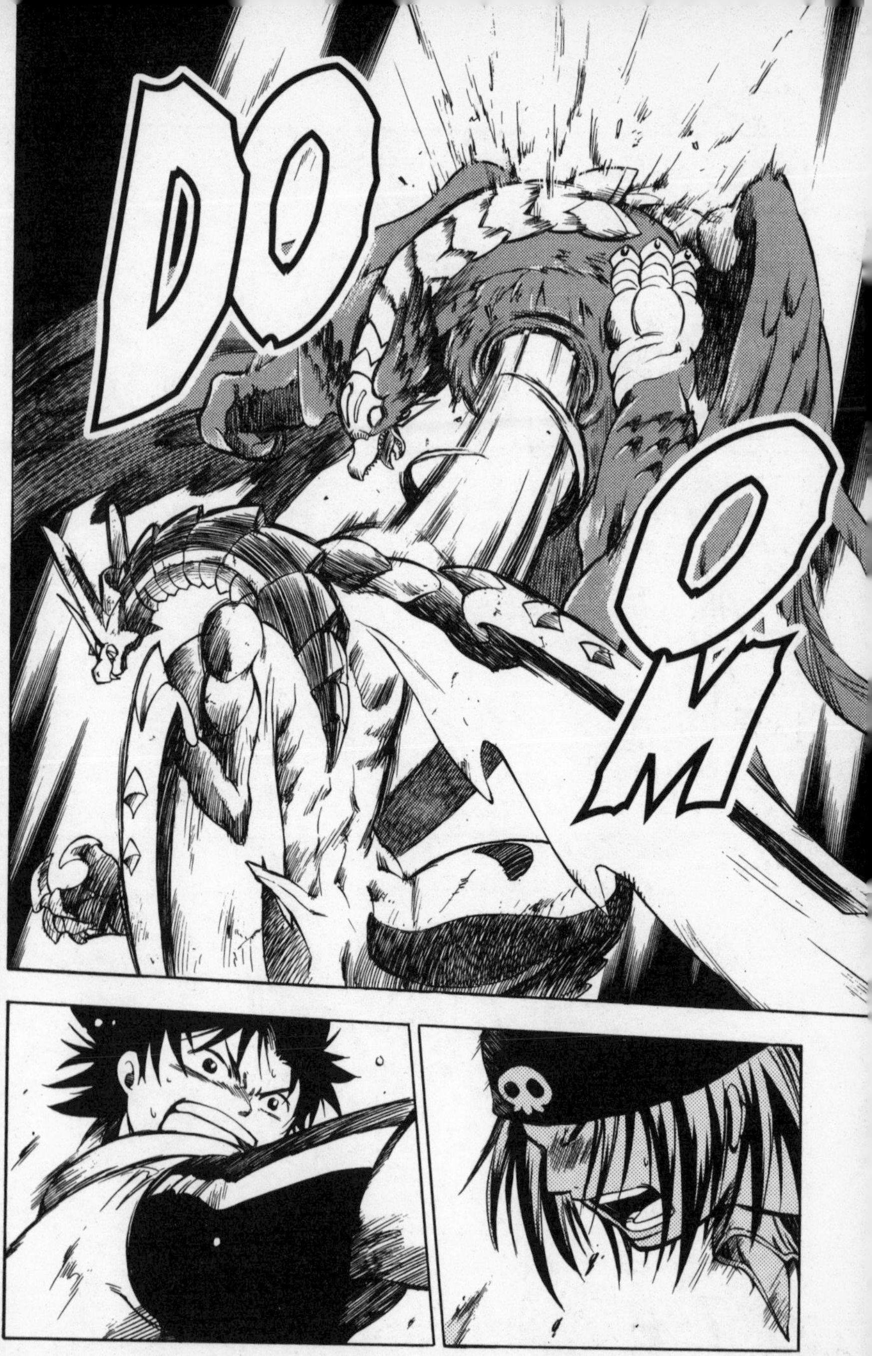
DOOM

READ THIS WAY

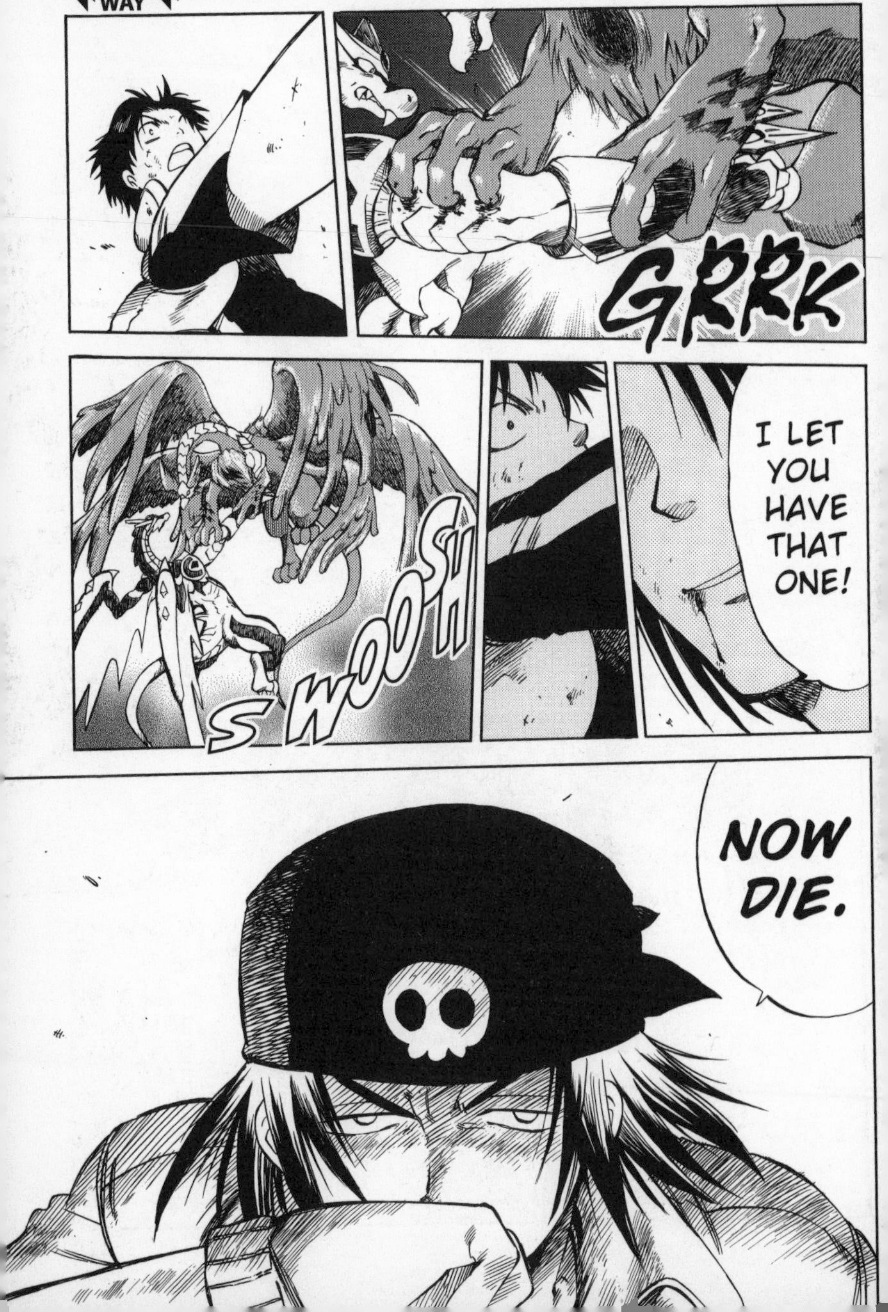
GRRK
I LET YOU HAVE THAT ONE!
SWOOSH
NOW DIE.

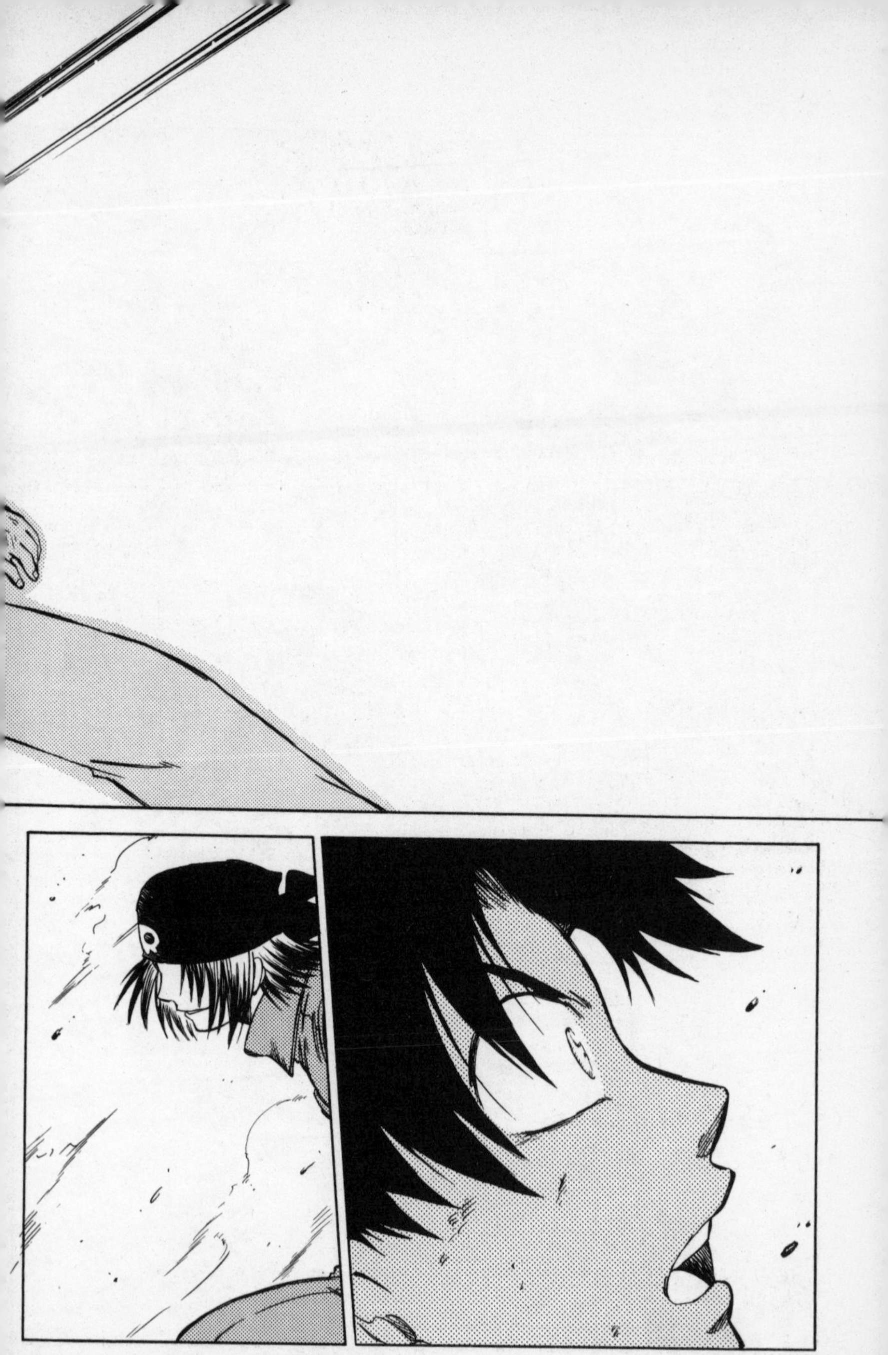

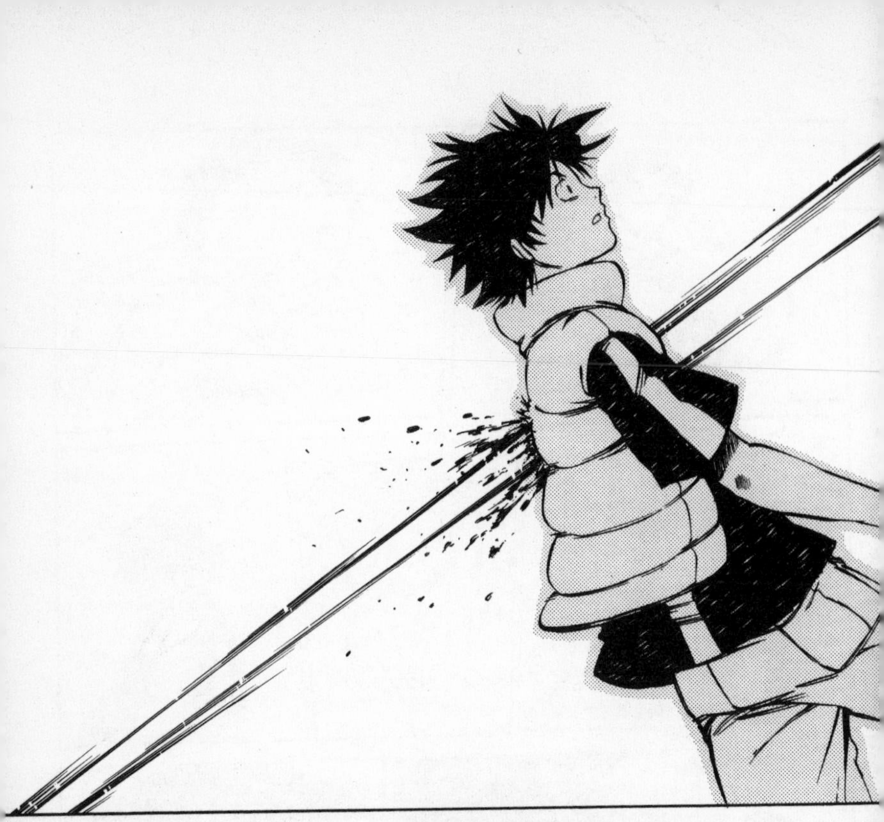
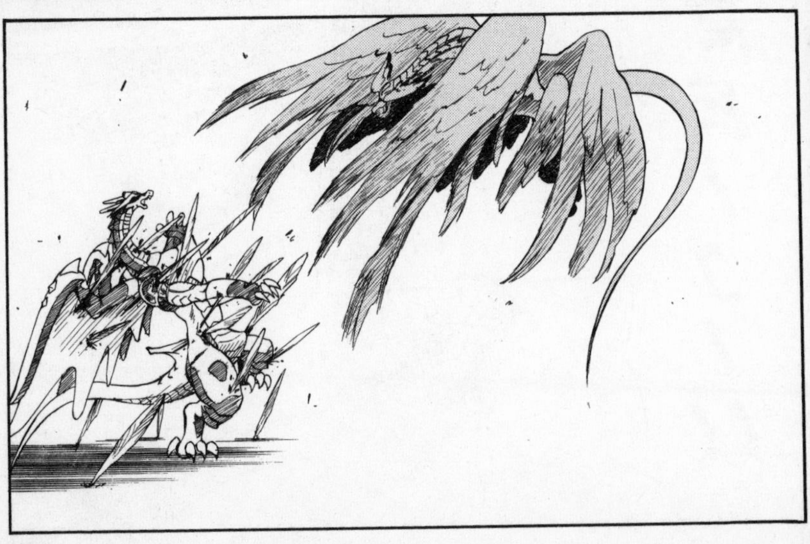

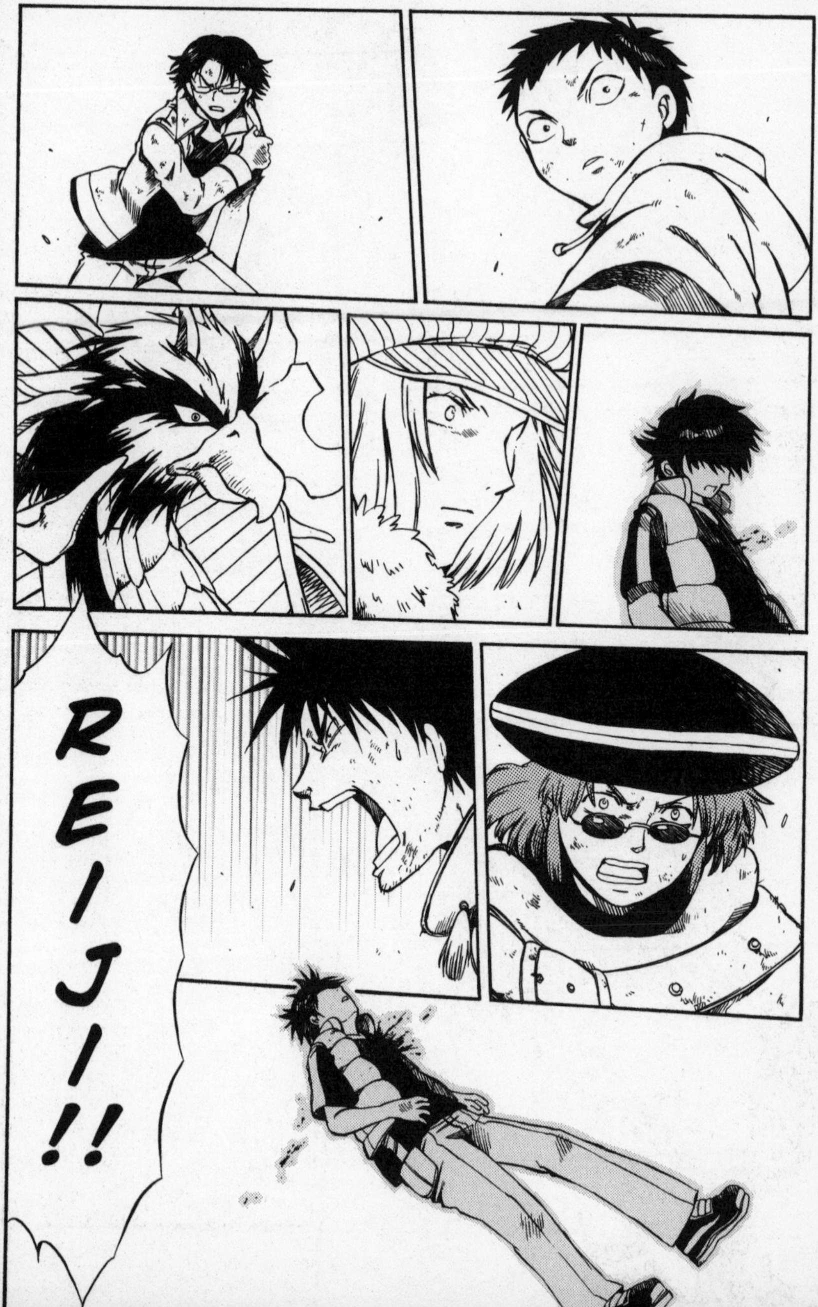
REIJI!!

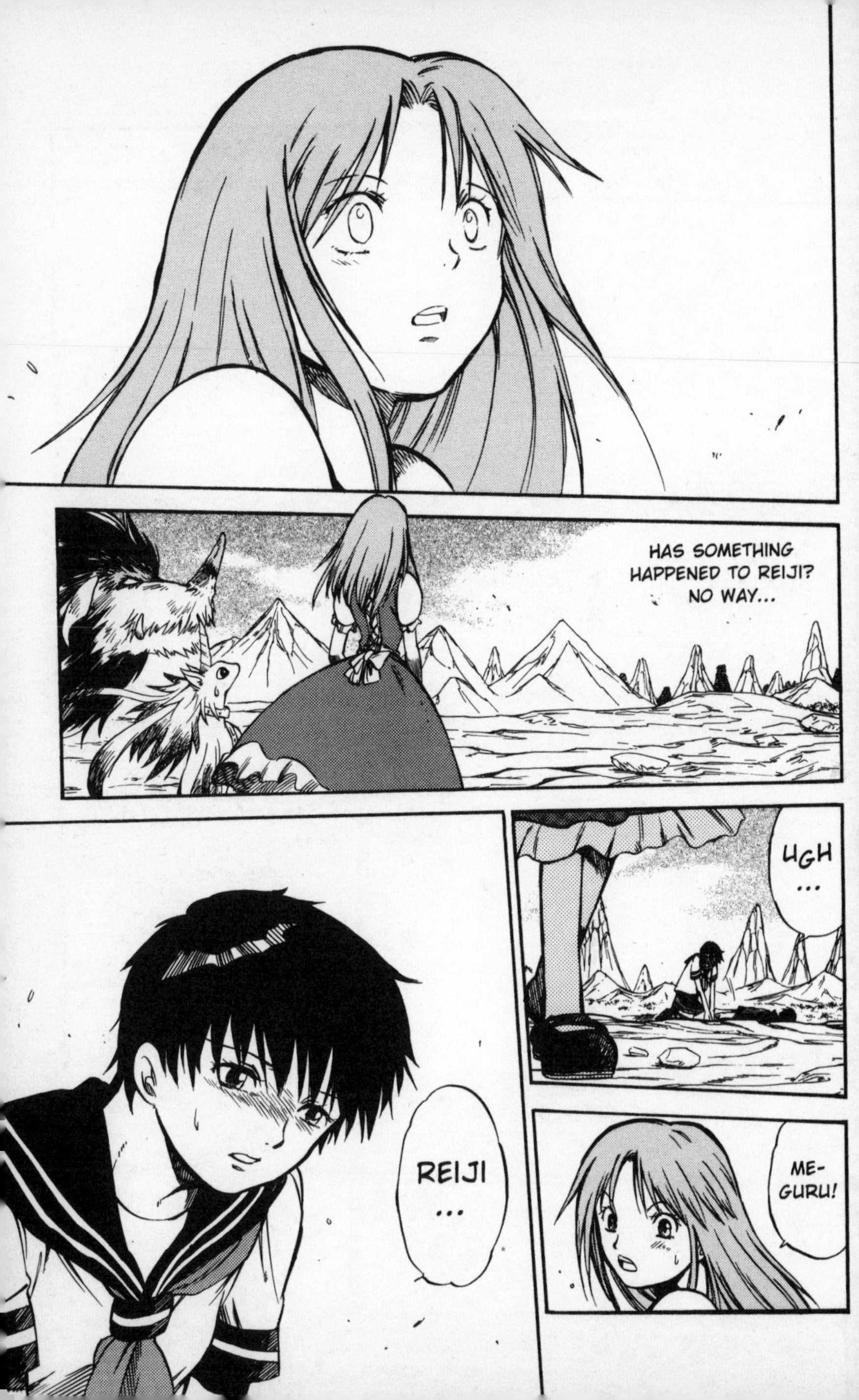
HAS SOMETHING HAPPENED TO REIJI? NO WAY...
UGH ...
ME-GURU!
REIJI ...

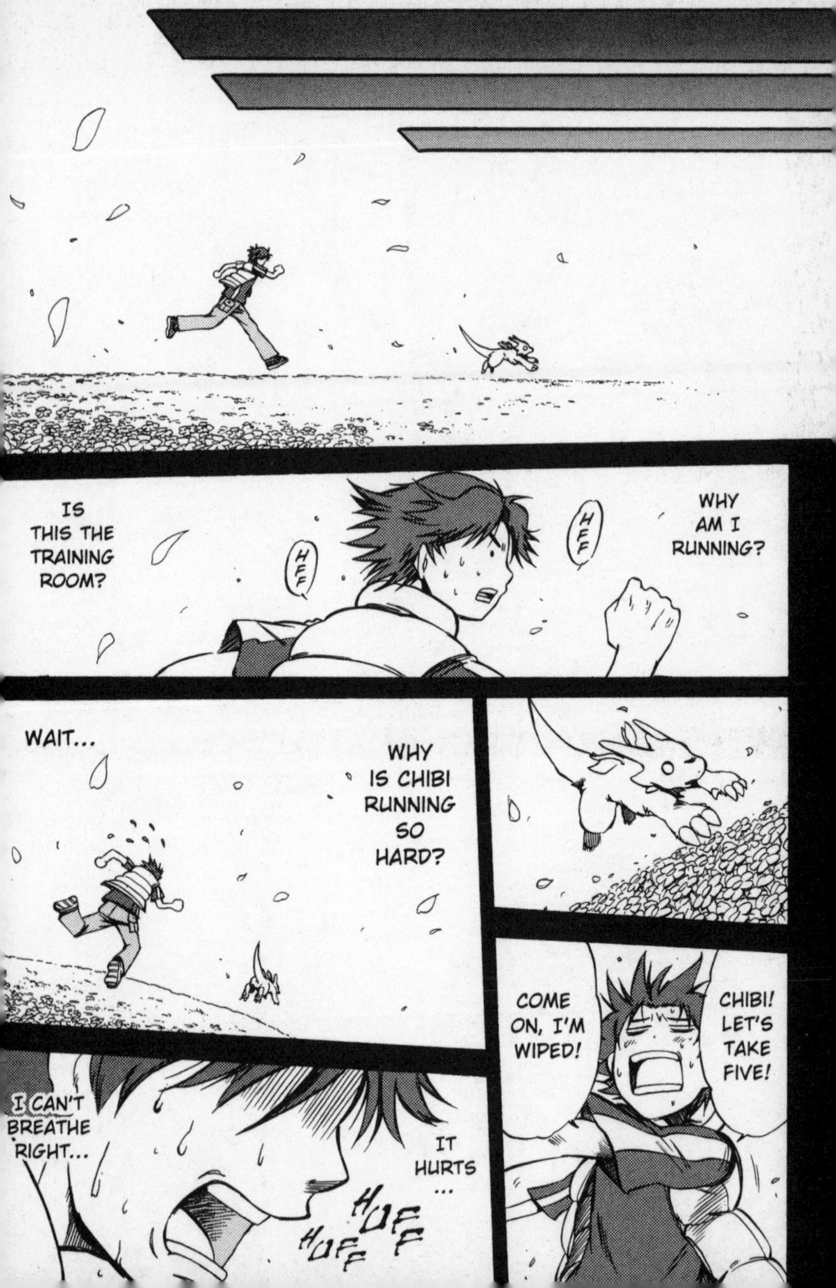
WHY AM I RUNNING?
HEF
HEF
IS THIS THE TRAINING ROOM?
CHIBI! LET'S TAKE FIVE!
COME ON, I'M WIPED!
WAIT...
WHY IS CHIBI RUNNING SO HARD?
I CAN'T BREATHE RIGHT...
IT HURTS...
HUFF
HUFF

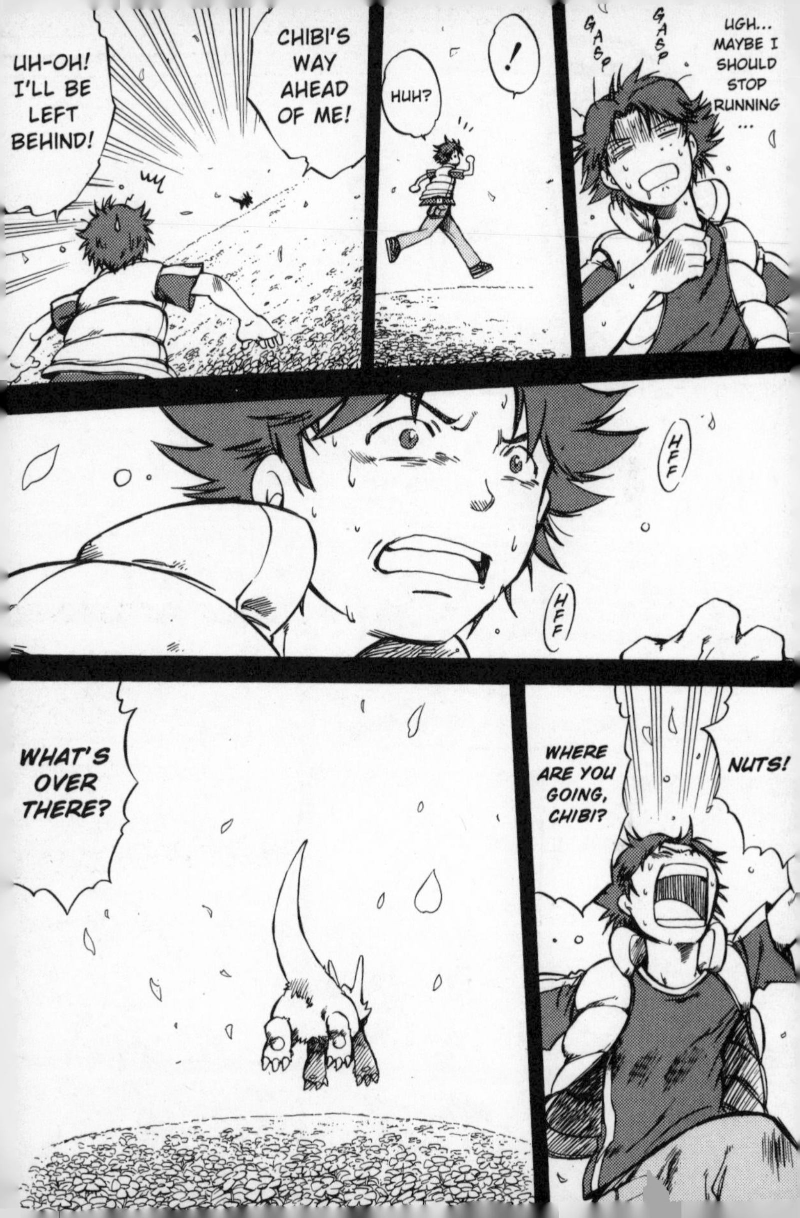
GASP
GASP
UGH... MAYBE I SHOULD STOP RUNNING...
!
HUH?
CHIBI'S WAY AHEAD OF ME!
UH-OH! I'LL BE LEFT BEHIND!
HFF
HFF
NUTS!
WHERE ARE YOU GOING, CHIBI?
WHAT'S OVER THERE?

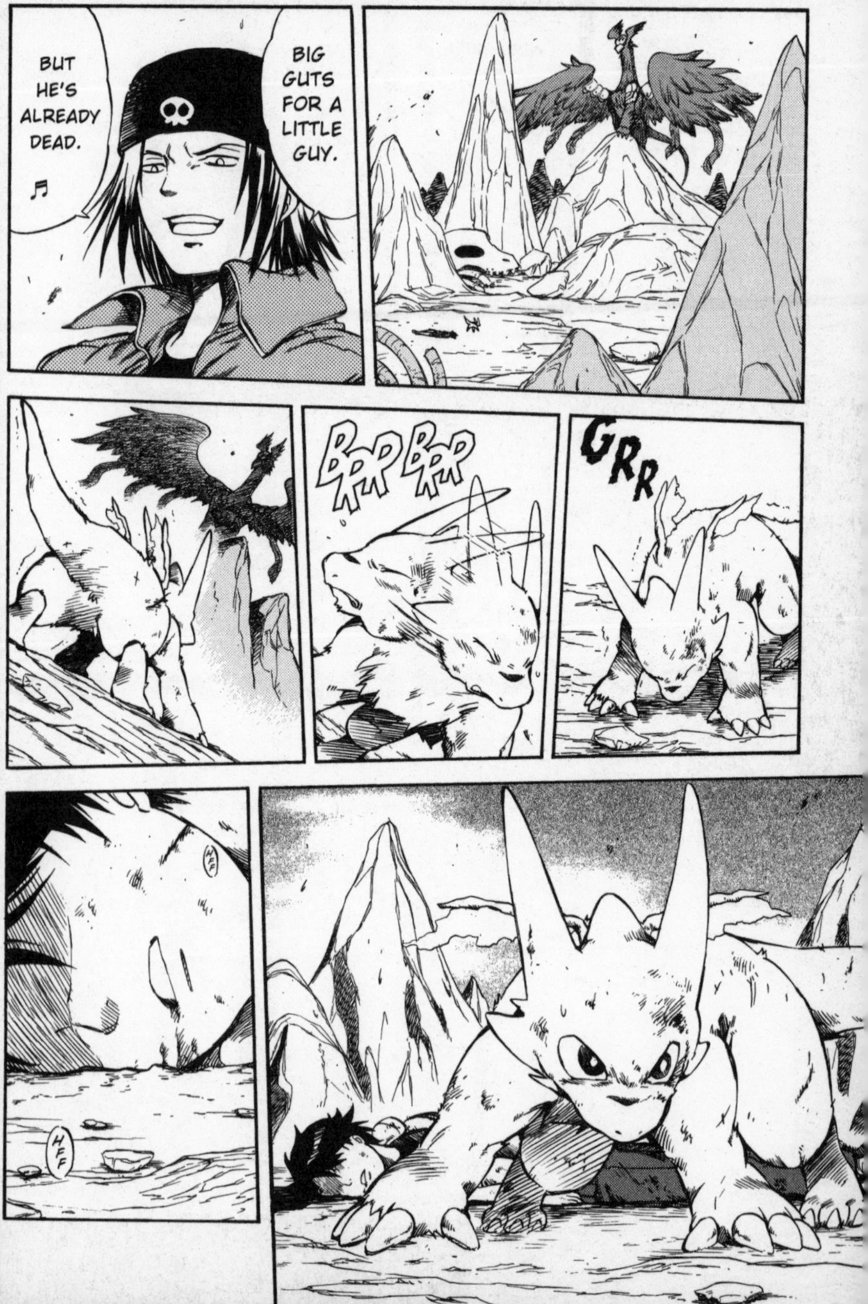
BIG GUTS FOR A LITTLE GUY.
BUT HE'S ALREADY DEAD. ♬
GRR
BRR BRR
HFF
HFF

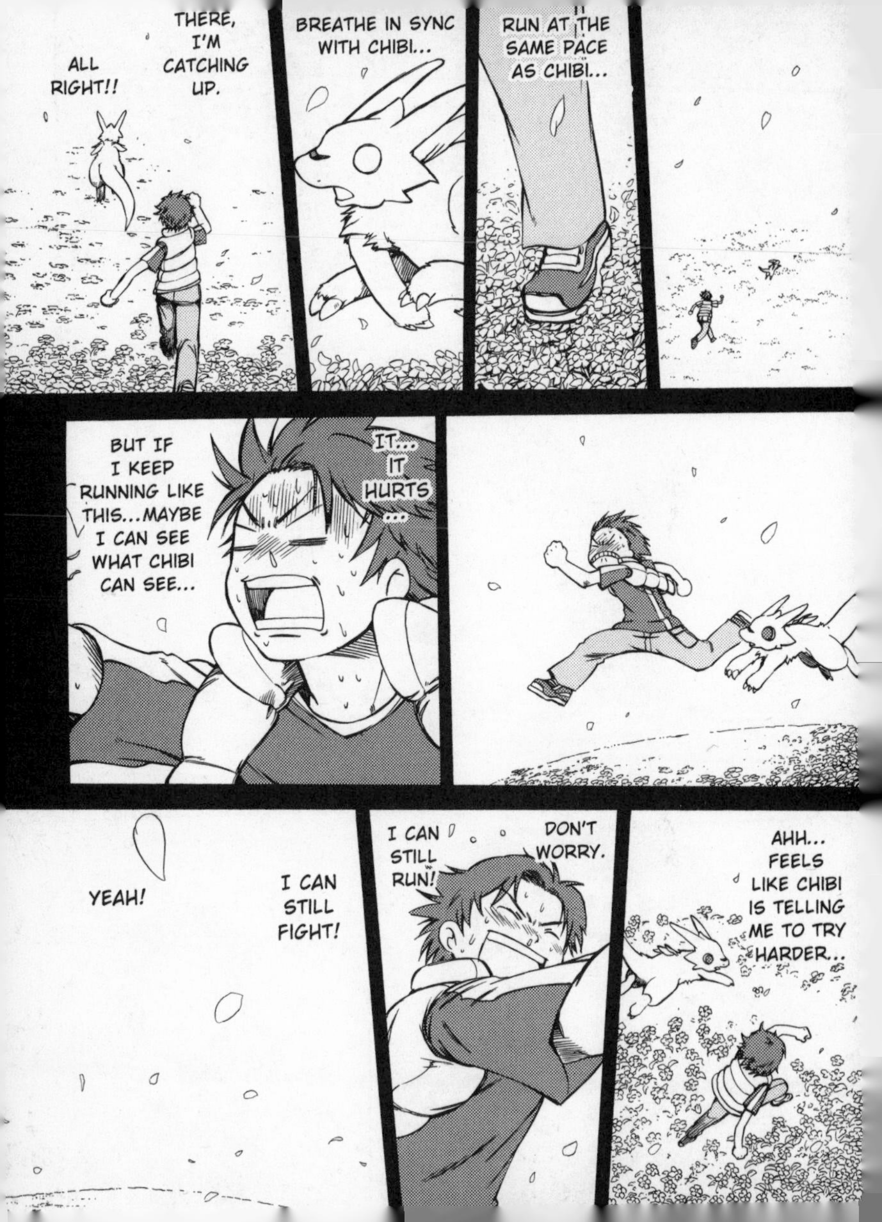
RUN AT THE SAME PACE AS CHIBI...
BREATHE IN SYNC WITH CHIBI...
THERE, I'M CATCHING UP.
ALL RIGHT!!
IT... IT HURTS...
BUT IF I KEEP RUNNING LIKE THIS...MAYBE I CAN SEE WHAT CHIBI CAN SEE...
AHH... FEELS LIKE CHIBI IS TELLING ME TO TRY HARDER...
DON'T WORRY.
I CAN STILL RUN!
I CAN STILL FIGHT!
YEAH!

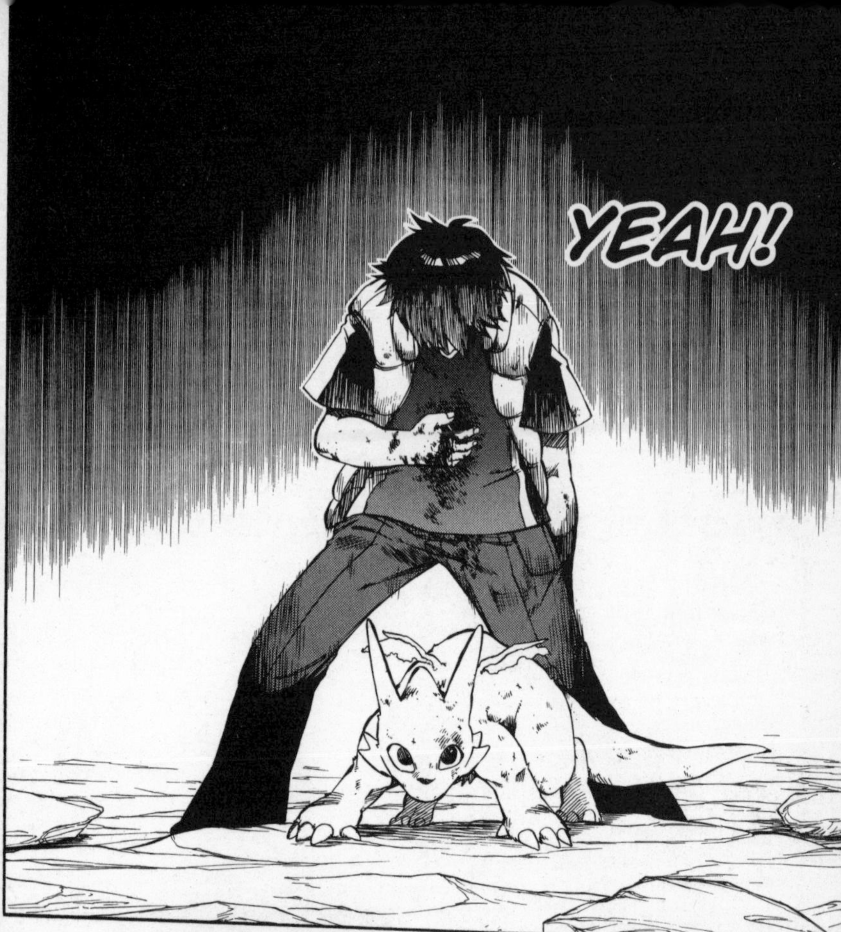
YEAH!
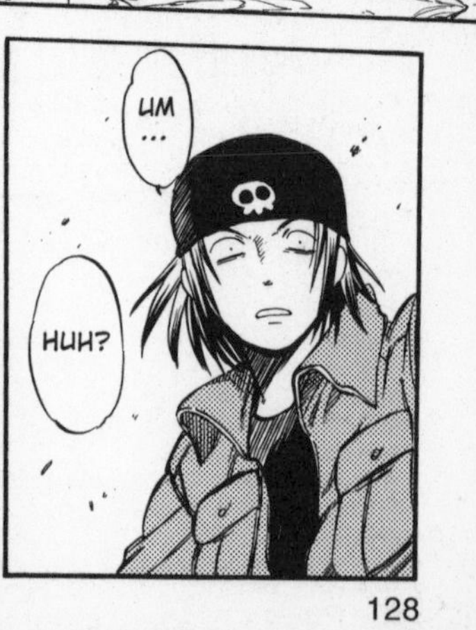
UM ...
HUH?
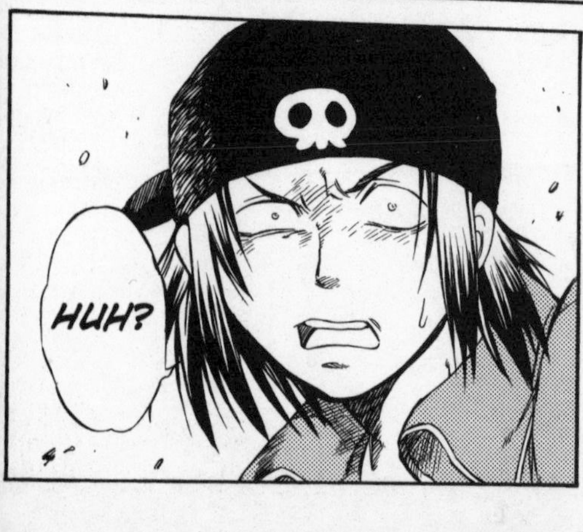
HUH?

READ THIS WAY

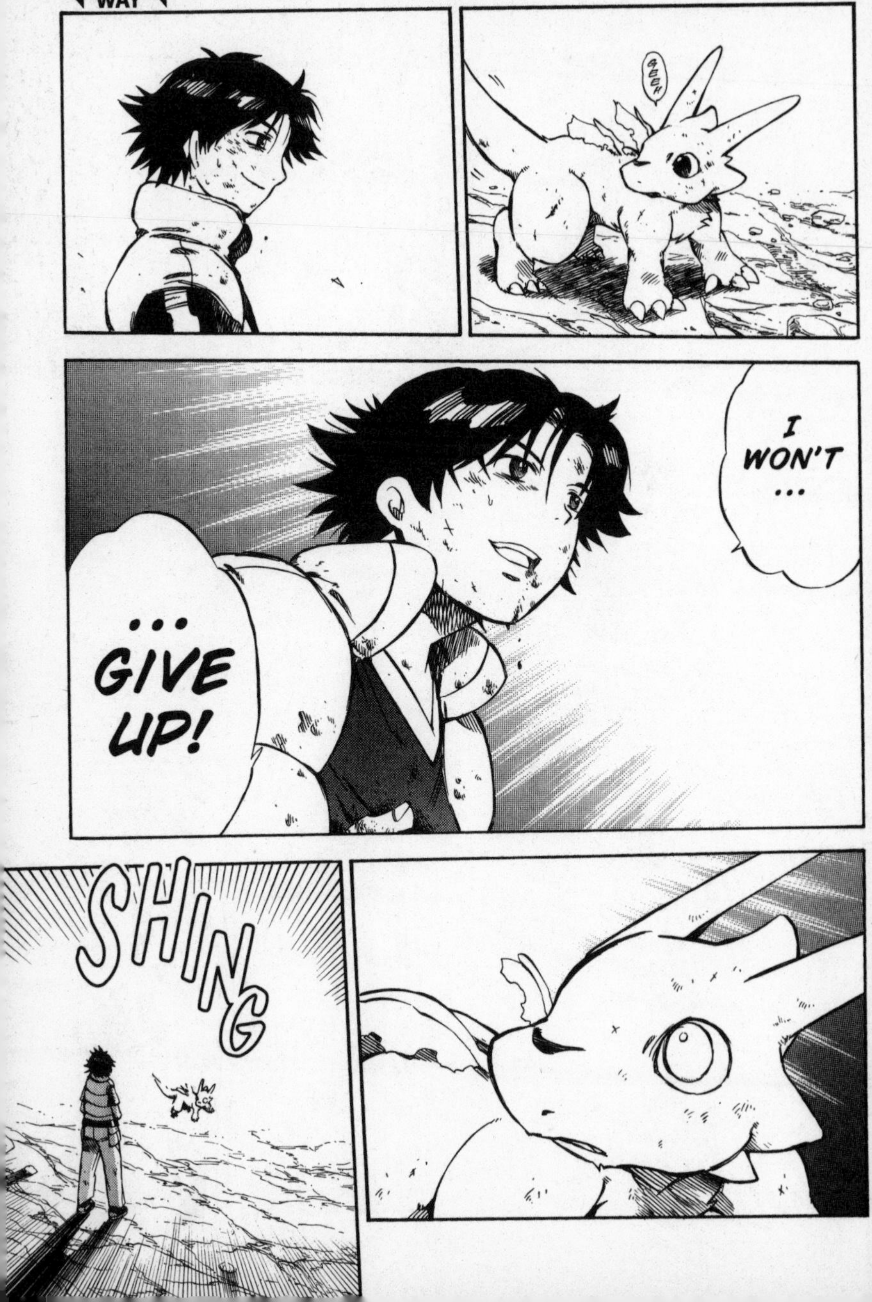
GEEH
I WON'T ...
... GIVE UP!
SHING

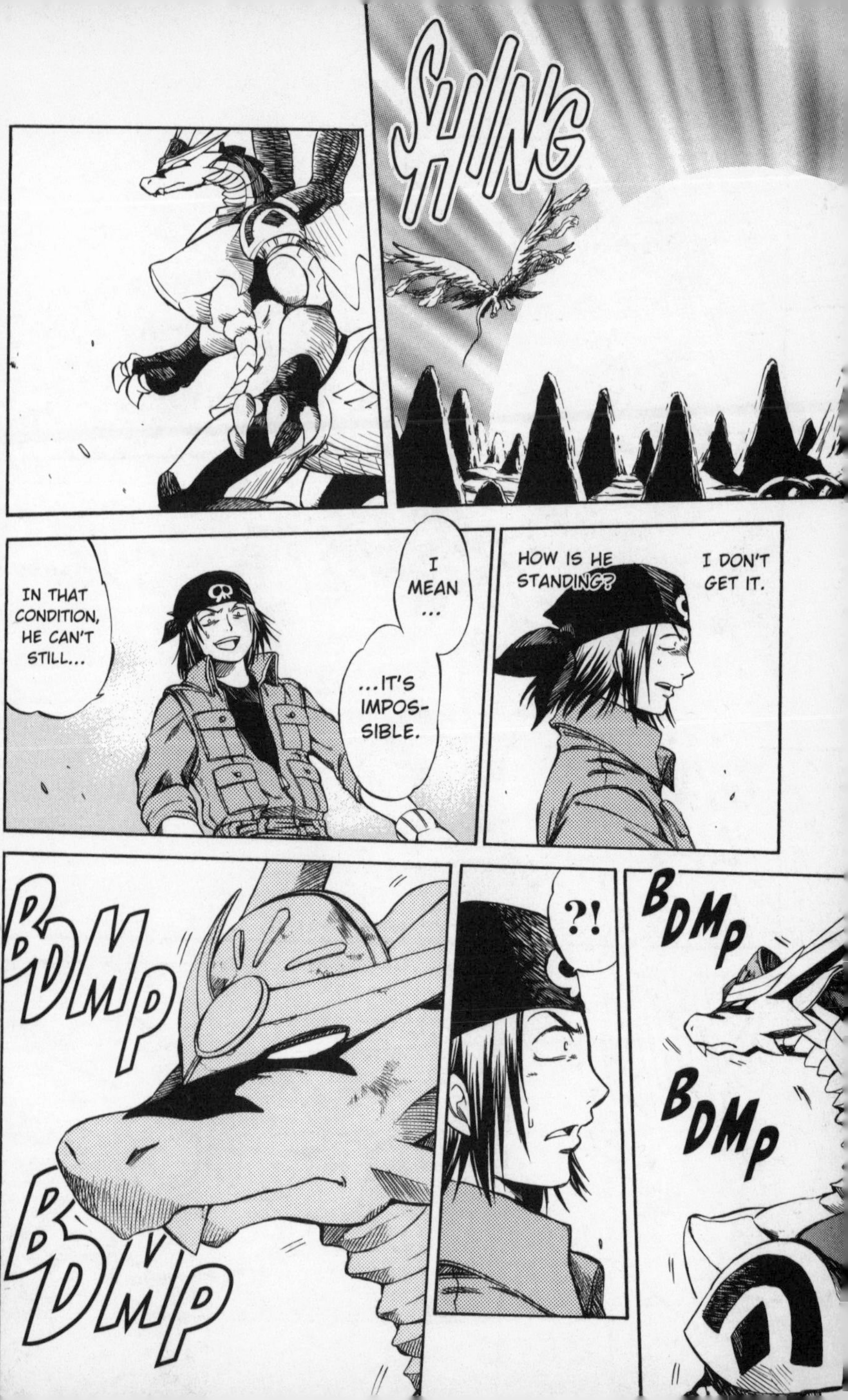
SHING
I DON'T GET IT.
HOW IS HE STANDING?
I MEAN ...
...IT'S IMPOSSIBLE.
IN THAT CONDITION, HE CAN'T STILL...
BDMP
BDMP
?!
BDMP
BDMP

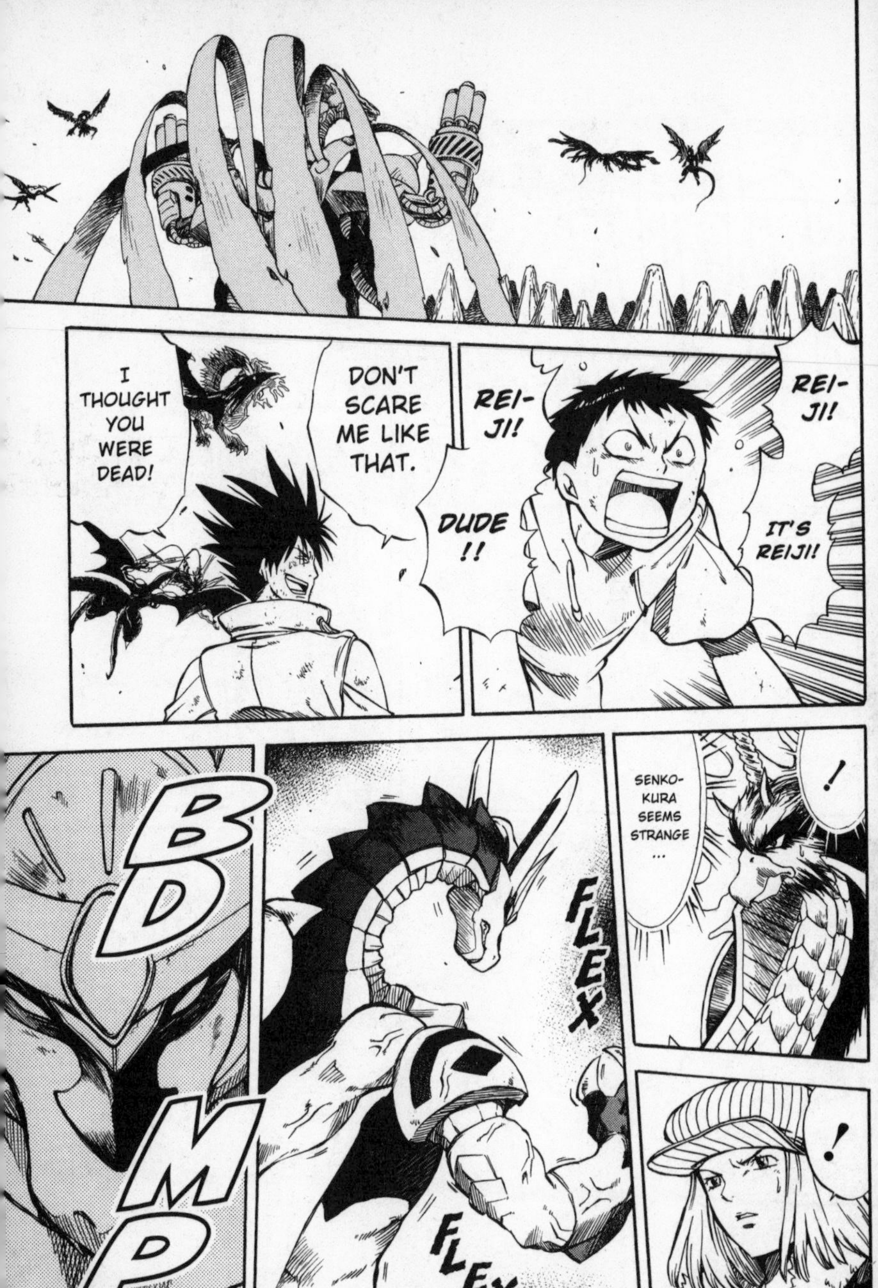
REI-JI!
REI-JI!
IT'S REIJI!
DUDE !!
DON'T SCARE ME LIKE THAT.
I THOUGHT YOU WERE DEAD!
!
SENKO-KURA SEEMS STRANGE ...
!
FLEX
FLEX
BDMP

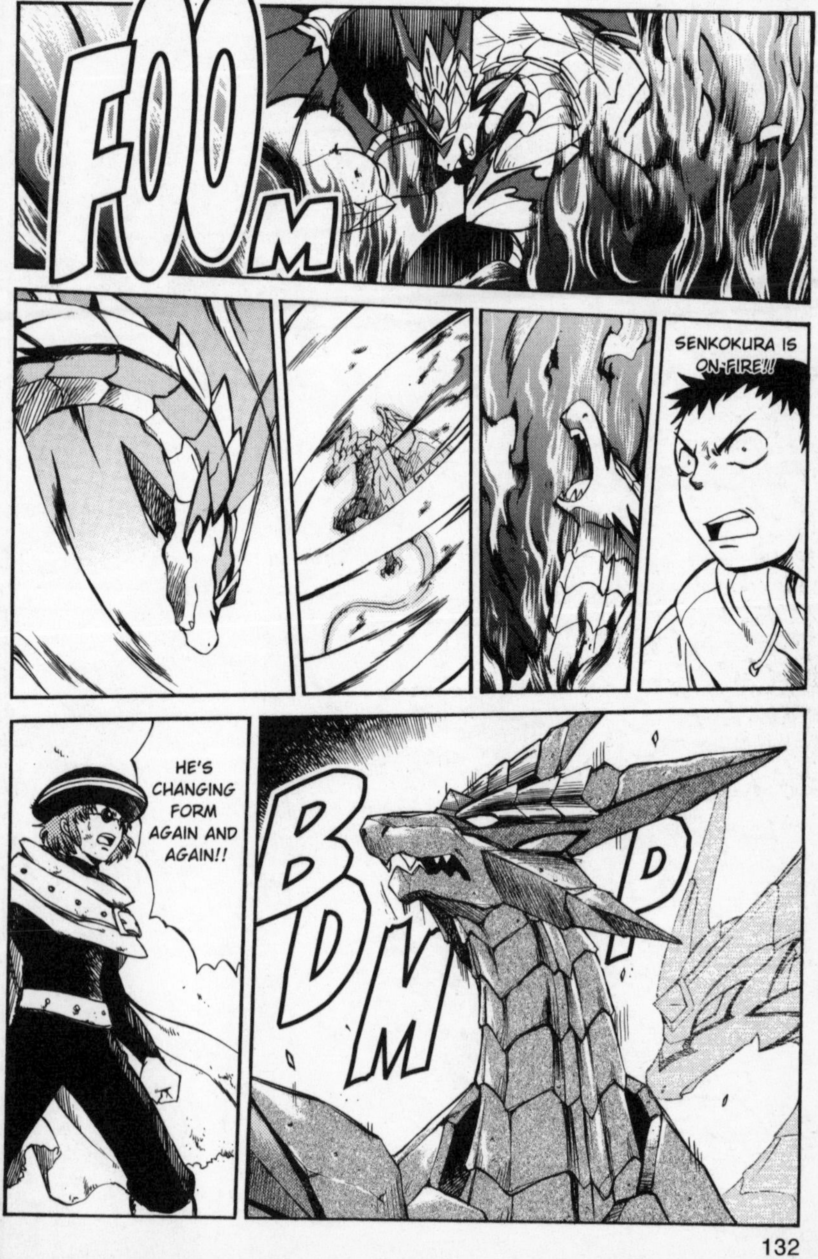
F-OOM
SENKOKURA IS ON FIRE!!
BDDM
HE'S CHANGING FORM AGAIN AND AGAIN!!

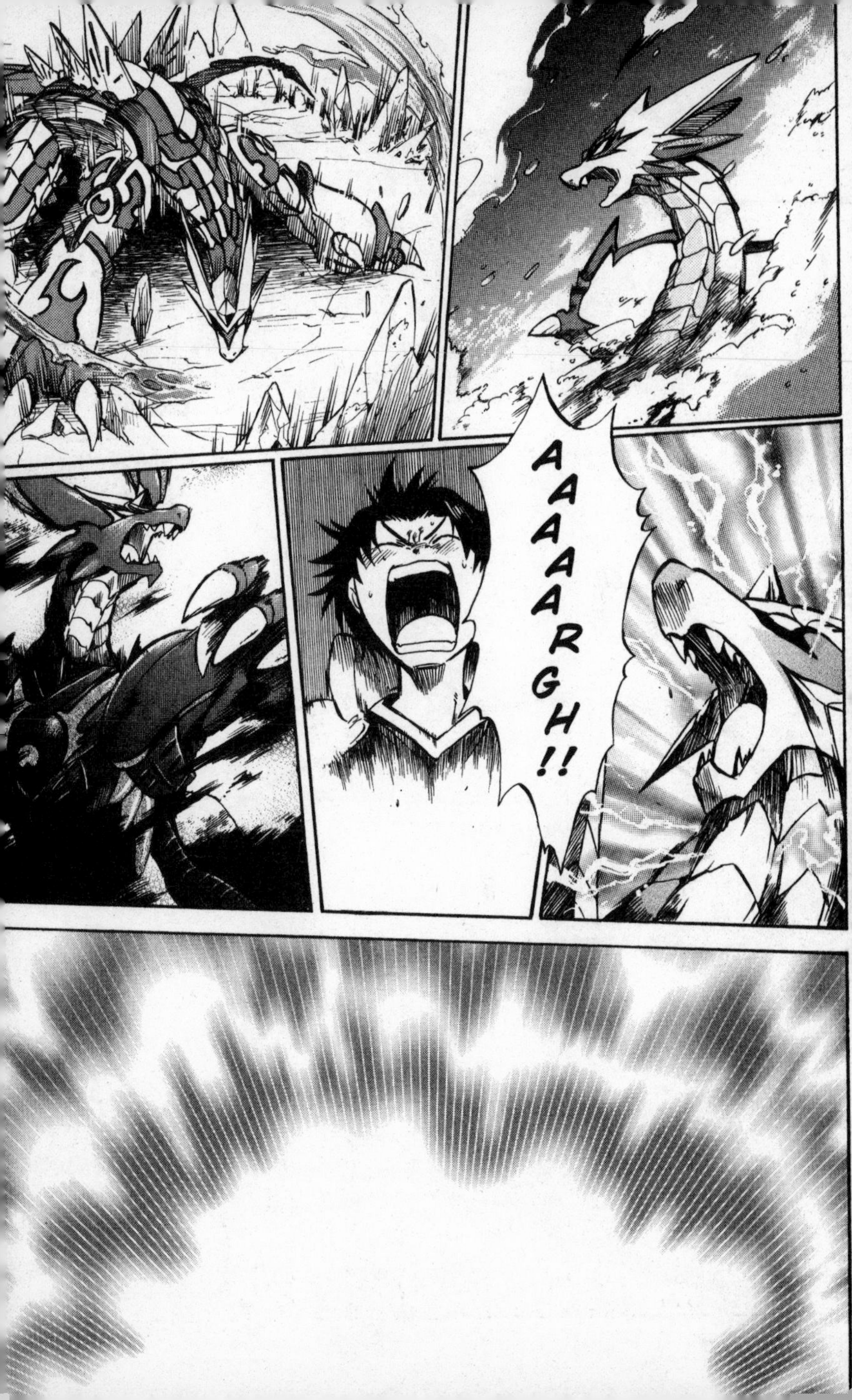
AAAAARGH!!

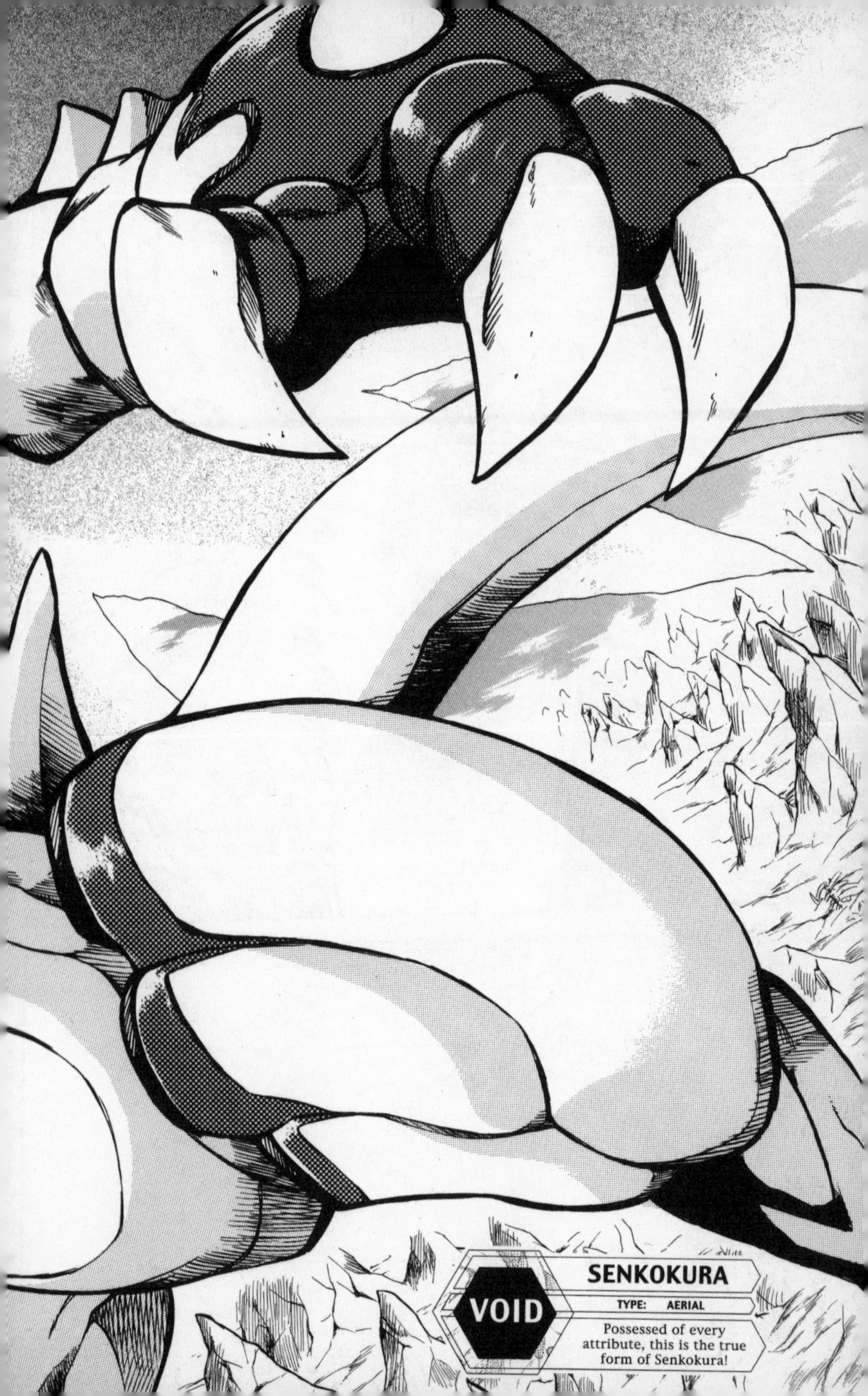
SENKOKURA
VOID
TYPE: AERIAL
Possessed of every attribute, this is the true form of Senkokura!

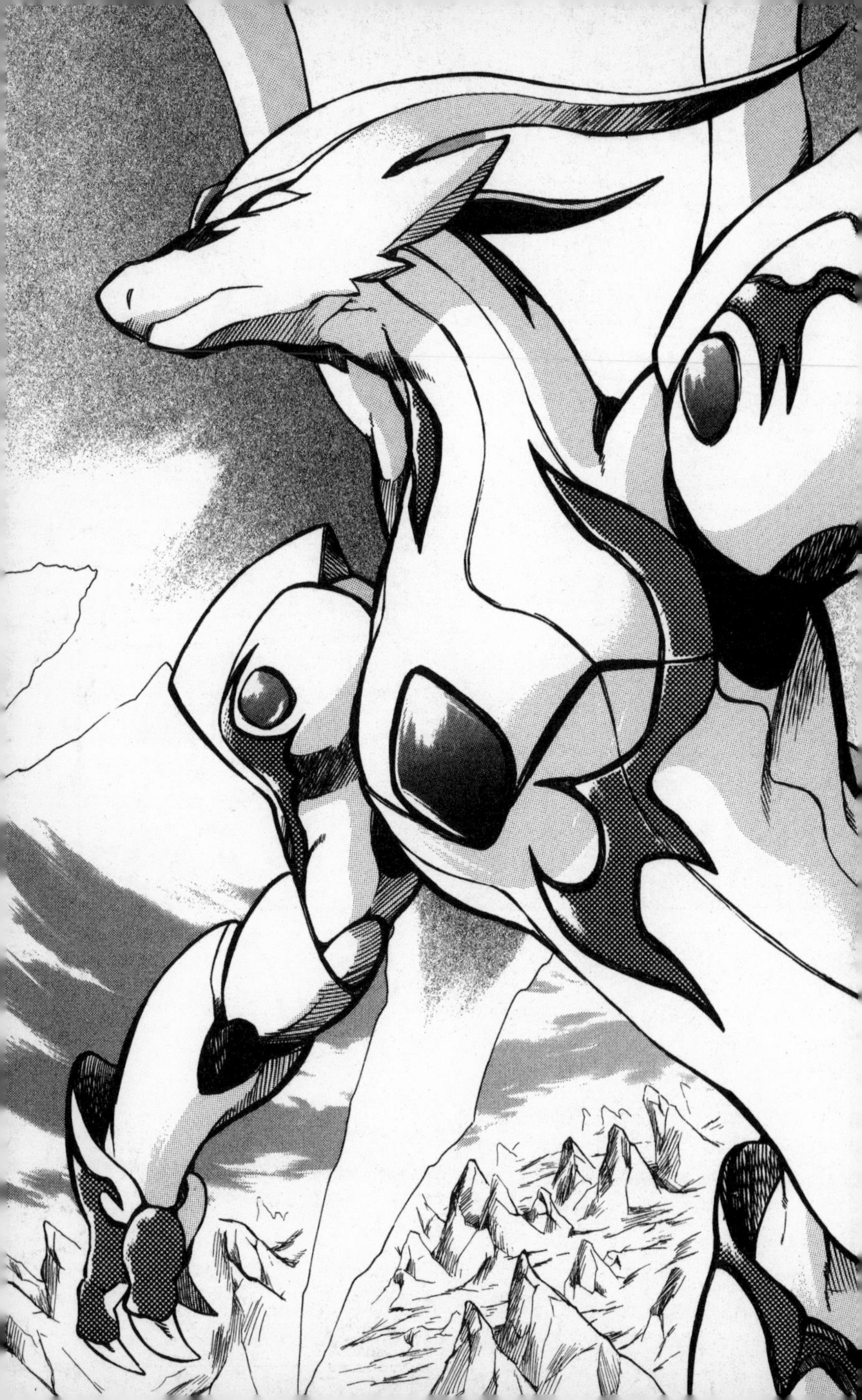

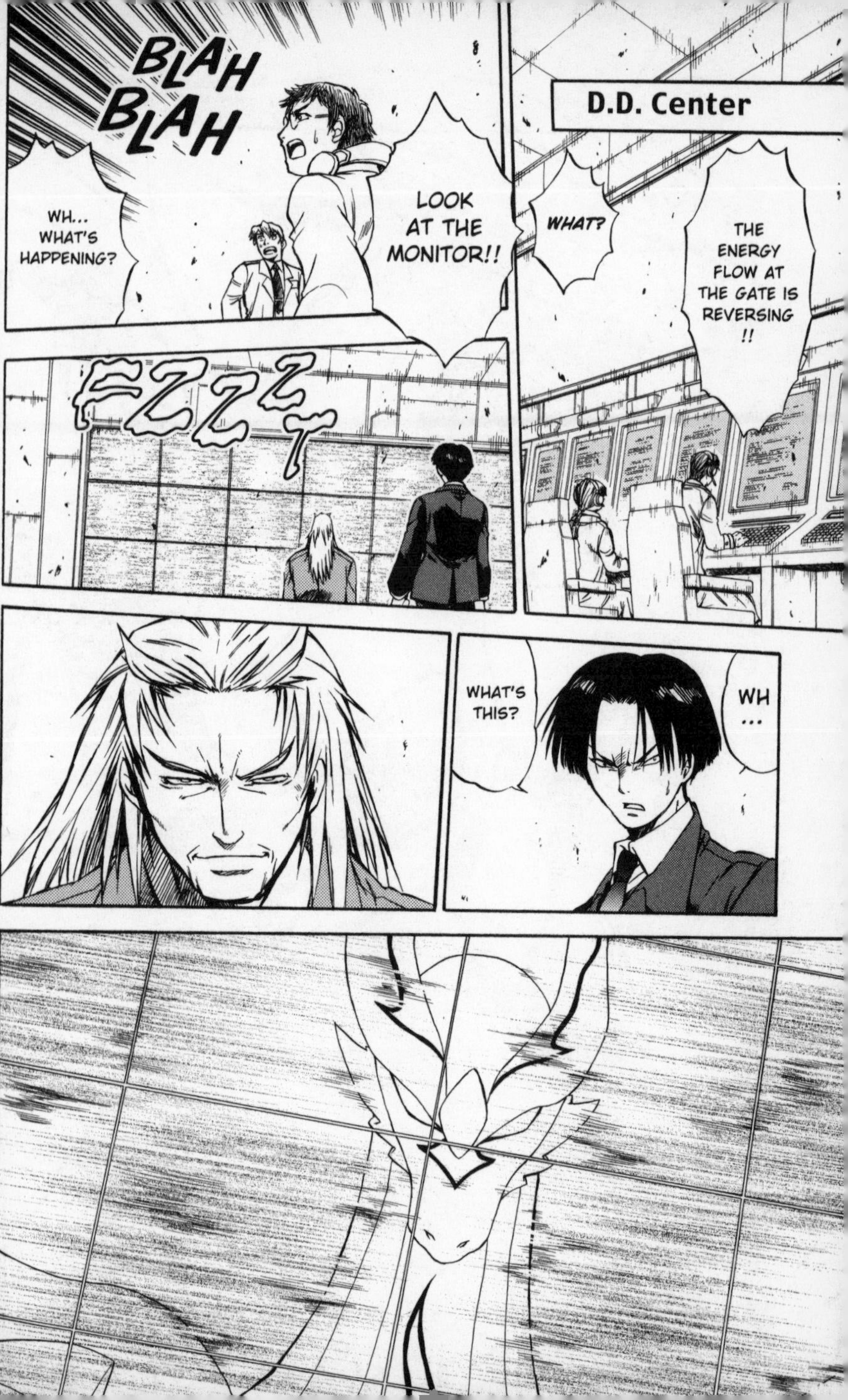
D.D. Center
WHAT?
THE ENERGY FLOW AT THE GATE IS REVERSING !!
LOOK AT THE MONITOR!!
BLAH BLAH
WH... WHAT'S HAPPENING?
FZZZT
WH ...
WHAT'S THIS?

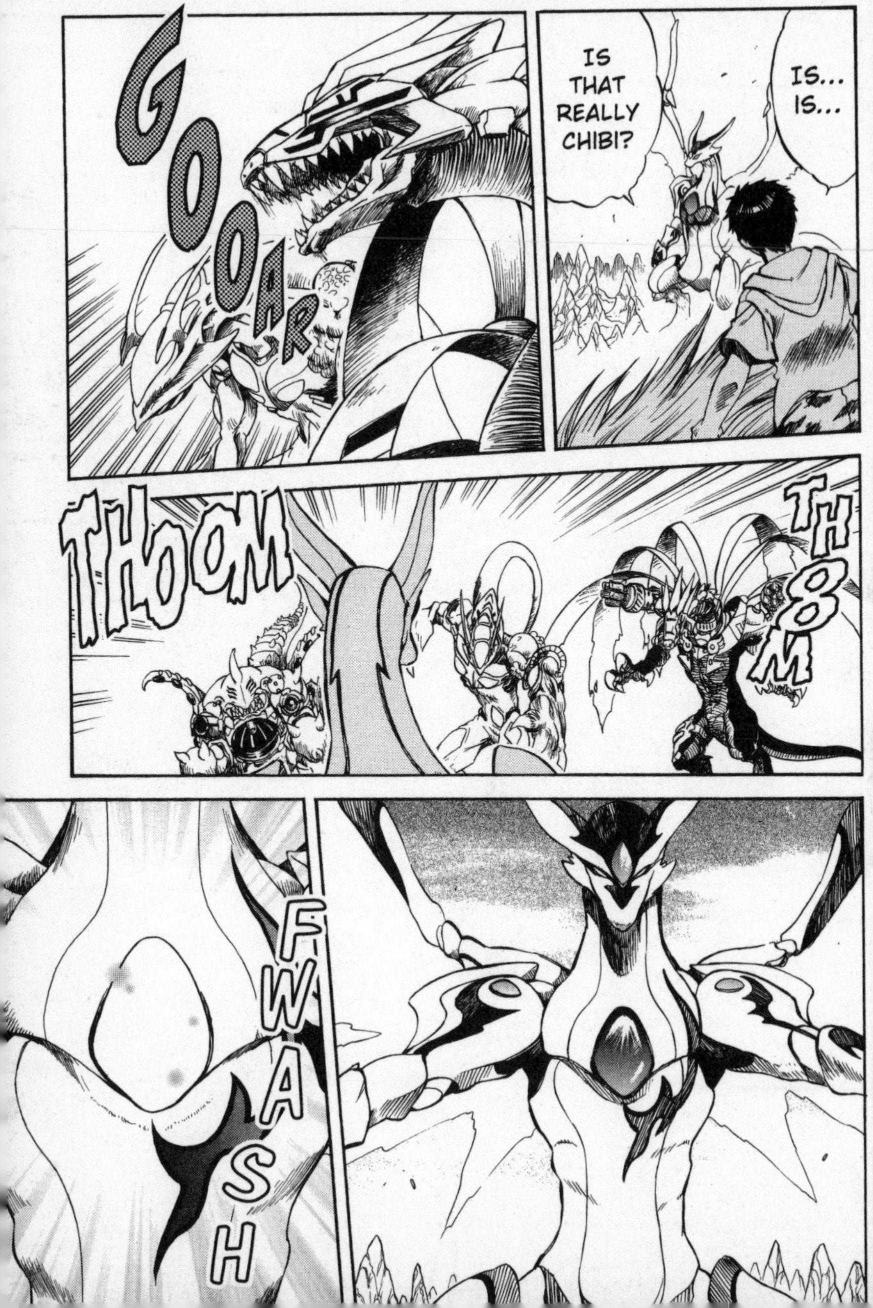
IS... IS...
IS THAT REALLY CHIBI?
GOOAR
THOOM
THOOM
FWASH

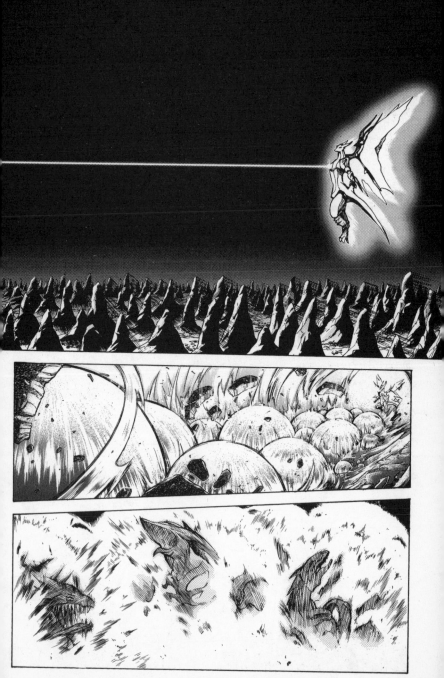

138

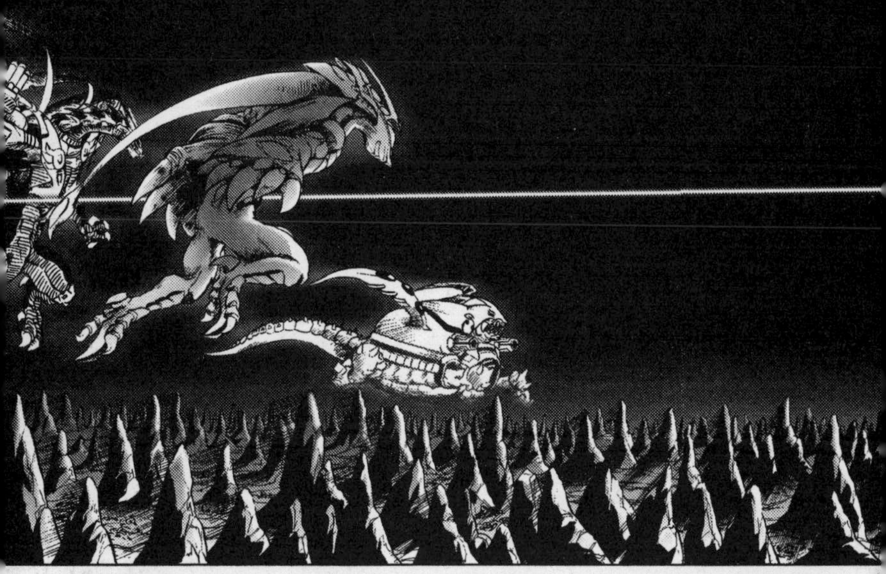

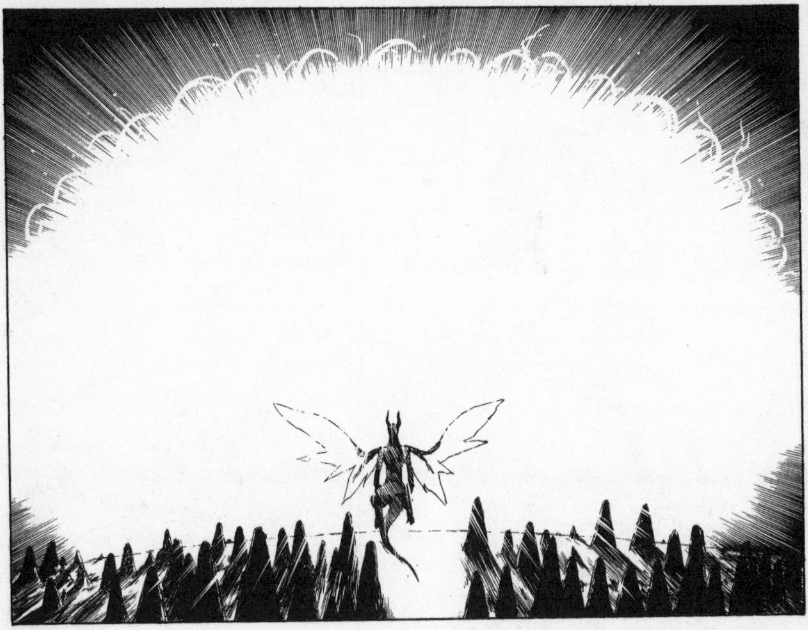

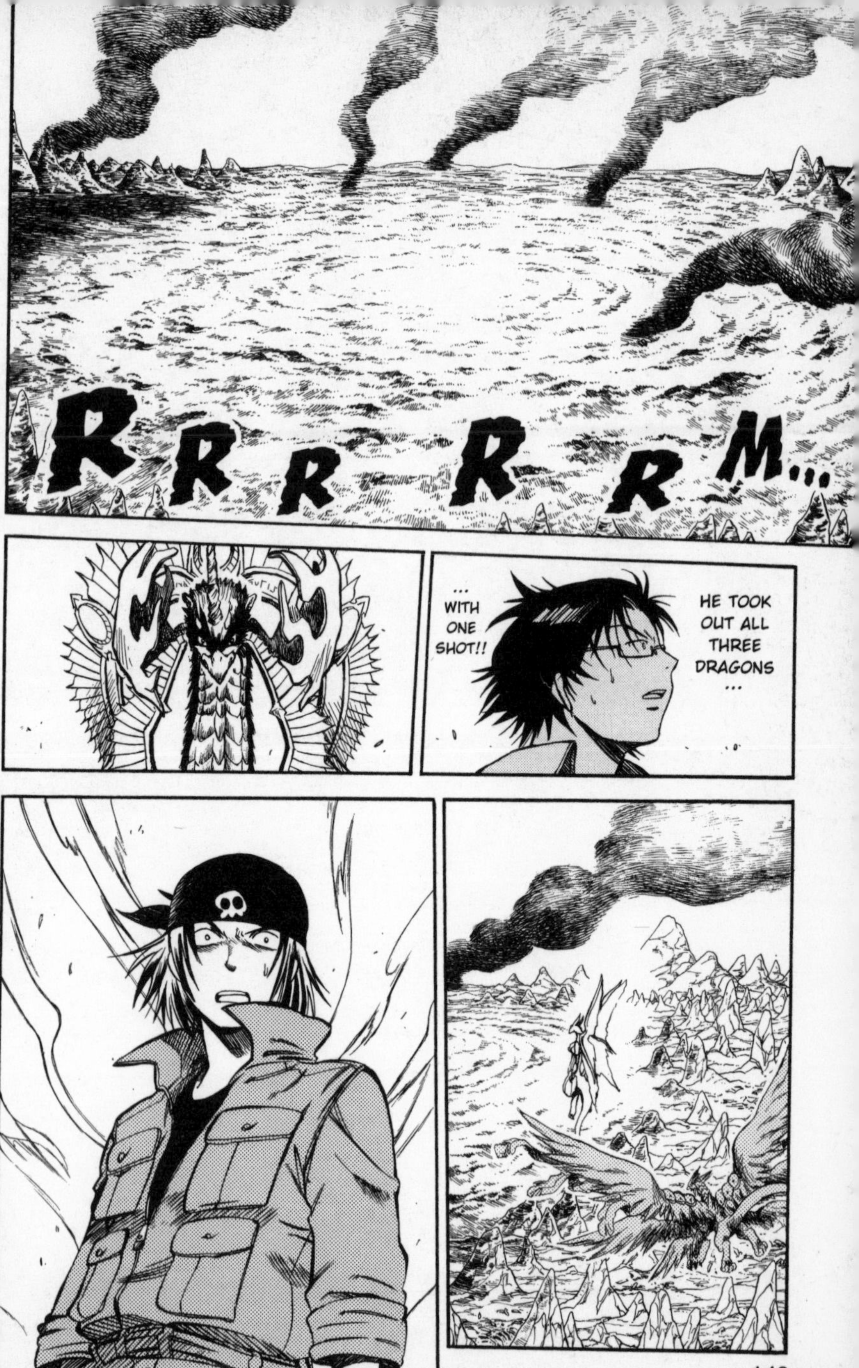
RRRRRRM...
HE TOOK OUT ALL THREE DRAGONS ...
... WITH ONE SHOT!!

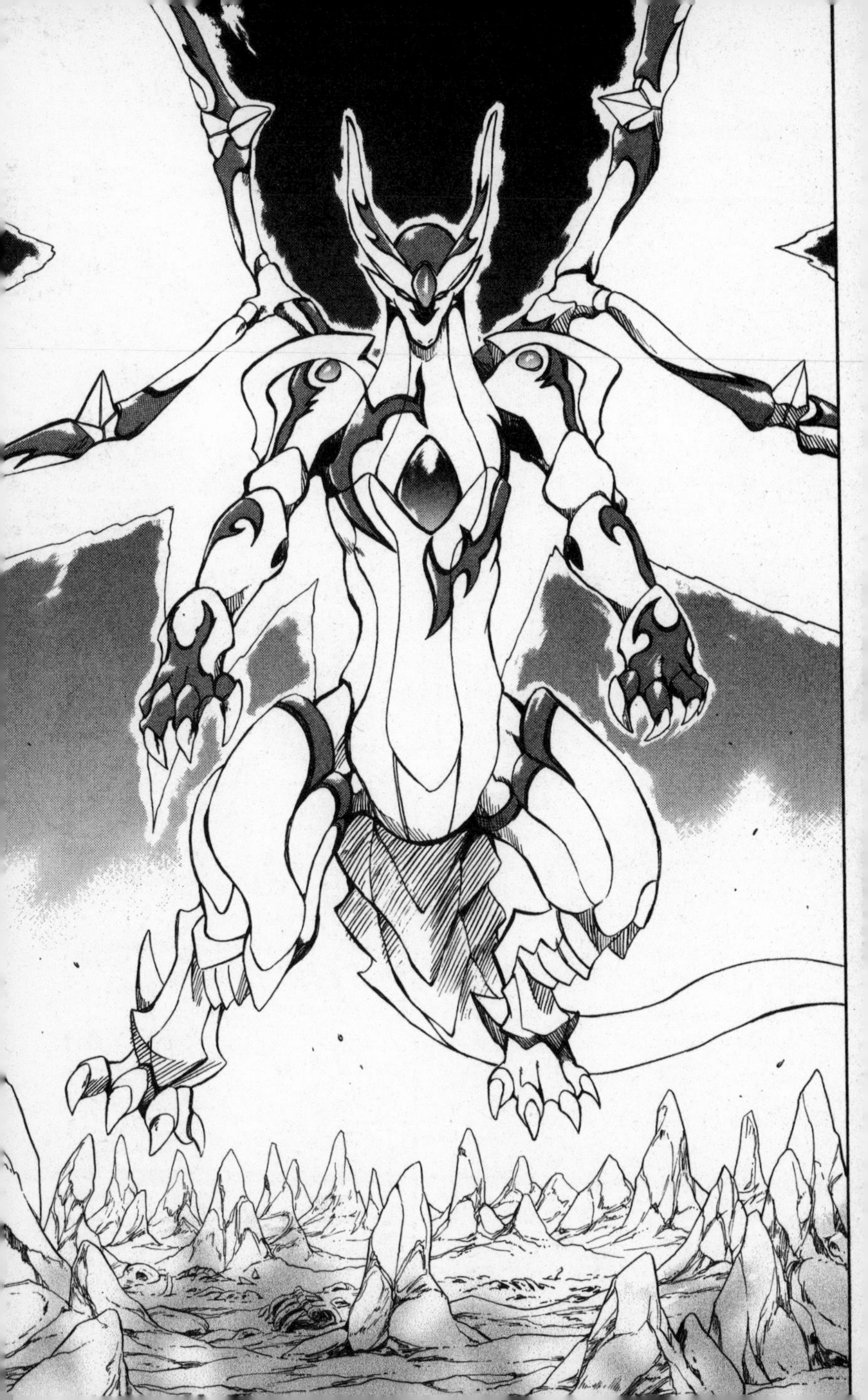

Go Agent S, Part 2 *BY TRA-SAN*

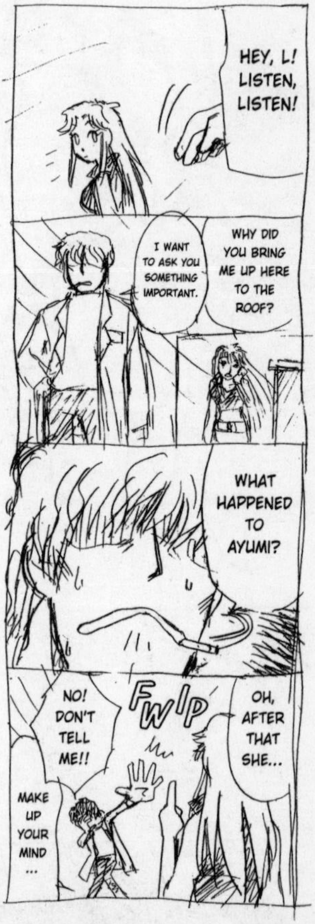
HEY, L! LISTEN, LISTEN!
WHY DID YOU BRING ME UP HERE TO THE ROOF?
I WANT TO ASK YOU SOMETHING IMPORTANT.
WHAT HAPPENED TO AYUMI?
OH, AFTER THAT SHE...
FWIP
NO! DON'T TELL ME!!
MAKE UP YOUR MIND...

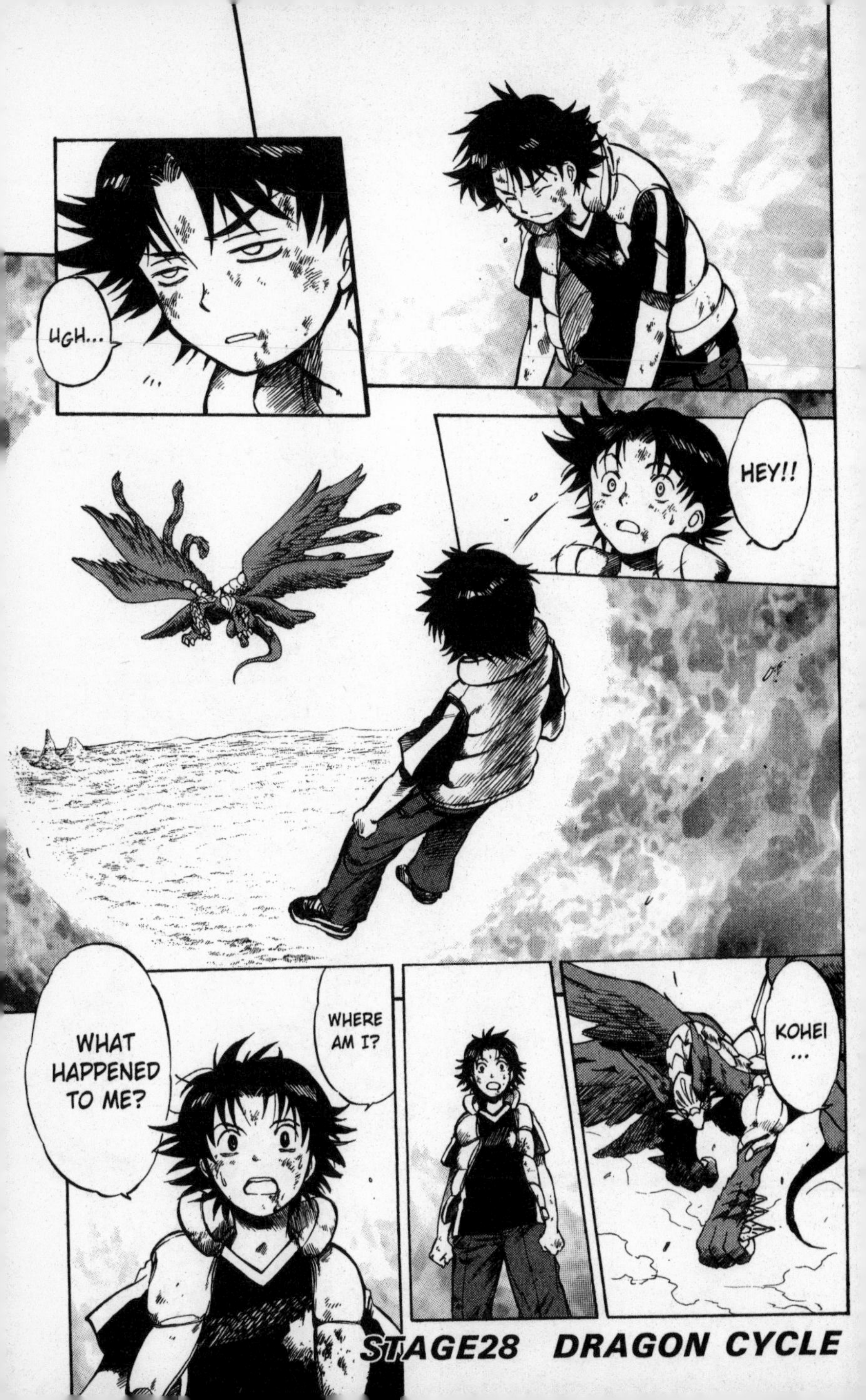
UGH...
HEY!!
KOHEI ...
WHERE AM I?
WHAT HAPPENED TO ME?

STAGE28 DRAGON CYCLE

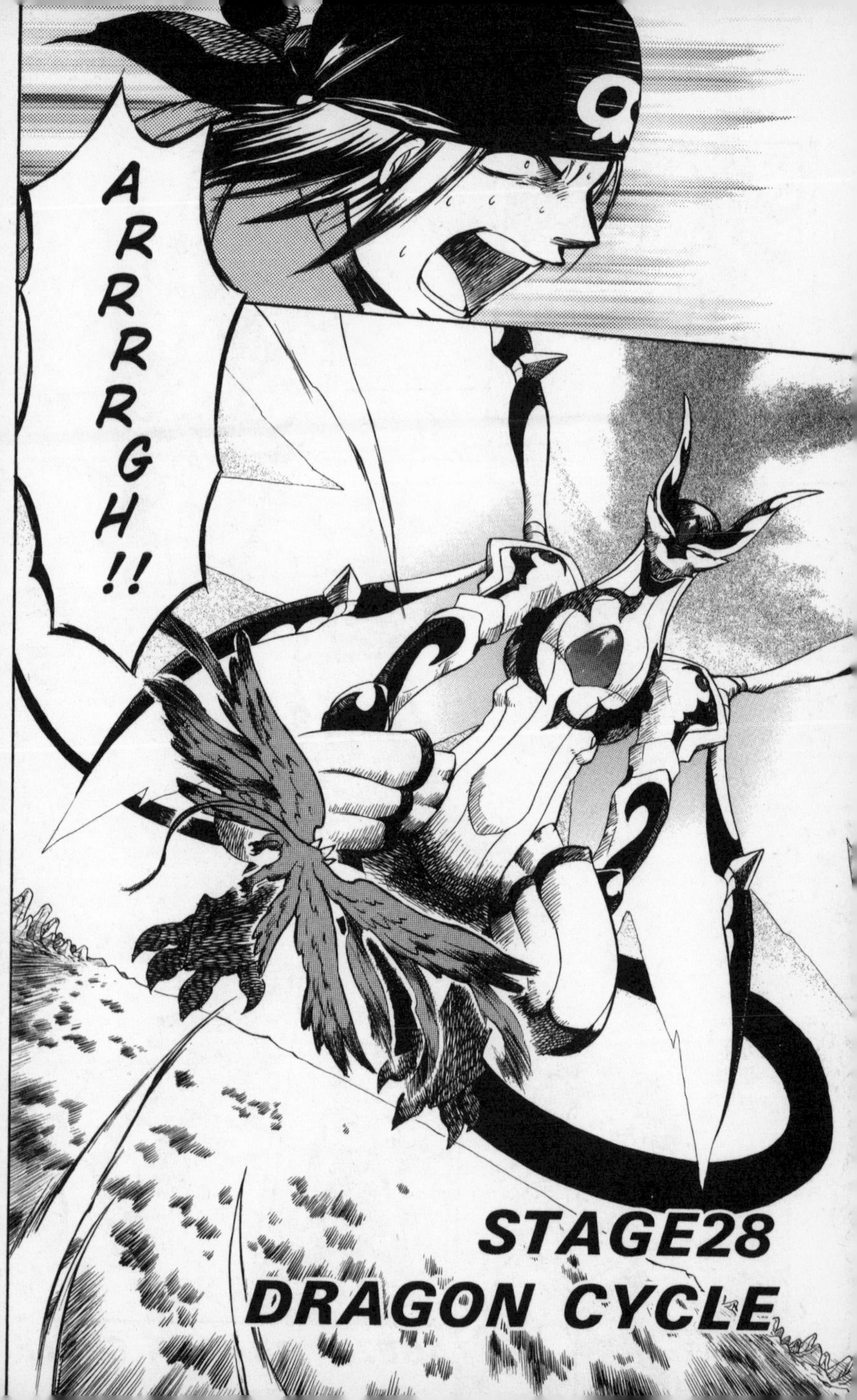
ARRRRGH!!
STAGE28
DRAGON CYCLE

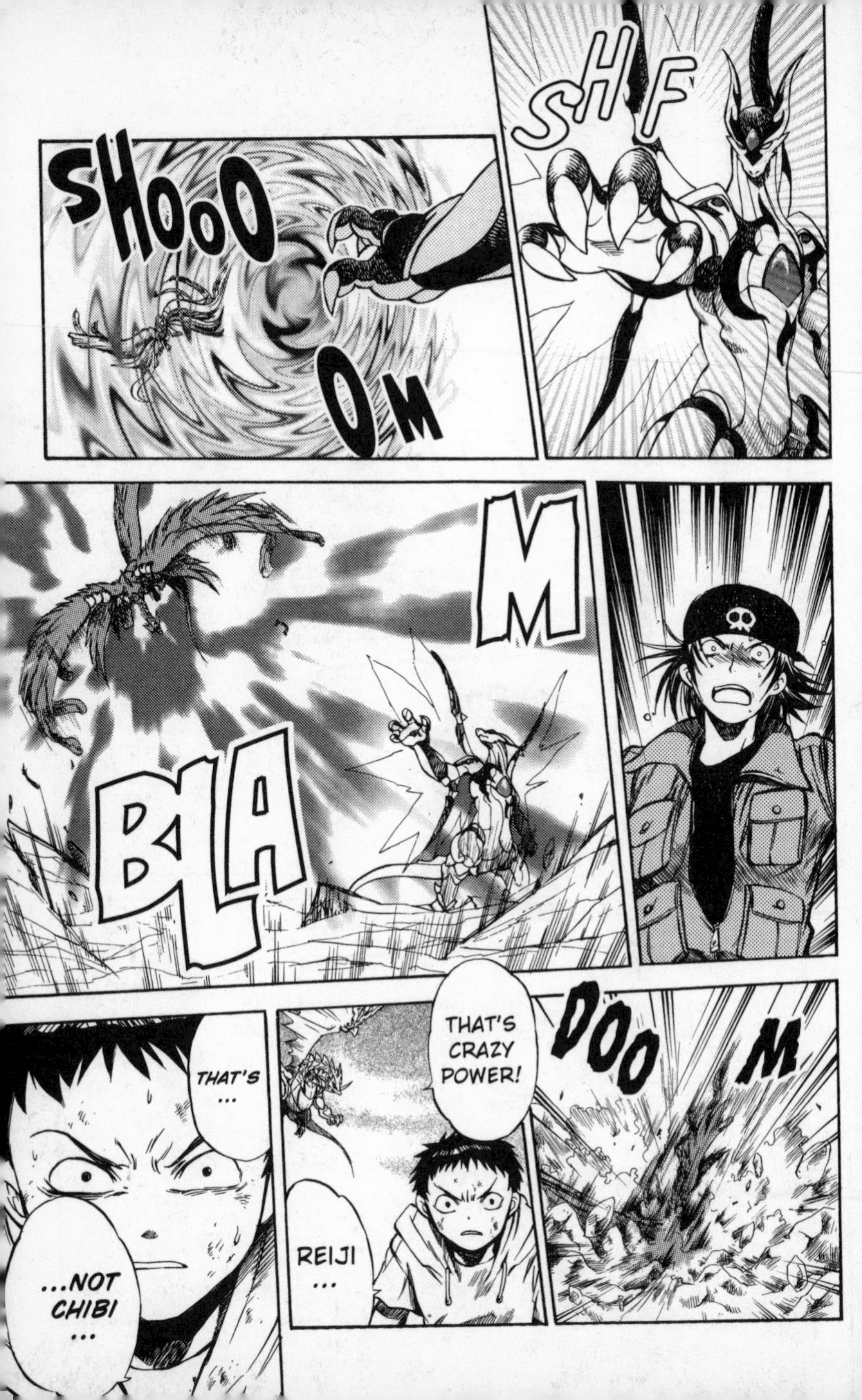
SHF
SHOOOOM
M
BLAM
DOOM
THAT'S CRAZY POWER!
REIJI ...
THAT'S ...
...NOT CHIBI ...

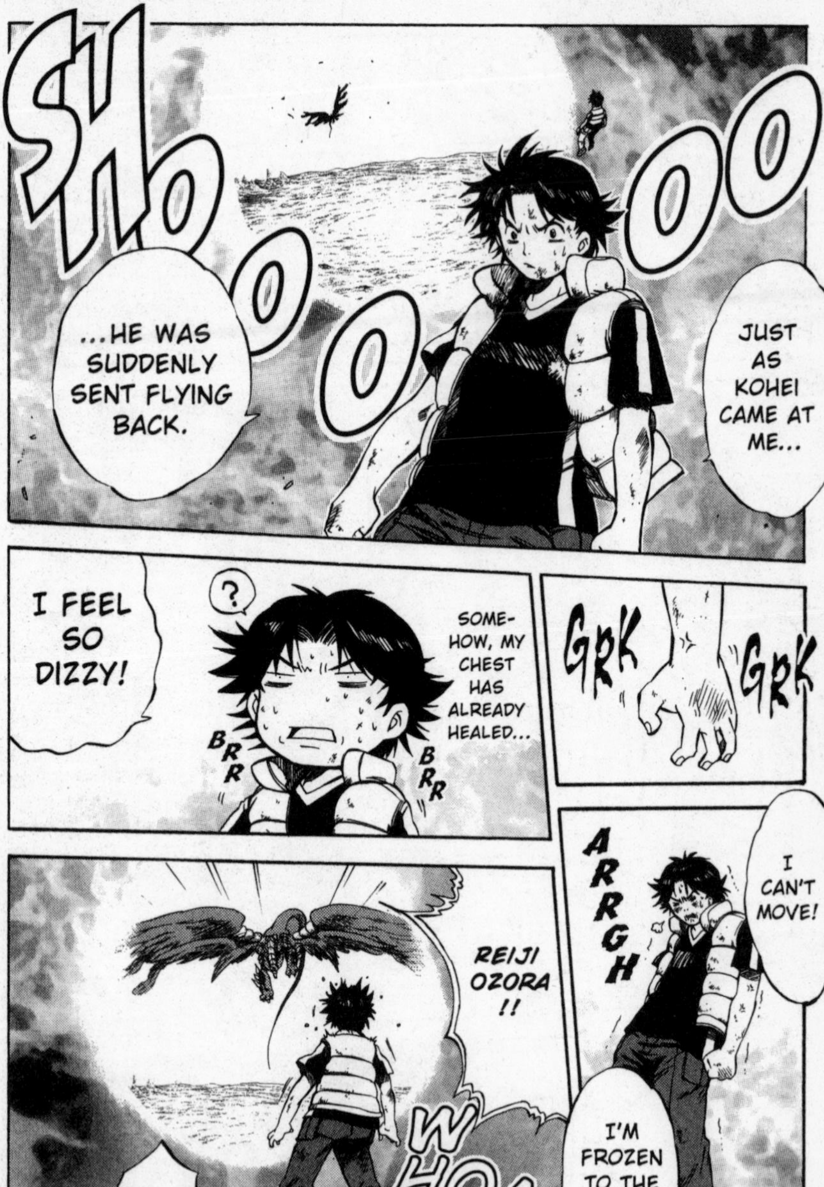
SHOOOOOOO
JUST AS KOHEI CAME AT ME...
...HE WAS SUDDENLY SENT FLYING BACK.
GRK
GRK
SOME-HOW, MY CHEST HAS ALREADY HEALED...
?
I FEEL SO DIZZY!
BRR
BRR
I CAN'T MOVE!
ARRGH
I'M FROZEN TO THE SPOT!!
REIJI OZORA!!
WHOA
WHAT?

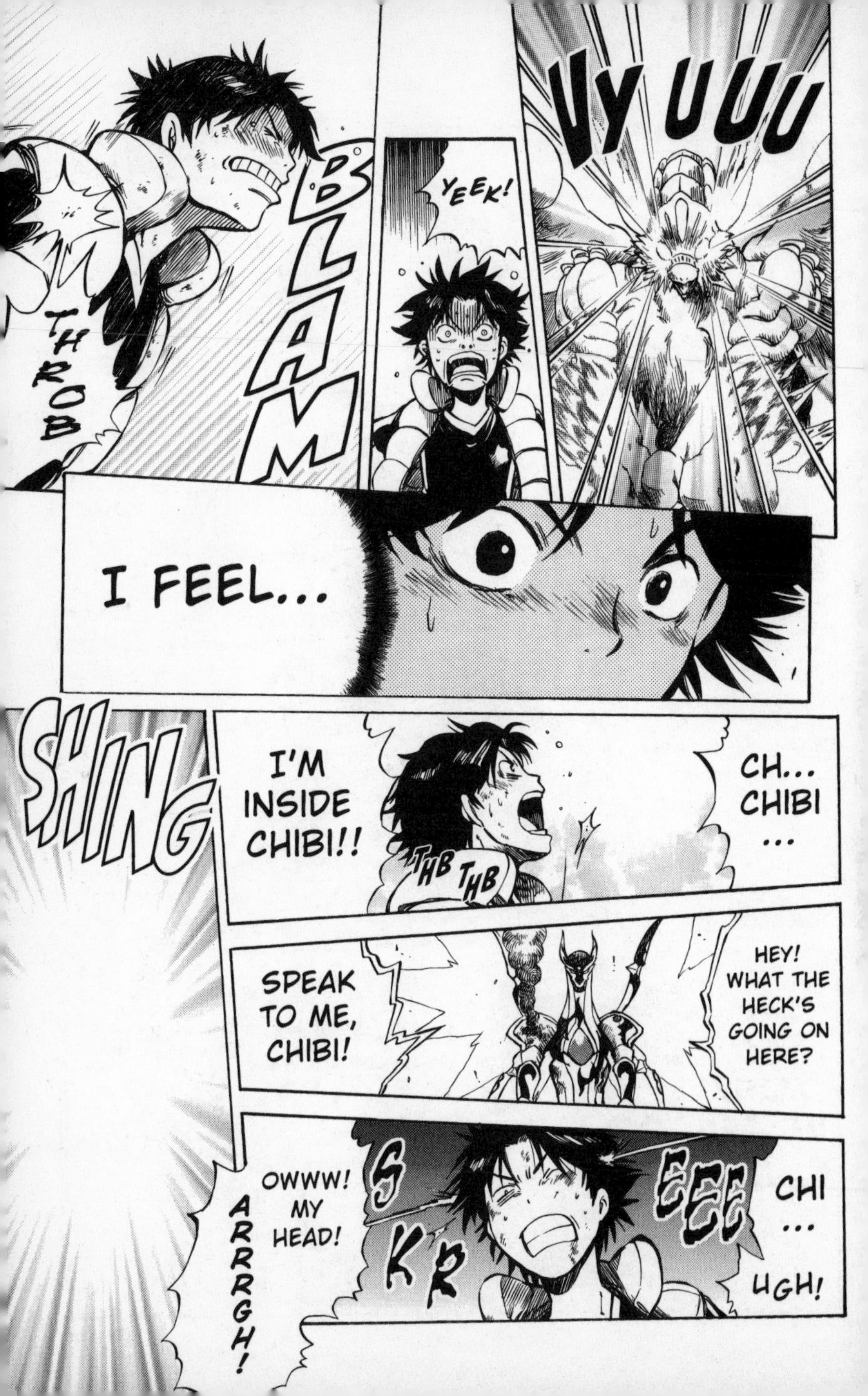
VYUUU
YEEK!
BLAM
THROB
I FEEL...
CH... CHIBI ...
I'M INSIDE CHIBI!!
THB THB
HEY! WHAT THE HECK'S GOING ON HERE?
SPEAK TO ME, CHIBI!
CHI ... UGH!
EEE
SKR
OWWW! MY HEAD!
SHING
ARRRGH!

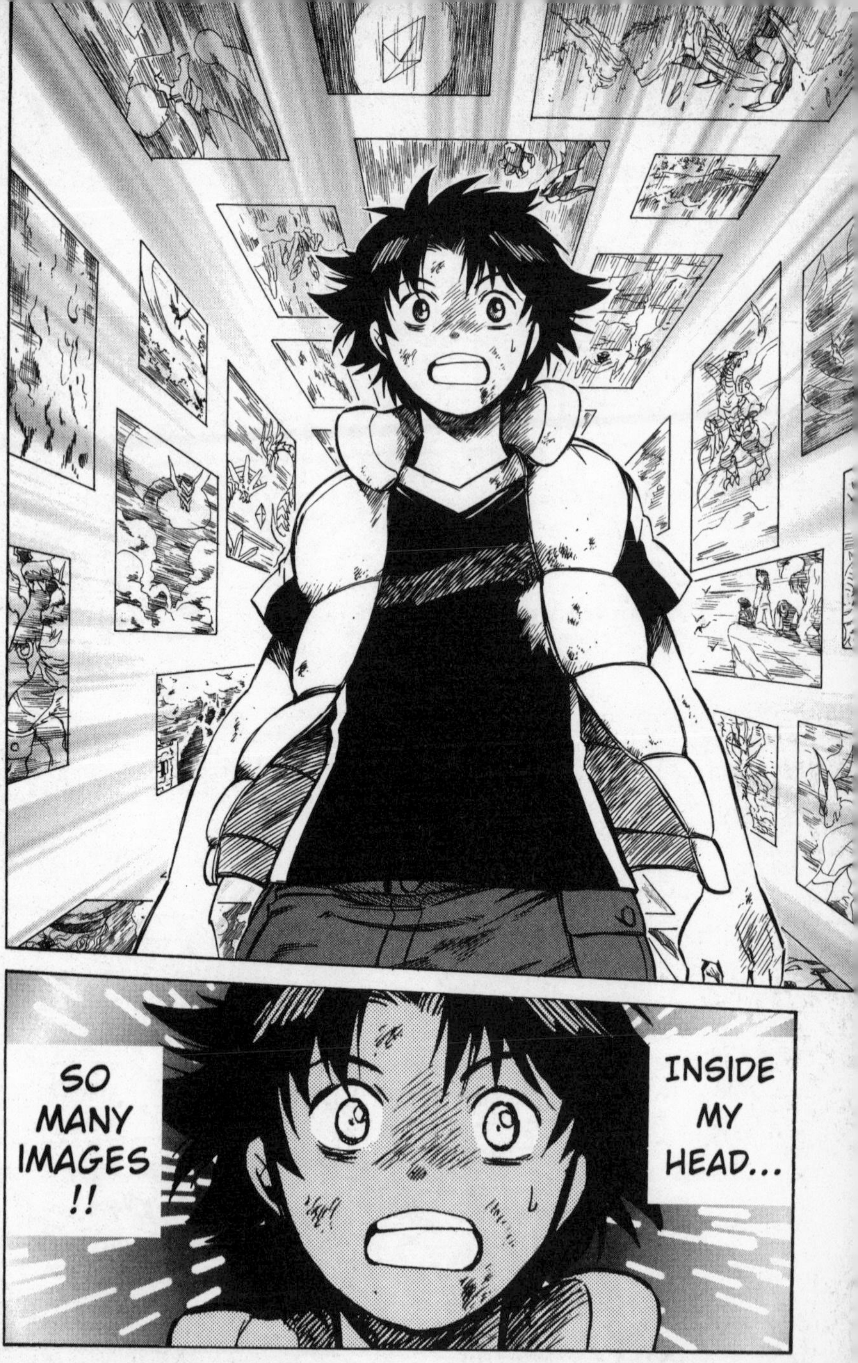
INSIDE MY HEAD...
SO MANY IMAGES !!

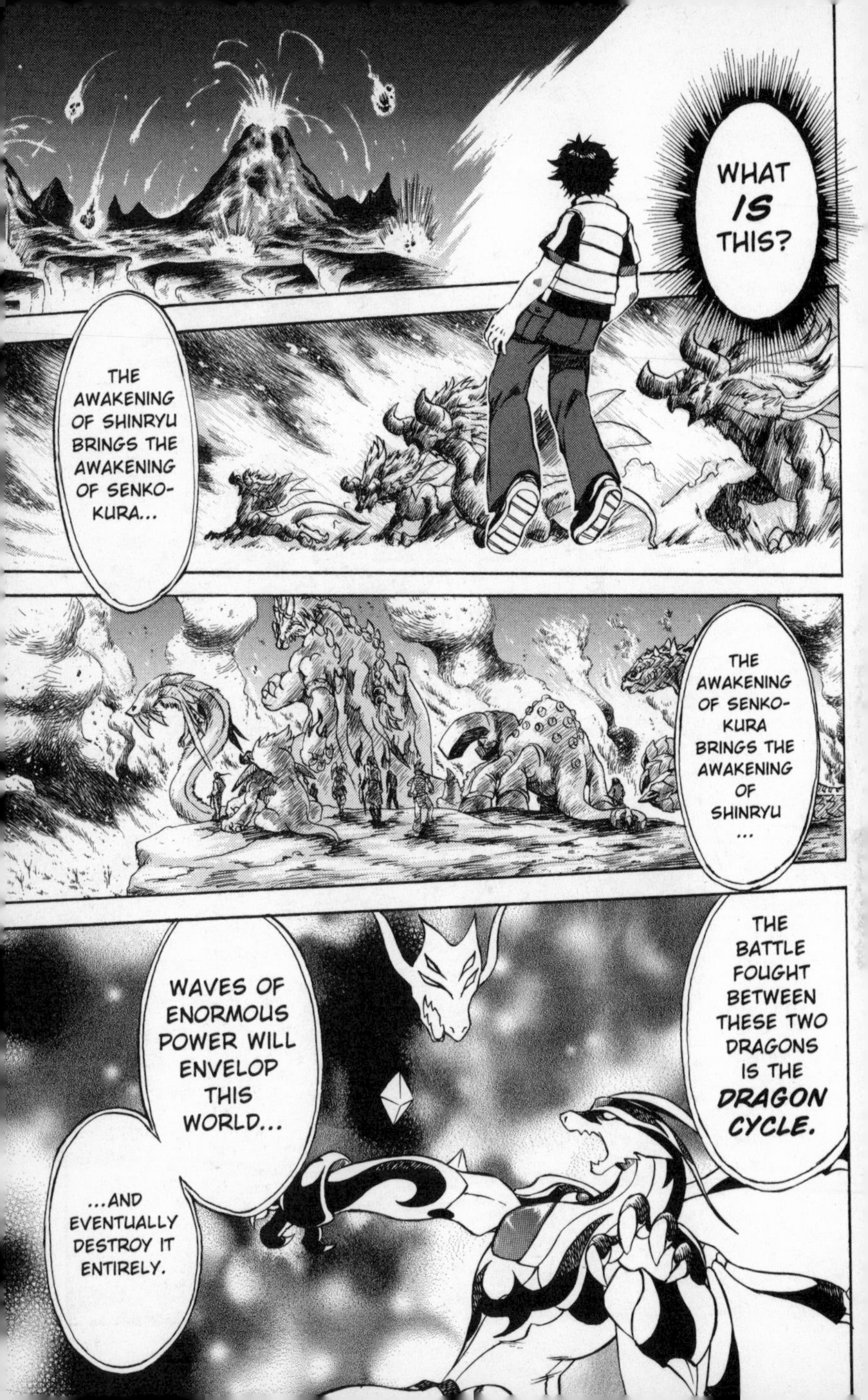
WHAT *IS* THIS?
THE AWAKENING OF SHINRYU BRINGS THE AWAKENING OF SENKO-KURA...
THE AWAKENING OF SENKO-KURA BRINGS THE AWAKENING OF SHINRYU...
THE BATTLE FOUGHT BETWEEN THESE TWO DRAGONS IS THE ***DRAGON CYCLE.***
WAVES OF ENORMOUS POWER WILL ENVELOP THIS WORLD...
...AND EVENTUALLY DESTROY IT ENTIRELY.

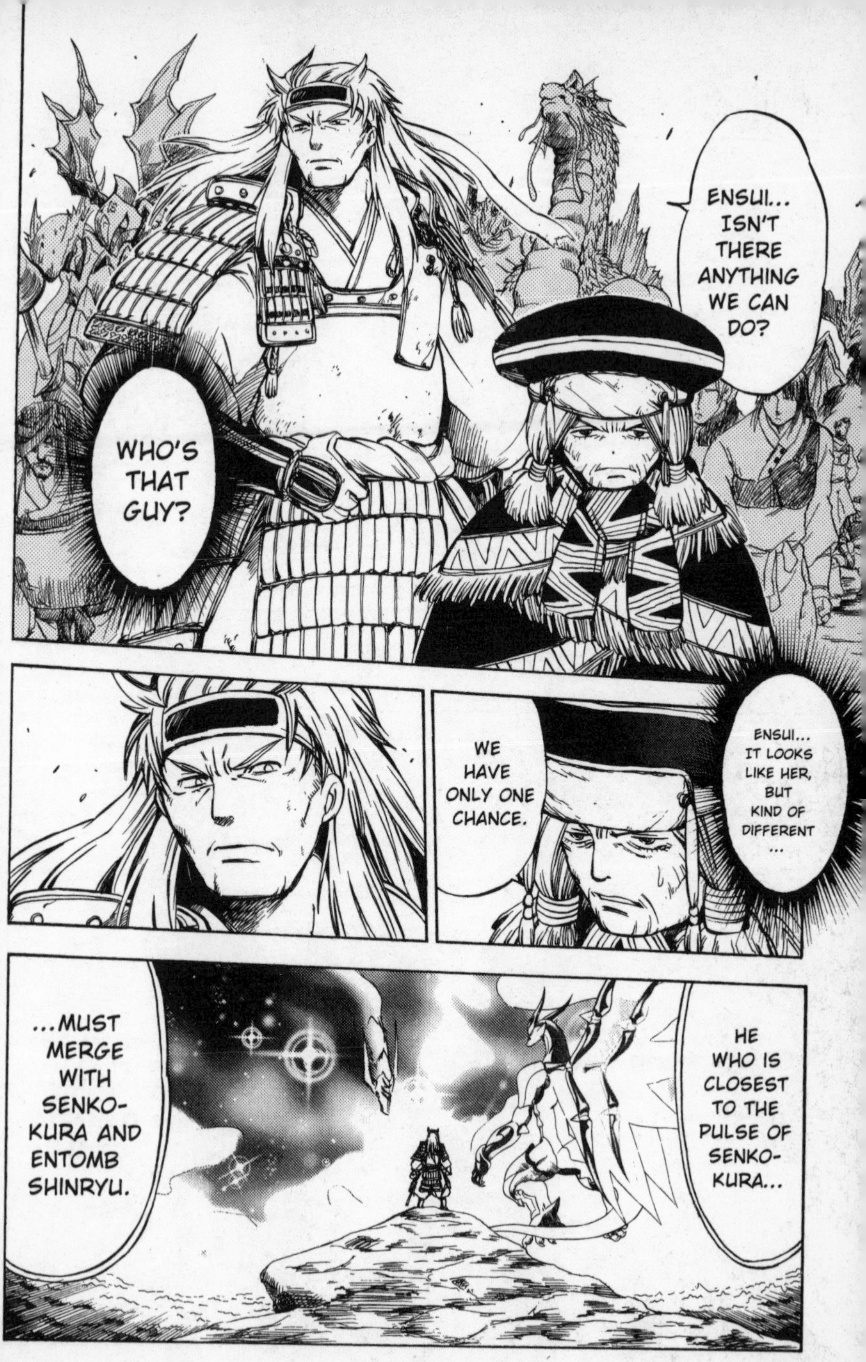
ENSUI... ISN'T THERE ANYTHING WE CAN DO?
WHO'S THAT GUY?
ENSUI... IT LOOKS LIKE HER, BUT KIND OF DIFFERENT ...
WE HAVE ONLY ONE CHANCE.
HE WHO IS CLOSEST TO THE PULSE OF SENKO-KURA...
...MUST MERGE WITH SENKO-KURA AND ENTOMB SHINRYU.

READ THIS WAY

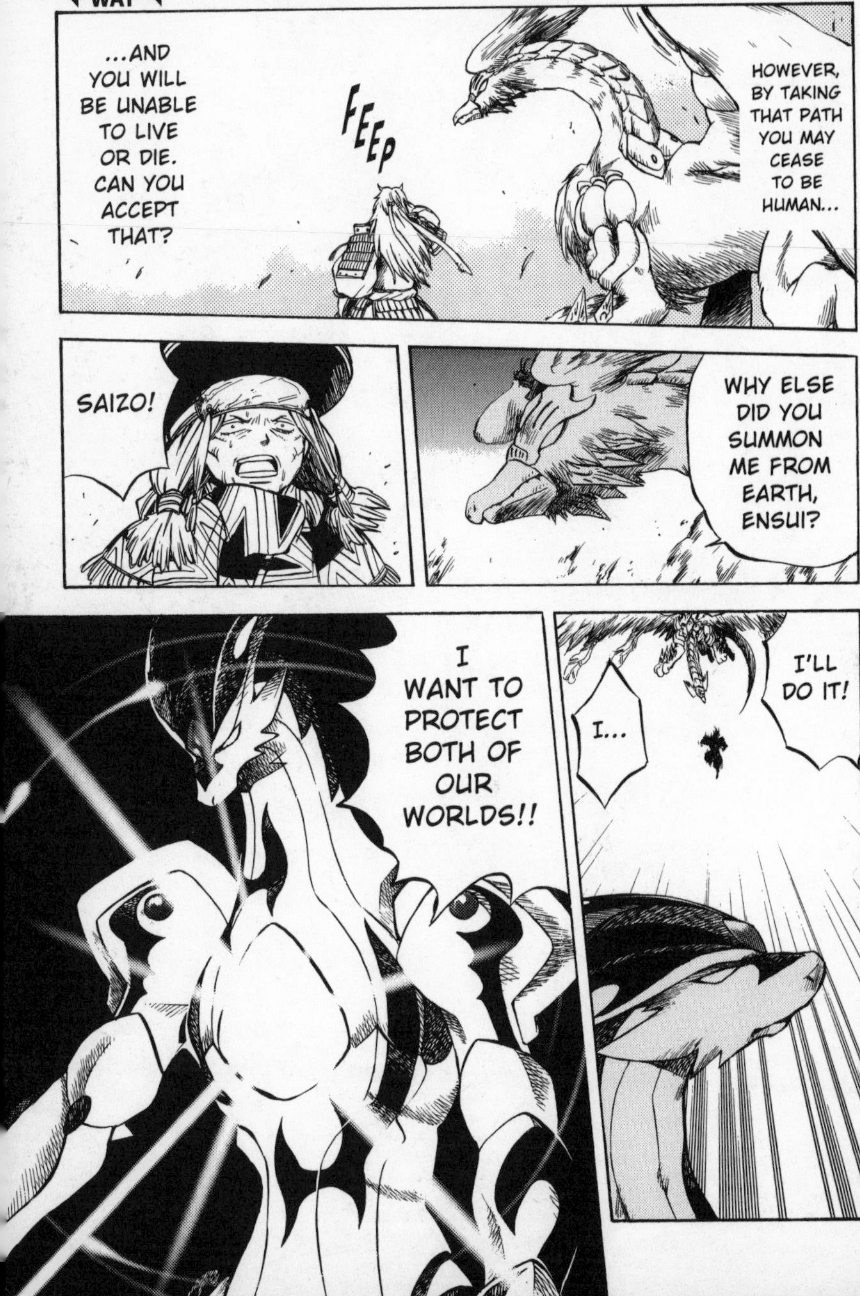
HOWEVER, BY TAKING THAT PATH YOU MAY CEASE TO BE HUMAN...
FEEP
...AND YOU WILL BE UNABLE TO LIVE OR DIE. CAN YOU ACCEPT THAT?
WHY ELSE DID YOU SUMMON ME FROM EARTH, ENSUI?
SAIZO!
I'LL DO IT!
I...
I WANT TO PROTECT BOTH OF OUR WORLDS!!

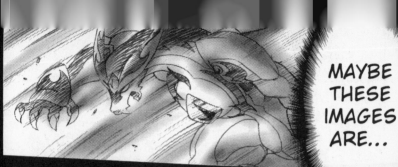

MAYBE
THESE
IMAGES
ARE...

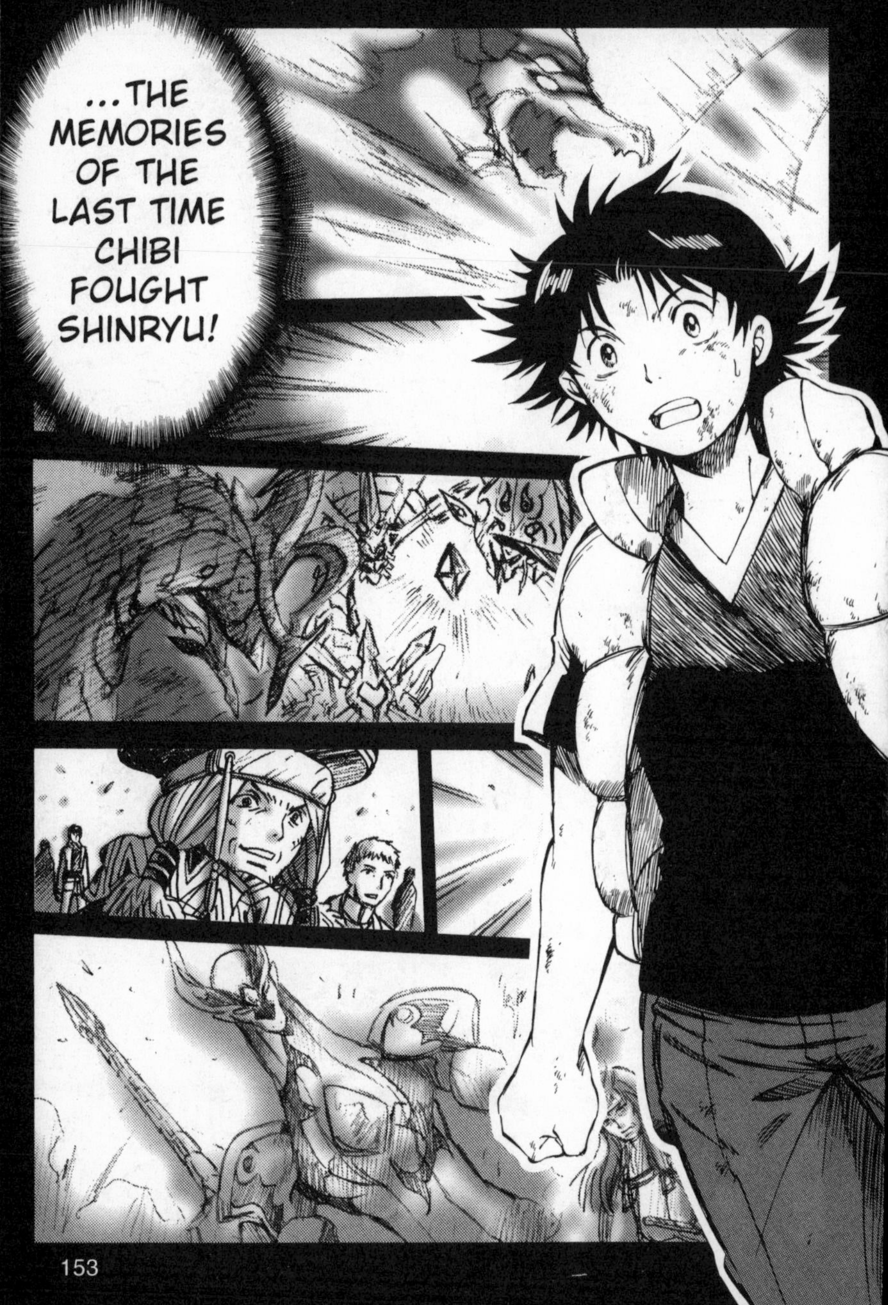
...THE MEMORIES OF THE LAST TIME CHIBI FOUGHT SHINRYU!

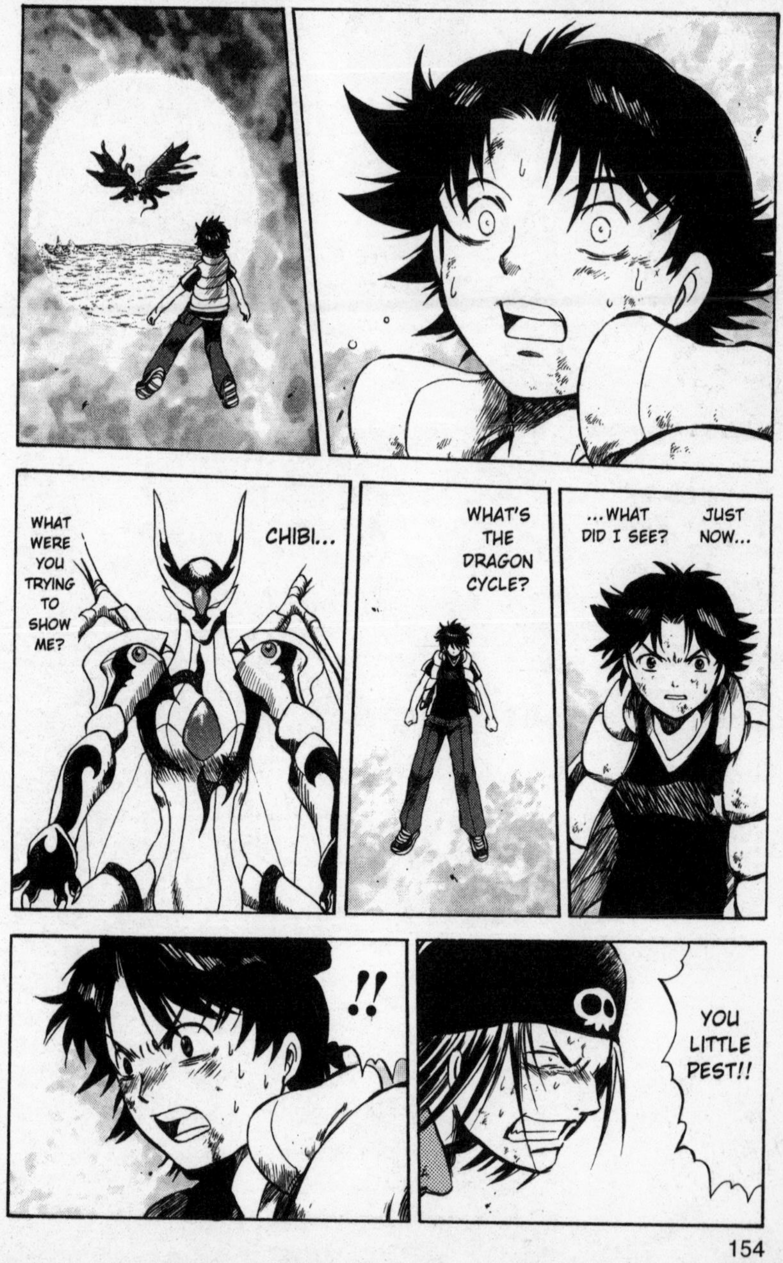
JUST NOW...
...WHAT DID I SEE?
WHAT'S THE DRAGON CYCLE?
CHIBI...
WHAT WERE YOU TRYING TO SHOW ME?
YOU LITTLE PEST!!
!!

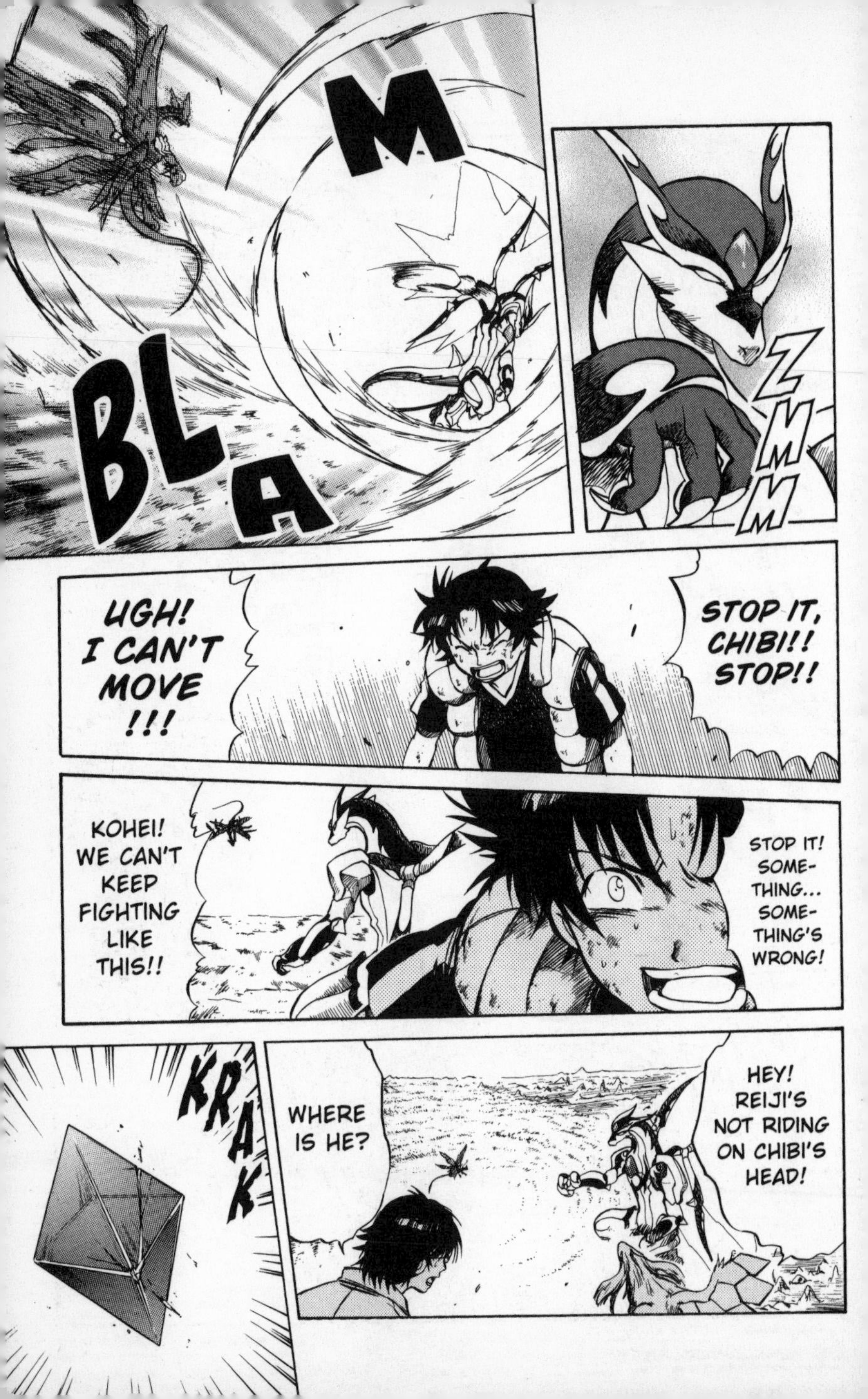
ZMMMM
BLAM
STOP IT, CHIBI!! STOP!!
UGH! I CAN'T MOVE!!!
STOP IT! SOMETHING... SOMETHING'S WRONG!
KOHEI! WE CAN'T KEEP FIGHTING LIKE THIS!!
HEY! REIJI'S NOT RIDING ON CHIBI'S HEAD!
WHERE IS HE?
KRAK

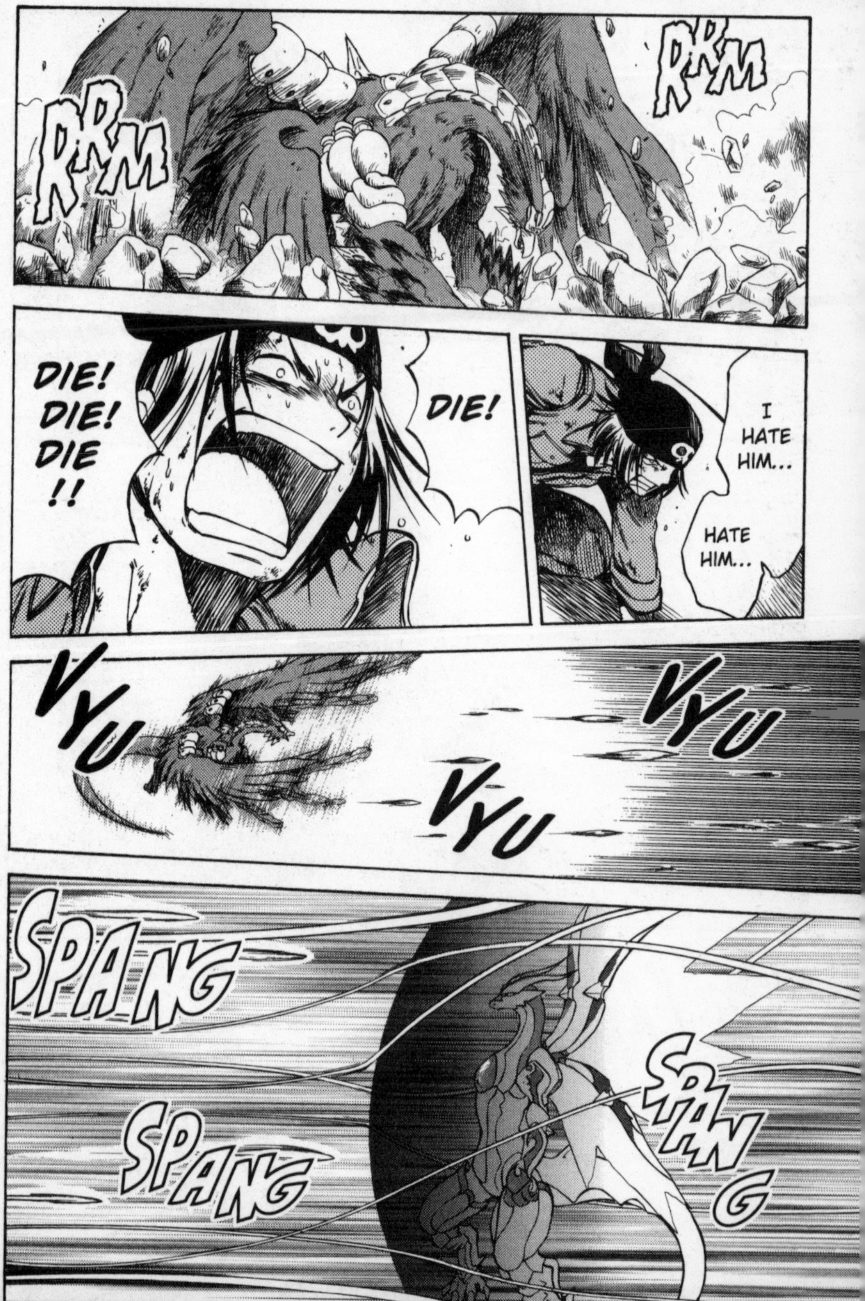
RRM
RRM
I HATE HIM...
HATE HIM...
DIE!
DIE! DIE! DIE!!
VYU
VYU
VYU
SPANG
SPANG
SPANG

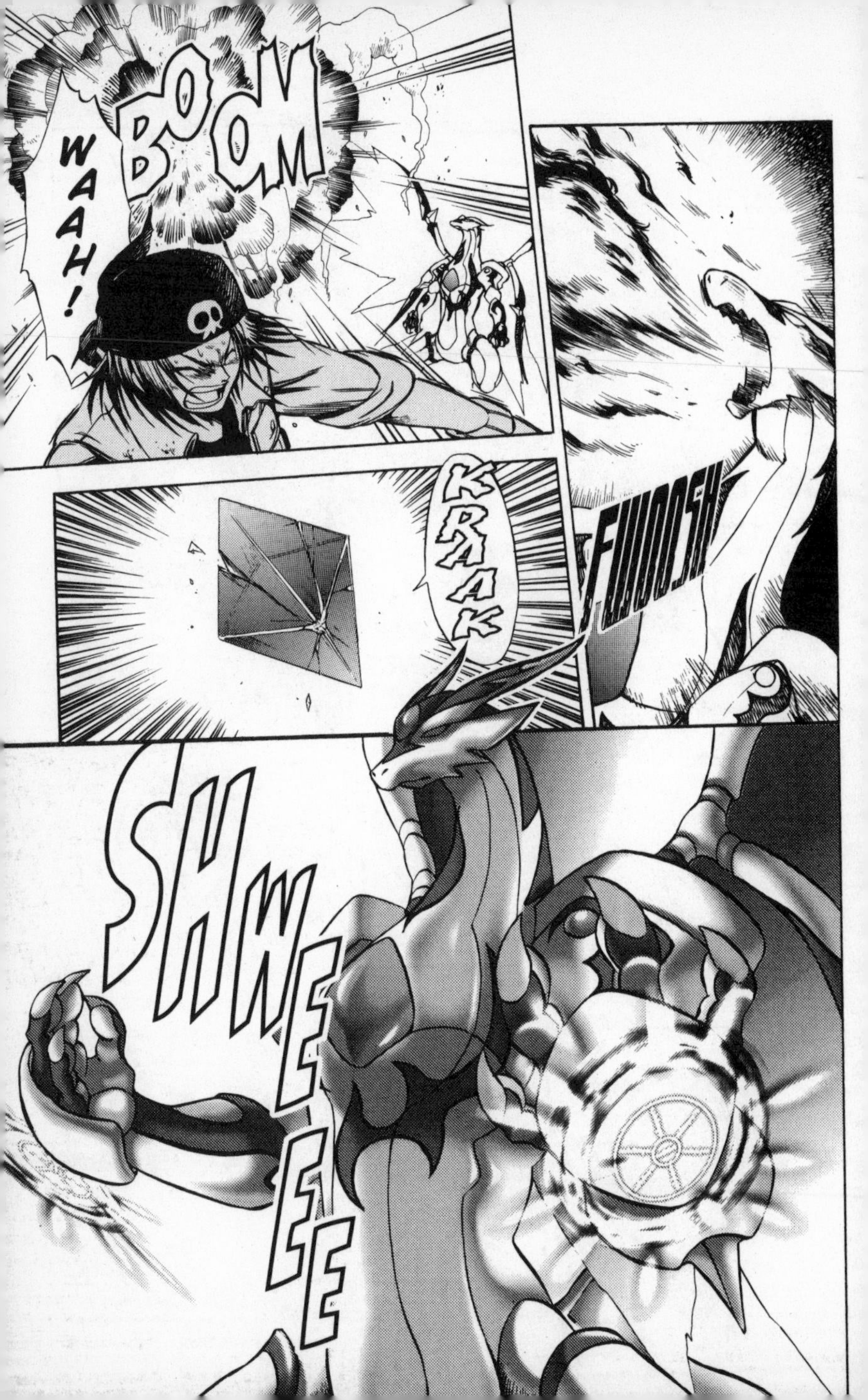
FWOOSH
BOOM
WAAH!
KRAAK
SHWEEEE

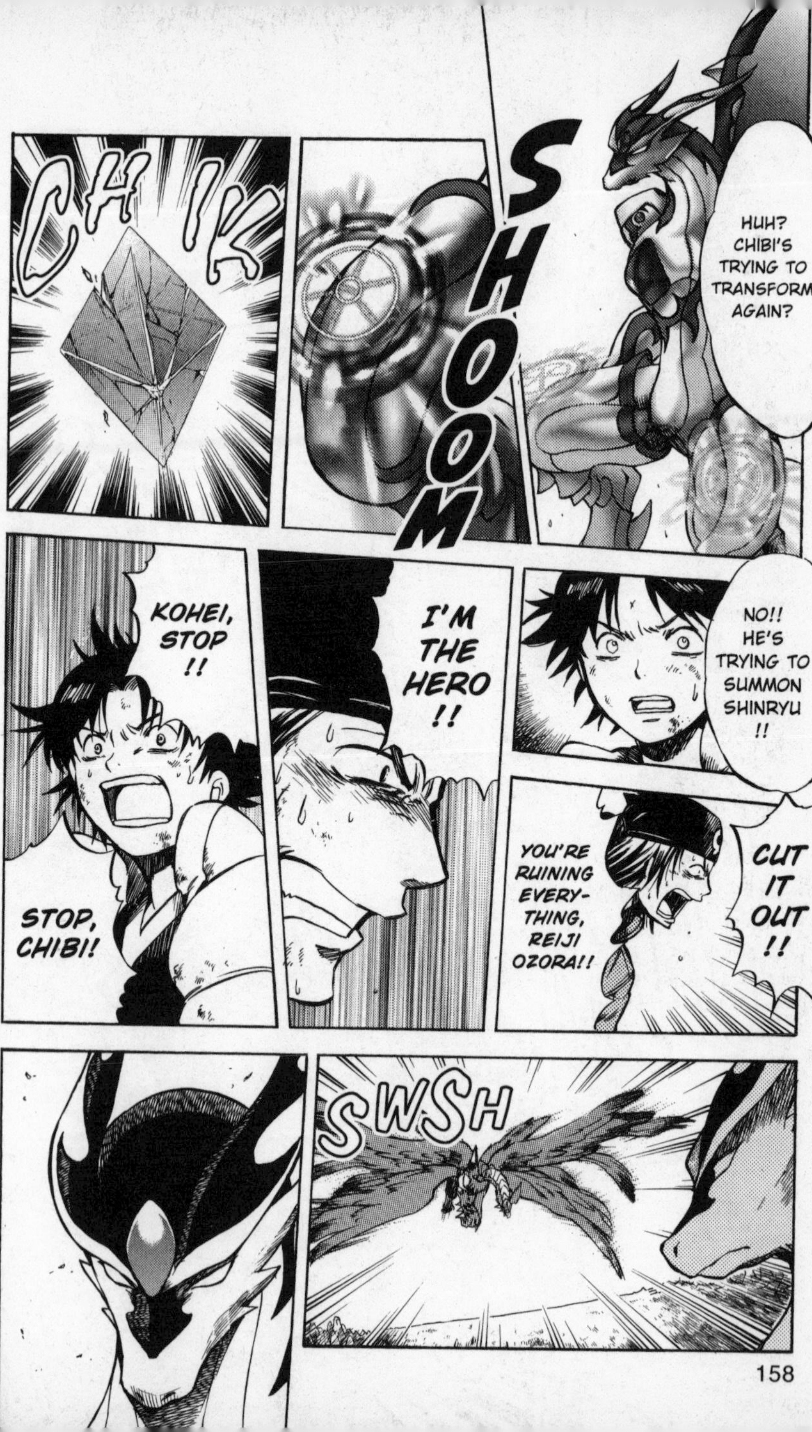
HUH? CHIBI'S TRYING TO TRANSFORM AGAIN?
SHOOM
CHIK
NO!! HE'S TRYING TO SUMMON SHINRYU !!
CUT IT OUT !!
YOU'RE RUINING EVERY-THING, REIJI OZORA!!
I'M THE HERO !!
KOHEI, STOP !!
STOP, CHIBI!
SWSH

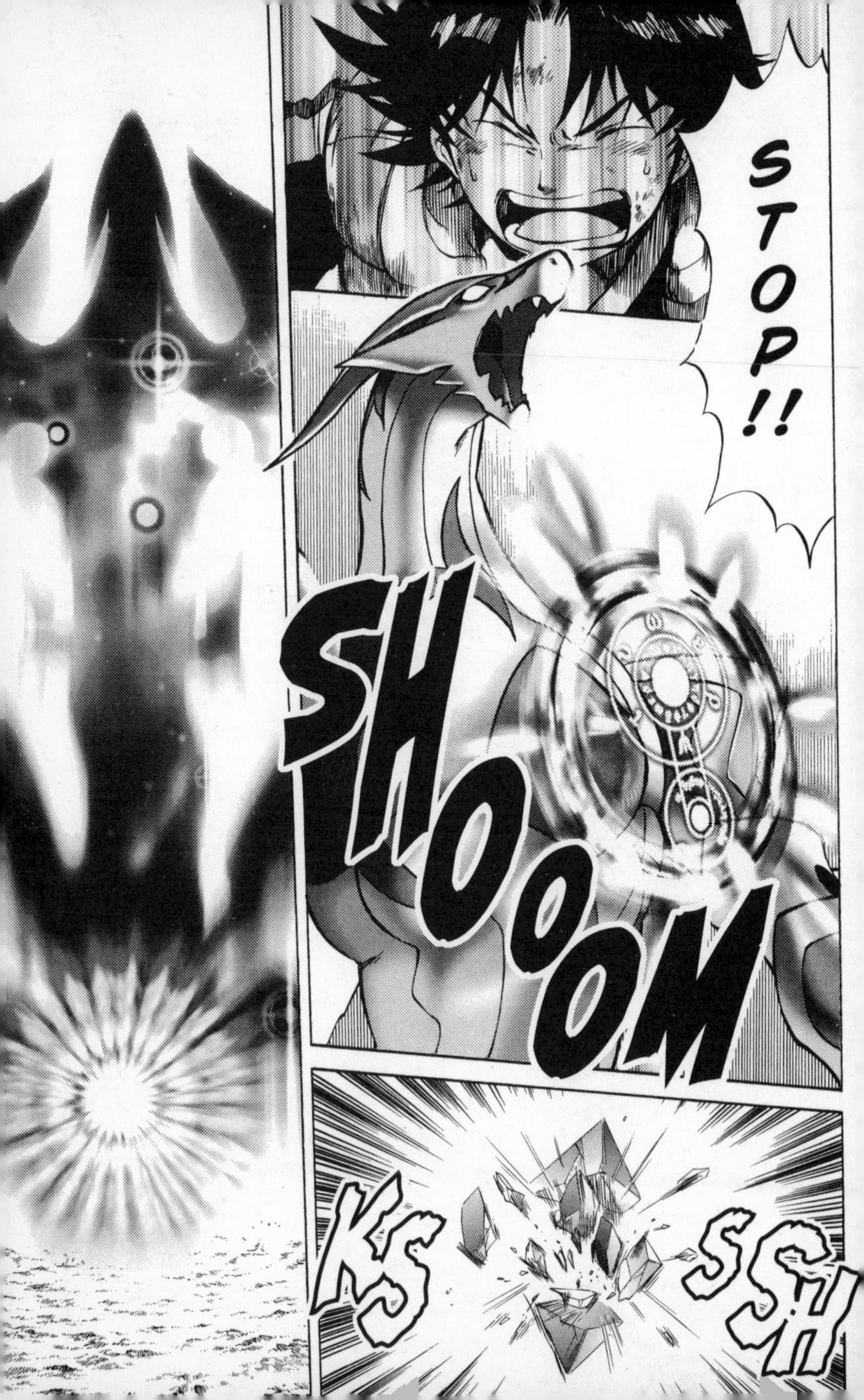
STOP!!
SHOOOM
KSSSH

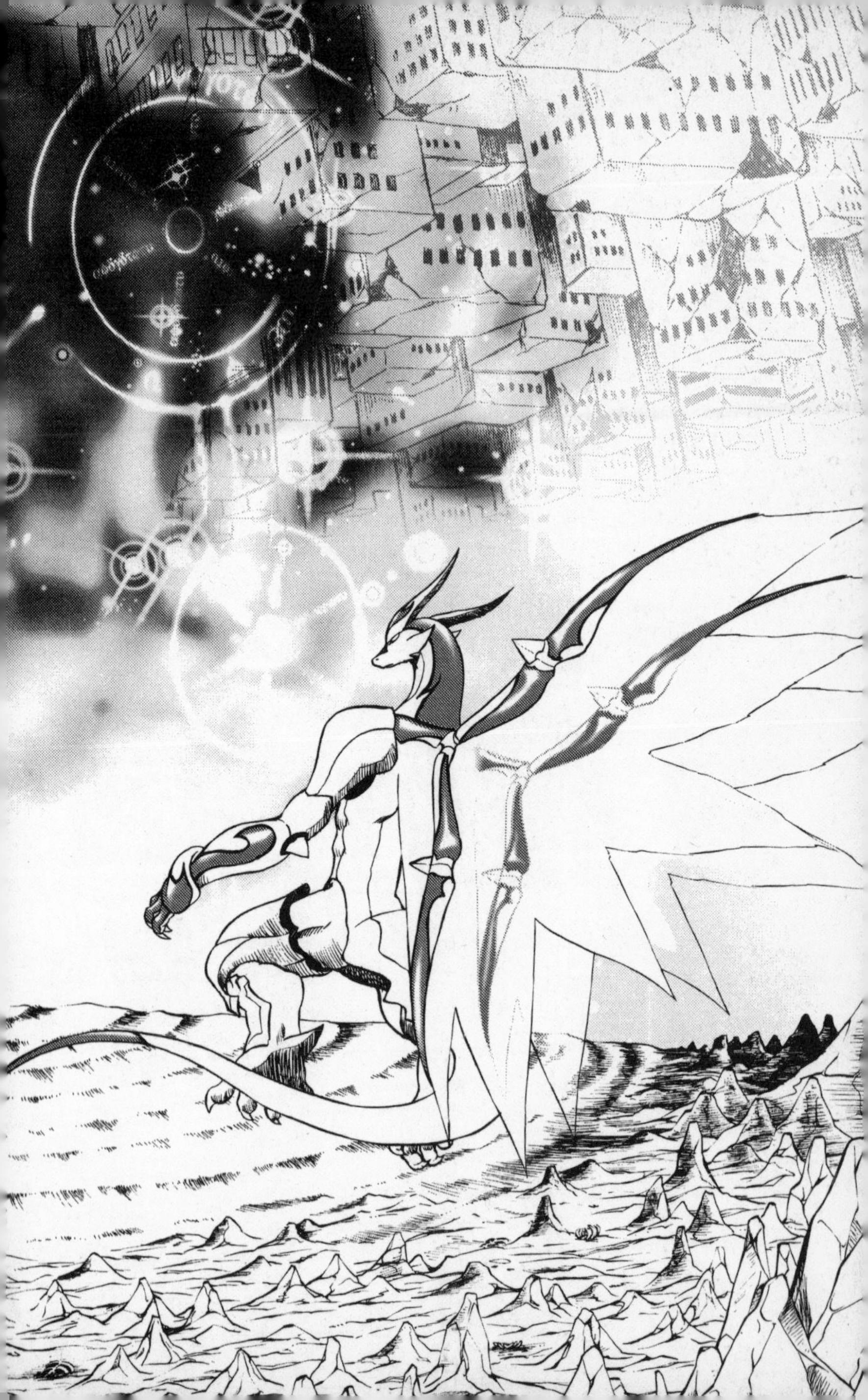

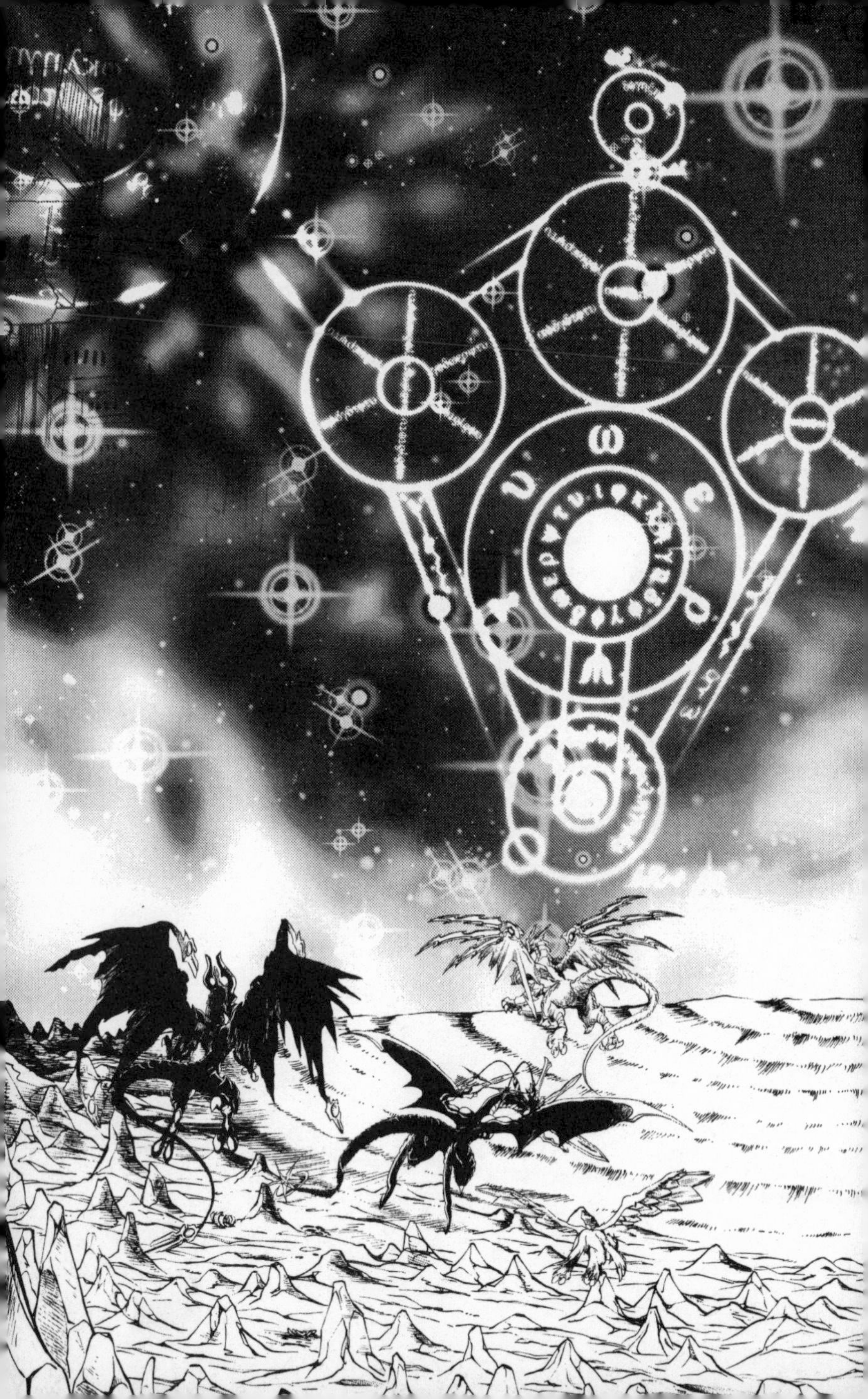

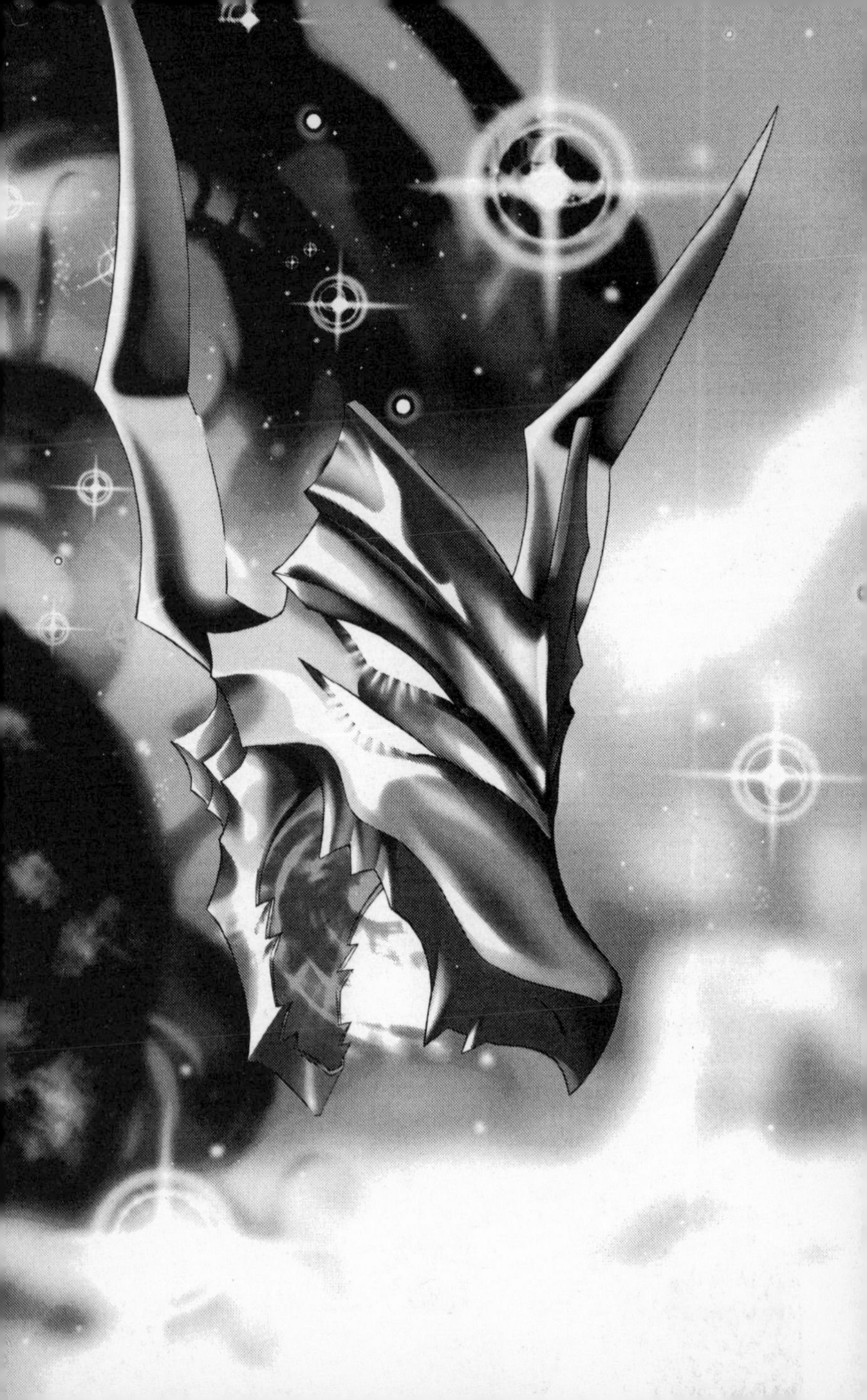

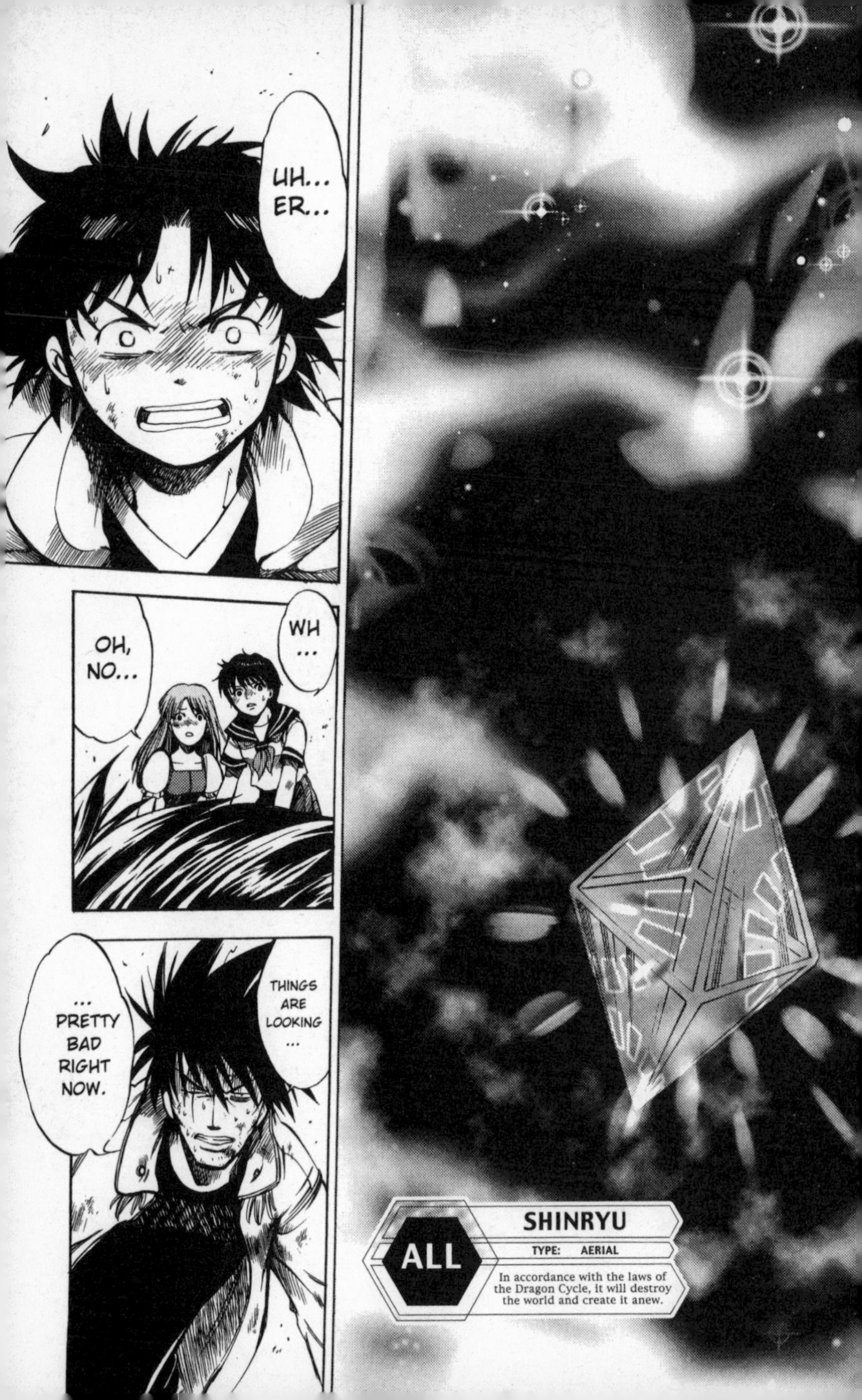
ALL
SHINRYU
TYPE: AERIAL
In accordance with the laws of the Dragon Cycle, it will destroy the world and create it anew.
UH... ER...
WH ...
OH, NO...
THINGS ARE LOOKING ...
... PRETTY BAD RIGHT NOW.

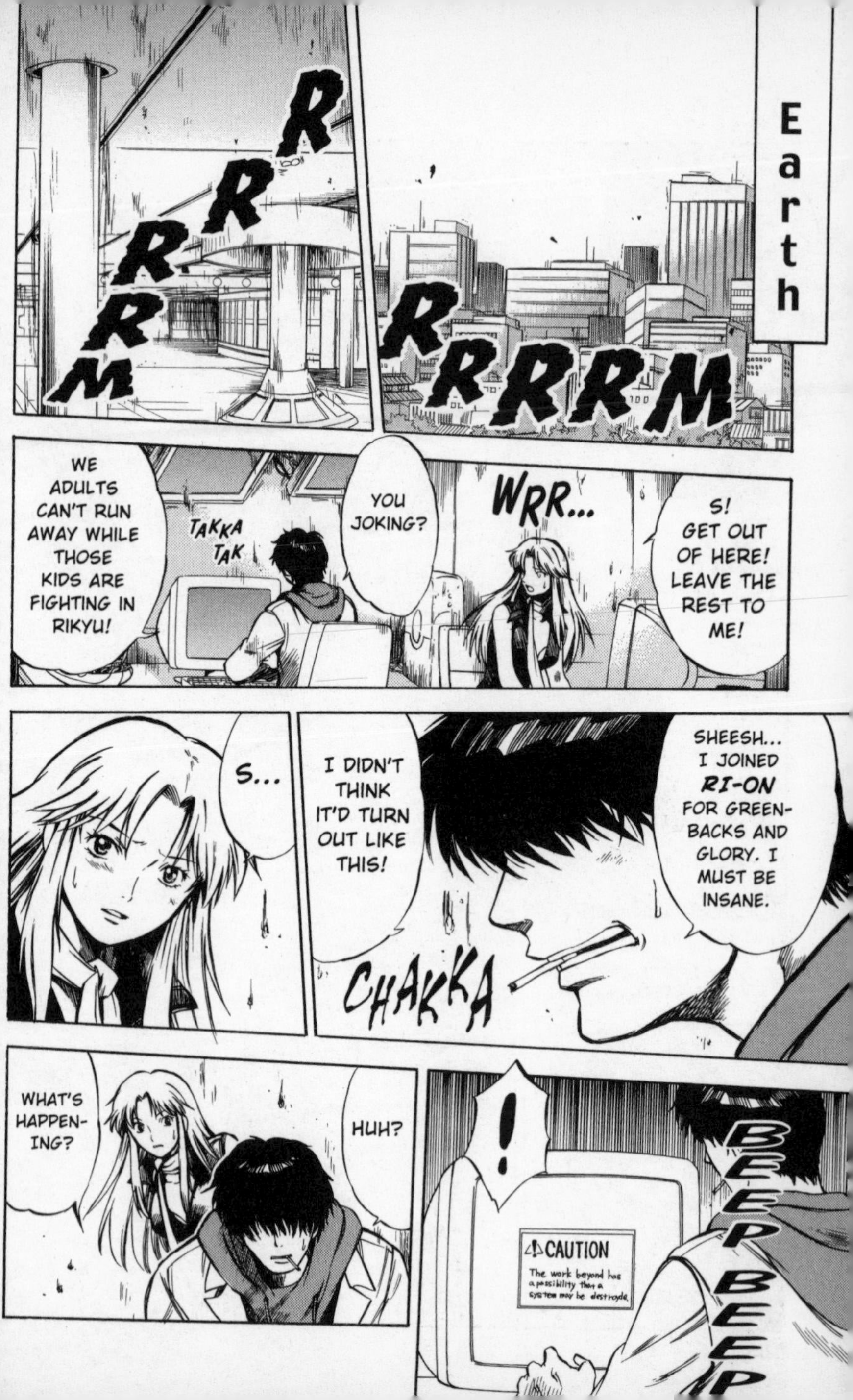
Earth
RRRRM
RRRRM
S! GET OUT OF HERE! LEAVE THE REST TO ME!
WRR...
YOU JOKING?
TAKKA TAK
WE ADULTS CAN'T RUN AWAY WHILE THOSE KIDS ARE FIGHTING IN RIKYU!
SHEESH... I JOINED RI-ON FOR GREEN-BACKS AND GLORY. I MUST BE INSANE.
I DIDN'T THINK IT'D TURN OUT LIKE THIS!
CHAKKA
S...
!
BEEP BEEP
⚠CAUTION
The work beyond has a possibility that a system may be destroyde.
HUH?
WHAT'S HAPPEN-ING?

READ THIS WAY

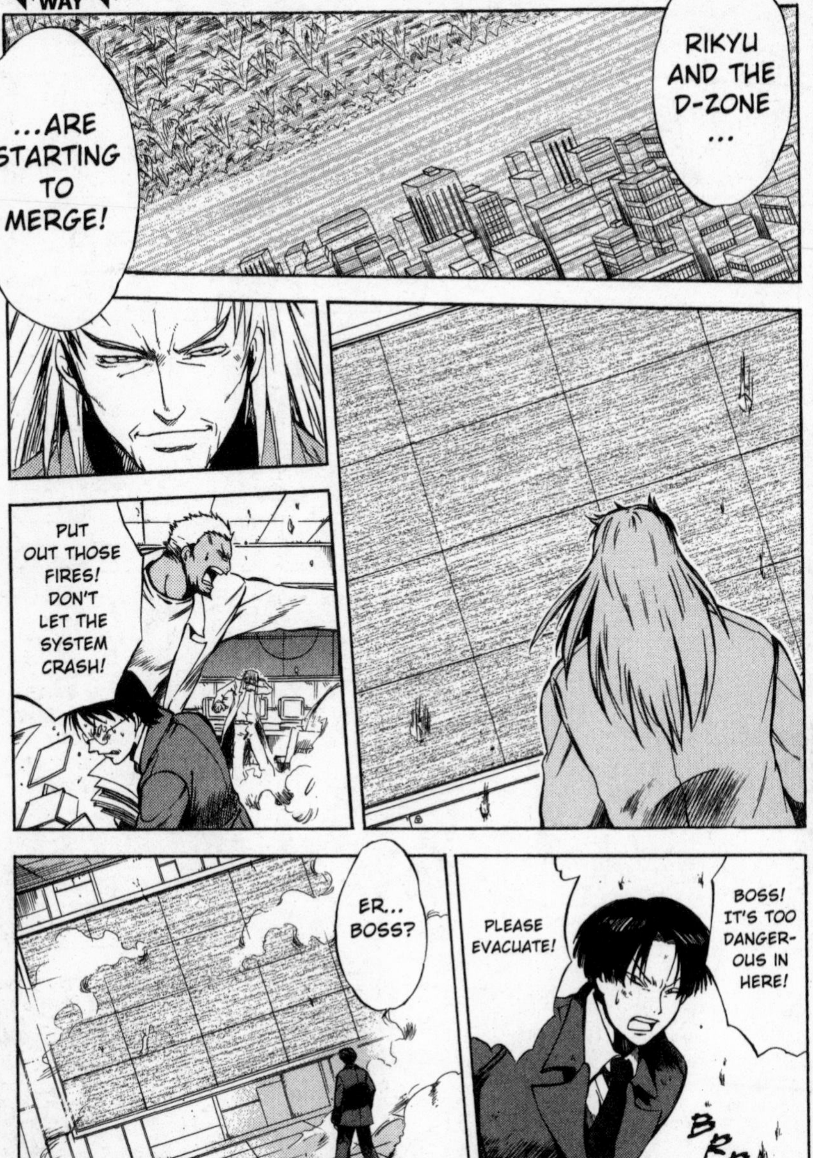
RIKYU AND THE D-ZONE...
...ARE STARTING TO MERGE!
PUT OUT THOSE FIRES! DON'T LET THE SYSTEM CRASH!
BOSS! IT'S TOO DANGER-OUS IN HERE!
PLEASE EVACUATE!
BRRR
ER... BOSS?

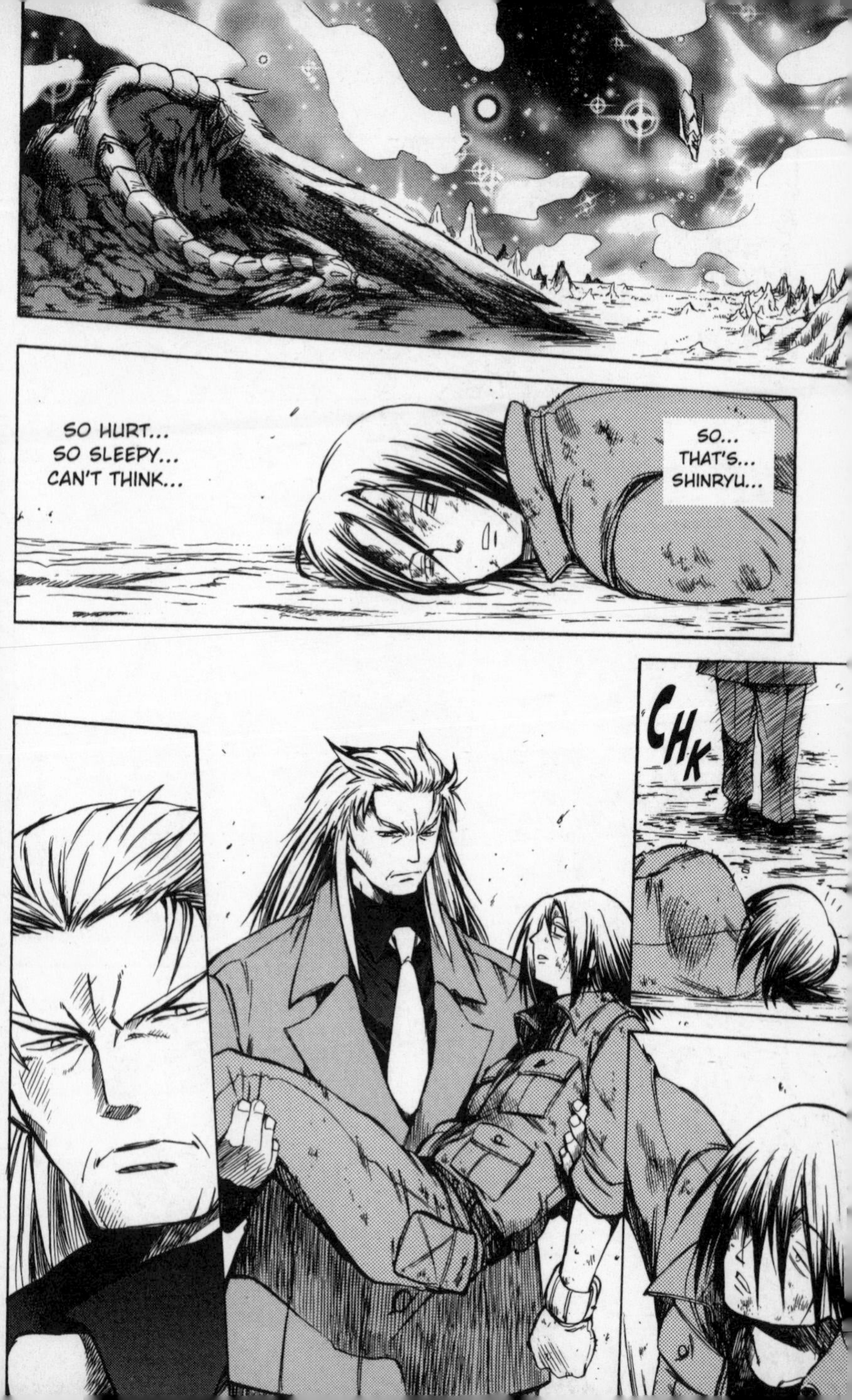
SO... THAT'S... SHINRYU...
SO HURT... SO SLEEPY... CAN'T THINK...
CHK

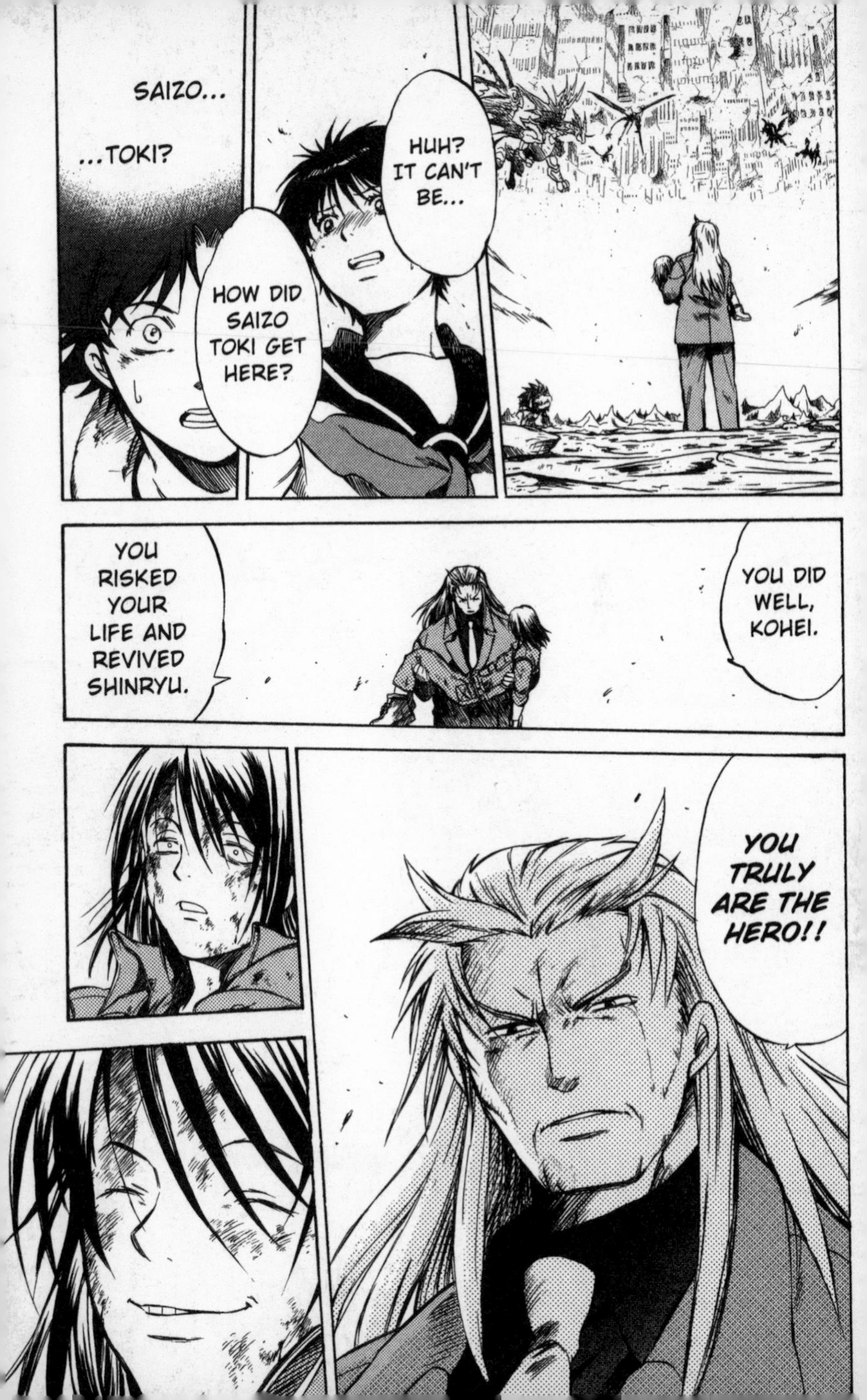
HUH? IT CAN'T BE...
HOW DID SAIZO TOKI GET HERE?
SAIZO...
...TOKI?
YOU DID WELL, KOHEI.
YOU RISKED YOUR LIFE AND REVIVED SHINRYU.
YOU TRULY ARE THE HERO!!

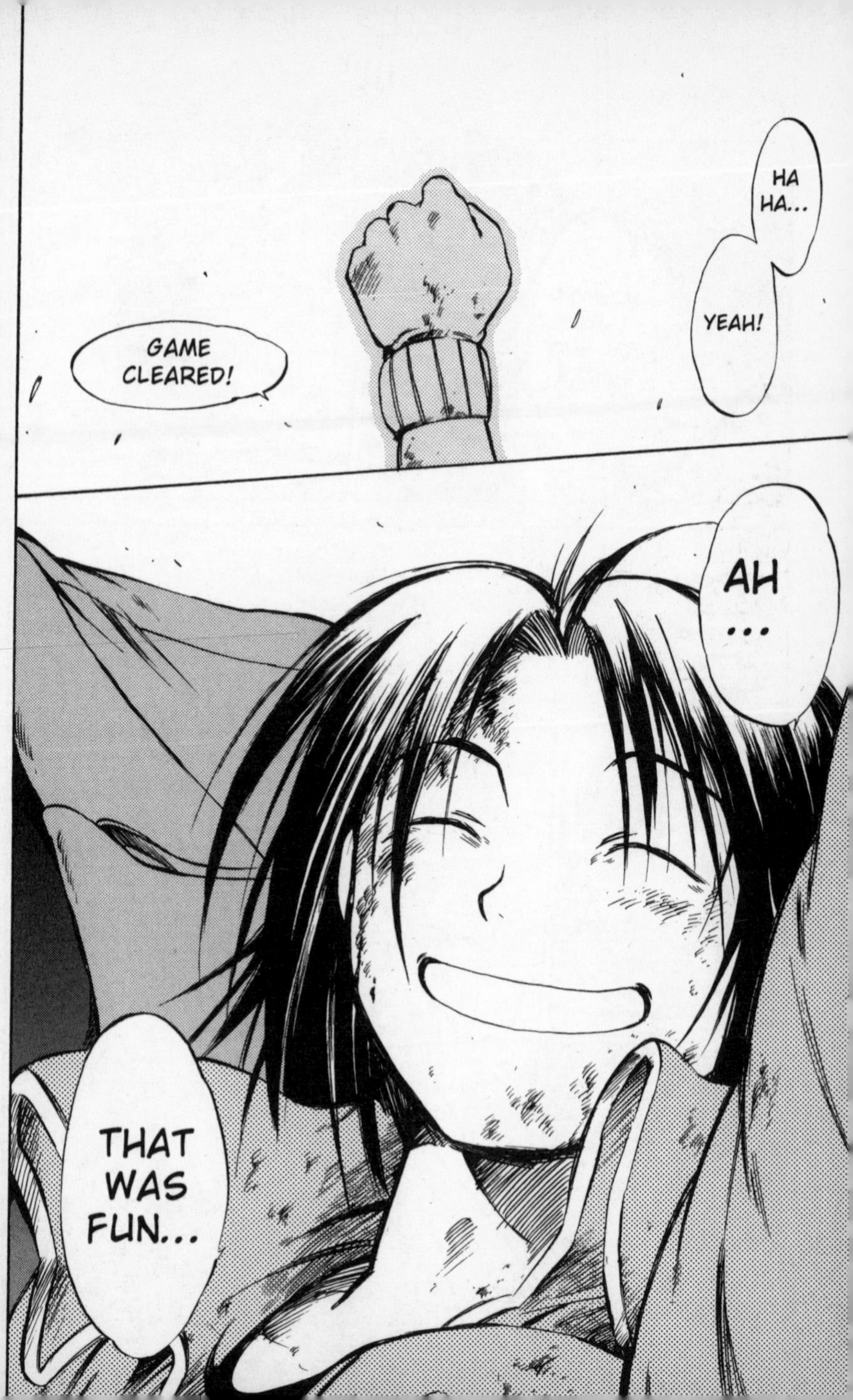
HA HA...
YEAH!
GAME CLEARED!
AH ...
THAT WAS FUN...

READ THIS WAY

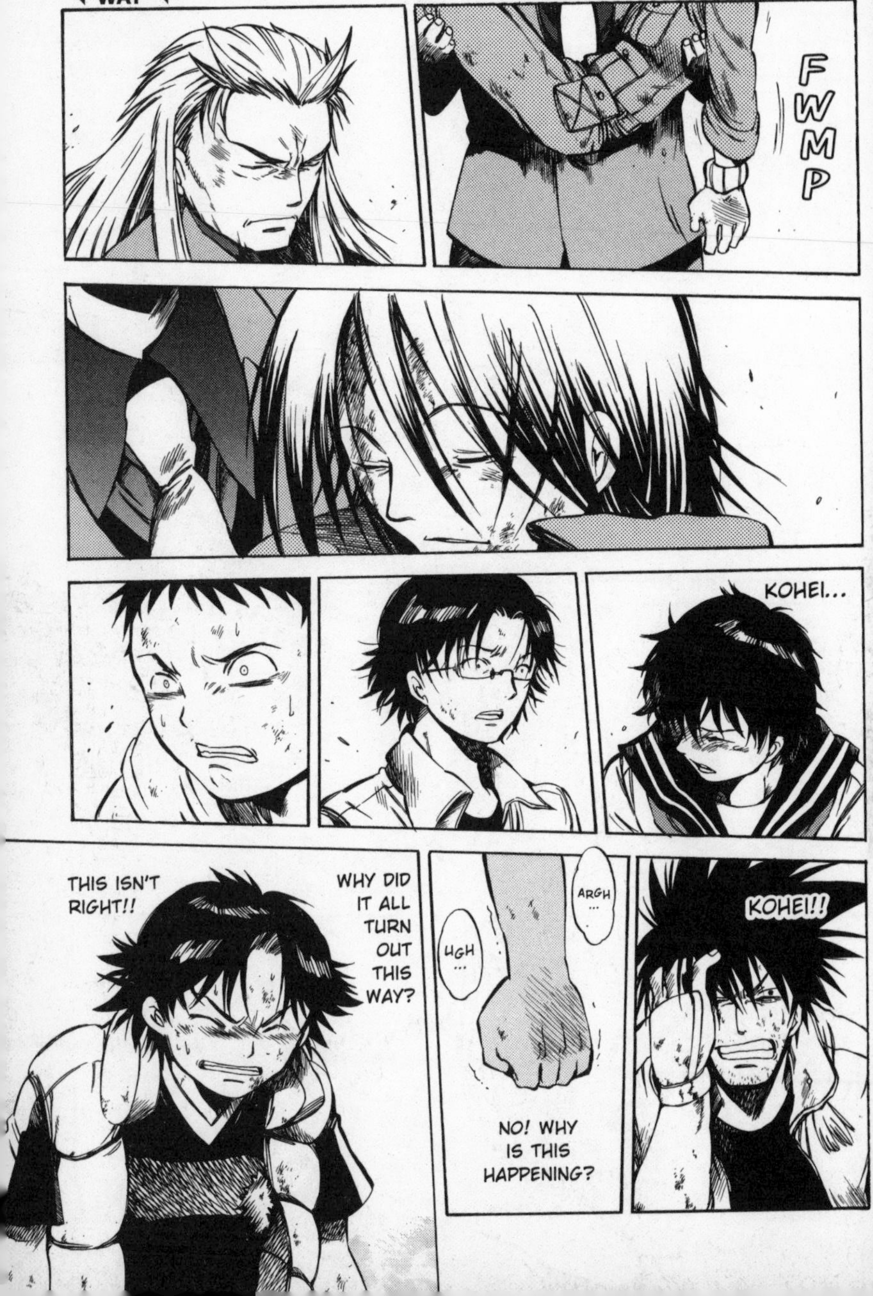
FWMP
KOHEI...
KOHEI!!
ARGH...
UGH...
NO! WHY IS THIS HAPPENING?
WHY DID IT ALL TURN OUT THIS WAY?
THIS ISN'T RIGHT!!

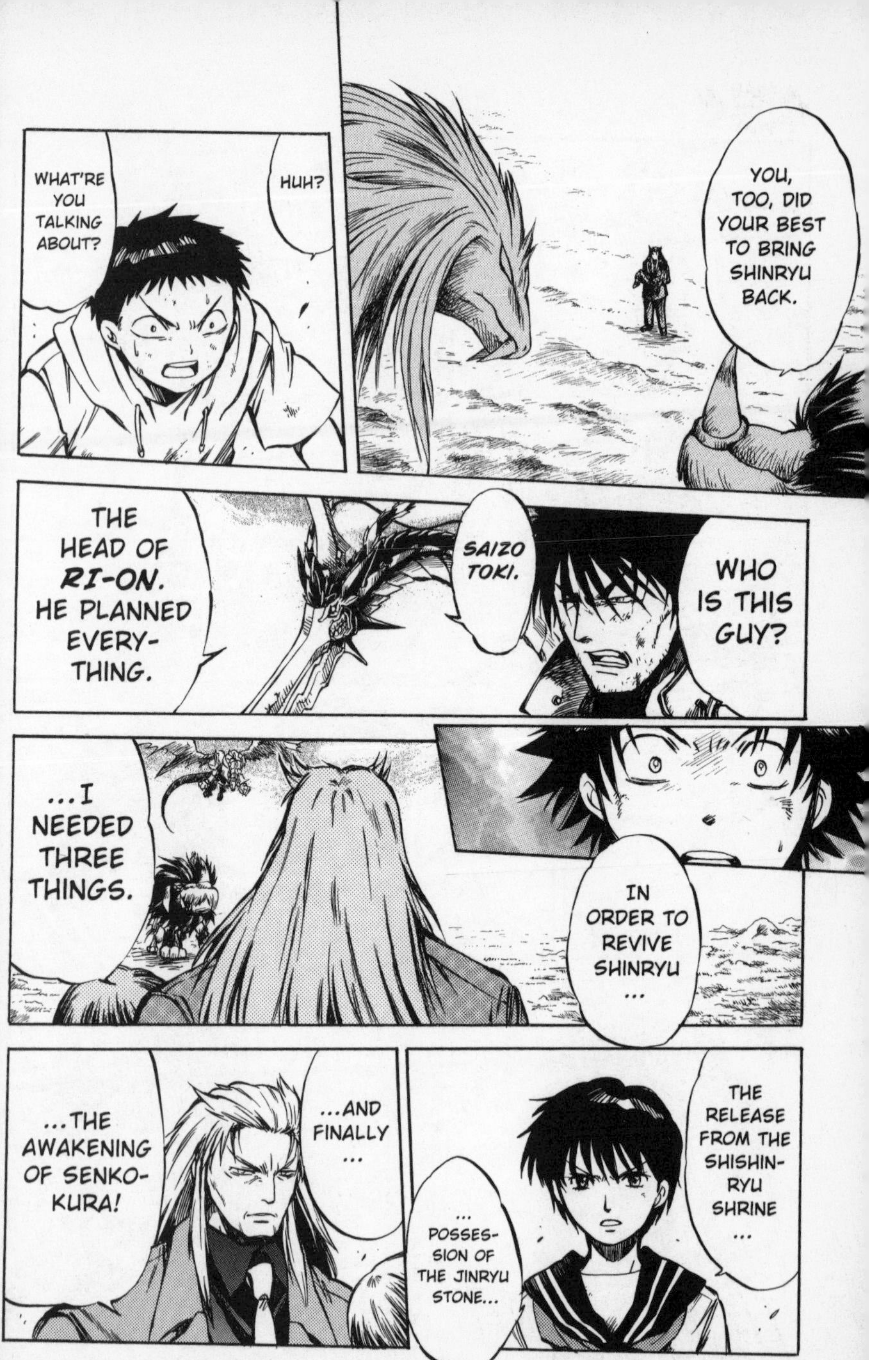
YOU, TOO, DID YOUR BEST TO BRING SHINRYU BACK.
HUH?
WHAT'RE YOU TALKING ABOUT?
WHO IS THIS GUY?
SAIZO TOKI.
THE HEAD OF RI-ON. HE PLANNED EVERY-THING.
IN ORDER TO REVIVE SHINRYU ...
...I NEEDED THREE THINGS.
THE RELEASE FROM THE SHISHIN-RYU SHRINE ...
... POSSES-SION OF THE JINRYU STONE...
...AND FINALLY ...
...THE AWAKENING OF SENKO-KURA!

READ THIS WAY

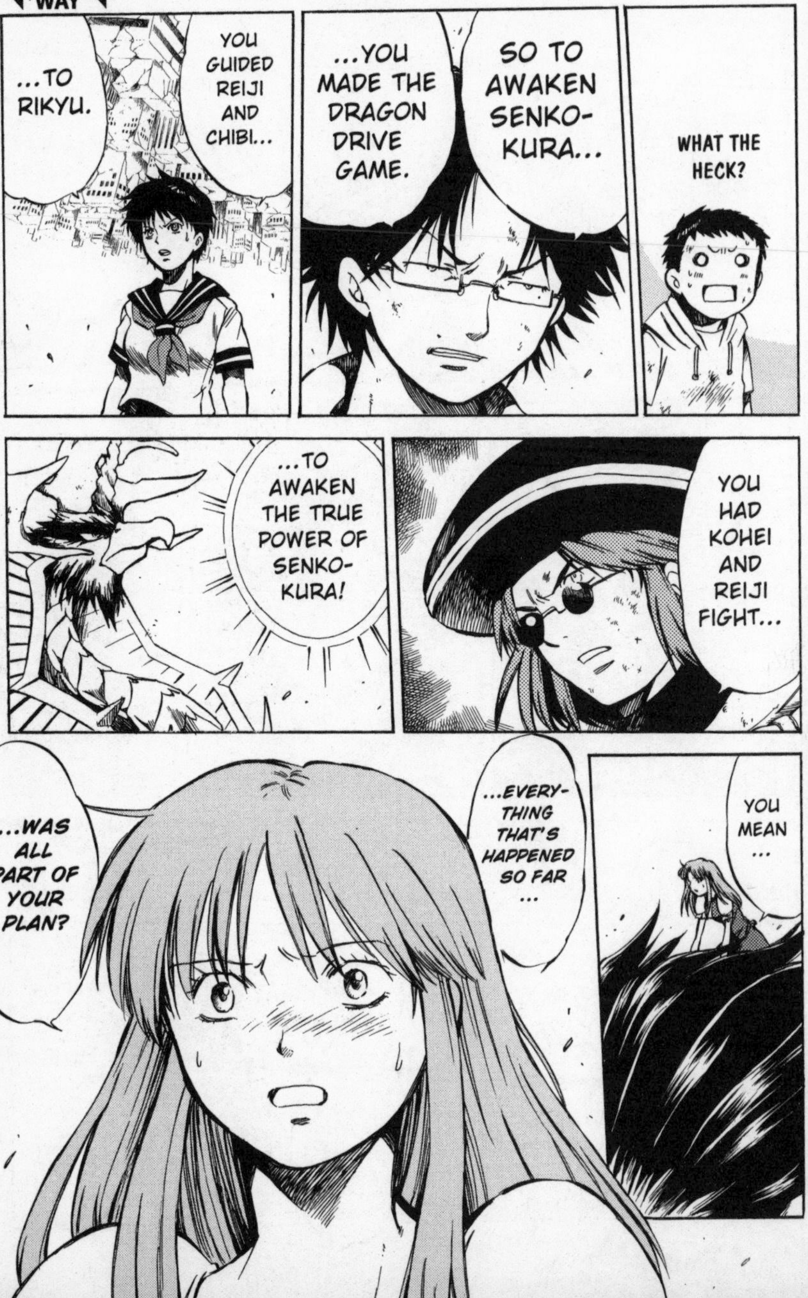
WHAT THE HECK?
SO TO AWAKEN SENKO-KURA...
...YOU MADE THE DRAGON DRIVE GAME.
YOU GUIDED REIJI AND CHIBI...
...TO RIKYU.
YOU HAD KOHEI AND REIJI FIGHT...
...TO AWAKEN THE TRUE POWER OF SENKO-KURA!
YOU MEAN...
...EVERYTHING THAT'S HAPPENED SO FAR...
...WAS ALL PART OF YOUR PLAN?

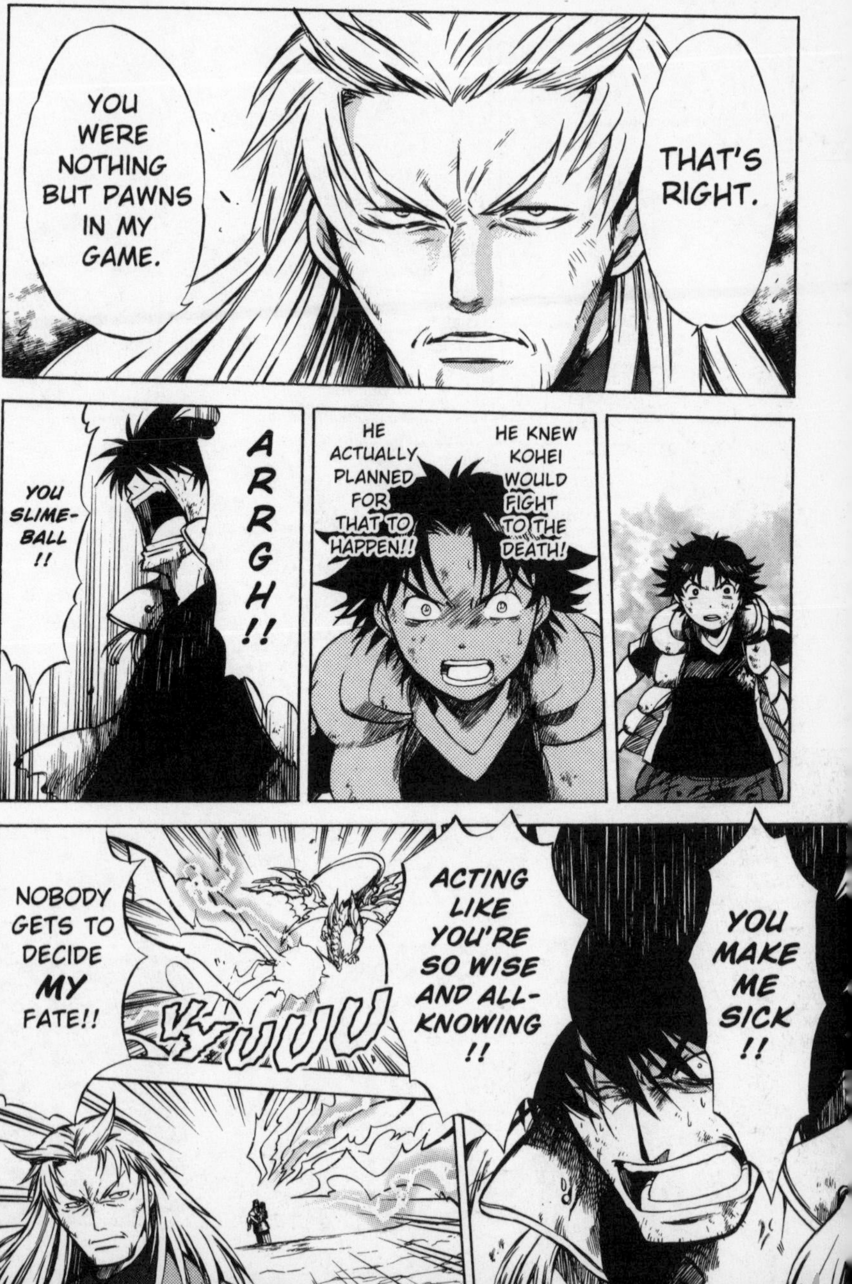
THAT'S RIGHT.
YOU WERE NOTHING BUT PAWNS IN MY GAME.
HE KNEW KOHEI WOULD FIGHT TO THE DEATH!
HE ACTUALLY PLANNED FOR THAT TO HAPPEN!!
ARRGH!!
YOU SLIME-BALL!!
YOU MAKE ME SICK!!
ACTING LIKE YOU'RE SO WISE AND ALL-KNOWING!!
NOBODY GETS TO DECIDE MY FATE!!
VWUUU

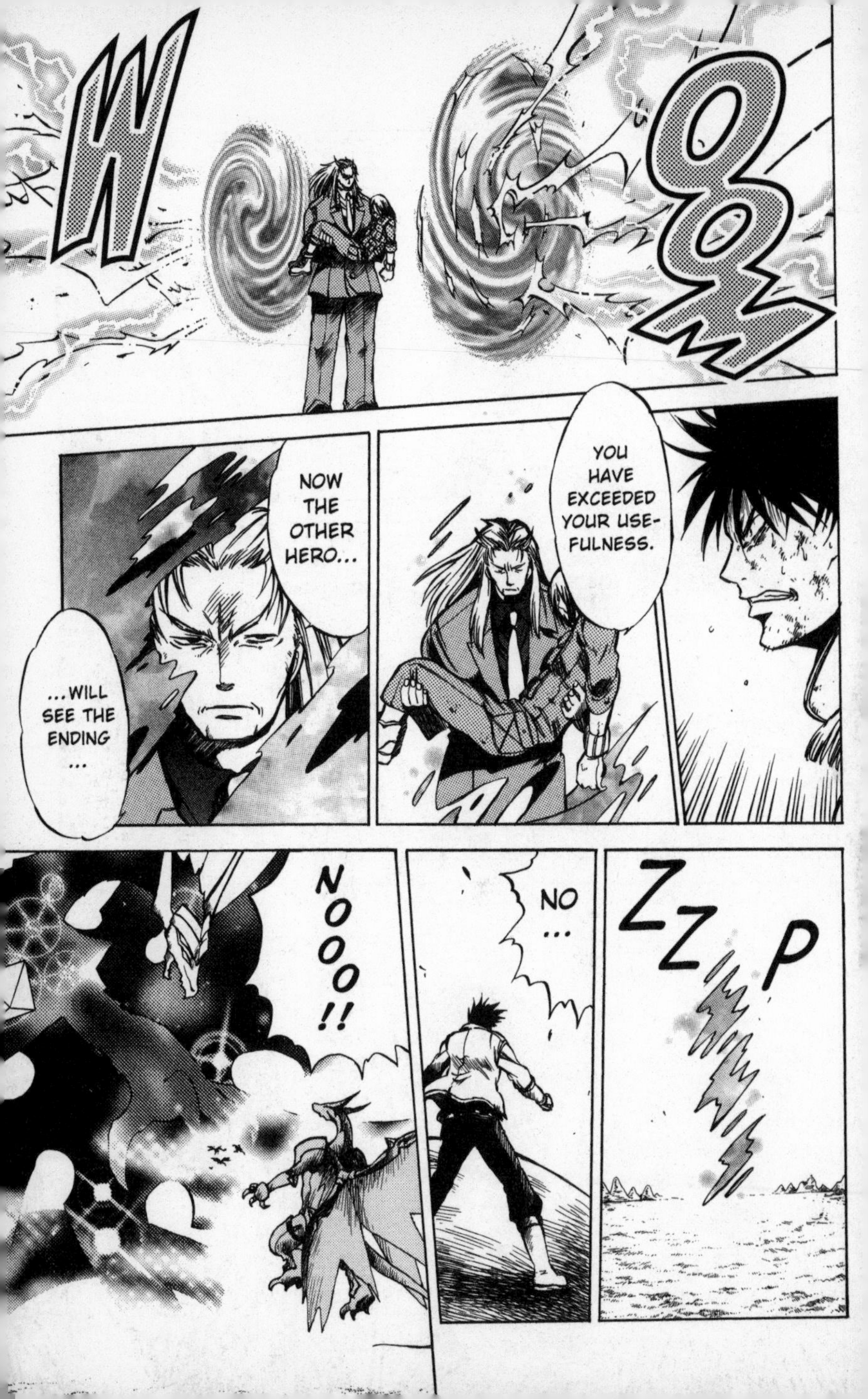
WOOOOM
YOU HAVE EXCEEDED YOUR USE-FULNESS.
NOW THE OTHER HERO...
...WILL SEE THE ENDING ...
ZZP
NO ...
NOOOO!!

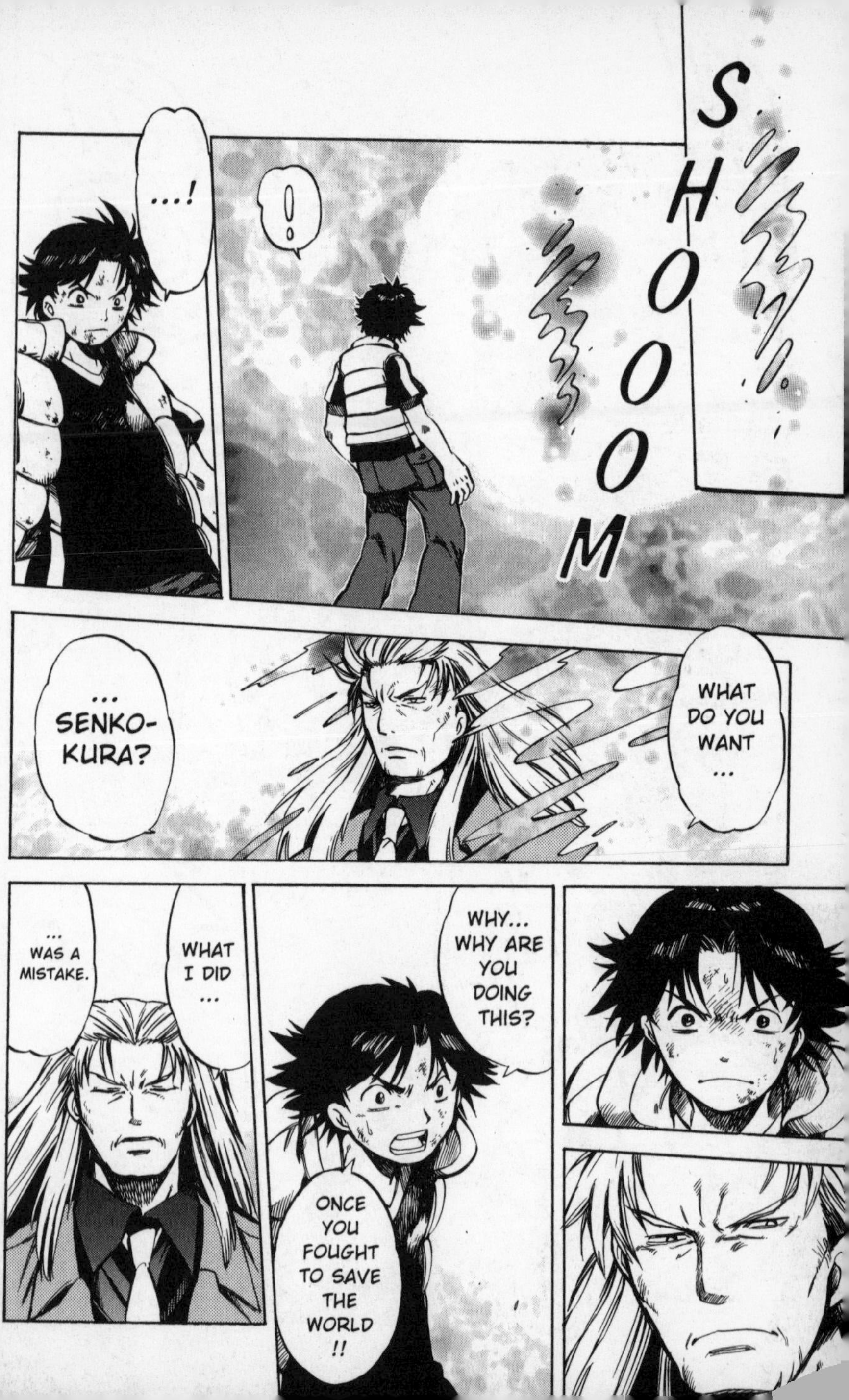
SHOOOOM
!
...!
WHAT DO YOU WANT ...
... SENKO-KURA?
WHY... WHY ARE YOU DOING THIS?
ONCE YOU FOUGHT TO SAVE THE WORLD !!
WHAT I DID ...
... WAS A MISTAKE.

READ THIS WAY

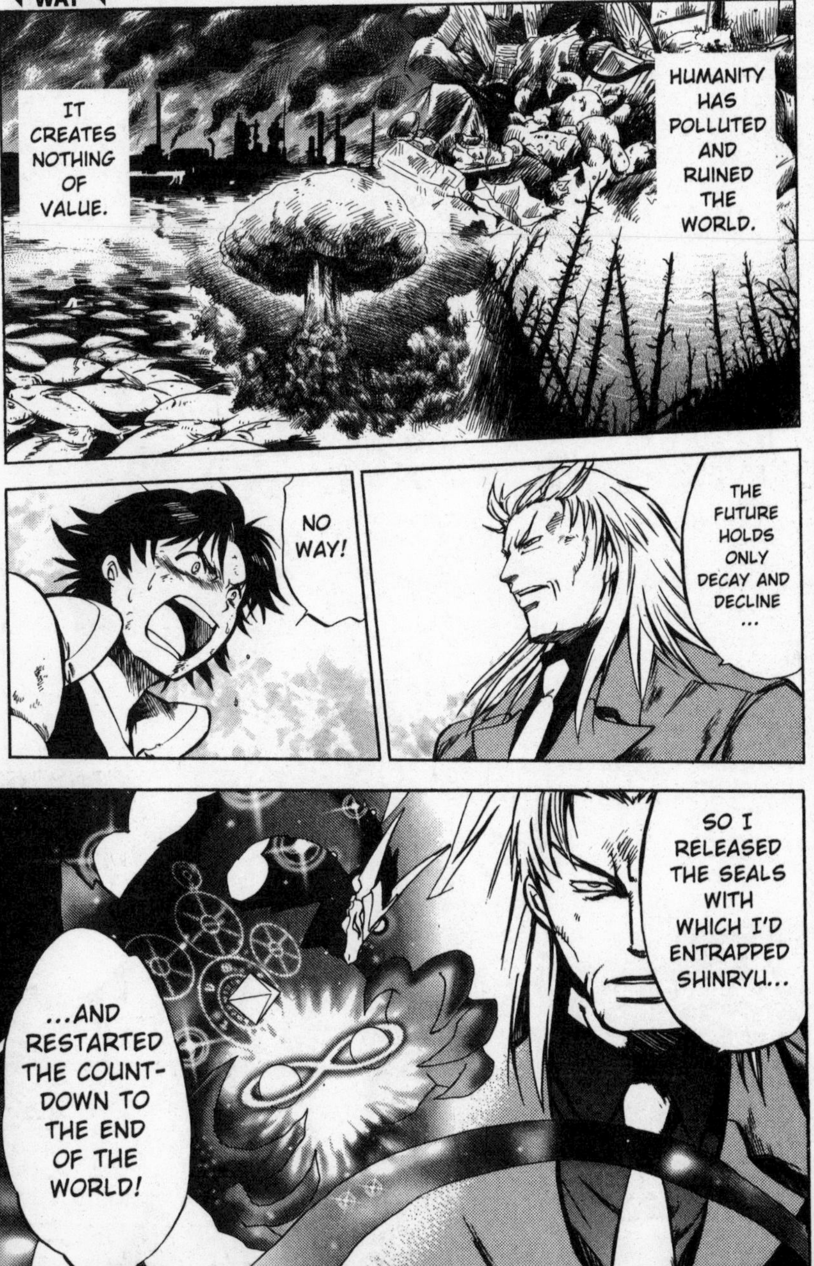
HUMANITY HAS POLLUTED AND RUINED THE WORLD.
IT CREATES NOTHING OF VALUE.
THE FUTURE HOLDS ONLY DECAY AND DECLINE ...
NO WAY!
SO I RELEASED THE SEALS WITH WHICH I'D ENTRAPPED SHINRYU...
...AND RESTARTED THE COUNT-DOWN TO THE END OF THE WORLD!

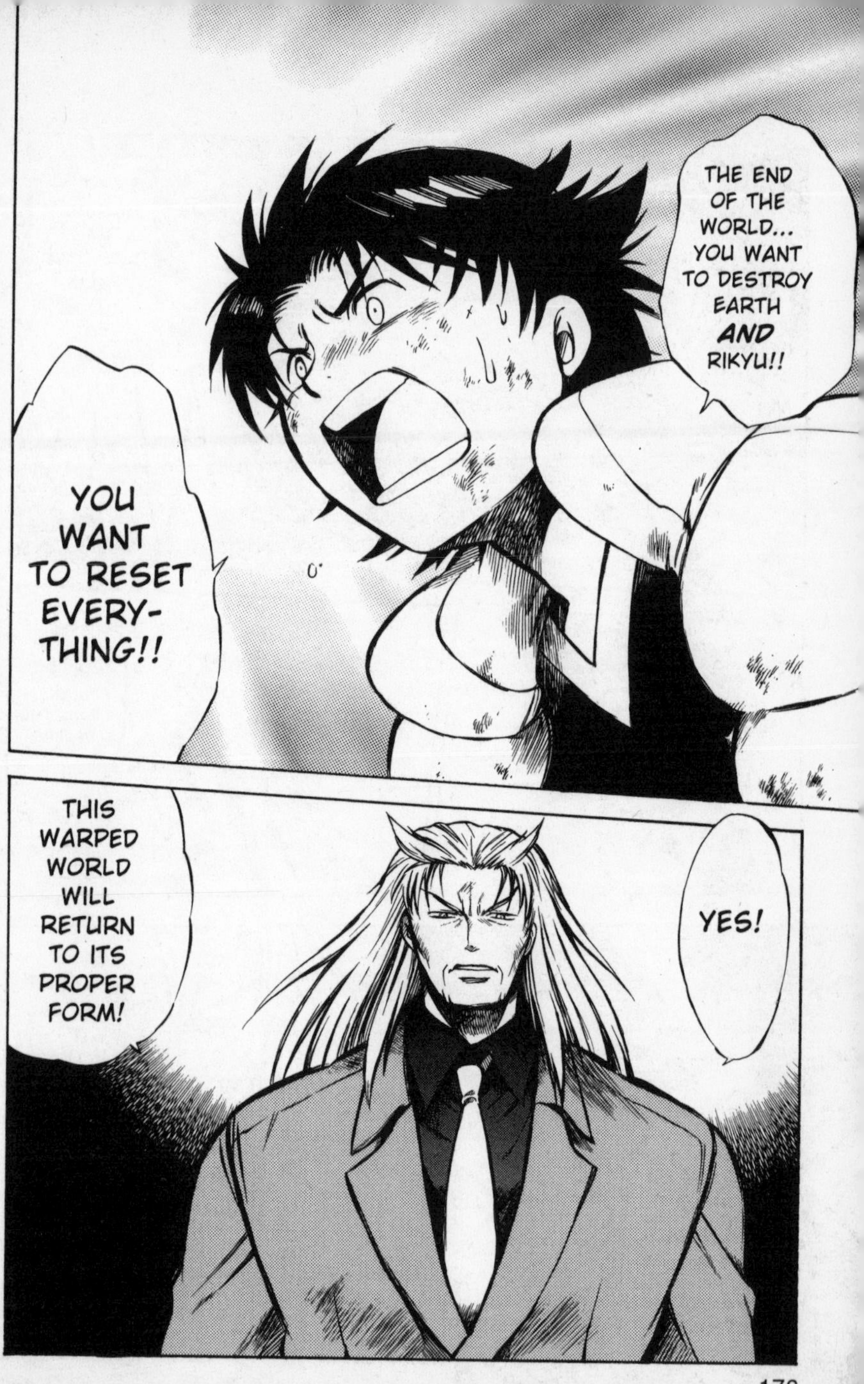
THE END OF THE WORLD... YOU WANT TO DESTROY EARTH AND RIKYU!!
YOU WANT TO RESET EVERY-THING!!
YES!
THIS WARPED WORLD WILL RETURN TO ITS PROPER FORM!

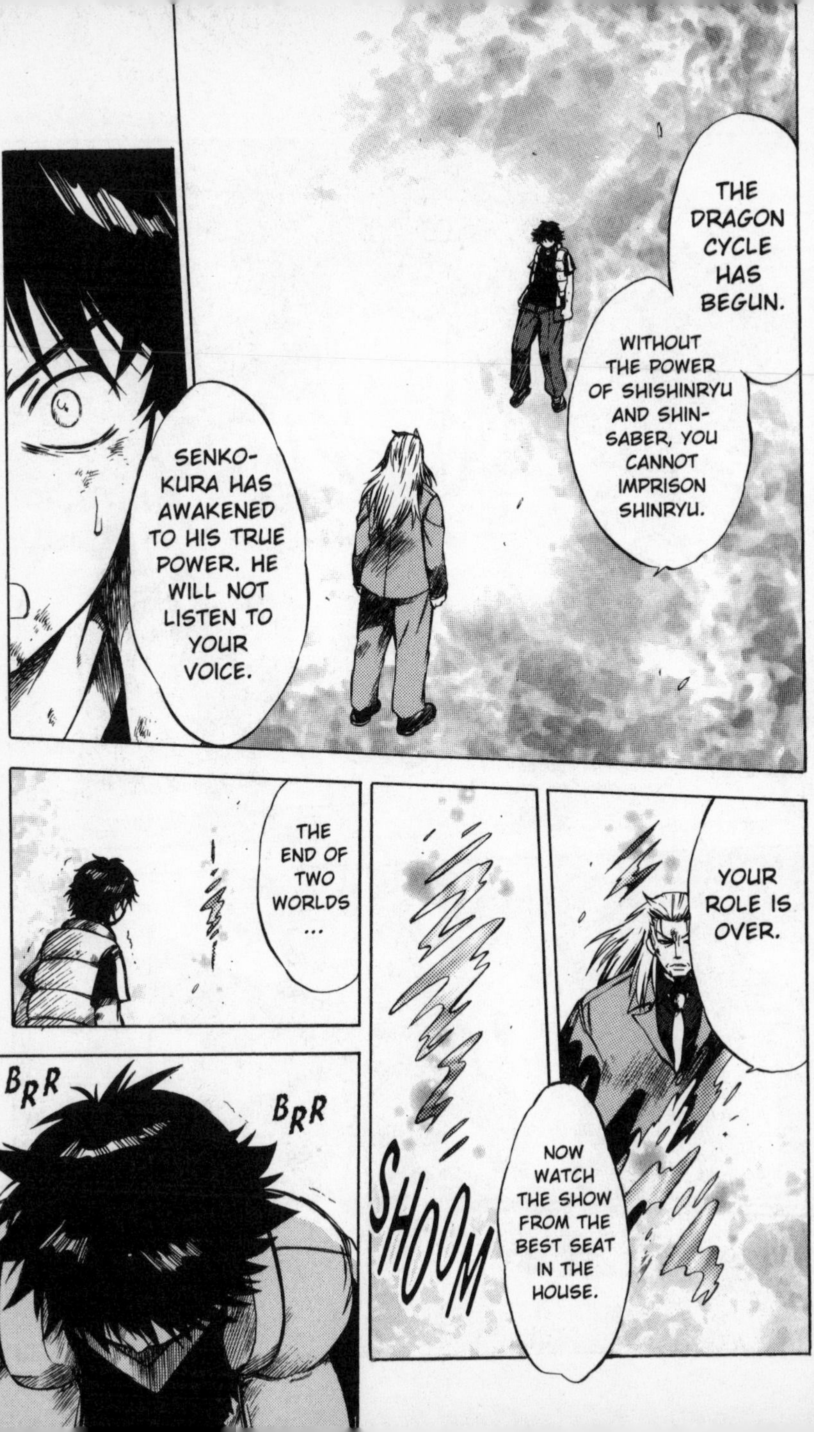
THE DRAGON CYCLE HAS BEGUN.
WITHOUT THE POWER OF SHISHINRYU AND SHINSABER, YOU CANNOT IMPRISON SHINRYU.
SENKOKURA HAS AWAKENED TO HIS TRUE POWER. HE WILL NOT LISTEN TO YOUR VOICE.
YOUR ROLE IS OVER.
NOW WATCH THE SHOW FROM THE BEST SEAT IN THE HOUSE.
SHOOM
THE END OF TWO WORLDS ...
BRR
BRR

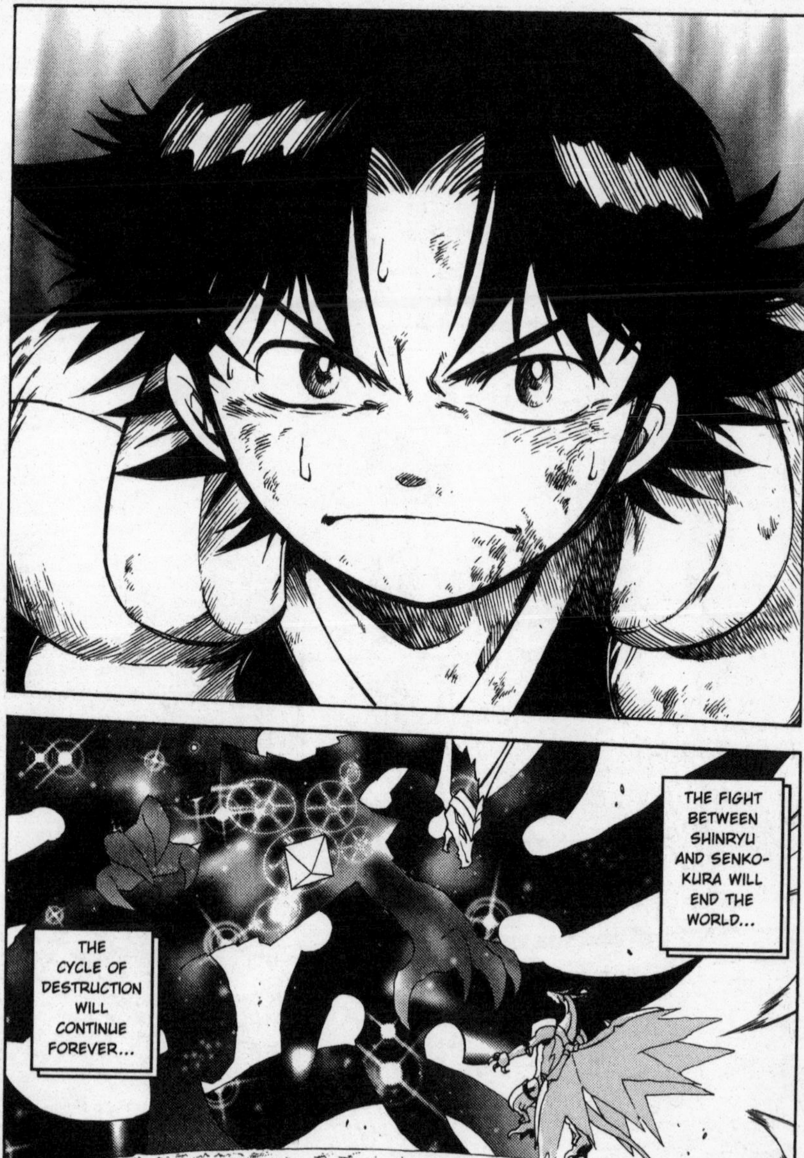
THE FIGHT BETWEEN SHINRYU AND SENKO-KURA WILL END THE WORLD...
THE CYCLE OF DESTRUCTION WILL CONTINUE FOREVER...

READ THIS WAY

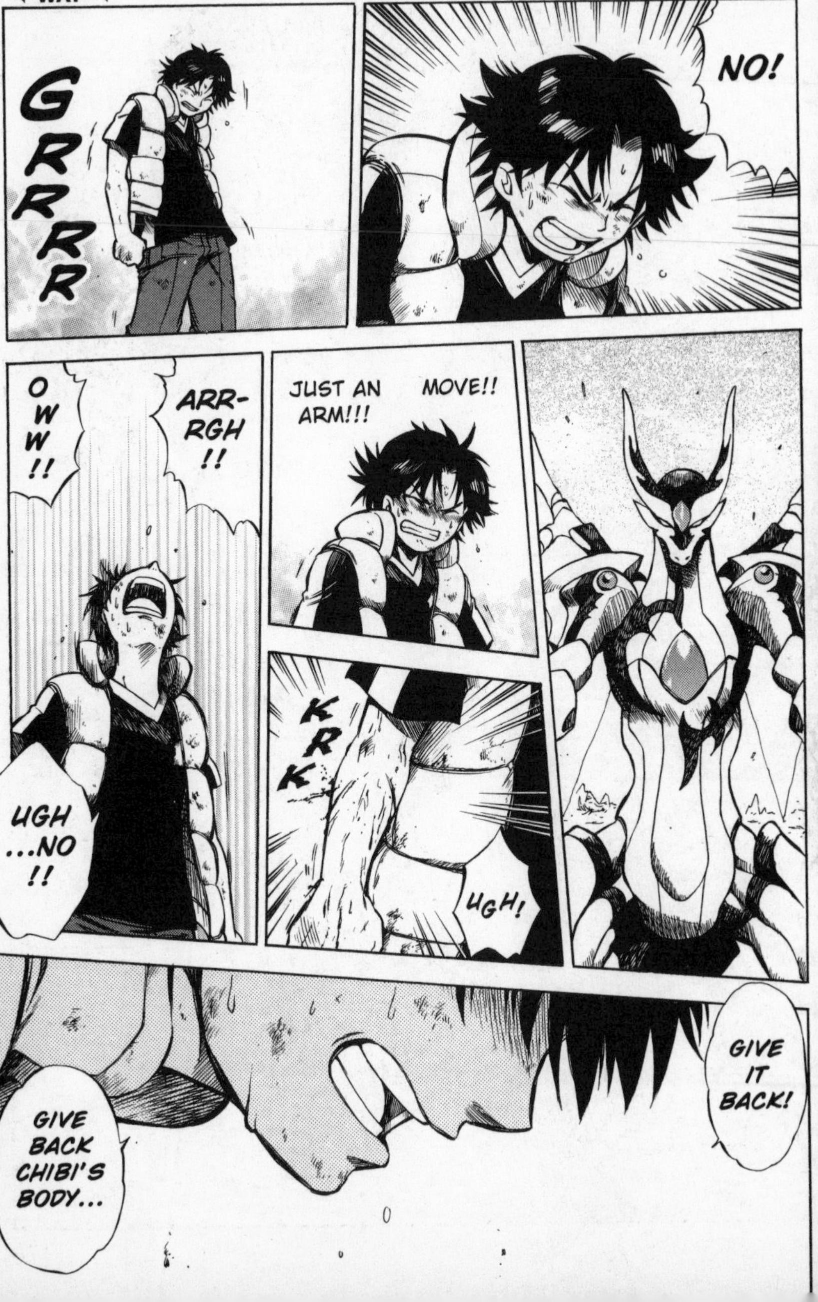
NO!
GRRRR
MOVE!!
JUST AN ARM!!!
KRK
UGH!
ARR-RGH!!
OWW!!
UGH...NO!!
GIVE IT BACK!
GIVE BACK CHIBI'S BODY...

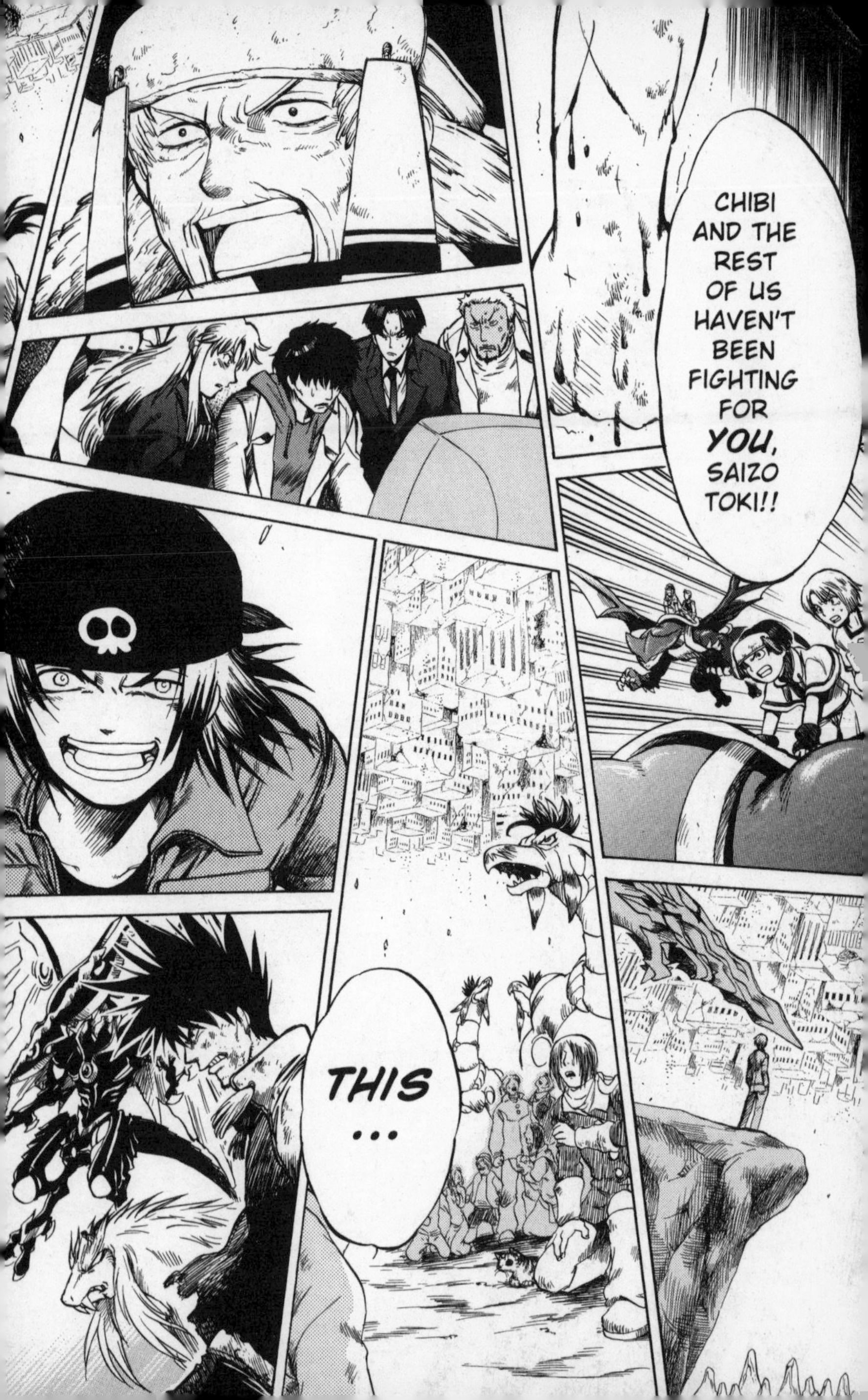
CHIBI AND THE REST OF US HAVEN'T BEEN FIGHTING FOR YOU, SAIZO TOKI!!
THIS ...

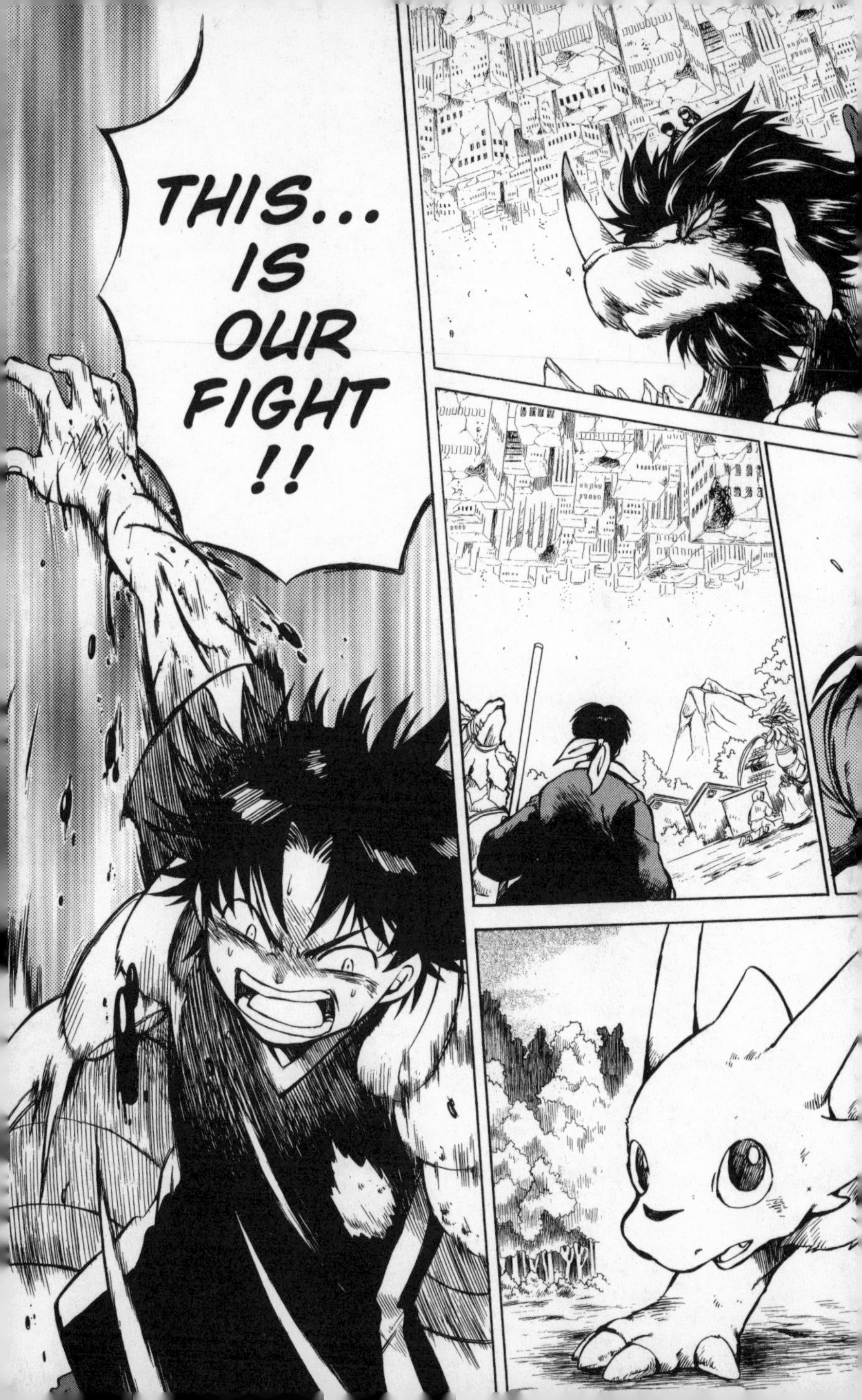
THIS... IS OUR FIGHT !!

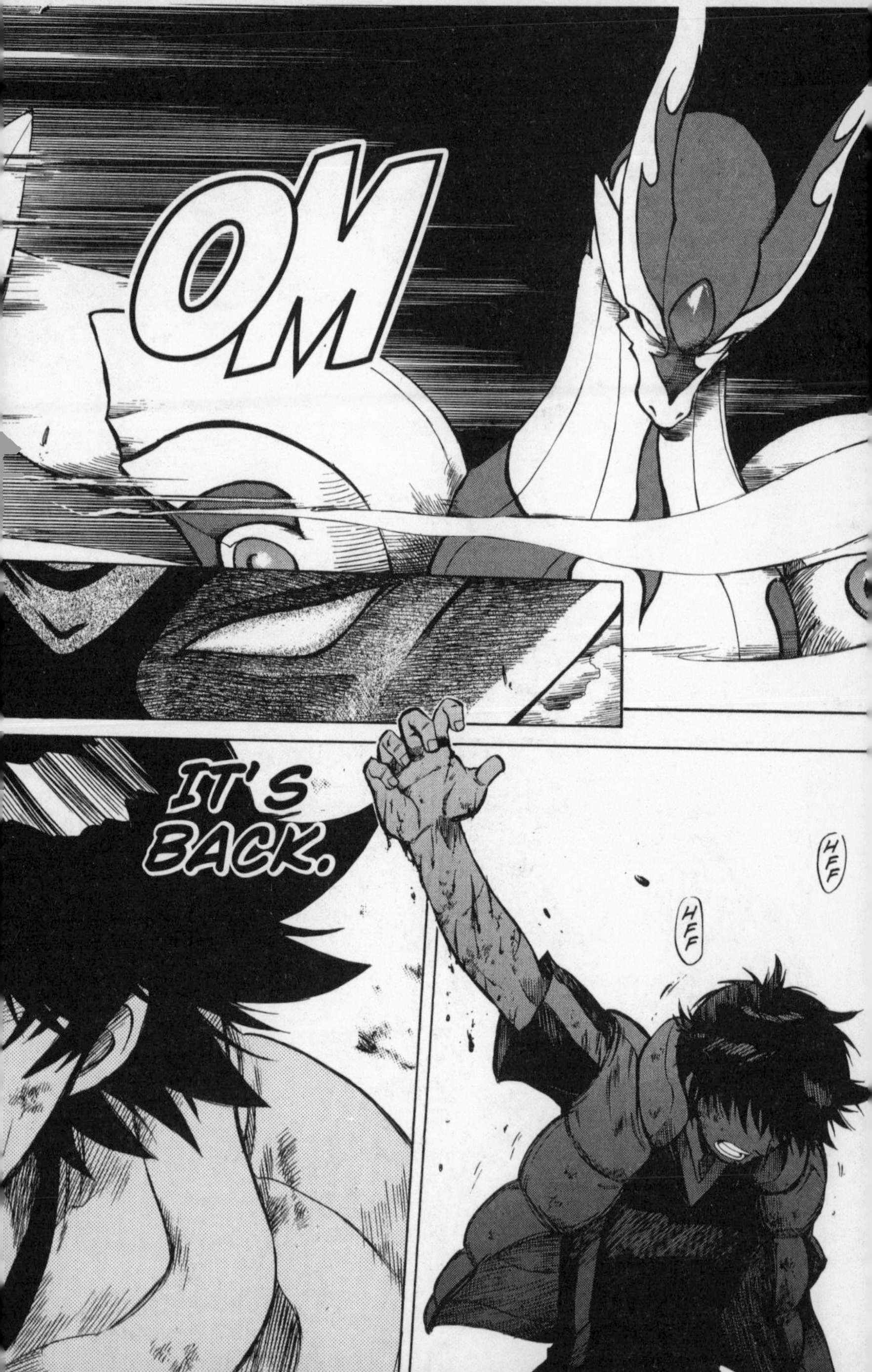
OM
HFF
HFF
IT'S BACK.

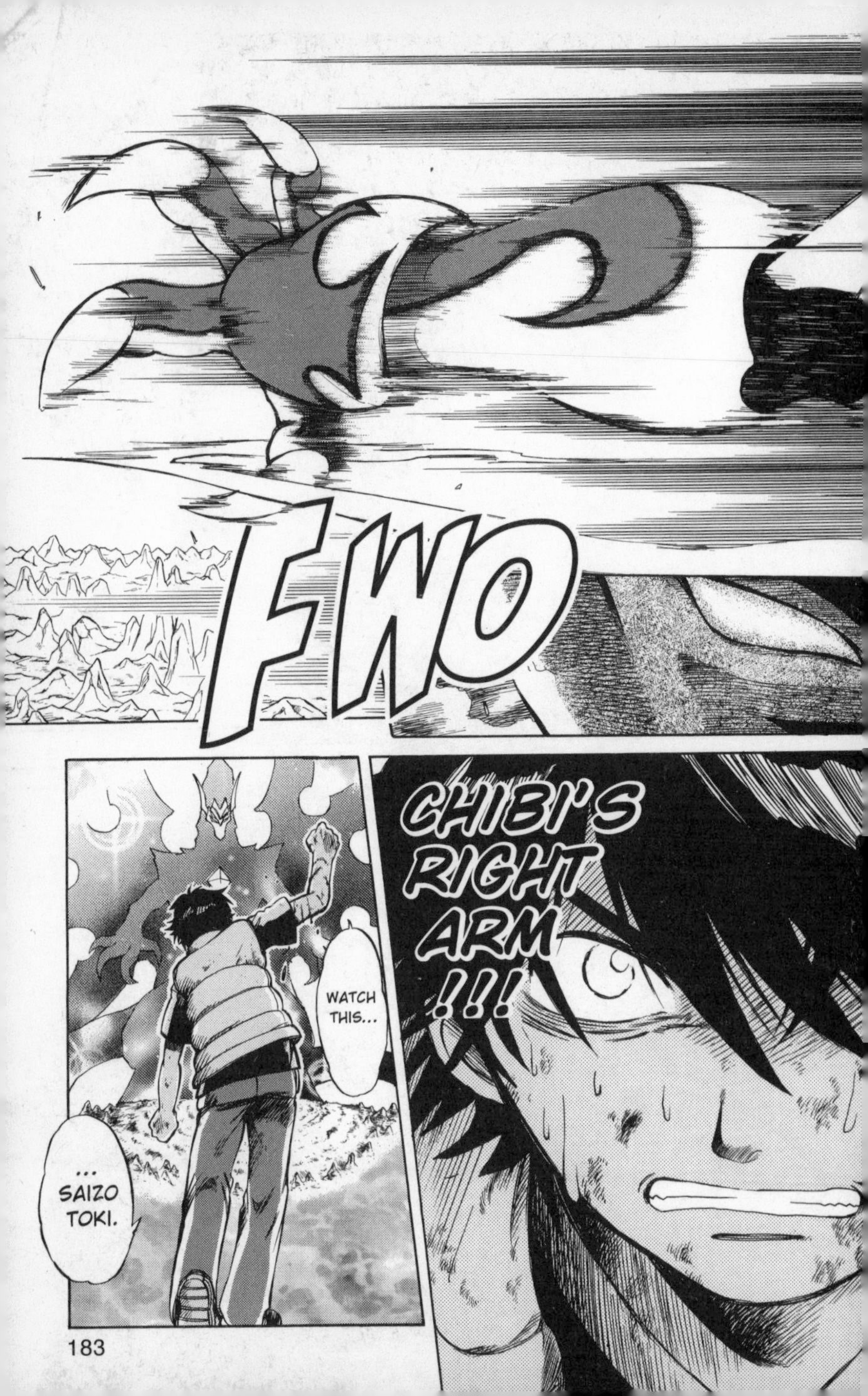
FWO
CHIBI'S RIGHT ARM!!!
WATCH THIS...
... SAIZO TOKI.

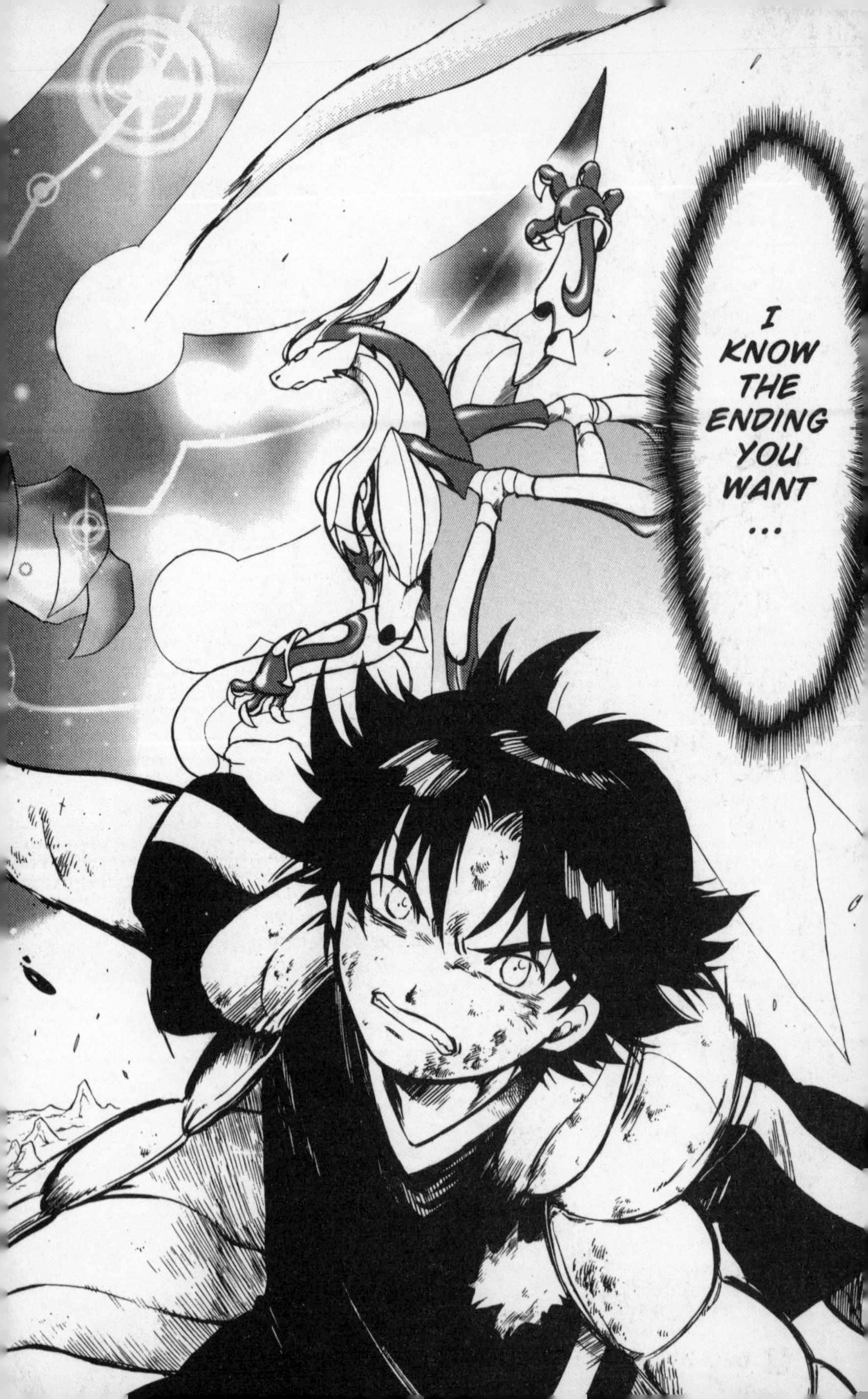
I KNOW THE ENDING YOU WANT...

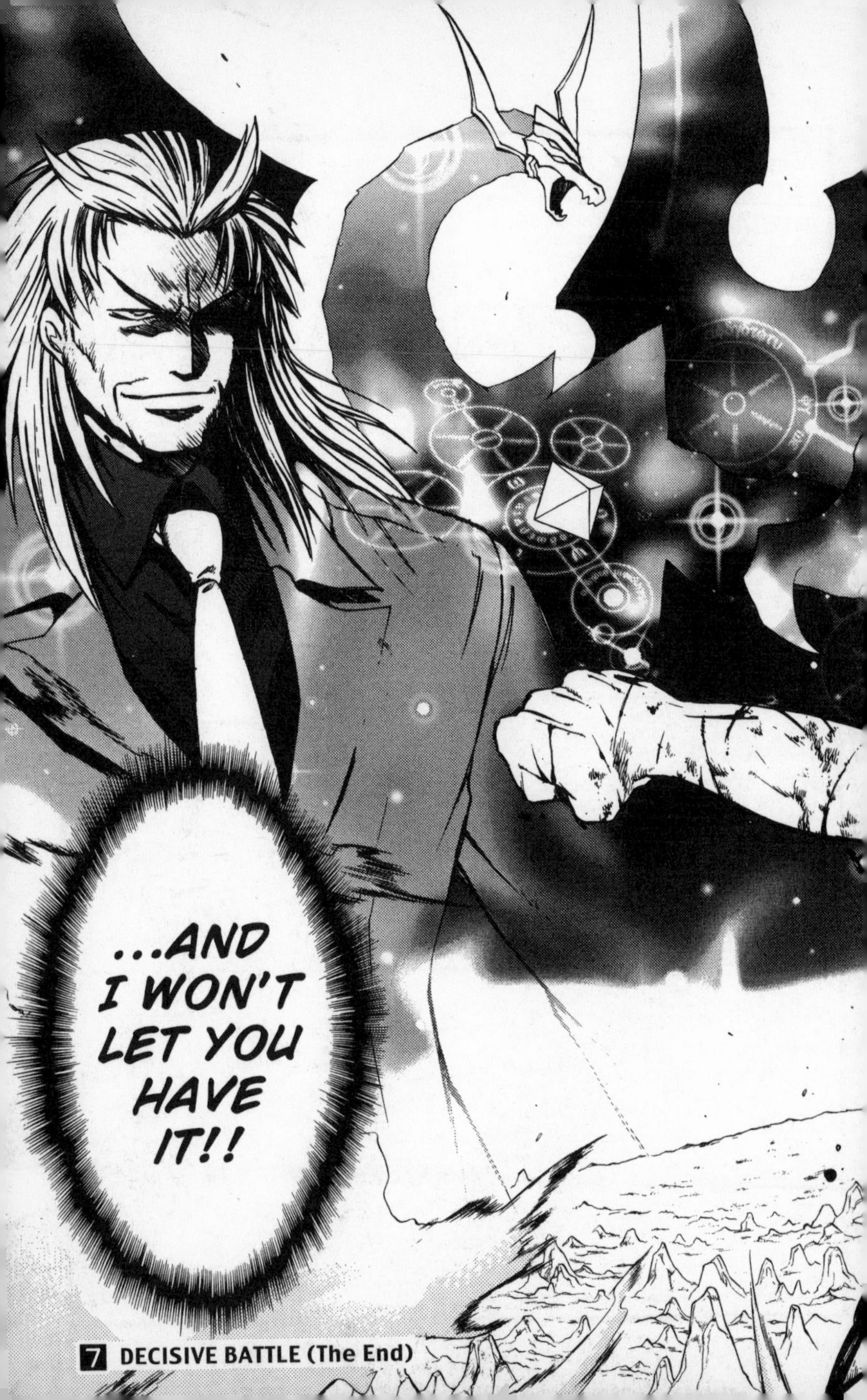
...AND I WON'T LET YOU HAVE IT!!

7 DECISIVE BATTLE (The End)

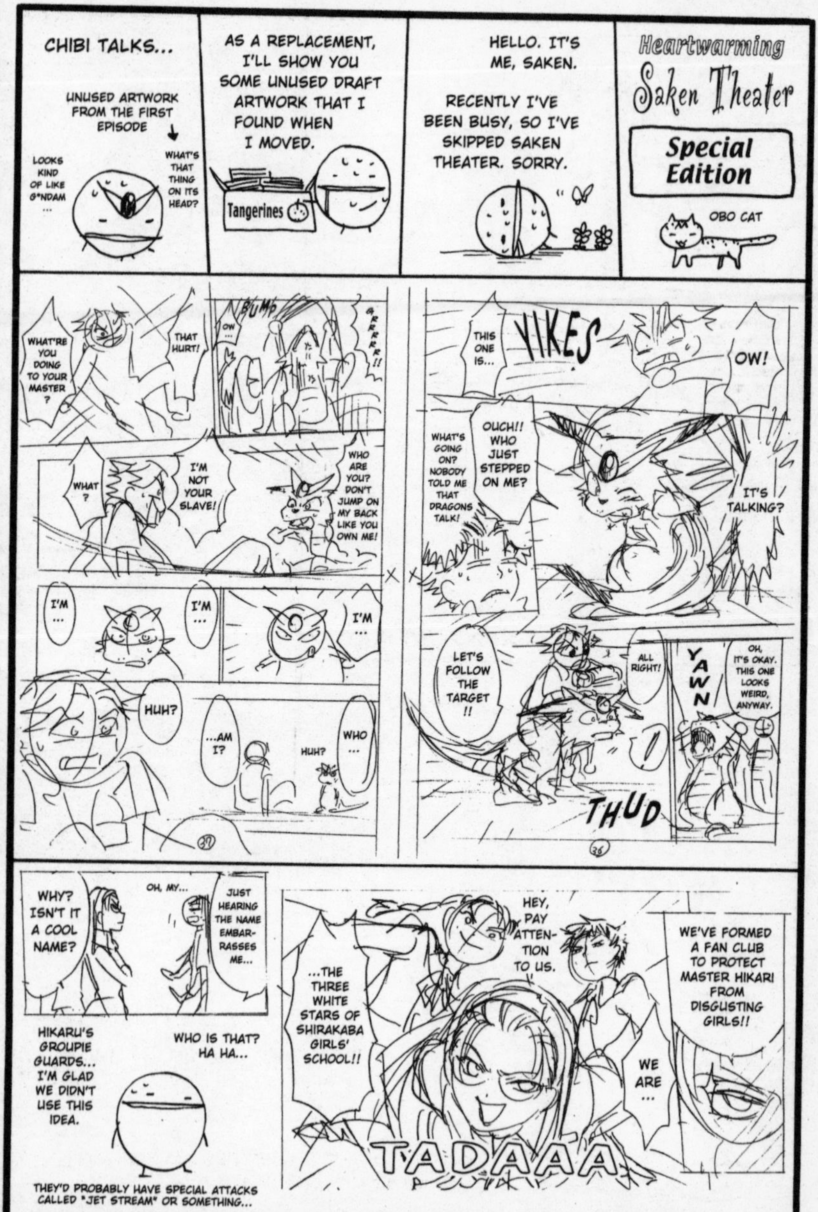
Heartwarming
Saken Theater
Special Edition
OBO CAT
HELLO. IT'S ME, SAKEN.
RECENTLY I'VE BEEN BUSY, SO I'VE SKIPPED SAKEN THEATER. SORRY.
AS A REPLACEMENT, I'LL SHOW YOU SOME UNUSED DRAFT ARTWORK THAT I FOUND WHEN I MOVED.
Tangerines
CHIBI TALKS...
UNUSED ARTWORK FROM THE FIRST EPISODE
WHAT'S THAT THING ON ITS HEAD?
LOOKS KIND OF LIKE G*NDAM...
OW!
YIKES
THIS ONE IS...
IT'S TALKING?
OUCH!! WHO JUST STEPPED ON ME?
WHAT'S GOING ON? NOBODY TOLD ME THAT DRAGONS TALK!
OH, IT'S OKAY. THIS ONE LOOKS WEIRD, ANYWAY.
YAWN
ALL RIGHT!
LET'S FOLLOW THE TARGET!!
!
THUD
GRRRR!!
BUMP
OW...
THAT HURT!
WHAT'RE YOU DOING TO YOUR MASTER?
WHO ARE YOU? DON'T JUMP ON MY BACK LIKE YOU OWN ME!
I'M NOT YOUR SLAVE!
WHAT?
I'M...
I'M...
I'M...
WHO...
HUH?
...AM I?
HUH?
WE'VE FORMED A FAN CLUB TO PROTECT MASTER HIKARI FROM DISGUSTING GIRLS!!
HEY, PAY ATTENTION TO US.
WE ARE...
...THE THREE WHITE STARS OF SHIRAKABA GIRLS' SCHOOL!!
TADAAA
JUST HEARING THE NAME EMBARRASSES ME...
OH, MY...
WHY? ISN'T IT A COOL NAME?
WHO IS THAT? HA HA...
HIKARU'S GROUPIE GUARDS... I'M GLAD WE DIDN'T USE THIS IDEA.
THEY'D PROBABLY HAVE SPECIAL ATTACKS CALLED "JET STREAM" OR SOMETHING...

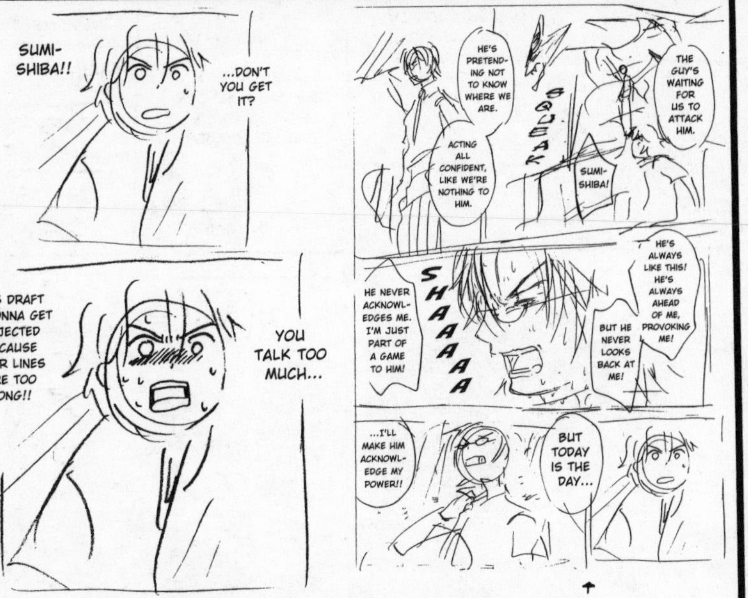
THE GUY'S WAITING FOR US TO ATTACK HIM.
SQUEAK
HE'S PRETENDING NOT TO KNOW WHERE WE ARE.
SUMI-SHIBA!
ACTING ALL CONFIDENT, LIKE WE'RE NOTHING TO HIM.
HE'S ALWAYS LIKE THIS! HE'S ALWAYS AHEAD OF ME, PROVOKING ME!
BUT HE NEVER LOOKS BACK AT ME!
SHAAAAA
HE NEVER ACKNOWLEDGES ME. I'M JUST PART OF A GAME TO HIM!
BUT TODAY IS THE DAY...
...I'LL MAKE HIM ACKNOWLEDGE MY POWER!!
...DON'T YOU GET IT?
SUMI-SHIBA!!
YOU TALK TOO MUCH...
THIS DRAFT IS GONNA GET REJECTED BECAUSE YOUR LINES ARE TOO LONG!!

THIS WAS TOO WORDY, SO WE EDITED IT OUT.

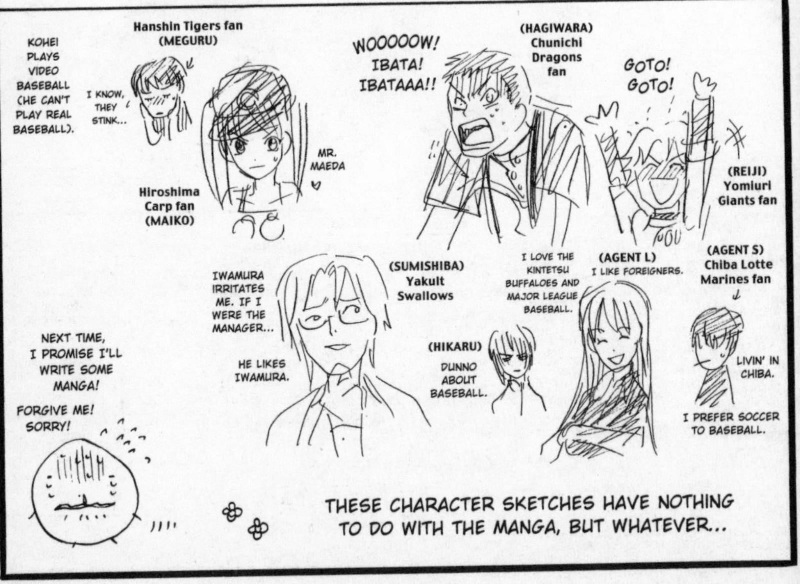
(REIJI) Yomiuri Giants fan
GOTO! GOTO!
(HAGIWARA) Chunichi Dragons fan
WOOOOOW! IBATA! IBATAAA!!
Hanshin Tigers fan (MEGURU)
KOHEI PLAYS VIDEO BASEBALL (HE CAN'T PLAY REAL BASEBALL).
I KNOW, THEY STINK...
MR. MAEDA
Hiroshima Carp fan (MAIKO)
(AGENT S) Chiba Lotte Marines fan
LIVIN' IN CHIBA.
I PREFER SOCCER TO BASEBALL.
(AGENT L)
I LIKE FOREIGNERS.
I LOVE THE KINTETSU BUFFALOES AND MAJOR LEAGUE BASEBALL.
(HIKARU)
DUNNO ABOUT BASEBALL.
(SUMISHIBA) Yakult Swallows
IWAMURA IRRITATES ME. IF I WERE THE MANAGER...
HE LIKES IWAMURA.
NEXT TIME, I PROMISE I'LL WRITE SOME MANGA!
FORGIVE ME! SORRY!

THESE CHARACTER SKETCHES HAVE NOTHING TO DO WITH THE MANGA, BUT WHATEVER...

COMING NEXT VOLUME...

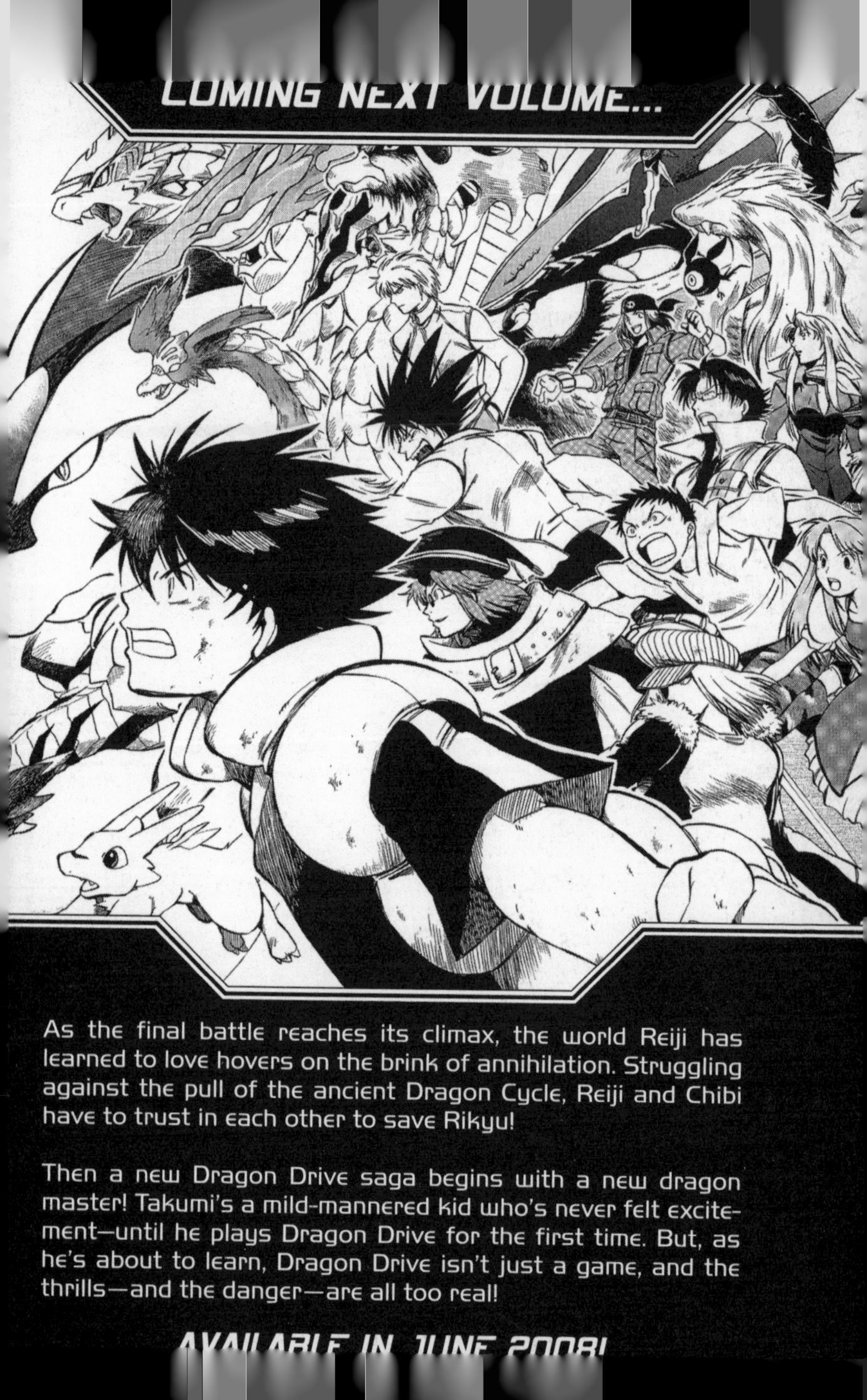

As the final battle reaches its climax, the world Reiji has learned to love hovers on the brink of annihilation. Struggling against the pull of the ancient Dragon Cycle, Reiji and Chibi have to trust in each other to save Rikyu!

Then a new Dragon Drive saga begins with a new dragon master! Takumi's a mild-mannered kid who's never felt excitement—until he plays Dragon Drive for the first time. But, as he's about to learn, Dragon Drive isn't just a game, and the thrills—and the danger—are all too real!

AVAILABLE IN JUNE 2008!

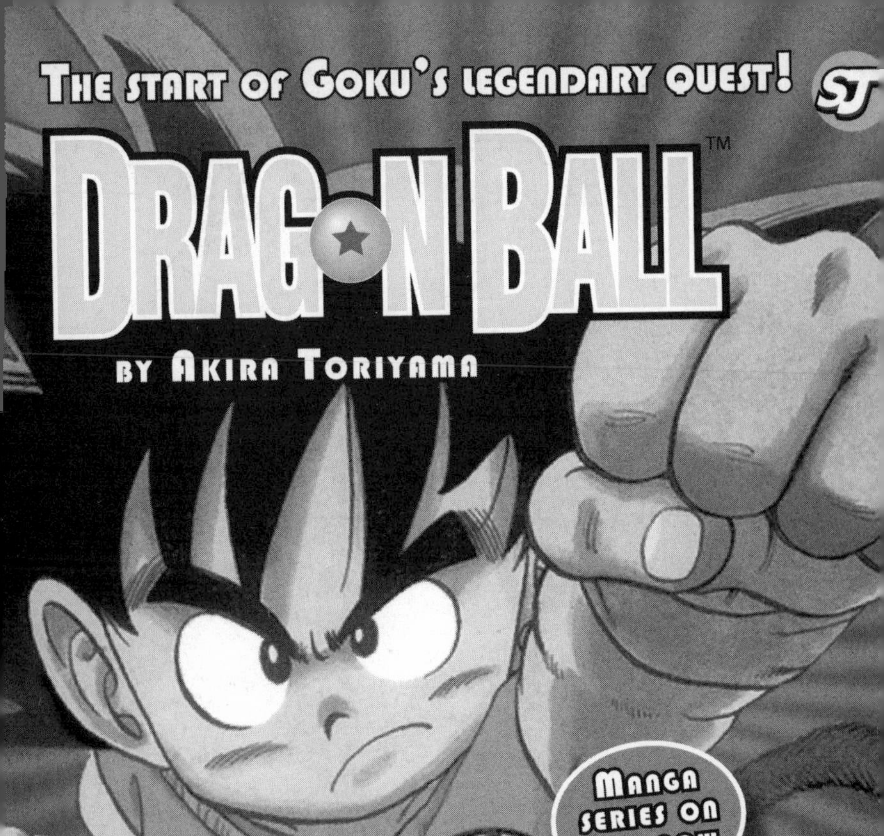
THE START OF GOKU'S LEGENDARY QUEST!
SJ
DRAGON BALL™
BY AKIRA TORIYAMA
MANGA SERIES ON SALE NOW
DRAGON BALL
Akira Toriyama
volume 1
DRAGON BALL
SHONEN JUMP GRAPHIC NOVEL
Akira Toriyama
volume 16

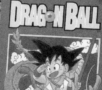

Save **50% OFF** the cover price!

SHONEN JUMP

THE WORLD'S MOST POPULAR MANGA

Over 300 pages per issue!

Each issue of SHONEN JUMP contains the coolest manga available in the U.S., anime news, and info on video & card games, toys AND more!

☑ **YES!** Please enter my one-year subscription (12 HUGE issues) to **SHONEN JUMP** at the LOW SUBSCRIPTION RATE of **$29.95!**

NAME _____

ADDRESS _____

CITY _____ STATE _____ ZIP _____

E-MAIL ADDRESS _____ P7GNC1

☐ **MY CHECK IS ENCLOSED** (PAYABLE TO SHONEN JUMP) ☐ **BILL ME LATER**

CREDIT CARD: ☐ VISA ☐ MASTERCARD

ACCOUNT # _____ EXP. DATE _____

SIGNATURE _____

 **CLIP AND MAIL TO**

SHONEN JUMP
Subscriptions Service Dept.
P.O. Box 515
Mount Morris, IL 61054-0515

Make checks payable to: **SHONEN JUMP**. Canada price for 12 issues: $41.95 USD, including GST, HST and QST. US/CAN orders only. Allow 6-8 weeks for delivery.

BLEACH © 2001 by Tite Kubo/SHUEISHA Inc. NARUTO © 1999 by Masashi Kishimoto/SHUEISHA Inc.
ONE PIECE © 1997 by Eiichiro Oda/SHUEISHA Inc.

ZOOOM

Ken-ichi Sakura

It's Volume 7!! Don't they say seven is a lucky number? Lucky, lucky! Just publishing seven volumes of manga is lucky in itself! However, my stay-at-home life means I never get lucky enough to find money dropped in the street.

Since I moved, my trash has doubled again! That's unlucky...

Ken-ichi Sakura's manga debut was *Fabre Tanteiki*, which was published in a special edition of *Monthly Shonen Jump* in 2000. Serialization of *Dragon Drive* began in the March 2001 issue of *Monthly Shonen Jump* and the hugely successful series has inspired video games and an animated TV show. Sakura's latest title, *Kotokuri*, began running in the March 2006 issue of *Monthly Shonen Jump*. *Dragon Drive* and *Kotokuri* have both become tremendously popular in Japan because of Sakura's unique sense of humor and dynamic portrayal of feisty teen characters.

DRAGON DRIVE

DRAGON DRIVE
VOLUME 7

The SHONEN JUMP Manga Edition

STORY AND ART BY
KEN-ICHI SAKURA

Translation/Martin Hunt, HC Language Solutions, Inc.
English Adaptation/Ian Reid, HC Language Solutions, Inc.
Touch-up Art & Lettering/Jim Keefe
Design/Sam Elzway
Editor/Shaenon K. Garrity

Editor in Chief, Books/Alvin Lu
Editor in Chief, Magazines/Marc Weidenbaum
VP of Publishing Licensing/Rika Inouye
VP of Sales/Gonzalo Ferreyra
Sr. VP of Marketing/Liza Coppola
Publisher/Hyoe Narita

Printed in the U.S.A.

Published by VIZ Media, LLC
P.O. Box 77010
San Francisco, CA 94107

SHONEN JUMP Manga Edition
10 9 8 7 6 5 4 3 2 1
First printing, April 2008

www.viz.com

THE WORLD'S
MOST POPULAR MANGA

www.shonenjump.com